LANDSCAPE OF THE SPIRITS

LANDSCAPE OF

Hohokam Rock Art at South Mountain Park

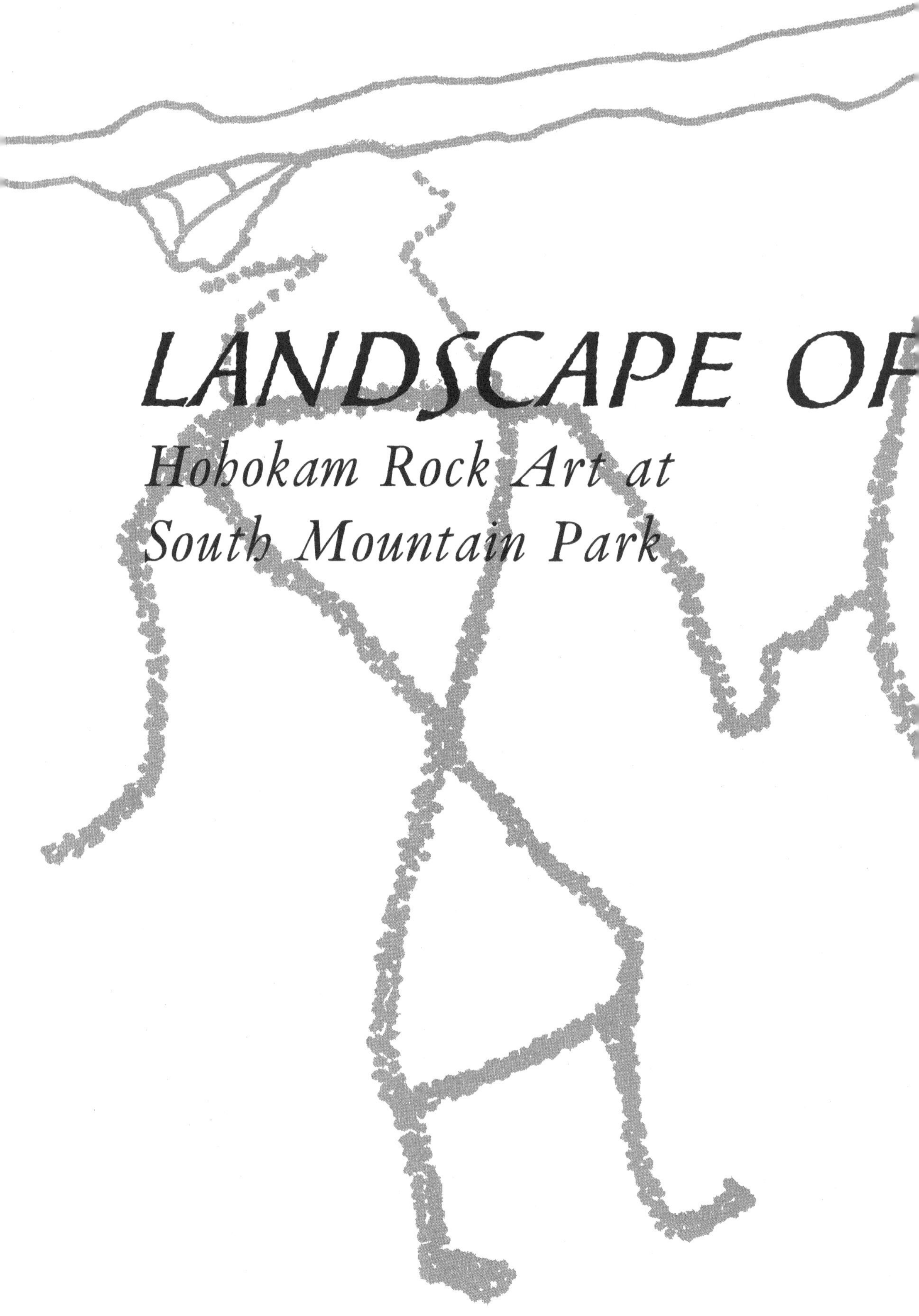

THE SPIRITS

Text by *Todd W. Bostwick*

Photographs by *Peter Krocek*

Illustrations by *Todd W. Bostwick and Peter Krocek*

The University of Arizona Press

Tucson

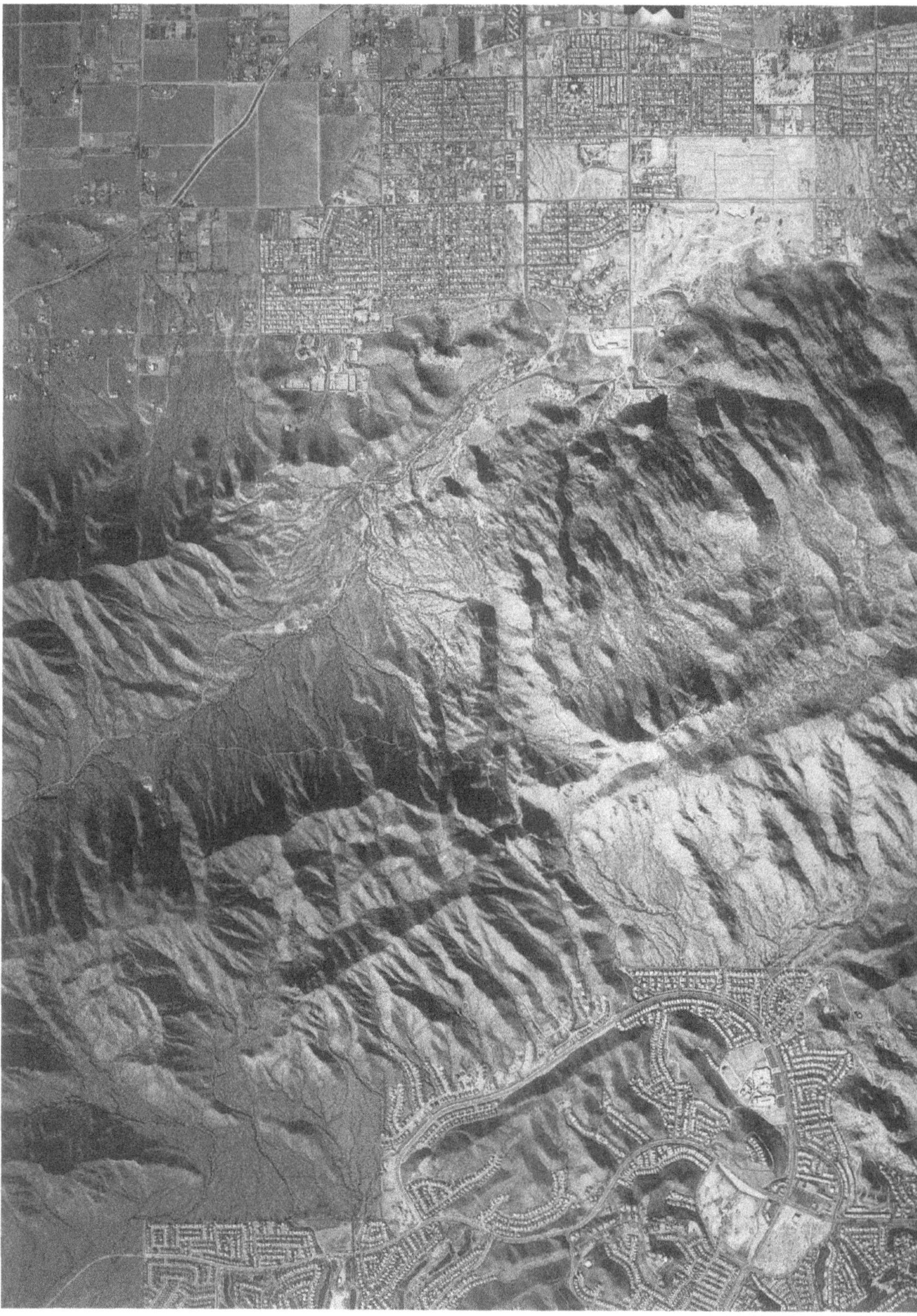

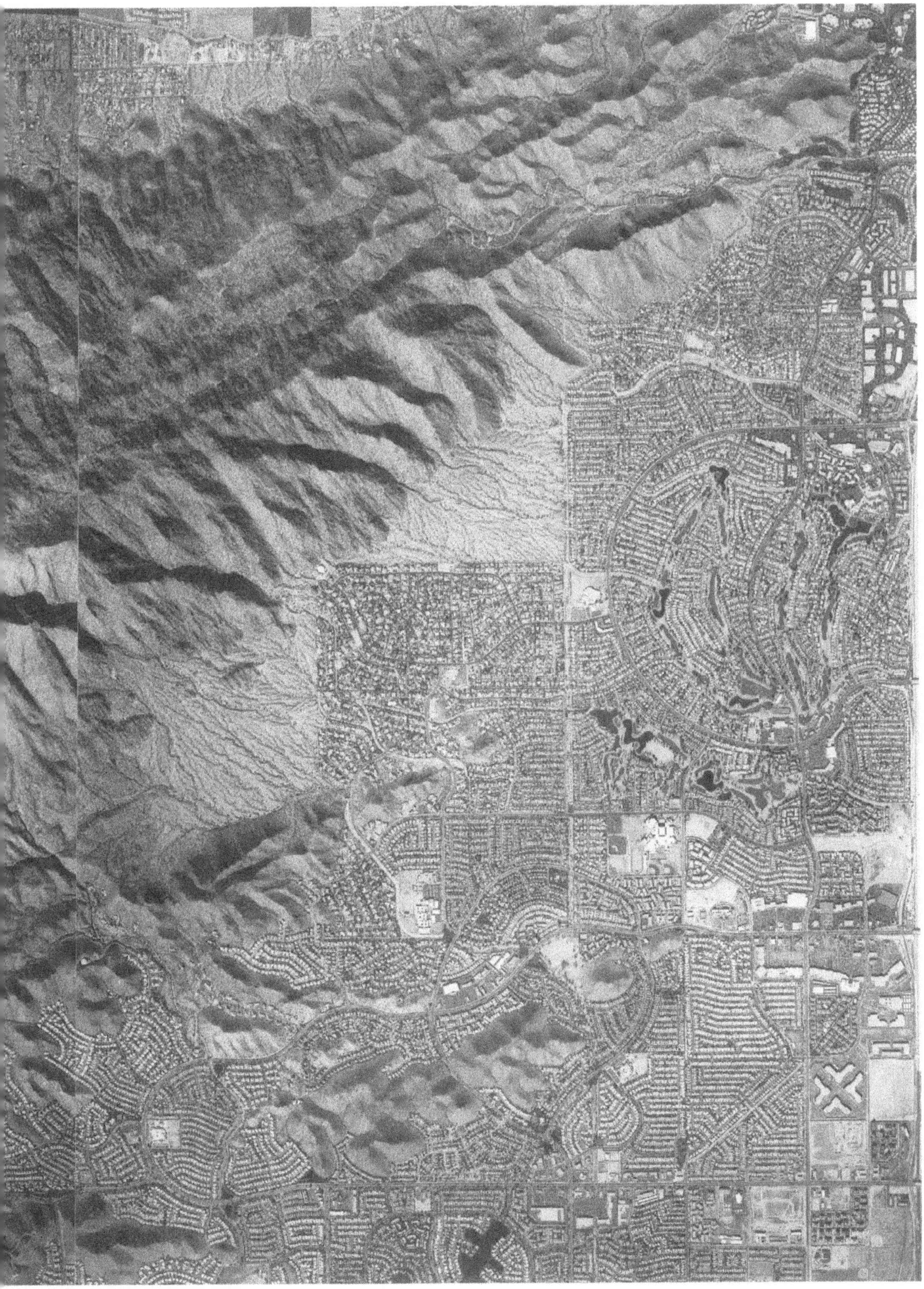

The University of Arizona Press

♾ This book is printed on acid-free, archival-quality paper.
Manufactured in the United States of America
First Printing

07 06 05 04 03 02 6 5 4 3 2 1

Library of Congress Cataloging-in-Publication Data

Bostwick, Todd W.
Landscape of the spirits : Hohokam rock art at South Mountain Park / Text by Todd W. Bostwick ; photographs by Peter Krocek ; illustrations by Todd W. Bostwick and Peter Krocek.
p. cm.
Includes bibliographical references and index.
ISBN 0-8165-2183-2 (cloth : alk. paper) — ISBN 0-8165-2184-0 (pbk. : alk. paper)
1. Hohokam culture—Arizona—South Mountains. 2. Petroglyphs—Arizona—South Mountains.
3. Rock paintings—Arizona—South Mountains. 4. South Mountains (Ariz.)—Antiquities.
I. Krocek, Peter, 1952– II. Title.
E99.H68 B67 2002
709'.01'1309791—dc21

2001007090

British Library Cataloguing-in-Publication Data
A catalogue record for this book is available from the British Library.

Publication of this book is made possible in part by the proceeds of a permanent endowment created with the assistance of a Challenge Grant from the National Endowment for the Humanities, a federal agency.

frontispiece: Aerial photograph of the South Mountains and surrounding area (courtesy of Landiscor Aerial Information)

CONTENTS

COLOR PLATES

Following page 28

FIGURES

MAPS AND TABLES

MAPS

TABLES

ACKNOWLEDGMENTS

THE AUTHORS WISH to express sincere appreciation for the helpful comments and constructive criticisms provided by Wes Holden, Walter "Dutch" Duering, and three anonymous reviewers. Many thanks also to Yvonne Reineke and Christine Szuter of the University of Arizona Press for their encouragement and help; to Sally Bennett, for her excellent technical editing of the draft manuscript; to Roger Lidman, director of Pueblo Grande Museum, for providing administrative support for the South Mountains rock art research project; to Heidi Bostwick for her patience and understanding; and to the City of Phoenix Parks, Recreation and Library Department for its commitment to protecting the South Mountains from inappropriate development. Individuals who assisted with the challenging task of locating rock art include Al Arpad, Dan Gronseth, Michael Goodman, Charles "Carlos" Sotomayor, and others. Stephanie Sherwood drafted the maps and site plan views. Robert Serocki assisted with the rock art element inventory.

Funding for this book was generously provided by the Arizona Humanities Council, the Michael P. Goodman Foundation for South Mountain Park/Preserve, Joanne S. Cline, Virginia "Ginger" Johnson, SWCA Environmental Services, the John F. Long Foundation, the Phoenix chapter of the Arizona Archaeological Society, Pueblo Grande Museum, and the Pueblo Grande Museum Auxiliary.

LANDSCAPE OF THE SPIRITS

CHAPTER ONE

LEARNING THE LANDSCAPE

The sacredness of land is first and foremost an emotional experience. It is that feeling of unity with a place that is complete, whatever the feelings it may engender in an individual.

—Vine Deloria Jr. (1991)

The urban metropolis of Phoenix is framed on its southern border by a rugged mountain range that rises 1,500 feet (457 m) above the surrounding desert terrain. This mountain range is currently known as the South Mountains. They were once called the Salt River Mountains, and before that the Pima (Akimel O'odham) Indians called them "Muhadag Du'ag," or Greasy Mountain. The Pima have a story about Trickster Coyote, who stole the heart of Rattlesnake's first victim from its cremation fire. Coyote had to outrun the people who chased him in pursuit. Resting after he crossed the Gila River, Coyote gobbled down his stolen food. Grease dripped from the hot meat, staining the landscape. That is why the mountains north of the Gila River are stained with a dark color.

This book is a story—actually, many stories—about the South Mountains. Hundreds of years ago, ancient desert people (whom archaeologists have called the Hohokam) pecked and scratched thousands of images, commonly referred to as rock art, into boulders and rock outcrops in these mountains. Rock art evokes a sense of excitement and awe from people of all ages and cultures. Symbols pecked into stone take on a sense of permanence and seem to produce a spontaneous, emotional connection with the past. Perhaps it is the notion that some lost secret language or communication system is displayed, challenging the viewer to decipher the meaning of the symbols.

The purpose of this book is to examine what the rock art in the South Mountains might mean, how it got there, and when it was made. These tasks are not easy, because rock art as a native tradition in the Americas has nearly disappeared. Fortunately, a rich ethnographic data base exists for the American Southwest, providing a framework for analysis and interpretation.

Native Desert Peoples

The Sonoran Desert has been home to a diversity of Native American groups for thousands of years. Piman-speaking people—including the Akimel O'odham (Pima), the Tohono O'odham (Papago), and others—occupied much of this desert region when the first Europeans arrived in the American Southwest in the sixteenth century. Spanish explorers also found the remains of ancient villages scattered within the same river valleys where the agricultural O'odham people lived. The O'odham today claim to be the descendants of the prehistoric Hohokam. However, archaeologists cannot all agree on this matter because a hundred-year gap separates the archaeological record, which ends in the late fifteenth century, from the first ethnographic accounts in the Sonoran Desert. No native people were living in the Salt River Valley when the Spanish arrived, possibly because of the danger of raids by the Apache and Yavapai living to the east and north. In addition, the Hopi of northern Arizona have migration legends that trace some of their ancestors' routes through southern Arizona. Furthermore, anthropologist Frank Hamilton Cushing (1890) saw connections in Hohokam material culture, which he had excavated in the late 1880s in the Salt River Valley, with the Zuni of east-central Arizona and western New Mexico. Archaeologists Lynn Teague (1993) and Judy Brunson (1989) have both reexamined Cushing's data and found that his observations merit consideration. Teague also sees similarities in some Hopi and late Hohokam material culture. Moreover, anthropologists David Shaul and Jane Hill (1998) have identified linguistic connections between the Zuni, O'odham, and Yuman-speaking Indians of western Arizona, and some interesting similarities are evident in Yuman and Hohokam cultures.

All these groups probably have ancient connections with the Hohokam. Trade was widespread during prehistoric times, and some groups are known to have migrated to new territories during droughts, especially in the late thirteenth century. We may never know what language or languages the Hohokam spoke. Archaeologist

David Wilcox (1980) argues that the Hohokam, with their complex society and vast territory, may have been an amalgamation of several different ethnic groups (a conclusion Shaul and Hill [1998] also reached). Therefore, we include traditional stories and ethnographic information from both O'odham and Pueblo people in our discussion of the rock art of the South Mountains, focusing on the O'odham because they actually mention the Hohokam in their oral traditions (Bahr et al. 1994; Lloyd 1911; Russell 1975; Saxton and Saxton 1973; Shaw 1968).

The Importance of Landscape

The highly eroded character of the South Mountains presents an imposing and challenging landscape, but one filled with beautiful and isolated canyons, springs, and outstanding elevated views. Archaeological evidence in the form of rock art and artifacts indicates that ancient people visited and possibly lived in that landscape. Several years ago a professional photographer, Peter Krocek, and I joined forces to study the rock art of the South Mountains. We came to learn the landscape of the mountains by spending a considerable amount of time exploring canyons, ridges, and mountain peaks. We wanted not only to locate all or at least most of the ancient petroglyphs, but also to become familiar with the resources and places within the mountains. Rock art must be studied in relation to its environmental context for potential meanings to be better understood. Archaeologist Thor Conway (1993:83) commented on the importance of landscape in his study of rock art in northeastern America:

> In the northern Woodlands, the erratic distribution of rock art has perplexed anyone who has searched for the elusive pictographs. Why has it been so difficult to predict the distribution of rock art sites? The Ojibwa and Cree shamans obviously preferred to record their dreams on sheer lakeside walls, but why would so many seemingly ideal locations remain unmarked, while the same type of cliffs and ledges only a few miles away bear red ochre symbols?
>
> The solution becomes simple when we learn to recognize sacred space, and then complicated again as we ponder the clever metaphors so poetically spoken by tribal shamans. For a long time I, like many others, treated rock art sites as distinct phenomena—unique expressions of native spirituality. My isolationist view was changed when the Elders revealed that pictographs and petroglyphs are a part of the detail woven onto the fabric of a spiritual landscape—a dream world filled with shrines, vision quest locations, animate rocks that spoke, immortals turned to stone and brought to life through mythology. Rock art sites suddenly become links in an entire spectrum of sacred sites.

M. Jane Young, a folklorist, spent several years studying Zuni rock art. She learned from her Zuni informants that rock art could only be understood as part of the landscape, in its full environmental setting (Young 1988). For the Zuni, rock art in its landscape encodes events that took place in the past and have the power to evoke that past. Rock art in the landscape links the Zuni with their ancestors and with mythic time. Certain places are considered sacred locations where the Zuni people emerged from the underground into this world. Other events in the distant past, such as the adventures of their Hero Twins, are recorded as rock art in special locations.

Learning the South Mountains Landscape

Learning a landscape takes time. Twenty-three years ago, my first visual impression of Phoenix was the view of the South Mountains with their huge communication towers. As a new graduate student in the Department of Anthropology at Arizona State University, I was told of ancient petroglyphs in some of the canyons of those desert mountains. The archaeology community at that time showed little interest in rock art, but mostly out of curiosity I visited a few of the more well known sites: Hieroglyphic Canyon, Pima Canyon, and Box Canyon. Rock art was rarely discussed in my classes, and opportunities to learn about these special types of archaeological sites were limited.

In 1986, I was given the job of directing an archaeological survey for Arizona State University around the southwestern and southern sides of the South Mountains as part of the planning for the Southwest Loop Freeway.[1] Among the scattering of archaeological sites discovered during that survey were three small but interesting rock art sites (Bostwick and Rice 1986). Five years later I conducted an archaeological survey for the City of Phoenix Archaeology Section along the National Trail, a seventeen-mile (27 km) east-to-west trail that traverses the higher ridges of the South Mountains (Bostwick and Howard 1992). To my surprise, a few small rock art sites were also present along this trail.

One of the most memorable experiences during those surveys was an early-morning encounter with a rattlesnake. As I slowly walked with my eyes to the ground, searching for traces of ancient life, I nearly stepped on a coiled rattlesnake warming itself in the morning sun. The startled snake struck at my foot but missed, stretching across the top of my boot for a moment before recoiling. Fortunately, the snake was not fully awake and did not strike again. It must have taken fifteen minutes for my heartbeat to become regular again. Because the South Mountains were the snake's home, I left it alone and moved on, happy to walk away unhurt. But I learned an important lesson that day—the South Mountains may be surrounded by a modern urban environment, but they are still a wilderness area.

Hohokam rock art sites in other mountains in the Salt River Valley occupied my attention for several years after that survey. Then I met Peter Krocek at an Arizona

Archaeological Society meeting in 1994 at Pueblo Grande Museum. A professional photographer with a passion for archaeology, Peter had already been exploring and photographing rock art in the South Mountains for several years but had found few people, including archaeologists, seriously interested in the rock art. We immediately joined forces to more intensively explore the rock art of the South Mountains. Over the next five years we made hundreds of trips into the mountains to locate, photograph, measure, and sketch the rock art. This process of returning to the mountains again and again, during different times of the day and in all seasons, became an educational experience. As we slowly learned the landscape, we were better able to predict where previously undiscovered rock art might be located. We discovered that in addition to being situated adjacent to canyon trails, rock art was also located along ridges that provided thoroughfares up into the mountains.

Day after day, Peter and I used our mornings and evenings to explore the mountains. Both of us encountered numerous animals and had dramatic and unforgettable experiences. On one occasion during a long exploration of the undeveloped southwestern side of the mountains, Peter underestimated the amount of water needed for the task. Warmer-than-usual weather and difficult terrain combined to seriously dehydrate him before he finally located some water within the park. The irony of dying of thirst only a few miles from a metropolitan area of more than 3 million people was forever etched upon Peter's mind.

Conversely, there is also the experience of too much water. During one of Peter's explorations, a sudden thunderstorm overcame the mountains, deluging the land with water. Peter took shelter under a rock overhang (with petroglyphs) to protect his equipment, only to have the deep wash next to the rock shelter rapidly fill with water. The deluge formed a raging flood down the wash, fed upstream by three other washes. The space in Peter's shelter shrank as the water rose higher. Deafening peals of thunder literally shook the stone outcrop, with lightning adding more drama to the moment. Fortunately, like most desert thunderstorms, the rain was soon over and the watery threat subsided to a memory.

On many occasions, we were visited by animals while recording and photographing rock art, especially on solo trips. Lizards were the most frequent visitors. They would often walk across the face of the rock, stopping to do pushups and laying claim to the panel we were recording. Their appearance next to a lizardlike petroglyph seemed eerie at times. Small birds also would fly by and converse with us. More than a few times, hummingbirds with their shimmering feathers hovered a few feet in front of my face as I concentrated on sketching a rock art panel. Large birds, especially hawks, also made their presence known, piercing the quiet solitude with their high-pitched screeches.

We each had many snake experiences in the mountains. More than a dozen different rattlesnakes announced their presence to Peter. One morning I was photographing a panel in Box Canyon and happened to look down to see a sleeping rattlesnake coiled up next to my shoe. Thankful that I hadn't disturbed it, I quietly stepped away to record that panel another day.

On another trip into a rugged canyon, I found a panel that contained mostly snake images. As I examined the art, I became aware of a large, white-colored rattlesnake next to the outcrop. The rattler did not move. Intrigued by its unusual lack of coloring, I abandoned my normal caution and moved toward it for a closer look. Suddenly annoyed by my presence, the snake raised up and rattled at me. I nearly had a heart attack! It then turned away and crawled into a hole under the boulder with the snake rock art. I wondered if it was distantly related to the snakes the Hohokam artist was thinking of when he depicted the design on the boulder a thousand years ago.

Peter and I also had numerous encounters with Mr. Coyote. On one occasion, Peter was uncharacteristically approached by two coyotes. Instead of trotting away, as they usually do, these coyotes barked louder and more aggressively as they moved toward him. Peter decided it was best that he leave, wondering what it was that they were protecting.

On a quiet winter solstice morning, I watched the sun rise over Four Peaks from a small knoll in the 32nd Street Locality. As the sun rose, a chicken coop off in the distance began to stir, and the roosters crowed nervously. Suddenly a coyote ran out of the canyon right past me toward the chicken coop. He was in such a hurry he seemed not to notice me. Moments later he yipped, and a second coyote raced out of the canyon to join his friend. I still wonder if they had a successful hunt.

On another early morning, I met a coyote on the trail, he leaving the mountains to go hunting, me entering the mountains in search of rock art. As we crossed paths a few feet apart, he stopped behind a rock and we stared at each other for what seemed like a long time. I was quite startled to realize that looking directly at me, the coyote's face appeared very humanlike. We then went our own ways, but the image of that face has stayed with me.

Not all of our experiences were positive. Parts of the mountains are rugged and remote, and mishaps occur. Both of us injured ourselves more than once on loose boulders. On one journey into a remote area, Peter found a human skeleton. Close inspection revealed a watch and a metal knife nearby, indicating that the skeleton was not Hohokam but relatively modern. Someone had chosen the South Mountains as his final resting place.

The rugged landscape of the South Mountains provides a variety of environmental contexts that create different emotional responses in different people. For us, the mountains are a sanctuary in which to escape the hectic pace of the urban jungle. But the mountains have different moods at different times of year. We experienced extreme heat, hail, lightning, and flash floods. On one occasion, in a summit valley, we encountered fog so thick that we could not see each other at thirty feet

(9 m) apart. We hiked the mountain's trails during full moons and in pitch dark and saw coyote markings along our shared trails. We watched springs gush with water, fill with tadpoles and other creatures, and then go dry. Each time we visit the mountains even after all our previous experiences we are struck by their beauty and wildness.

Our study resulted in thousands of photographs, sketches, and field notes on the fascinating rock art in the South Mountains.[2] We recorded more than 1,500 "panels" (discrete clusters) of petroglyphs but do not believe we have found them all; for on many trips to examine known sites, we found previously unknown petroglyphs. Rock art is present in areas with good visibility but also in not-so-easily-seen, difficult-to-reach places. The Hohokam rock artists used large boulders with flat faces ideally suited to rock art but ignored a surprising number in favor of boulders or outcrops nearby with less obvious qualities. Certain rocks and locations appear to have been selected for reasons other than the suitability of their rock face. The "quality of place" within the landscape clearly influenced site selection.

Physical Characteristics of the South Mountains

Geologists tell us that the Phoenix area is located within the Basin and Range Physiographic Province, a region of the western United States characterized by broad alluvial basins bordered by steep-sided mountains. The Salt River Valley is one of

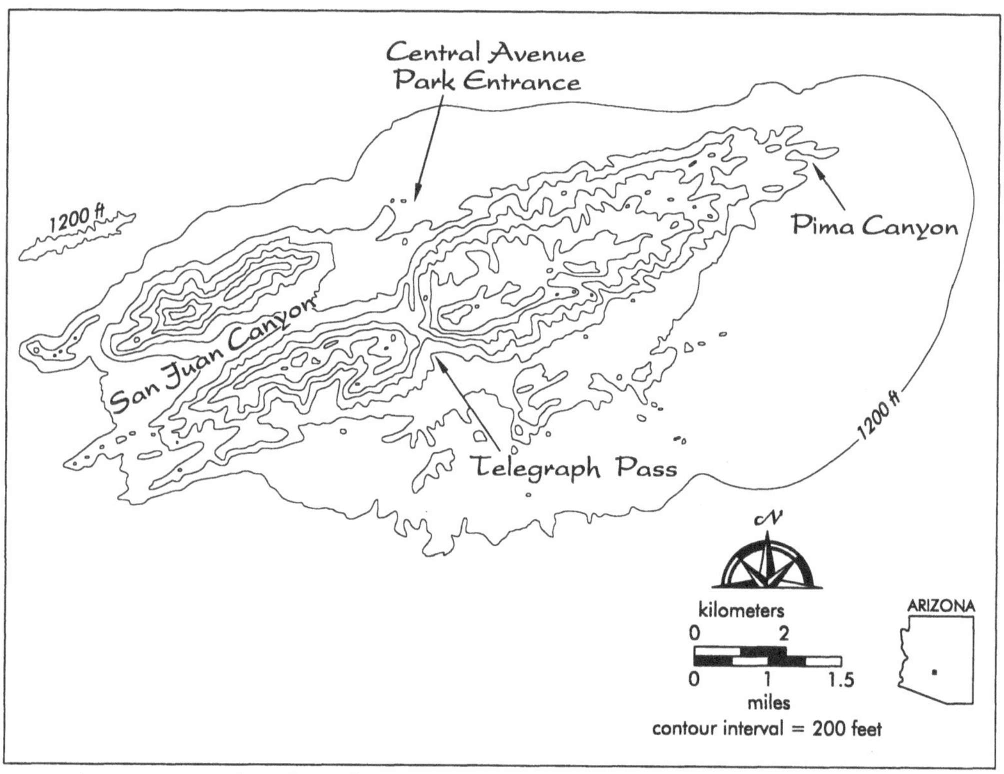

1. South Mountains in their physical setting

those basins. At the southern edge of that basin, a series of parallel ridges oriented southwest to northeast create the South Mountains. Together the ridges are approximately 11.5 miles (18.5 km) long and 4.5 miles (7.2 km) wide. The main ridge towers over the alluvial basins created by the Salt River, about 3 miles (4.8 km) to the north, and the Gila River, 4 miles (6.4 km) to the south. Extensive block faulting of the parent bedrock material has created four main ridges (map 1). The northwesternmost ridge is relatively small and lower in elevation than the other ridges. Guadalupe Ridge, the largest and highest ridge, is located in the middle of the mountains, with elevations ranging from 1,300 feet (396 m) at the base of the north face to 2,690 feet (820 m) at the top of Mount Suppoa. To the immediate northwest of Guadalupe Ridge is the Alta Ridge. A long, narrow corridor that slopes to the southwest, the San Juan Valley, lies between Guadalupe and Alta Ridges. To the southeast of Guadalupe Ridge are the southern foothills, near the rapidly growing residential areas of Ahwatukee and Mountain Park Ranch.

Several different rock types are present in the South Mountains, representing different geologic eras (Reynolds 1985). The western half is a very old metamorphic and granitic rock dating to the Precambrian period, with the oldest rocks dating back 1.6 billion years. Common rock types in this portion of the mountains include gneiss, schists, and granite. The eastern half comprises younger rocks that geologists have termed granodiorite, granite, diorite, and alaskite. These materials date to the mid-Tertiary period and are around 25 million years old. At the northeastern end of the main ridge is the rock termed chloritic breccia. In some of the highly fractured areas of the South Mountains, dikes have intruded the parent rock. Mineralization associated with these dikes has produced veins of gold, silver, and copper in the bedrock materials. From the 1880s to 1942, when all gold mines were shut down because of the war, numerous hardy individuals labored in search of this hardrock gold. Most mines yielded little profit after expenses, bursting the miners' dreams of easy fortunes (Bostwick 2001a).

Erosion of the rock materials, mainly granite and granodiorite, has created a rugged and wild landscape in the South Mountains. Dozens of steep canyons have been eroded into the exterior slopes of the range, as well as in upper, interior areas. Intermittent washes cut the canyons, generally perpendicular to the main ridge. In addition, a large wash traverses the mountains in a northeastern direction from the upper, interior canyons and out onto the pediment at the eastern end. The sandy bed of this drainage, called Pima Wash, provides a major east-west travel route into the mountains. Other canyon washes and their adjacent ridges also provide access into the mountains. Easy north-south travel over the mountains is generally restricted to a pass, known as Telegraph Pass, at an elevation of 2,000 feet (610 m) in the middle of Guadalupe Ridge. Generally, west of this pass is the older rock, with the eastern portion being younger.

Exposed bedrock in the eastern portion of the mountains has been eroded into millions of various-sized boulders, most having familiar forms, but some having bizarre shapes. These boulders have taken on a desert varnish, called "patina," that makes them appear dark brown or, when wet, greasy. Rock art designs were pecked through this patina, revealing the lighter-colored rock underneath. Eroded outcrops along the sides of canyons offer shaded overhangs and protection from the summer heat. Boulder-covered talus slopes provide natural tunnels, rock shelters, and rock chambers.

At least eight intermittent seeps or springs are present within the inner canyons of the South Mountains, in Pima Canyon, upper Pima Canyon, Goodman Canyon, Hieroglyphic Canyon, Mormon Loop Trail, Javelina Canyon, Valle Bonita Canyon, and 24th Street Canyon. With the exception of a permanent one in Hieroglyphic Canyon, all of these produce water only during the wetter periods of the year. Nearby petroglyphs and scatters of broken pottery indicate that all of these water sources were visited by ancient people.

The Pageantry of Life in the Sonoran Desert

Despite their arid and forbidding appearance, the South Mountains are full of life. More than 274 species of plants and 157 species of animals have been identified here, including 51 species of birds and 54 kinds of mammals. Biologists do not know if all these creatures were present in past times, but most probably were (Daniels and Butterwick 1992). Common animals are listed below (courtesy of Joe Yarchin, Arizona Game and Fish Department).

shrews
bats (18 species)
rabbits
hares
squirrels
pocket gophers
pocket mice
other mice
kangaroo rats
wood rats
other rats
porcupine
coyote
gray fox
kit fox
skunks (4 species)
badger
mountain lion
bobcat
collared peccary
mule deer
mountain sheep
salamanders
frogs
toads (5 species)
turtles
tortoise
Gila monster
other lizards
snakes (26 species)

The South Mountains are located in the northern portion of the Sonoran Desert, one of the four major deserts of North America. The other three are the Mojave, Great Basin, and Chihuahuan Deserts. Studies of Sonoran Desert vegetation have shown that, except for changes brought about by modern people, the desert environment has been relatively stable for the last 4,000 years.

The Sonoran Desert covers an area of nearly 120,000 square miles (310,800 km^2) in four states: Arizona and California in the United States and Sonora and Baja California in Mexico (McGinnis 1981; MacMahon 1985). Nearly all of this desert drains into the Gulf of California. The climate is generally warm with regional differences due to latitude, elevation, and geographic configuration. Annually, more than 90 consecutive days with a maximum of 100°F (38°C) are common throughout the region.

The South Mountains are located in the Arizona Upland Division of the Sonoran Desert, where the vegetation includes larger perennials, more numerous plants, and a greater diversity than in all other deserts. The wide range of plant species in the South Mountains reflects this biological diversity. Common plants include palo verde, mesquite, ironwood, and catclaw trees; barrel, prickly pear, and cholla cacti; ocotillo; jojoba; brittlebush, burro bush, and creosote bush; and various grasses and forbs. The stately saguaro, the blossom of which is the Arizona state flower, can be found on the slopes and in the upper, interior canyons. An unusual tree found in the South Mountains is called the elephant tree *(Bursera microphylla);* it has a thick, stocky trunk and a crown of richly green leaves. Though common along the Mexican border in southeastern Arizona, the elephant tree is rare in these parts, and the South Mountains are its northernmost growing range (M. Johnson 1992).

A wide variety of plants within the South Mountains can be eaten. Thomas Daniels and Mary Butterwick (1992) have identified more than 65 different plants that are edible for their seeds, flowers, fruit, leaves, or stems.

One of the seemingly magical phenomena of the Sonoran Desert is the biseasonal rainfall pattern. Rain falls in the desert primarily in winter and again during the hottest time of the year when it is desperately needed, in midsummer. Winter rains originate over the Pacific Ocean and travel east into the desert. These rains are generally gentle and soak into the ground. Summer rains, which come from the Gulf of California, are typically brief but violent. They usually are preceded by dramatic displays of towering clouds, dust storms, thunder, and lightning. Despite these two seasons of rain, however, the Sonoran Desert remains arid. The tallest point in the South Mountains, Mount Suppoa, receives an average of 7.2 inches (18 cm) of rain annually.

Much like their appeal to modern desert dwellers, the South Mountains of prehistoric times must have beckoned to the Hohokam, who lived in hot, dusty villages along the Salt and Gila Rivers. Cooler, and with a greater diversity of creatures than the river basins, the South Mountains would have been an attractive place to visit for ancient desert farmers. In wetter years, small areas were farmed along the washes and on some of the mountains' alluvial slopes. A variety of wild resources would have been available, and in some locations precious spring water was obtainable.

Reporting Our Study

In this book we emphasize the range of different rock art elements and compositions through generous use of descriptions, illustrations, and photographs. We try to avoid dwelling on absolute numbers of each element, except for the more infrequent motifs, partly because there are likely more yet to be found. Throughout the book, we discuss various theories about rock art in general, as well as about particular elements, basing possible meanings for certain elements on the rich ethnographic data base of native peoples in the American Southwest and on other rock art studies throughout the Southwest, in South Africa, and in Australia. To summarize the large amount of information we uncovered, we have grouped our discussion of element types into several categories: insects and arthropods, amphibians and reptiles, mammals, birds, humans, and geometric designs. This approach has limitations, particularly that in such groupings, important element variability or style deviations can be overlooked. Archaeologist Thor Conway (1993:123) has discussed this problem:

> Rock art can be puzzling, challenging, and contradictory. An imaginary catalogue that presented several hundred thousand rock art images could be divided into many broad categories, yet the idiosyncratic and often highly individualized subjects would remain distinct, uncomfortable with their neighbors. Any formal inventory of rock art faces this problem: How can it be divided into meaningful groupings? I don't think it can.
>
> Most schemes reduce these inspired creations into mundane classifications beyond recognition or meaning. It is easy to assign many of the apparently recognizable depictions to common categories. . . . Yet ambiguity will always remain, for science is not yet prepared, by its nature or vocabulary, to master the dreams, visions, and insights gained from aboriginal culture.

In organizing the scattered rock art sites, we defined more than fifty different geographic localities in the South Mountains (number of known panels in parentheses):

Beverly Canyon (26)
Box Canyon (242)
Canyon Drive (13)
Central Avenue (25)
Chandler Boulevard/32nd Street (13)
Chandler Boulevard/19th Way (4)
Clubhouse (12)
Desert Foothills (8)
Far West (21)
Goodman Canyon (52)
Graffiti Rock Canyon (12)
Hidden Valley (19)
Hieroglyphic Canyon (105)
Holbert Trail (19)
Javelina Trail (19)
Kiwanis Trail (23)
Los Lomitos (5)
Mormon Loop Trail (20)
Mormon Trail (22)
National Trail (2)
Pecos Road (10)
Pima Canyon (18)
River View (2)
San Juan East (21)
San Juan North (23)
San Juan South (2)
South-Central (4)
Southeast Side (50)
Southwest Side (14)
Summit (6)
Sunset View (10)
Telegraph Pass (28)
Twin Buttes (14)
Upper Pima Canyon (74)
Valle Bonita (3)
Water Tank Hill (10)
7th Street (19)
12th Street (22)
Upper 12th Street (3)
16th Street (27)
20th Street (2)
24th Street (54)
27th Street (39)
28th Place (89)
32nd Street (214)
34th Street (35)
35th Avenue (18)
36th Street (96)
40th Street (10)
43rd Street (26)
47th Avenue (3)
48th Street (76)
51st Avenue (11)

These localities are based on discrete geographic areas such as canyons and major trails; they are spread across the entire range but are concentrated mostly in the eastern half. Names for the localities were chosen from existing names of the canyon or the major street near the location (map 2).

Our exploratory efforts have located most of the rock art panels. However, we are convinced that others still exist along ridgetops or in yet-to-be-explored canyons.

We have found that similar rock art life-forms and geometric symbols are spread throughout the mountains, although the same ones are not present in all locations. Nor are the executions of the petroglyphs uniform, which suggests that they may have been made by different artists. Yet some of this variability in style could be intentional and laden with meaning or could have chronological significance.

The study of rock art in the South Mountains is still ongoing. But years of exploring, sketching, and photographing the designs have provided a fundamental

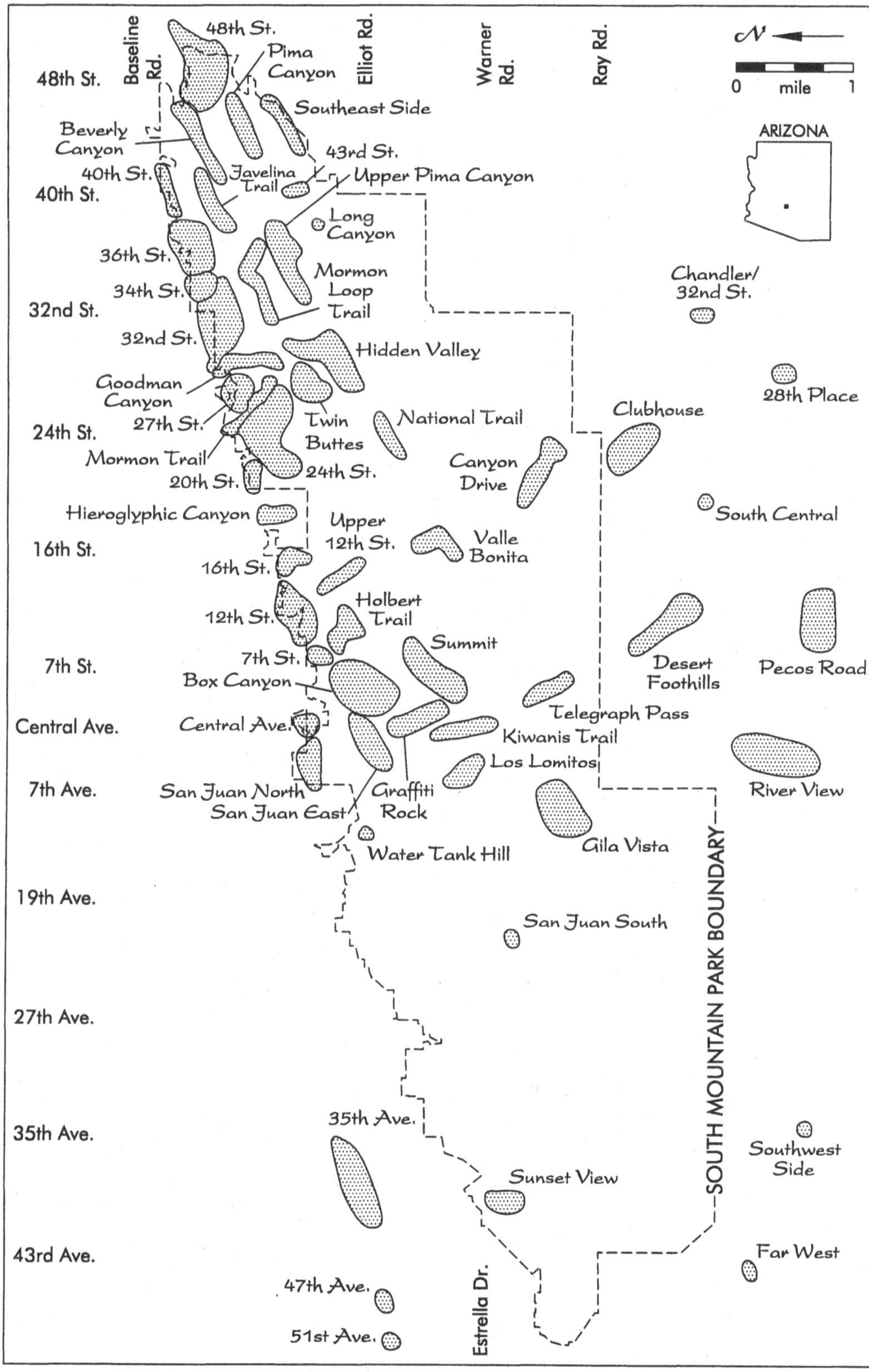

2. Locality map for South Mountains rock art

understanding of the variety of ancient images and of the landscape. On the basis of this knowledge, we propose that much of this rock art represents dreams, memories, and signs. The petroglyphs appear to be records of individual dreams or vision quests; memories of important historical or mythological events; and signs relating to local resources and to the heavens. To others, these mysterious designs may spark interesting ideas that we have not explored. We offer a large sample of South Mountains petroglyphs so that readers can see for themselves this magnificent collection of ancient art.

Preserving a Mountain Landscape

The South Mountains create a dramatic visual backdrop to the ever-expanding sprawl of buildings, streets, and parking lots in the Phoenix metropolitan area. Showing great vision, a small group of civic-minded individuals were able to convince the City of Phoenix in the 1920s to purchase a large portion of the South Mountains from the federal Bureau of Land Management. With several additions since then, the park has grown to nearly 17,000 acres, making it the largest municipal park in the world.[3] As a nature preserve for desert wildlife, South Mountain Park stands in serene contrast to the sea of development that surrounds it. The strange and wonderful rock art discussed in this book is part of the mystique that permeates the mountains.

A wide variety of people, all of whom have their own expectations about a mountain preserve, visit South Mountain Park. Park visitors consist of hikers, joggers, equestrians, cyclists, hang gliders, picnickers, partiers, romance-seekers, and stargazers. In addition, various civic and cultural events are held in the park, and telecommunication personnel use the park roads in route to a cluster of giant towers on the mountain's summit. An estimated 3 million people visit South Mountain Park annually. It is not uncommon for a thousand or more cars a day to drive into the park. The variety and number of visitors create many challenges for the management of rock art sites and other cultural resources within the park (Bostwick 1998a).

Many people in the Phoenix metropolitan area see the South Mountains as a desert playground. Indeed, the 1924 act of Congress that established the park stated that the land was to be used by the City of Phoenix for "municipal, park, recreation, playground, or public convenience purposes." However, using as a playground an area containing numerous rock art sites without damaging them requires that the public be educated about the unique values of rock art.

Vandalism to rock art sites is a long standing problem in South Mountain Park. In 1991, J. J. Golio and friends (1993) reexamined 401 of the rock art panels recorded by Ernest Snyder in 1964. They found that approximately 22 percent of the panels had been stolen or damaged, including petroglyphs destroyed by graffiti and gunfire. Boulders containing petroglyphs had been stolen, and individual petroglyph elements had been removed from panels. Public sites easily accessible to human traffic have been damaged, especially those located in the southern and eastern foothills, where recent housing development is extensive. Some examples seem pathological: in Box Canyon, a full-figured female was pecked into a Hohokam rock art panel and then shot full of holes with a gun. The City of Phoenix has taken steps to address many of the problems, but spray-paint graffiti remains a challenge at the edges of the park (Bostwick and Dean 2000).[4]

South Mountain Park is a special place with an amazing collection of ancient rock art whose meanings are complicated and layered but in some ways approachable and seemingly understandable. This rock art needs to be preserved so that it retains its power to touch individuals through personal encounters. These experiences may even mitigate the depersonalizing urban sprawl that surrounds the park.

When visiting the rock art in the South Mountains, please refrain from touching or climbing on the petroglyphs, and do not remove any artifacts. The protection and care of this rock art is everyone's responsibility. Park visitors are required to stay on the established trails, but a variety of rock art can be seen along many of the major trails (e.g., Desert Classic, Holbert, Javelina, Kiwanis, Mormon, Mormon Loop, Pima Canyon, and Telegraph Pass Trails). For information about other petroglyphs that are accessible to the public, visit the South Mountain Environmental Education Center, located near the Central Avenue entrance to the park.

CHAPTER TWO

INVESTIGATING ANCIENT ART IN THE SONORAN DESERT

The graphic imagery of rock art contains within itself a great deal of information about past societies, thus rendering it an important part of the archaeological record. . . . Ideographic systems expressed in rock art may reflect important aspects of social organization, illuminate issues of social change, document ceremonial practices linked to subsistence strategies (such as prayer for rain, calendrical celebrations, or organization of the supernatural realm), and identify relationships with outside groups. At the same time, rock art is a material artifact from a nonmaterial realm that can tell us something about how peoples viewed their world and gave it meaning.

—POLLY SCHAAFSMA (1980)

THE DESERT DWELLERS who farmed the Salt River Valley before Columbus arrived in the New World are called the Hohokam, a Pima word translated by ethnographer Frank Russell (1975) as "those who have gone." The Hohokam were a resourceful people who constructed impressive canal systems that carried water from major desert rivers to fields of maize, beans, squash, cotton, and other plants. Beginning about the time of Christ and continuing for a millennium and a half, the Hohokam built and maintained hundreds of miles of canals in the Salt River Valley. These canals, some up to 20 miles (32 km) in length, delivered life-giving water to tens of thousands, perhaps hundreds of thousands, of acres of farmland along both sides of the Salt and Gila Rivers.

The Hohokam were also familiar with the available native plant resources, as is evident in the diversity of plant remains found in archaeological deposits. They utilized dozens of plant species for food, medicine, ceremonies, and countless utilitarian products. These plant resources include agave hearts and fibers, mesquite tree bean pods, cholla cactus buds, prickly pear fruits, saguaro fruits, and a variety of grass seeds and leafy plants.

Although archaeologists have defined the Salt and Gila river valleys as the core area of the Hohokam (Doyel 1991), ruins of this culture are scattered throughout most of the Sonoran Desert of central and southern Arizona and in northern Sonora, Mexico. Dozens of villages were built in the Phoenix region, each containing from a hundred to a thousand inhabitants. More than twenty thousand Hohokam probably occupied the region during the height of the Classic period (ca. A.D. 1150–1450).

The Hohokam were an artistic people who made a variety of useful and beautiful craft items. They also constructed oval ball courts, where ritual games were played, and earthen platform mounds, where important ceremonies were held. More than two hundred ball courts have been recorded throughout Arizona, the great majority being Hohokam courts (Wilcox 1991a). In addition, as many as one hundred platform mounds may have been built by the Hohokam and their neighbors to the east, the Salado (Doelle et al. 1995). The ball courts and platform mounds may place the Hohokam into a larger regional system, possibly with economic and religious underpinnings (Wilcox 1991b).

Hohokam Art Designs

Well-crafted objects left behind by the Hohokam reveal a rich art tradition expressed in a variety of materials including stone, ceramics, shell, bone, textiles, and wood. Living creatures provided inspiration for Hohokam artists. An assortment of animal forms were delicately carved into stone ornaments and bowls, shell jewelry, finely incised schist palettes, and elaborately carved hairpins made from animal bones.

Animal, human, and geometric shapes appear as red designs on buff-colored or brownware pottery. Delightful plain and painted pottery effigy vessels were made in the shape of humans and animals. Naturally, changes in artistic styles became evident over time. These changes provide a framework within which to examine changes in Hohokam culture as a whole.

Emil Haury, one of the pioneers of archaeology in the American Southwest, conducted an in-depth analysis of red-on-buff pottery designs from the important site of Snaketown, located about 12 miles (19 km) southeast of the South Mountains along the Gila River. Haury tracked the use of different art motifs over time and made suggestions concerning the possible origins of particular elements. He (1976:229) characterized Hohokam pottery designs as follows: "Much of the uniqueness and charm of Hohokam pottery rises from the emphasis the artists put on the simple but dynamic rendering of life forms: birds, reptiles, mammals, and human figures. They also devised a bewildering array of small geometric figures, often repeated over and over again. The latter have been frivolously called the 'Hohokam alphabet.'" Haury (1976:229) recognized that art styles can provide important information about a culture: "In the life form category, modes of portrayal, associated elements and detail related to the representation of the human form, are hints of Hohokam customs. In fact, cultural elements can be added to the inventory on the basis of 'pictures' when the objects themselves have not survived, as for example, flutes and fancy headdresses."

Although constrained by the shape and size of the pottery vessel, Hohokam painted designs have a certain freedom about their execution. One of the first archaeologists to systematically study Hohokam pottery designs, Charles Amsden (1936:43–44), stated that the Hohokam potter was a "master of the extemporaneous stroke, using her brush in truly creative delineation." Design analysis has identified a relatively narrow range of life-forms on Hohokam pottery compared to the diversity of living creatures in the desert. Perhaps this reflects some shared standards or conventions relating to the appropriate use of certain life-forms. Identified forms include humans, deer, antelope, coyote or dog, quail, hummingbirds, waterbirds, lizards, turtles, scorpions, snakes, and a small number of fish. Early Hohokam painted wares did not have life-forms but, for unknown reasons, used only geometric designs. Painted pottery from the site of Snaketown indicates that life-form designs were introduced several hundred years after geometric designs came into vogue. According to Haury (1976), birds and lizards were the first life-forms depicted on Hohokam pottery. Bird images are sometimes found in association with snakes. Reptiles as pottery designs are not as detailed as those carved in stone or etched in shell ornaments, the latter sometimes representing the sidewinder rattlesnake and the horned lizard. Mammals depicted include deer, antelope, and dog or coyote. Archaeological data from a number of village sites have shown that the Hohokam had the domesticated dog. This animal probably served as a companion, assisted with hunting, and guarded village perimeters. Sticklike human figures are occasionally portrayed on Hohokam pottery, sometimes in association with other elements that appear to be activity scenes.

Strangely, animal designs completely disappeared from the Hohokam painted pottery tradition during the Classic period (ca. A.D. 1150–1450), and complex geometric designs became the norm. However, animals continued to be important in other mediums such as carved stone and shell ornaments. At the site of Pueblo Grande, located 4 miles (6 km) north of the South Mountains, birds, frogs, lizards, snakes, and other life-forms are represented in Classic period jewelry (Bostwick and Downum 1994; Foster 1994).

Haury (1976:241) suggested that Hohokam potters were "in the beginning stages of a story-telling art" with their use of life-forms in activity scenes. The source of this artistic tradition may have been in western Mexico, where artisans of the Chalchihuites Culture painted life-forms on pottery as early as the sixth century

(Kelley and Abbott 1966). Haury (1976:242) provided a possible explanation for the meaning of this art:

> In varying degrees throughout Mesoamerica, the isolated element, geometric or animal, portrayed in whole or in abbreviated fashion, stood as a symbol for a cosmological, calendrical, or numerical value. Initially, most of these were expressed on stone or native paper, less frequently on pottery. However, a mode of communication was established in which the unit element was thought of as a vehicle for expressing an idea. As this concept spread northward to the Mesoamerican frontier, it is likely that the symbolic meaning and the precise form of elements were lost or modified as functions of the distance over which they were diffused. The orientation of the recipient culture would also have had its effect.

Haury (1976:242) further argued that original calendrical or numerical values of the artistic elements were likely lost among the Hohokam, with the meaning perhaps "best explained as mythological and secular inspirations."

Hohokam Rock Art

More than 550 major Hohokam rock art sites have been recorded in the Sonoran Desert (Thiel 1995; see for example, Bostwick 1998b, 1999, 2000, 2001b; Ferg 1979; Golio et al. 1995; Hamann 1995; Hedges and McDaniel 1986; Rodgers 1985; Wallace 1983; Wallace and Holmlund 1986; Weaver 1985; Weaver and Rosenberg 1978). Other rock art sites are likely still to be found. The vast majority recorded thus far are petroglyphs, made by the removal of the darkly patinated surface of rocks to expose a lighter color underneath. Designs made in this method were created either directly with a hammerstone or, most often, indirectly with a hammerstone and pebble chisel. Occasionally, the Hohokam also painted designs in alcoves or places protected from weathering. Archaeologists call painted rock art "pictographs."

Southwestern art historian and rock art specialist Polly Schaafsma (1980) has labeled Hohokam rock art the "Gila style," to distinguish it from more than two dozen other distinctive styles identified in the American Southwest. Nonetheless, some images are common to both Hohokam rock art and other rock art styles. These images consist primarily of geometric or abstract designs and representational elements such as life-forms and artifacts. Differences in execution, elaboration, and certain unique designs distinguish Hohokam rock art from other styles. Schaafsma (1980:83–88) has summarized the general characteristics of Hohokam rock art:

> Life forms in Hohokam art include a variety of human figures, large game animals, and perhaps dogs. Quadrupeds [four-legged mammals] are pictured both as stick figures and as more solid forms. The latter are sometimes shown with a pendant half-circle in the abdominal area, perhaps signifying pregnancy. . . . The heads of Hohokam

petroglyph quadrupeds have pointed noses and prominent ears, which together define a V shape. Turtles, snakes, birds, and insects are also depicted. Occasionally animal tracks and bows also occur. . . .

Abstract elements are important. . . . Abstract designs are primarily curvilinear, although some rectilinear elements do occur. Wavy lines, some of which represent snakes, curvilinear meanders, and mazes composed of meander segments are characteristic elements in the Gila Petroglyph Style. A few one-pole ladders . . . and rectilinear grids appear at these sites. Some of the grids seem to be of Hohokam origin, while others are more heavily patinated than [more recent] Hohokam work in the same group and thus seem to be older. Occasionally there are highly formalized patterns such as terraces, frets, outline crosses, diamond patterns, and large rectilinear motifs, particularly in the northern Hohokam. Everywhere there are circle designs—small single circles, circles joined by lines, circle clusters, figure eights, circles with central dots, sunbursts, and concentric circles.

Although the number of different rock art elements or motifs used by the Hohokam in their rock art seems infinite, they are actually limited to slightly over fifty basic element types.

Rock Art Research in the South Mountains

Archaeologists have been familiar with petroglyphs in the South Mountains for more than a century, but detailed research on this rock art has been limited.[1] During his 1887–1888 excavations of several Hohokam villages in Phoenix and Tempe, Zuni ethnographer Frank Hamilton Cushing made two sketches of rock art panels in Pima Canyon (1890:178). One of these rock art panels depicts several dancing humans, four-legged mammals, and other life-forms (figure 1). Cushing thought it might represent a Zuni "pasture dance."

A decade later, Warren K. Moorehead briefly explored the South Mountains

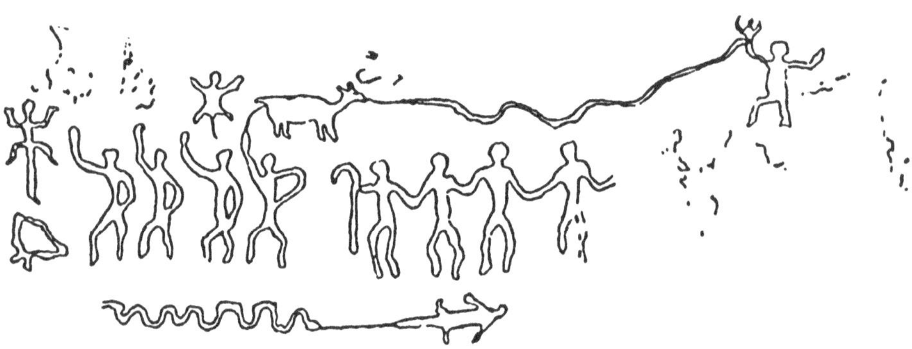

1. Frank Hamilton Cushing's (1890:178) sketch of a petroglyph panel in Pima Canyon, South Mountain Park.

during his excavations in Hohokam platform mounds in Phoenix. Moorehead's (1906:Figs. 48–50) report included sketches of rock art images from "bluffs south of Phoenix," most of which appear to be from Box Canyon. His sketches of individual images are relatively accurate, although he extracted those images from their panels and combined them into composite figures (figure 2).

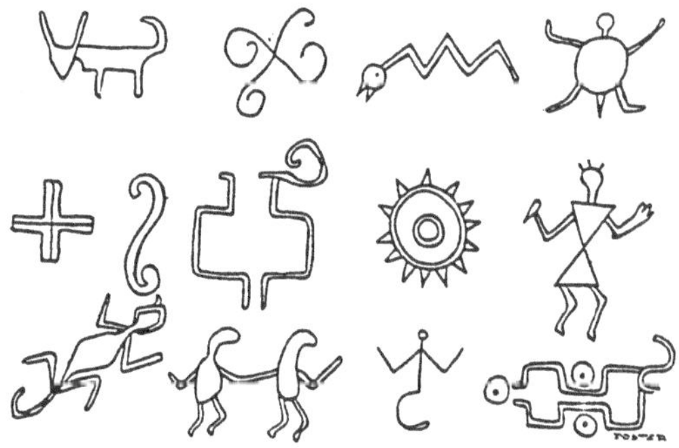

2. Warren King Moorehead's (1906:Fig. 49) sketch of several petroglyphs in the South Mountains.

In 1912, Jesse Walter Fewkes reported on his excavations at the Hohokam ruin of Casa Grande near present-day Coolidge, about 30 miles (48 km) southeast of Phoenix. Fewkes (1912:Pl. 40) included two photographs of "pictographs from Casa Grande and vicinity." Both of these rock art panels are located in Box Canyon on the northern side of the South Mountains.

Anthropologist Julian Steward's 1929 publication of a survey of rock art in California and the Southwest included photographs of rock art in the South Mountains. Steward did not personally visit this rock art but instead relied on the rock art files at the University of California and on photographs and sketches provided to him by local citizens. Steward (1929:Pl. 86c) included an 1899 photograph by M. A. Bolton of the same rock art panel in Pima Canyon that Cushing had sketched a few years earlier. He also provided sketches of more than a hundred designs, which he acknowledged in the captions were "not natural groupings." Steward's (1929:Figs. 76 and 77) sketches appear to represent rock art panels located in Box Canyon and in an area near the south end of 48th Street.

During the late 1930s, Frank Mitvalsky (aka Midvale) was hired as park naturalist. In a 1937 *Arizona Republic* newspaper article, Mitvalsky commented on the rock art, associating it with the ancient people of the Salt River Valley. Mitvalsky discussed a large panel near the Holbert Trail (7th Street Locality), first recorded by Warren Moorehead, which Mitvalsky called "Story Rock" because "the many groups of figures enscribed there seem to represent incidents and scenes from primitive life and reveal a story of the past." Mitvalsky also mentioned the dancers in the rock art panel in upper Pima Canyon and panels in Hieroglyphic Canyon. Curiously, Mitvalsky suggests that the geometric designs called "large rectangles" by him, but now called "pipettes," represent sacred shrines.

Byron Cummings, first chair of the Department of Archaeology (later changed to Anthropology) at the University of Arizona, authored a textbook on Southwestern archaeology called the *First Inhabitants of Arizona and the Southwest* (1953). In a chapter on prehistoric religion, Cummings (1953:224) included a photograph taken by J. C. McClintock of a large rock art panel at the entrance to Pima Canyon.

The systematic study of rock art in the South Mountains did not begin until the 1960s, when Ernest Snyder, an avocational archaeologist, located and photographed 119 rock art sites with 2,031 separate designs. His results were published in 1966 in a five-page article in *American Antiquity.* At that time, archaeologists knew little about Sonoran Desert rock art. Consequently, Snyder's work stands as a pioneering effort in Hohokam rock art research.

Snyder focused on classifying the various rock art elements he found based on a system of analysis developed by two California archaeologists, Robert Heizer and Martin Baumhoff (1962), for their study of rock art in the Great Basin of California and Nevada. Snyder identified thirty-eight different element types:

human figure
concentric circles
circle
lizard
curvilinear abstract
quadruped
spiral
rectilinear abstract
deer
sun disc
cross (X)
snake
bighorn sheep
turtle
figure eight
swastika
bird
connected circle
square
zigzag lines
connected squares
ladder
chevron
centipede
disc
cactus
skunk
wavy lines
tailed spiral
turkey
scorpion
asterisk
pinwheel
rabbit
fish
antelope
rake
squirrel

Human figures, called "anthropomorphs" by archaeologists, were the most common element, followed by circles. Lizards and quadrupeds also were frequently recorded. Rock art sites were found at the bottoms of washes, in the areas where rock outcrops meet the sloping river basin, in passes, and on the summits of hills or ridges. When Polly Schaafsma published her landmark book on Southwestern rock art in 1980, her chapter on Hohokam rock art included six of Snyder's photographs of rock art in the South Mountains.

The Current Study of Rock Art

Understanding rock art involves locating it in the landscape, documenting it, and analyzing and interpreting it. Five issues to consider are identification, representation, composition, meaning, and interpreting the system (Morphy 1989: 1–17).

- The full range of elements in an area must first be identified, with motifs segregated. Those elements should be organized into sets according to time and space.
- Representation is the process by which meaning is encoded, and how it is intended to be seen and by which audience. Some geometric elements may have been schematic forms of figurative elements.
- Composition consists of the way in which elements are combined together or organized as a whole in the same panel or in a series of related panels. A single rock art panel could have evolved or developed over time, and modifications may reflect reinterpretation. Superpositioning of elements could have been fortuitous or intentional, sometimes created as an illusion of perspective. Compositions can be studied by charting the frequency and distribution of elements, and their relationships with each other.
- Revealing the meaning of rock art is difficult, involving the merging of symbols and metaphors that will never be known or understood with certainty.
- Interpreting the system requires a long-term effort and involves system modeling to examine the range of possible relationships and interpretations for each of the system's components.

Many people are intrigued by what rock art may mean. Only recently have archaeologists devoted serious study to this matter. A variety of theories have been proposed, none of which taken individually seems entirely satisfactory. We may never know exactly what all rock art was meant to communicate, but that should not deter the pursuit of possible explanations. Garrick Mallery of the Smithsonian Institution's Bureau of Ethnology conducted a detailed study of American Indian art in the late nineteenth century. His design study (Mallery 1893), which included an extensive sample of rock art, indicates that this art had a wide range of functions and meanings including mnemonic devices, chronological counts, notices, declarations of war, declarations of peace, challenges, totems, titles, individual names, mythological beings, supernatural animals, religious ceremonies, cult societies, daily life or games, records of battles, migration events, sociological events, biographies, personal exploits, abstract ideas, and signs, symbols, or emblems.

Archaeologist Henry Wallace (1983) has proposed six possible functions for Hohokam rock art, which are not necessarily exclusive. These are (1) doodling or graffiti, (2) mnemonic devices, (3) clan or totem symbols, (4) decoration, (5) trail or boundary markers, and (6) ceremonial or religious significance.

The once-popular idea that rock art is simply the product of idle hands is no longer given much credence. Experiments have shown that the creation of most petroglyphs requires considerable skill and patience. Particular designs are found over broad areas, suggesting the sharing of recognizable images.

Mnemonic devices help persons remember a particular location for a specific reason. Pima calendar sticks, into which designs were carved or burned to record important community events, are one example. Some of the carved symbols in the calendar sticks, such as certain geometric forms, look similar to Hohokam petroglyphs. Interpreting the meaning of mnemonic devices in rock art is difficult without ethnographic information.

Some rock art appears to represent clan symbols. Hopi clan symbols have been identified as repeated petroglyphs at a rock art site along a major trail, as well as near cliff dwellings. Archaeologists do not know whether the Hohokam had clans, but the repeated occurrence of certain images, such as animals, could represent Hohokam clan designs or other social groups. The O'odham have two named moieties (dual divisions): Red Ant and White Ant for the Akimel O'odham, and Vulture and Coyote for the Tohono O'odham.

In recent years archaeologists have become increasingly certain that rock art was not created simply to make a residential area more attractive. Rock art is often found next to trails, travel routes, game paths, or resource procurement areas. This rock art could have told a traveler important information about the people or resources of the region crossed by the trail. For example, a Hohokam rock art panel in the Picacho Mountains resembles the local topography and looks like a map of the area (Wallace and Holmlund 1986:Fig. 9.2).

Shamanism and the Neuropsychological Model

The association of rock art with religious activities is a common theme in rock art research in the American Southwest. One of the current theories used to interpret geometric rock art designs involves shamanism and the neuropsychological model, which is most clearly described by anthropologists John David Lewis-Williams and Thomas Dowson (1988). Based on clinical medical studies of altered states of mind, this model proposes the existence of a universal set of geometric shapes, called entoptic phenomena, that are seen by individuals under altered states of consciousness (Fischer 1975; Huffman 1983; Hunchak 1980; Oster 1970; Tyler 1978). The altered state can most commonly be generated by sensory deprivation and fatigue (e.g., sleepless fasting in a dark chamber), intense concentration and rhythmic movements (e.g., ceremonial dances), schizophrenia, and chemical stimuli such as hallucinogenic plants.[2]

A powerful hallucinogen used by Southwestern Native Americans is jimsonweed, also called datura. The O'odham were cautious of the dangerous effects of this member of the nightshade family (Curtin 1949; Underhill 1946). Zuni rain priests administered datura with great care, putting "the powdered roots into their eyes to see at night, to commune with the feathered kingdom, and to commune with the spirits of the dead to intercede for rain" (Schultes 1972:47). The Hopi used datura to induce visionary diagnosis of illness (Whiting 1939). Datura seeds have been found in prehistoric Pueblo sites, suggesting that this plant has been used for centuries (Yarnell 1959).

Another desert plant used as a stimulant is native tobacco, a variety of which *(Nicotiana trigonophylla)* grows in the South Mountains (Daniel and Butterwick 1992). Hopi initiates fasted for four days in the kiva, an underground ceremonial chamber, before ritually smoking tobacco and performing songs and dances (Stephen 1936). Tohono O'odham shamans smoked tobacco to bring them into the supernatural world, face to face with the rain god (Underhill 1938). Among the Pima, tobacco smoke was intended to enhance vision or deepen perceptions (Rea 1997:317).

Three stages of trance experiences have been identified. The first stage involves the spontaneous visualization of entoptic forms, seen by individuals during altered states of consciousness and originating from the structure of the optic system. These may take the form of a limited number of common geometric shapes (figure 3). These recurring shapes are also called "form constants" or "phosphenes." Common entoptic forms include grids, parallel lines, dots and circles, zigzags, nested curves, filigrees, meanders, and vortices (spirals, concentric circles, and circle with dot). Individuals undergoing altered states of consciousness—such as initiates, religious specialists, and shamans entering trances—reportedly experience the entoptic forms as incandescent, moving, rotating, and shimmering patterns that may combine in bewildering ways.

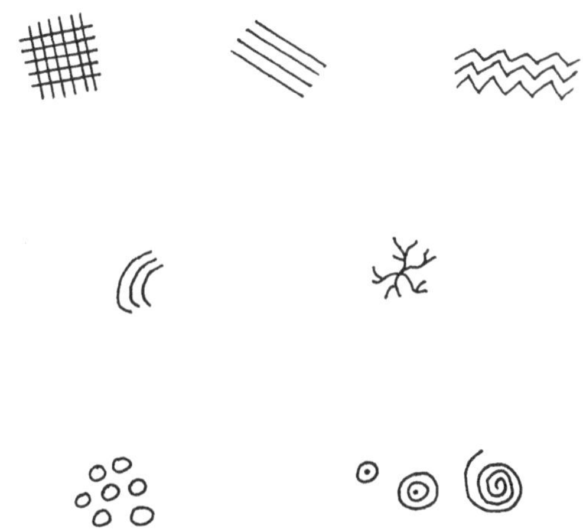

3. Common entoptic forms (from Lewis-Williams and Dowson 1988). These forms appear as petroglyphs and pictographs at many Hohokam rock art sites.

During a second trance stage, entoptic forms can become elaborated or stylized and are combined with human and animal designs. These combined geometric and animal forms, called "construals," are constructed as patterns that make sense to the individual who has had the trance experience. It is his or her effort to interpret the trance images.

In the third stage, the trance images appear spontaneously as combined animal and geometric patterns. These combined patterns eventually take on iconographic importance, appearing as cultural symbols in a variety of mediums, with their meanings recognized by different members of a society. Thus, according to the neuropsychological model, an artistic tradition such as that of the Hohokam could have originated with images generated by the trance or dream experiences of shamans and other religious leaders. Earlier Archaic period rock art is dominated by abstract geometric designs, and the Hohokam may have connections with this ancient art tradition.

Geometric images, which may have originated as entoptic forms, become embedded into an artistic tradition and acquire layers of meaning specific to that culture. Hence, simple geometric designs become symbols representing complex abstract concepts. The association of a geometric design with other rock art elements may help inform on the possible meaning of the geometric design.

The O'odham and Shamanism

The Piman-speaking Indians of the Sonoran Desert once practiced a form of religion called shamanism by many researchers. Shamans are religious specialists who communicate with the supernatural for the benefit of an individual or the community as a whole. The shaman's world is multilayered, with an underworld, a middle world where humans live, and an upper world. Through a variety of methods, such as fasting and sensory deprivation, shamans enter a trance state and travel to the upper world or into the underworld where spirits and demons dwell. In these sacred other worlds, the shaman is taught special knowledge by guardian spirits. This knowledge, in turn, is used for initiation, curing, divination, and prophesy.

Shamans played an important role in O'odham society (Bahr 1983; Underhill 1946). Historically, the O'odham recognized three kinds of shamans, each with different skills or powers: *si-atcokam* treated diseases using supernatural powers; *makai* had power over weather, crops, and war; *hai'-tcottam* used roots and other remedies to treat illnesses (Russell 1975:256). A village typically had as many as three to five shamans, who would work alone or sometimes together. Both men and women could be shamans, although the shamans were mostly men. A shaman's power came primarily from dreams in which supernatural animal spirits contacted the shaman and taught him or her songs. Individuals could seek their own visions in isolated places, such as remote canyons, or they could apprentice themselves to other shamans. An individual bitten by a rattlesnake was considered chosen and often had no choice but to become a shaman. Experiences received during salt gathering expeditions, scalping an enemy, or killing an eagle also could induce dreams in which an individual obtained power songs.

Ethnographer Ruth Underhill, in her book *Singing for Power* (1938:5–6), comments on the importance of song and its relationship to the supernatural in the Tohono O'odham religion:

> Song was not simply self-expression. It was a magic which called upon the powers of Nature and constrained them to man's will. People sang in trouble, in danger, to cure the sick, to confound their enemies, and to make crops grow. They sang as they fought and as they worked, all together.
>
> The power of song was an honor to be earned; it could not be assumed lightly at the mere whim of an individual. The describing of a desired event in the magic of beautiful speech was to them the means by which to make that event take place. All their songs describe such desired events, and besides the songs there are stately ritual orations intended for the same purpose. The songs are from every department of life and in many moods: solemn, wistful, humorous, wild. The mood does not matter. Magic will be worked if the description is vivid and if the singing or the recitation is done, as it should be, at the right time and with the right behavior, on behalf of all the people.
>
> Such a magic spell is never consciously composed: it is "given" by the supernatural powers. A man who desired a song did not put his mind on words and tunes: he put it on pleasing the supernaturals.

The O'odham people once considered animals to be superior to humans because animals are more at home on earth than man. They could act and talk like humans if they chose to do so. It was very important to win the friendship of some animal, who, in turn, would talk to the person and teach him their magic songs during a dream or under conditions of extreme hardship. But animals could also cause disease, as vengeance on careless humans, for failing to remember the ancient ways, for mistreating animals, or for not believing in their power. Only shamans could cure a person of such a disease by singing their own animal songs and calling for aid from their animal spirit helpers. Underhill (1938:141) provided a colorful description of a Tohono O'odham shaman: "A person to be feared is a Papago [Tohono O'odham] medicine man. He gains his power in dreams, as other men do, but his dreams go further into the unknown. He flied *[sic]* with eagles; he visits magicians beneath the sea; he hears songs which can bring rain and bring death. Great power passes through him."

With help from O'odham informants, anthropologist Donald Bahr (1974) conducted an in-depth study of O'odham shamanism. He confirmed Underhill's ethnographic work that the concept of shamanism in the O'odham world was based on the belief that sickness in humans was caused by ceremonial lapses or by the ill will of animals. Ceremonial lapses include the touching of sacred objects that are too powerful for individuals who are not shamans or priests. For the O'odham, at least twenty different animals—including mammals, birds, reptiles, and amphibians—have the power to cause or cure human sickness.

Bahr and his colleagues (1994:233) have described a "landscape of the spirits," where shamans seek out lost souls and spirit helpers. These landscapes of the spirits are located where "the mountains are standing." The spirits' domain is considered to be inside mountains or in darkness outside a patient's house, the portion of the world set aside for visions, apparitions, or supernatural entities. Great battles take place between shamans and "spiritualized causal agencies" within those landscapes. Spirits are invoked as a last resort, when lesser curing methods have proven inadequate. Spirits are thought to be enduring and individualized and can be encountered in this world. Spirits can be animals, humanlike beings, or other creatures. According to Bahr and others (1994:232), "Pimans know where to go and what to do if they wish to meet them."

The South Mountains are one of those places.

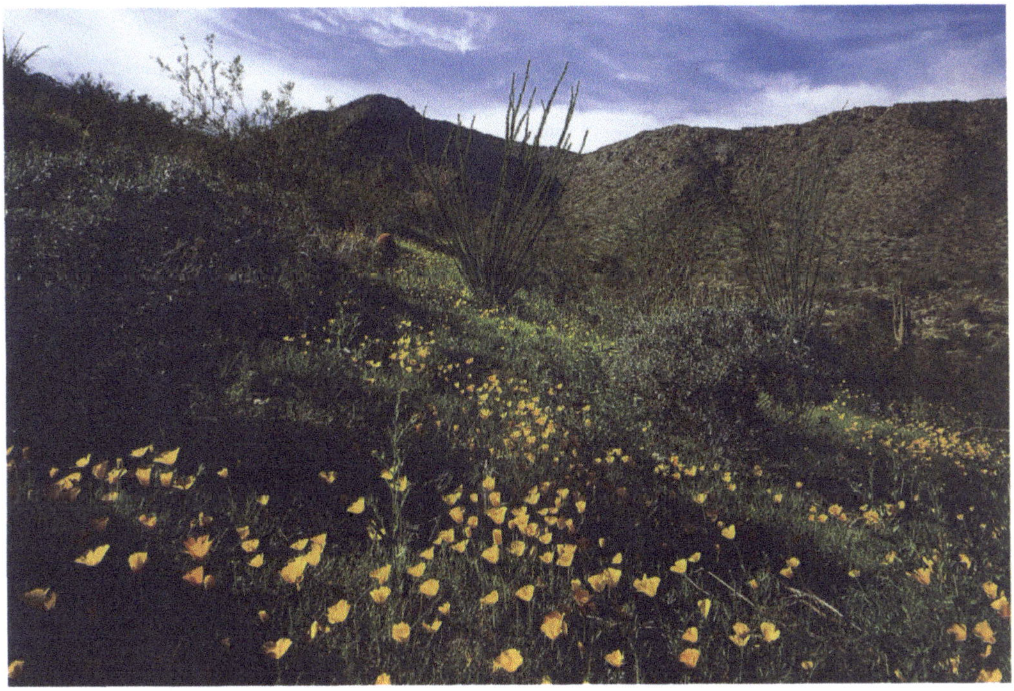

The northern entrance into South Mountain Park near Central Avenue. The desert vegetation in the South Mountains is diverse and can be very verdant after a rain.

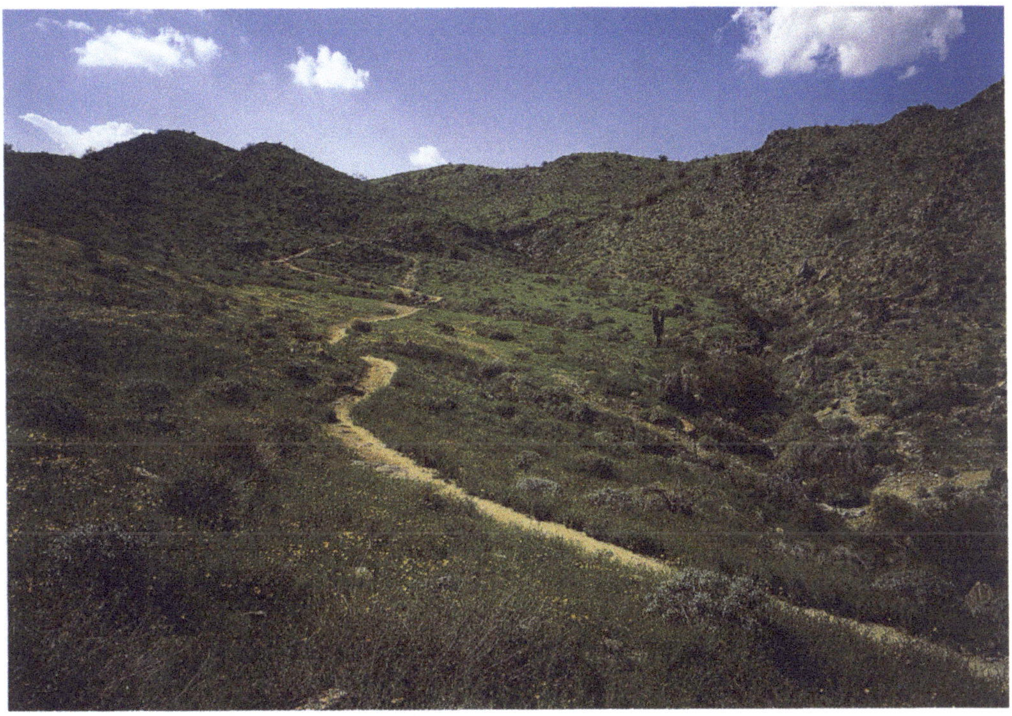

Javelina Trail, northeastern side of South Mountain Park. The presence of Hohokam artifacts and rock art sites along the many washes indicates that they have served as travel routes into the mountains for centuries.

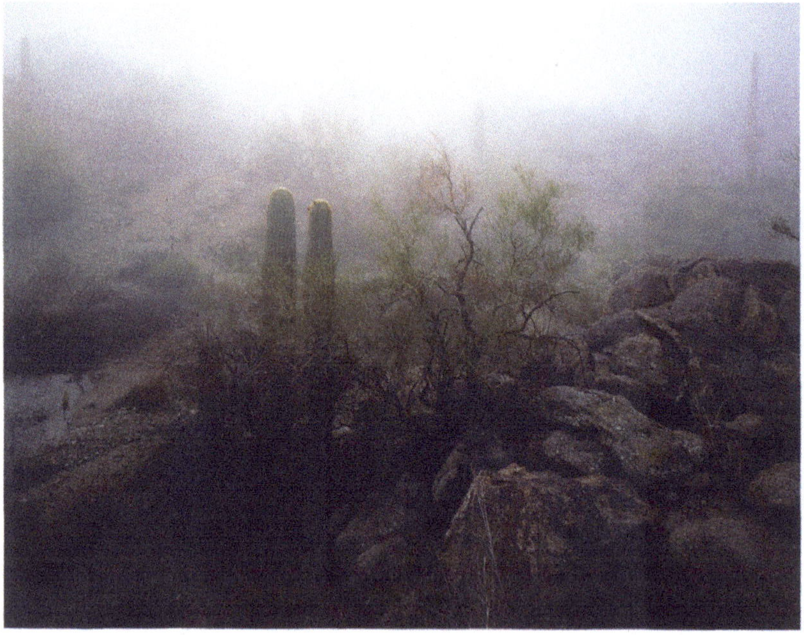

Dense fog in the upper canyons of the South Mountains, summit area. The weather in the upper part of the mountains can be quite dramatic at times, especially during summer thunderstorms.

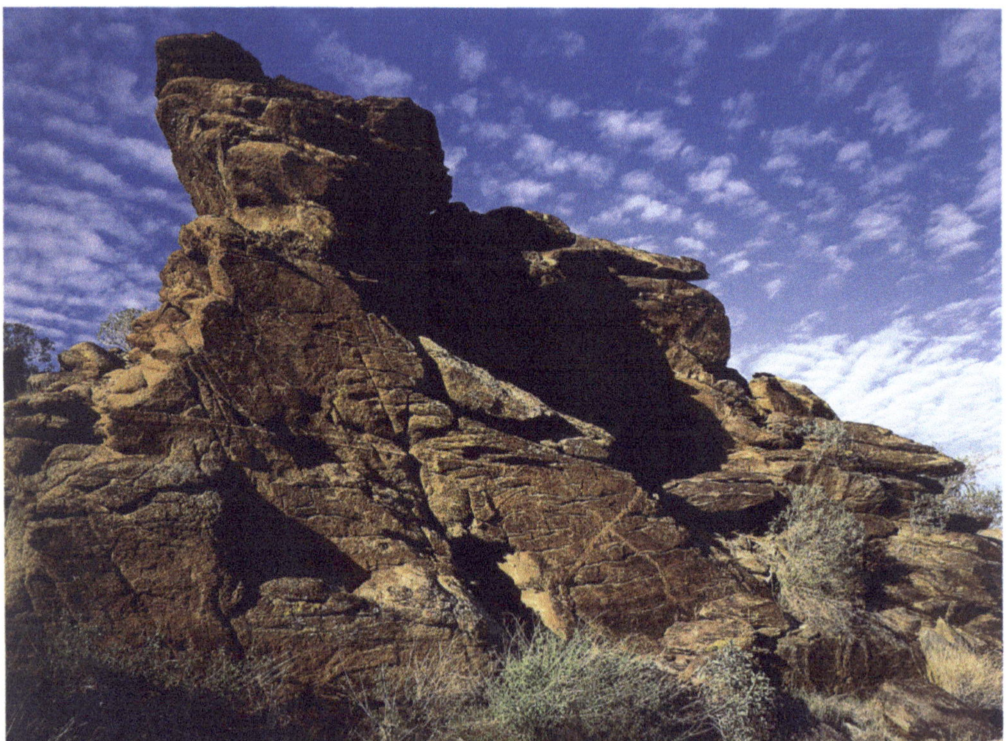

Dramatic rock formation and cloudy sky at the Yellow Rock Site, 24th Street Locality. The highly eroded rock in the South Mountains has created many beautiful rock formations. Rock art is sometimes associated with these formations.

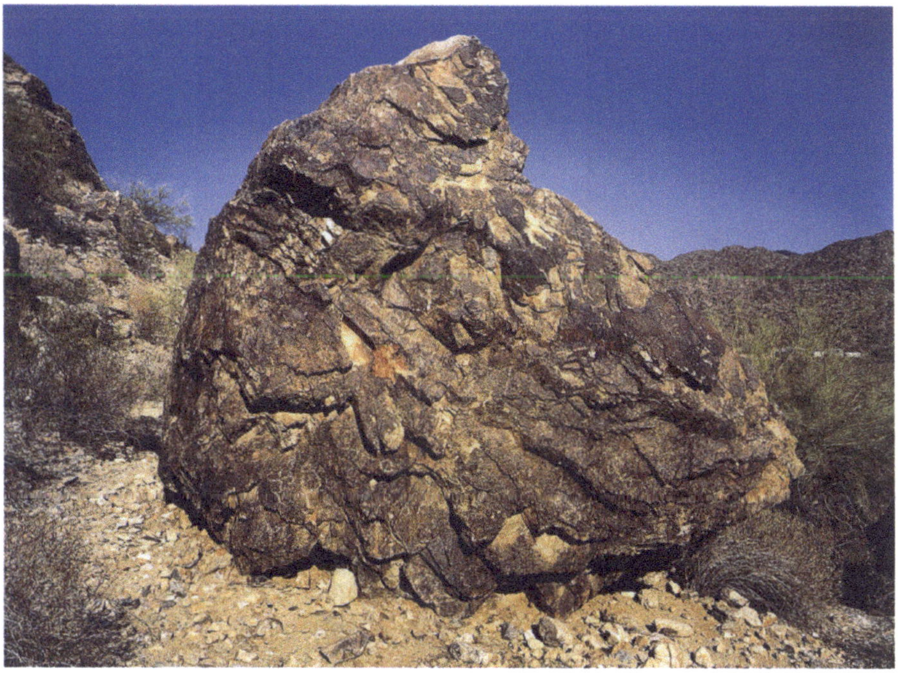

Large boulder with rock art located in mountain saddle, San Juan Canyon. Petroglyphs on this boulder include interesting geometric designs.

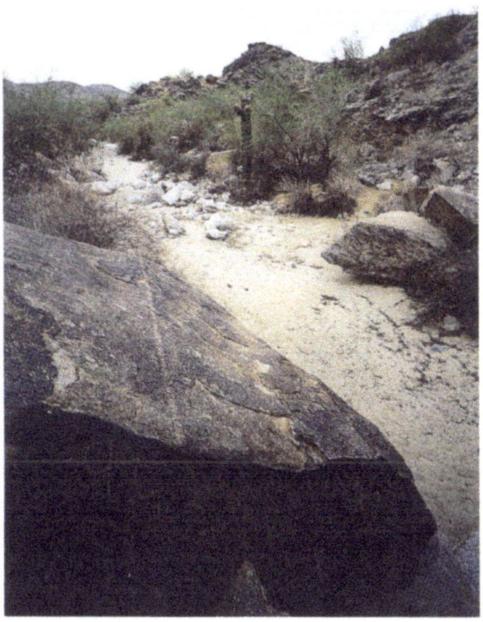

Boulder with rock art in wash, near Holbert Trail. This panel has an elaborate diamond chain design.

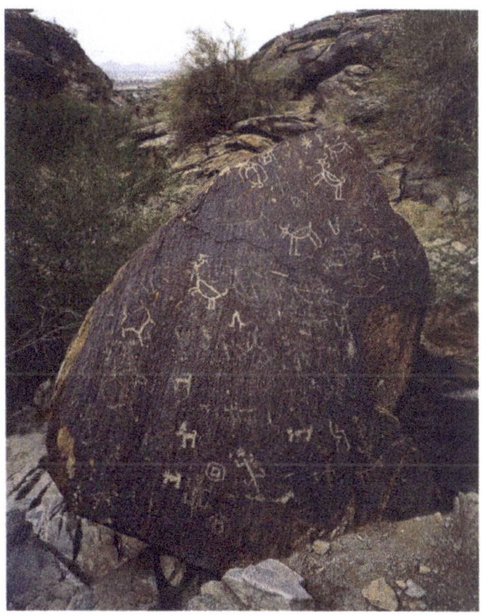

Large boulder in the middle of a wash, 16th Street Locality. Petroglyphs have been pecked on all sides of this boulder, and the main panel has had multiple pecking episodes.

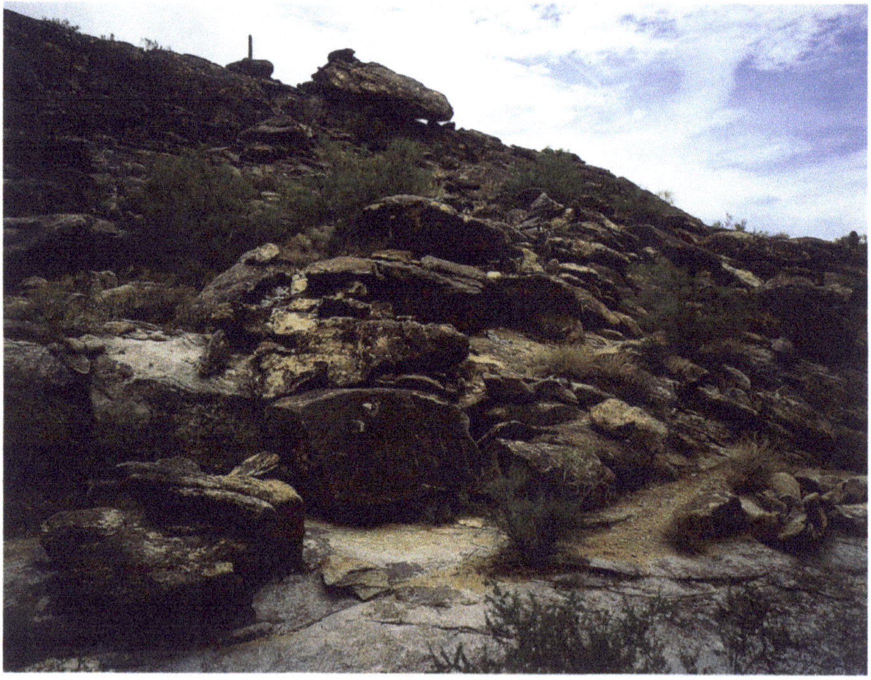

Boulder-strewn wash in an upper canyon of the South Mountains, summit area. A rock art panel on a large boulder adjacent to the wash contains bird petroglyphs.

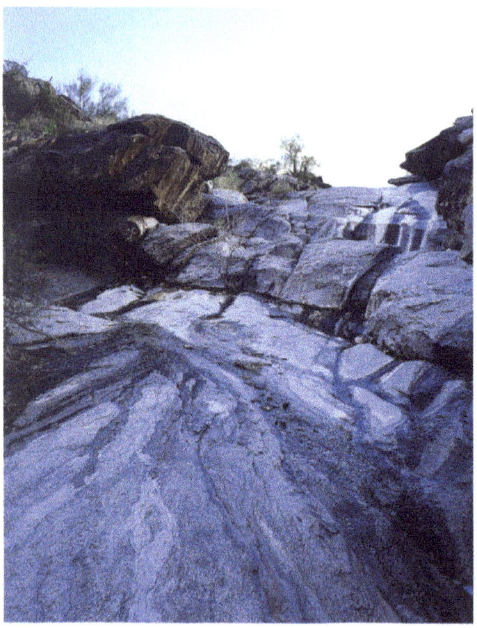

Hieroglyphic Canyon spring flowing during the wet season. This canyon has the most permanent spring in the South Mountains and contains one of the densest concentrations of rock art. Most of the canyon is owned by the Boy Scouts of America.

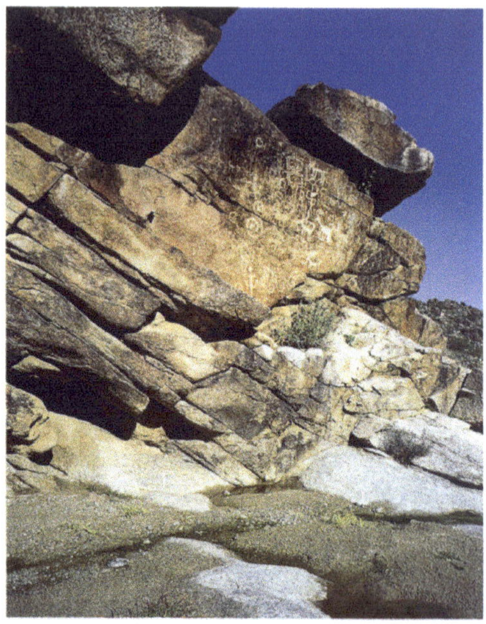

Natural water tank full of water at the southern end of Box Canyon. A rock art panel containing a pipette design and other petroglyphs overlooks the water tank.

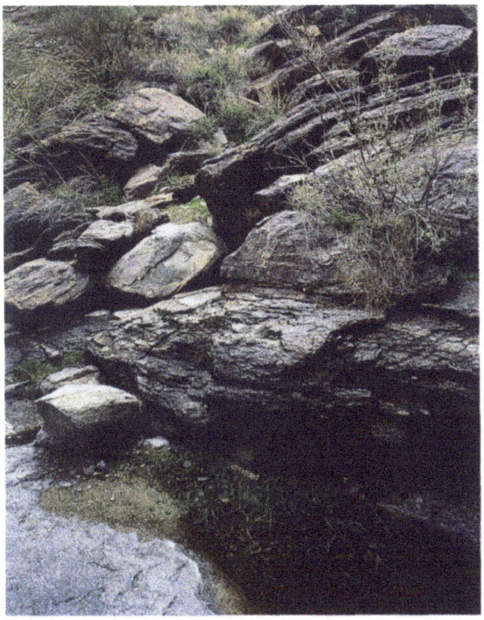

Natural water tank full of water in Goodman Canyon. Petroglyphs representing anthropomorphs and spirit beings are present above the water tank. This canyon was named after Michael Goodman, who lives at the base of the canyon and watches over the well-preserved rock art located within the canyon.

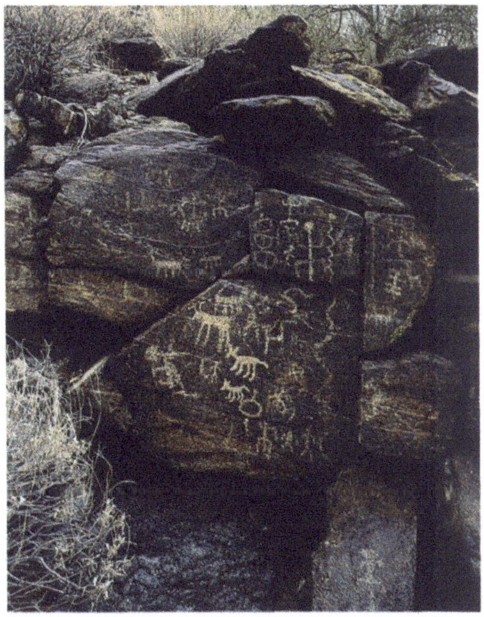

Rock art panel next to a spring in Goodman Canyon. Anthropomorphs, quadrupeds, snakes, and other designs are present in this panel.

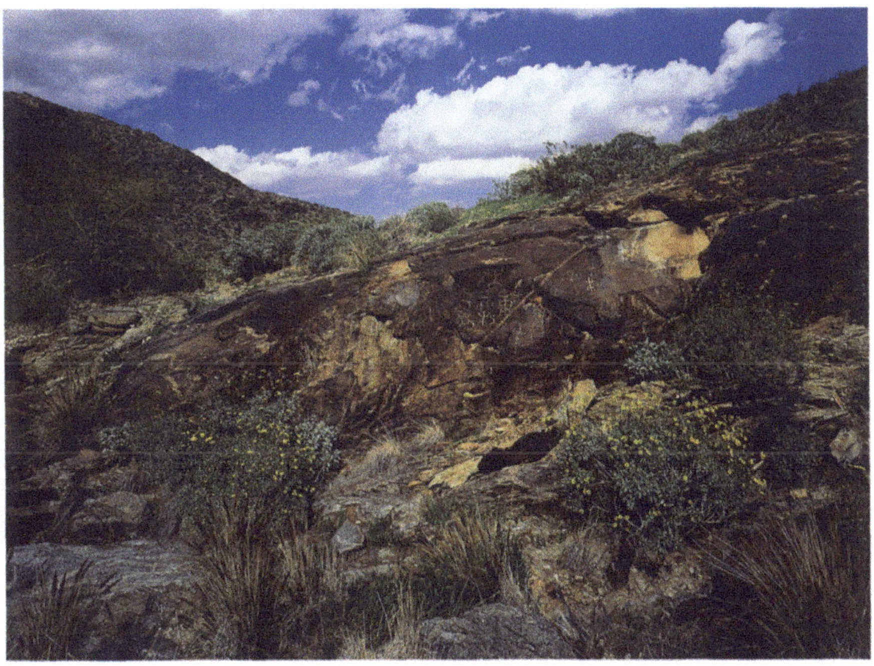

Rock art panel located next to natural water tanks in Javelina Canyon. The upper portion of this canyon contains a series of natural water tanks.

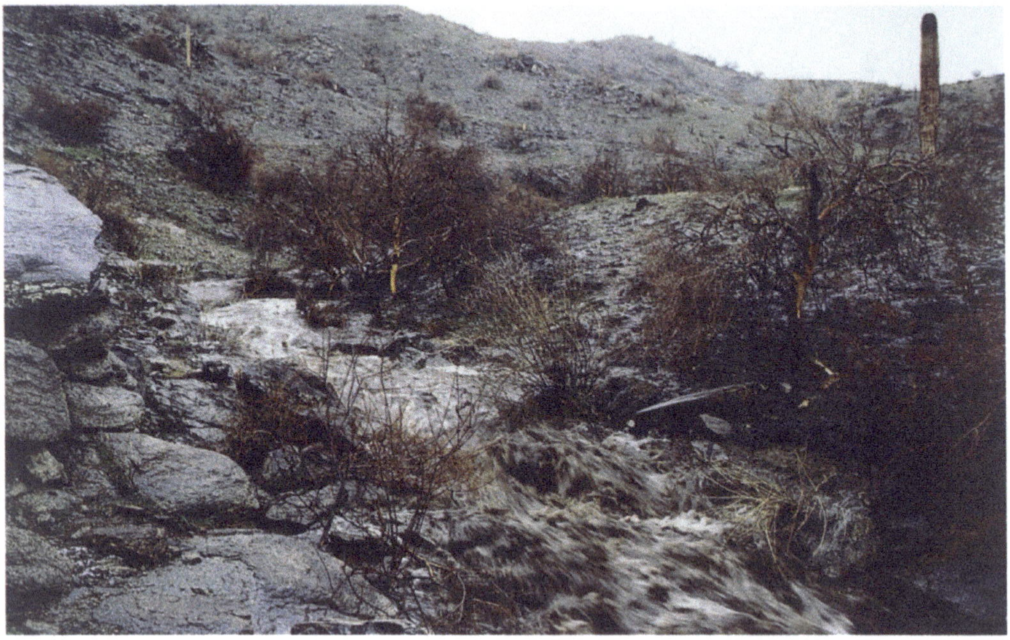

Wash in Javelina Canyon rushing with water from a summer thunderstorm. Vegetation in the area was badly damaged by a lightning-caused wildfire.

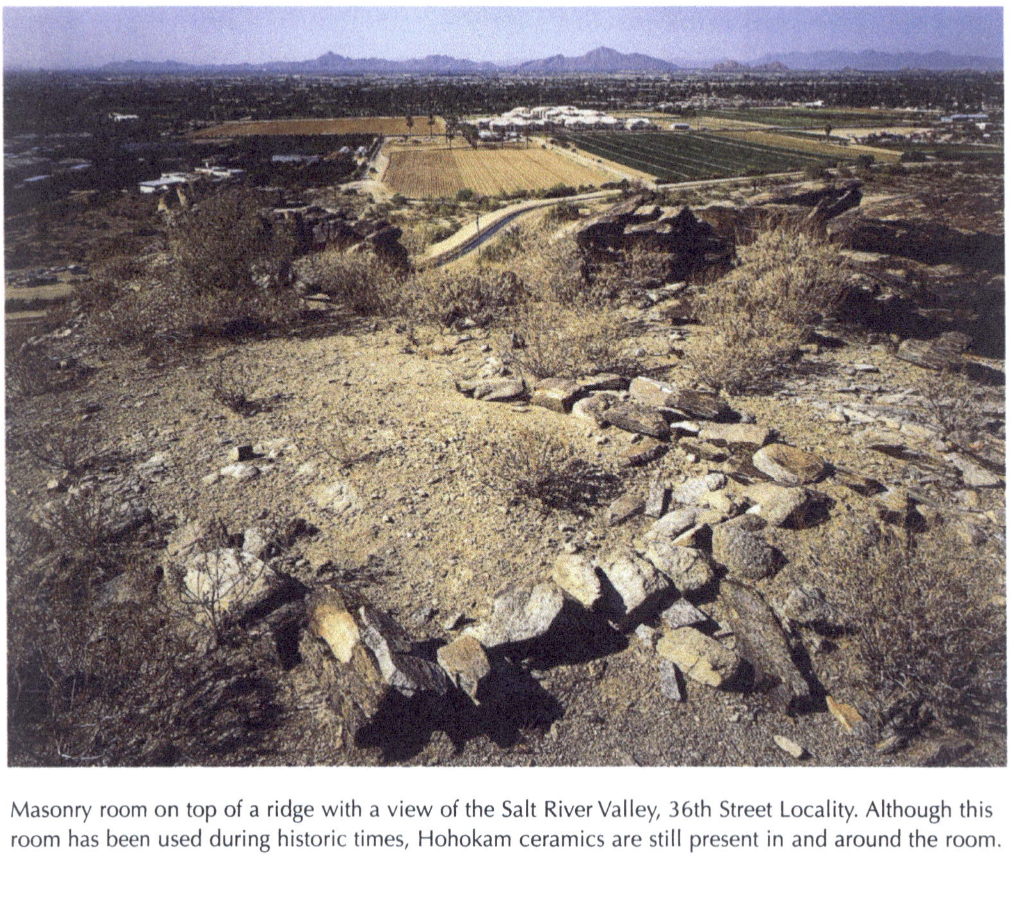

Masonry room on top of a ridge with a view of the Salt River Valley, 36th Street Locality. Although this room has been used during historic times, Hohokam ceramics are still present in and around the room.

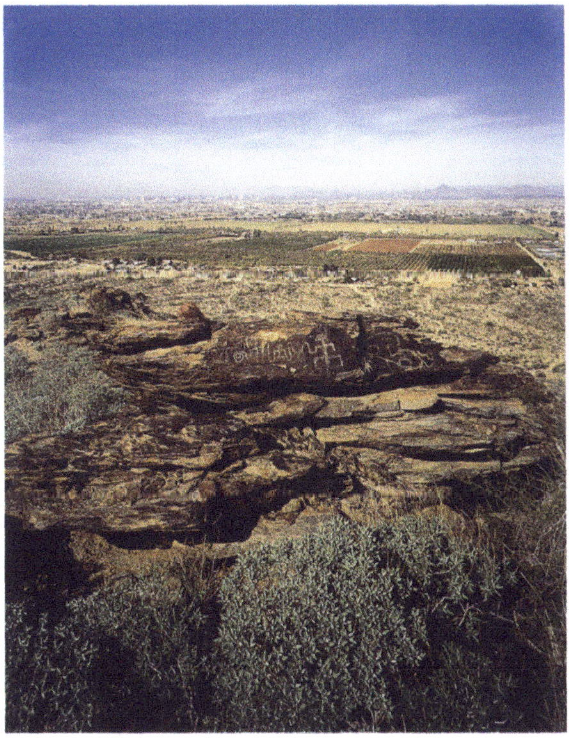

Rock art panel high up on the northeastern side of the South Mountains with a view of the Salt River Valley, 32nd Street Locality. This panel is one of many that are spread across the northeastern face of the South Mountains around 1,500 feet (450 m) in elevation.

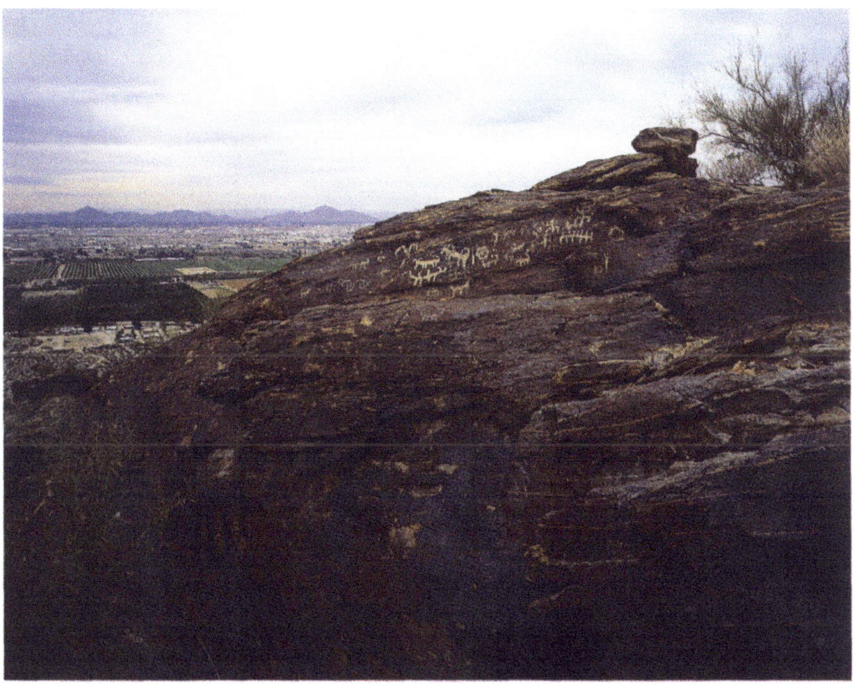

Rock art panel in the upper portion of Goodman Canyon with a view of the Salt River Valley.

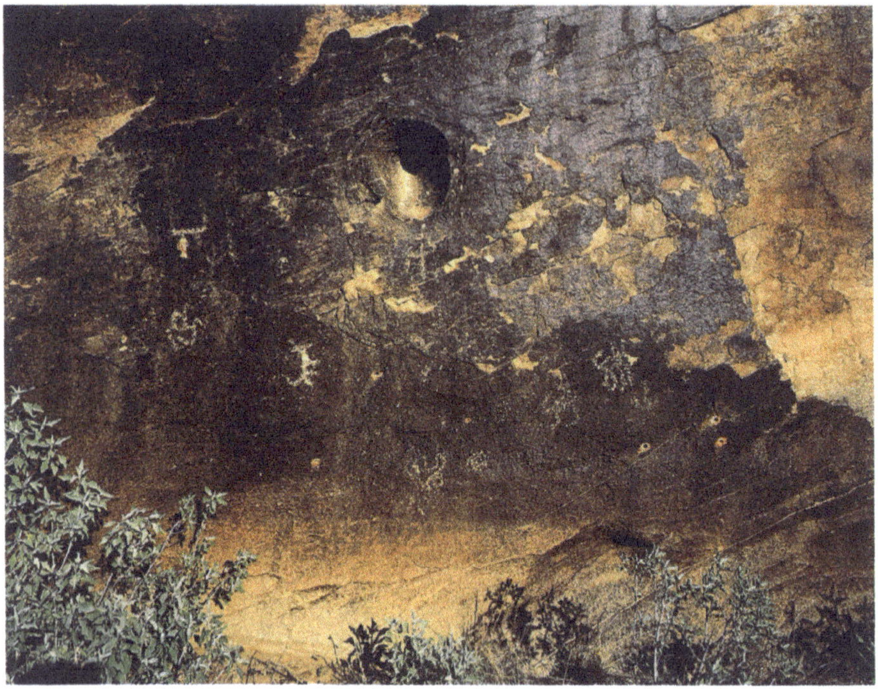

Petroglyphs next to a large natural hole in an outcrop next to a wash, upper 32nd Street Locality. Below the hole is an anthropomorph who seems to be entering into the hole, which may represent a portal into the stone.

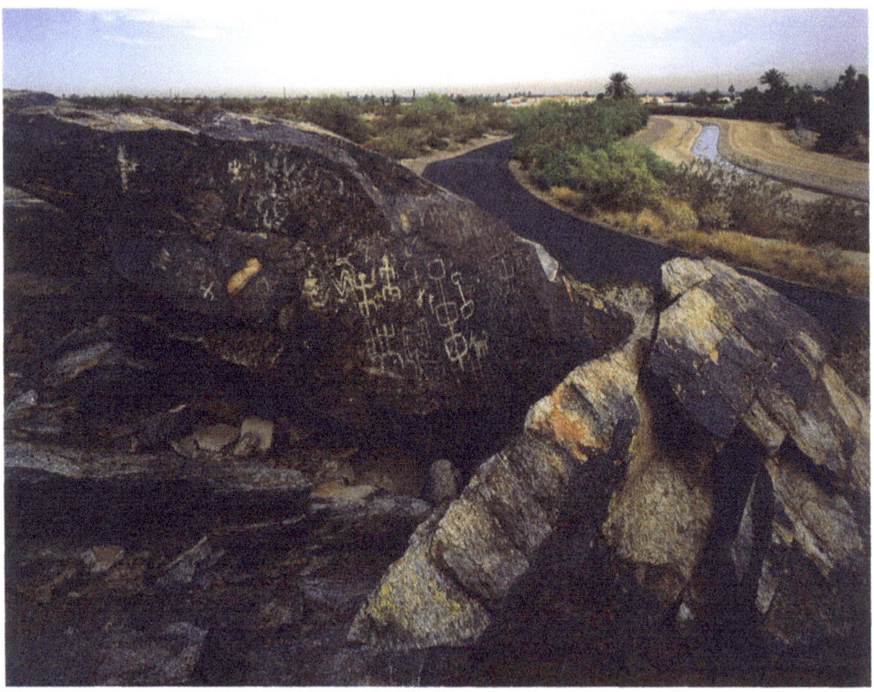

Rock art panel in a rock cleft at the northern base of the South Mountains, 36th Street Locality. This panel has multiple pecking episodes in which anthropomorphs appear to have been added into an existing scene.

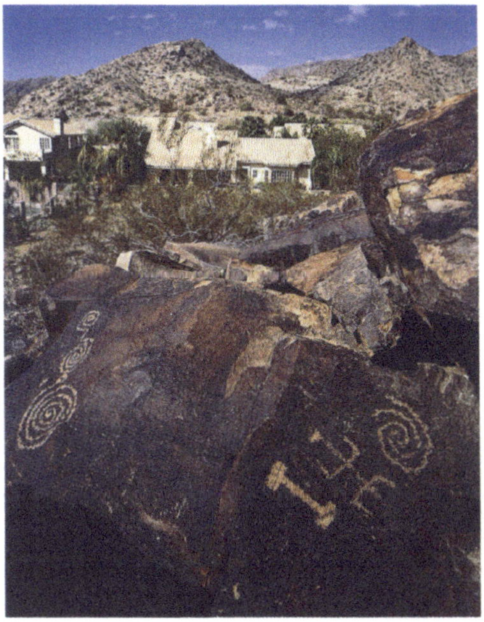

Rock art site located in a residential area on the southern side of the South Mountains, outside the park's boundaries. The spirals appear to be coiled snakes.

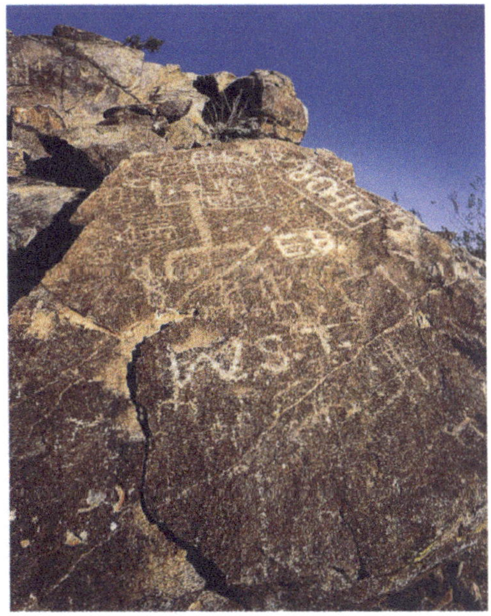

Vandalized rock art panel in Beverly Canyon in the northeastern end of the park. This panel contains two of the largest anthropomorph petroglyphs in the South Mountains; both are more than 1 m in length. Modern initials cover portions of both anthropomorphs.

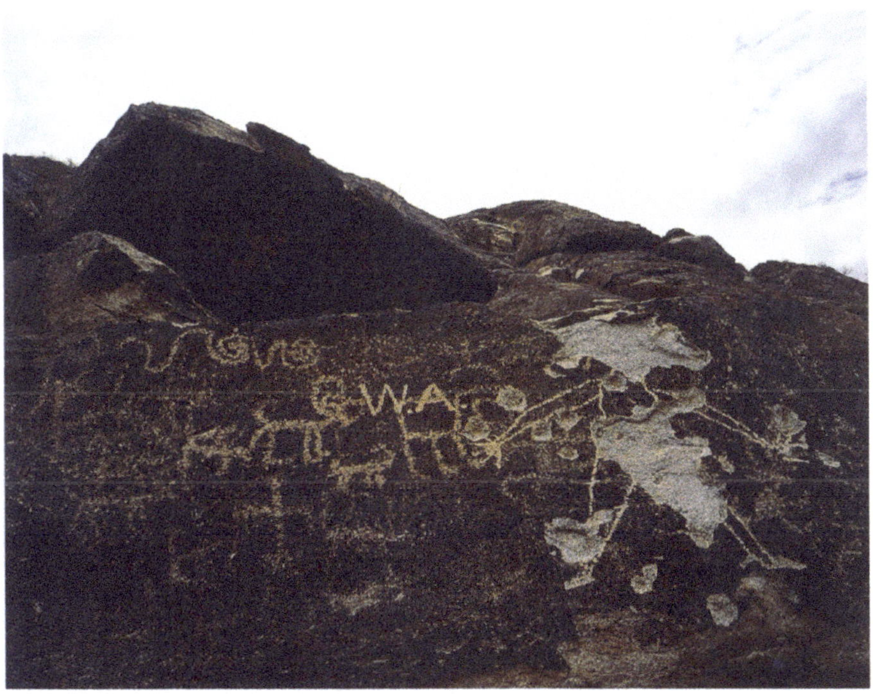

Vandalized rock art panel in Box Canyon. In modern times, someone pecked a female human figure on top of a prehistoric Hohokam rock art panel and then shot the petroglyph full of holes with a gun.

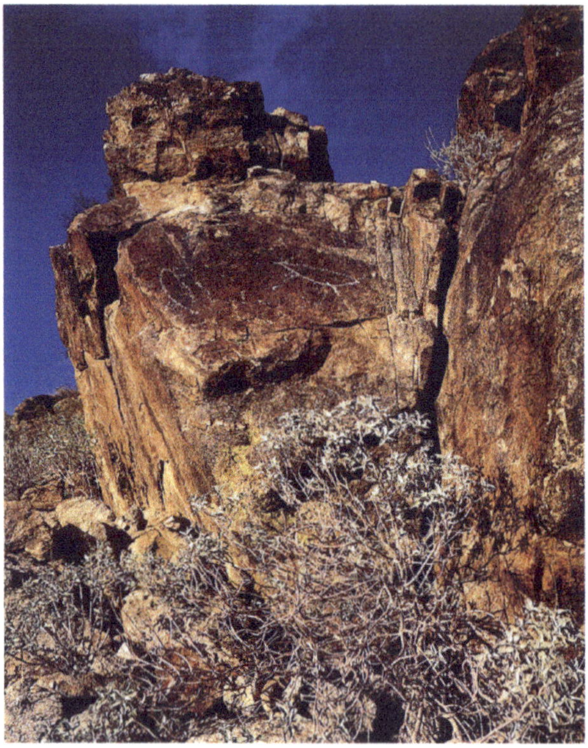

Rock outcrop with mountain sheep petroglyphs at the San Juan North Locality. A trail into the South Mountains passes close to this outcrop.

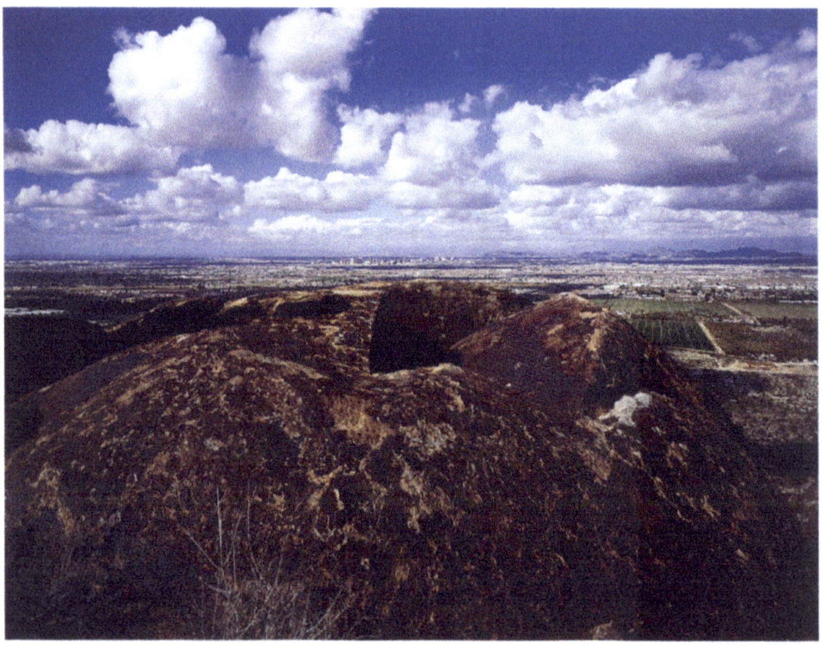

View north over the city of Phoenix from a large split boulder that contains rock art. This massive, fragmented boulder is located high up the mountain near the Mormon Trail.

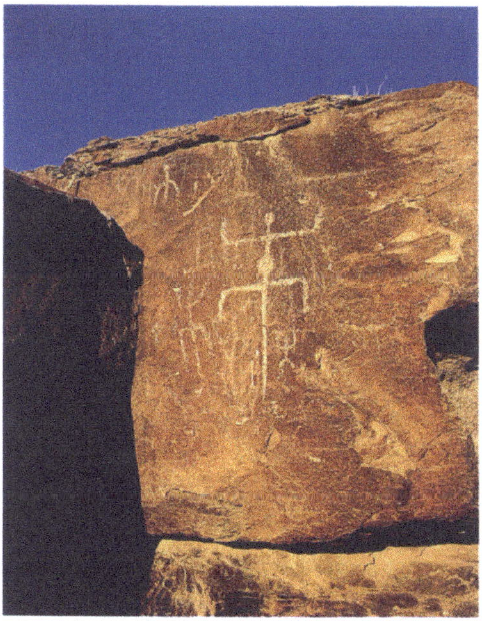

Large lizard petroglyph in lower Pima Canyon. A smaller anthropomorph below the lizard has upraised arms as though saluting the lizard. The summer solstice sun rises over this rock art panel.

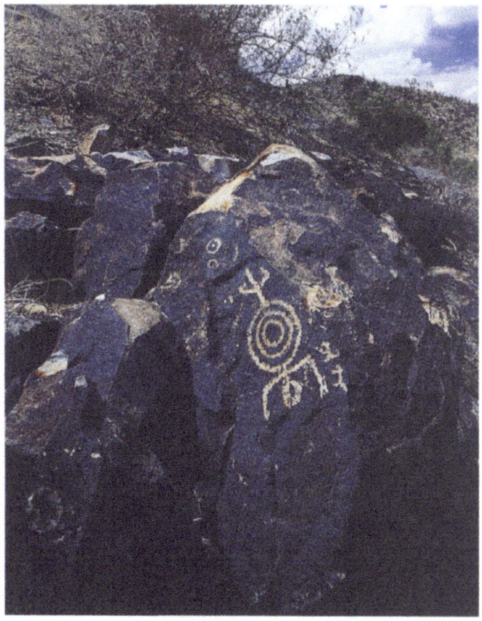

Large lizard petroglyph with concentric circles for a body, 28th Place Locality. This petroglyph may represent one of several lizard species that live in the South Mountains.

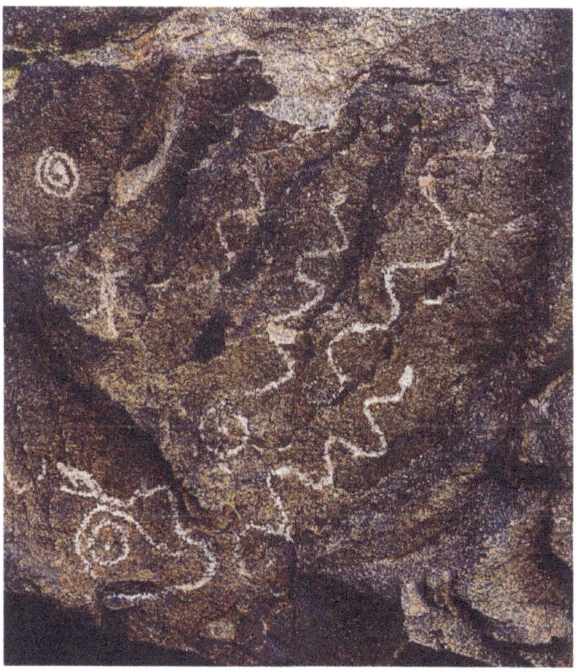

Rock art panel with multiple snakes that appear to be in motion, Southeast Side Locality. Many kinds of snakes inhabit the South Mountains, and perhaps it is not surprising that snake petroglyphs are the fourth most common rock art design in the South Mountains (behind anthropomorphs, various circles, and quadrupeds).

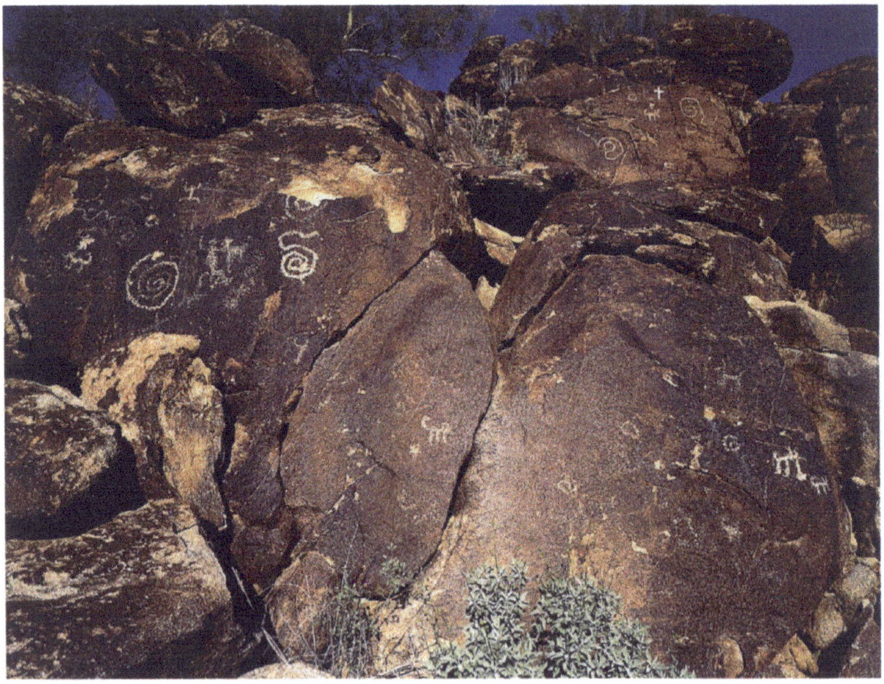

Coiled snake petroglyphs in Box Canyon. This cluster of panels is located high up on the side of the canyon. A stick-figure cross that may be more recent is present in the uppermost panel.

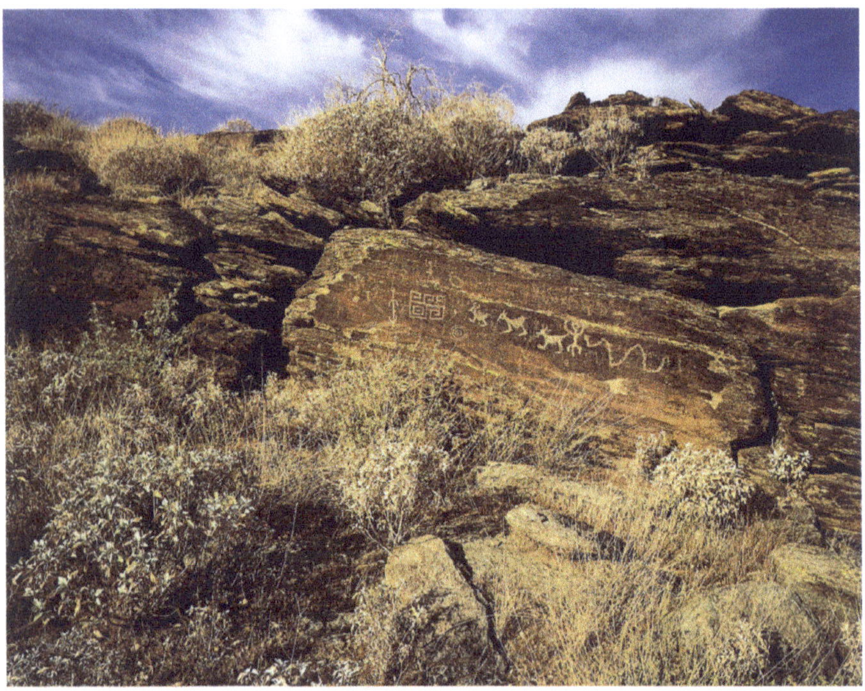

Rock art panel with snakes, anthropomorphs, quadrupeds, and geometric designs at the 32nd Street Locality. The designs are arranged in a line as though they are in a procession. A flat area containing Hohokam ceramics is present in front of this panel.

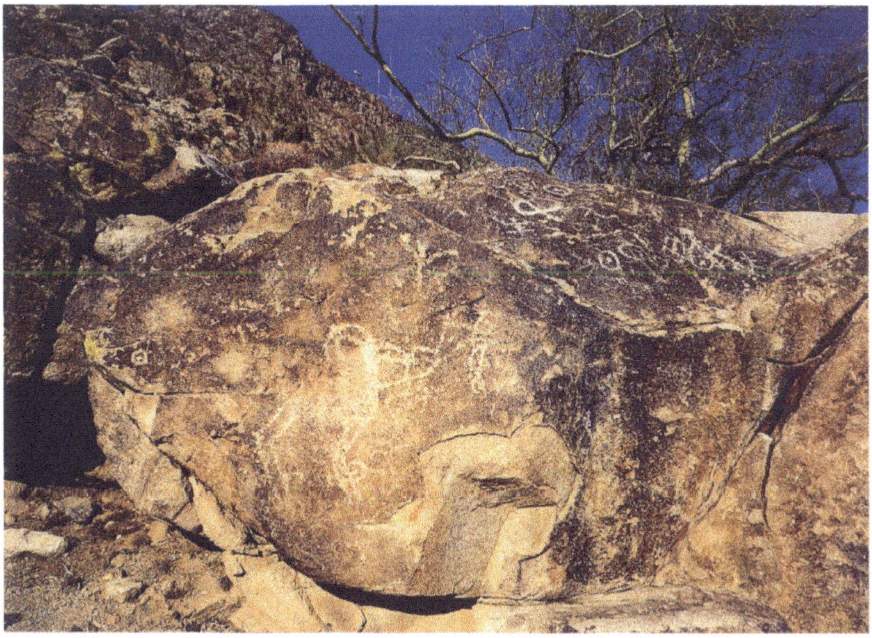

Large boulder containing multiple rock art panels and located along the trail to Telegraph Pass on the southern side of the South Mountains. One of the panels contains a well-executed mountain sheep holding a snake in its mouth. Hohokam ceramics have been found near this panel, indicating that Telegraph Pass has been used for centuries as a travel route.

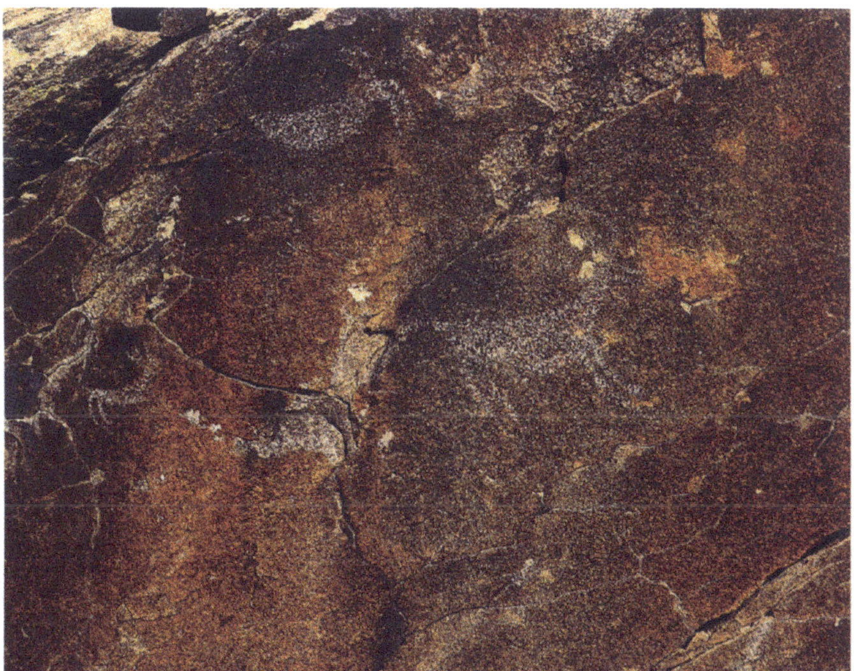

Delicately pecked mountain sheep petroglyphs in a boulder alcove, lower 12th Street Locality. A flat boulder is located in front of this panel. Similar rock art settings are found throughout the South Mountains, suggesting that rock alcoves and other isolated spaces were considered special places.

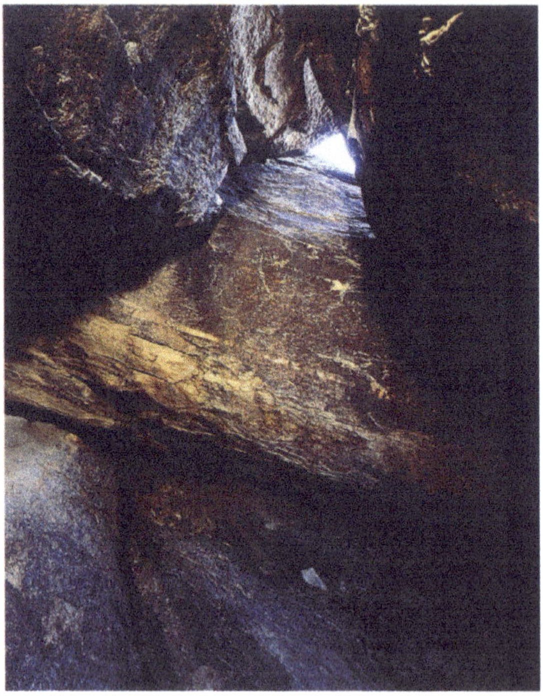

Mountain sheep petroglyph inside a large rock shelter in the upper portion of Goodman Canyon. The rock shelter is created by a cavity in the middle of a pile of massive boulders. The mountain sheep petroglyph is illuminated by a ray of light that streams through a hole in the roof of the rock shelter.

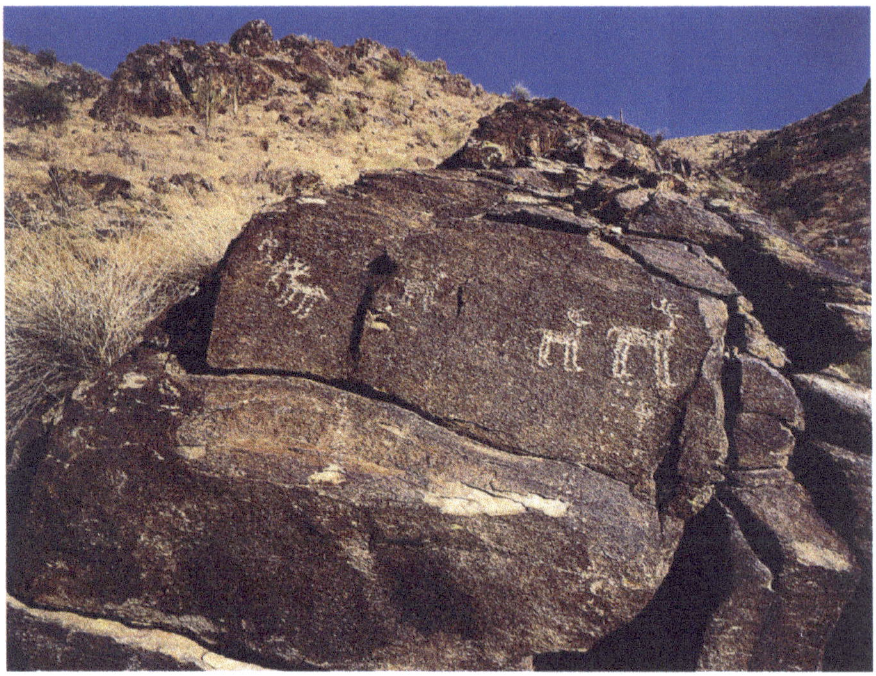

Four deer and their tracks, 36th Street Locality. A hunter is located below the deer on the right side of the panel, and another anthropomorph is wrestling with the deer on the left side of the panel. Animal track petroglyphs are uncommon in the South Mountains.

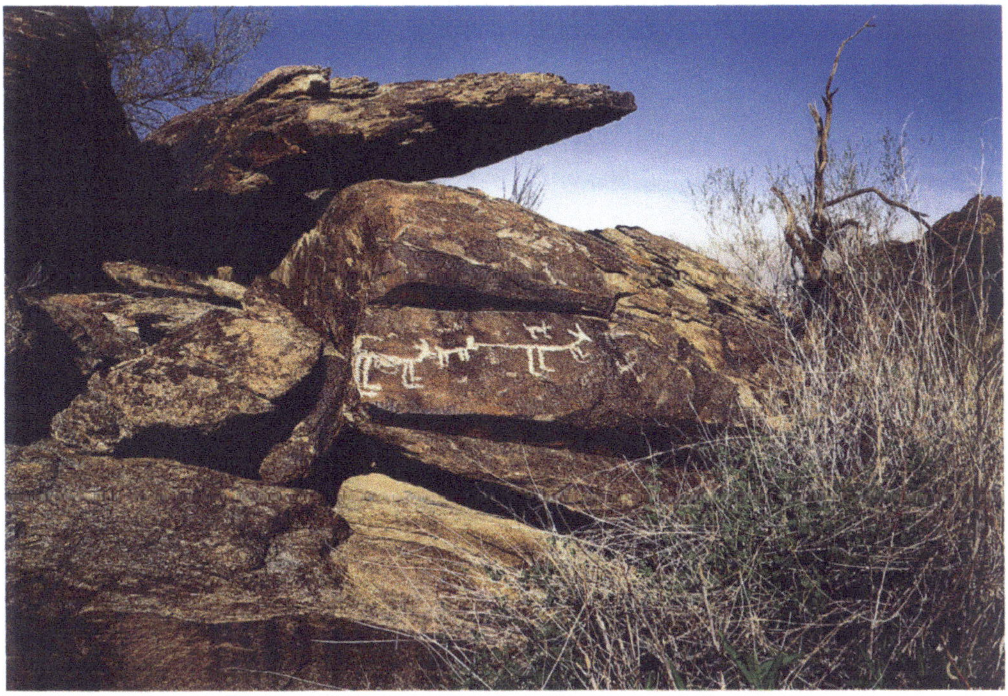

Four-legged mammals that may represent coyotes or dogs, upper Goodman Canyon. This panel is located in a wash near a spring.

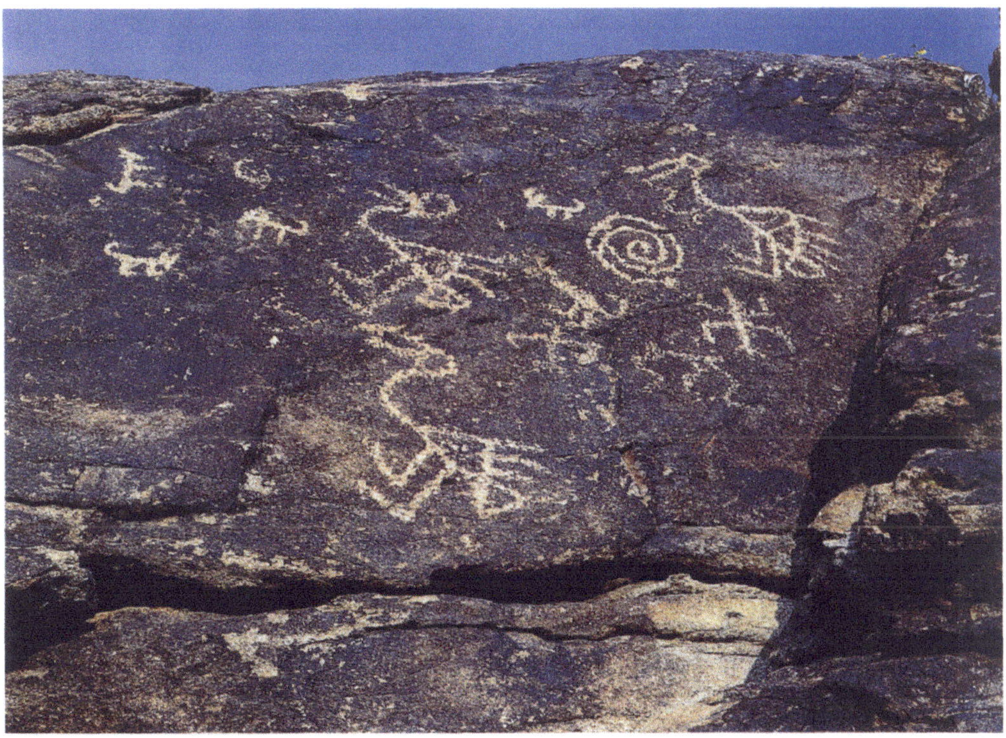

Waterbird petroglyphs in Box Canyon. This panel is located high up on the western side of Box Canyon and faces east.

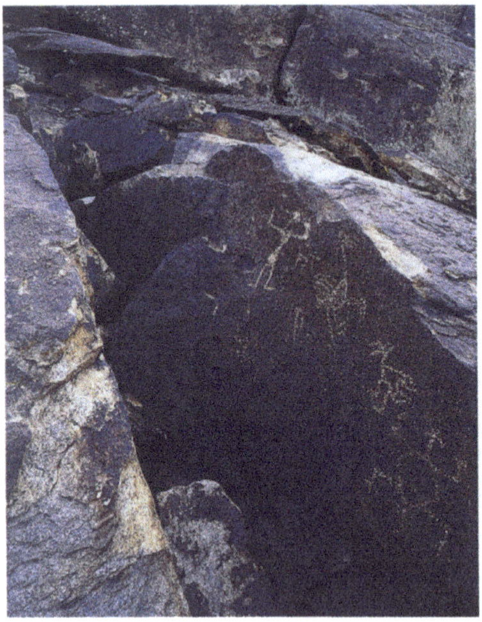

Rock art panel inside a boulder cleft in Box Canyon. Two unusual birds, a large lizard, and several anthropomorphs are depicted. One of the birds has four legs.

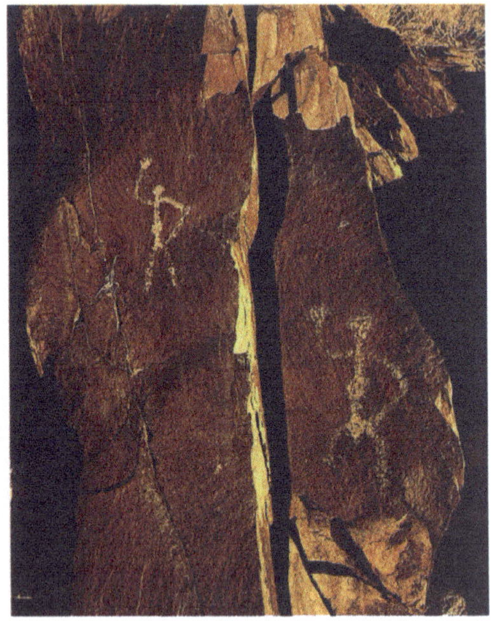

Two anthropomorphs, both with expanded midbodies and one upraised arm, upper 32nd Street Locality. The anthropomorph on the right has facial features, including two eyes and a mouth. Many of the anthropomorphs with solidly pecked heads in the South Mountains have hollow eyes.

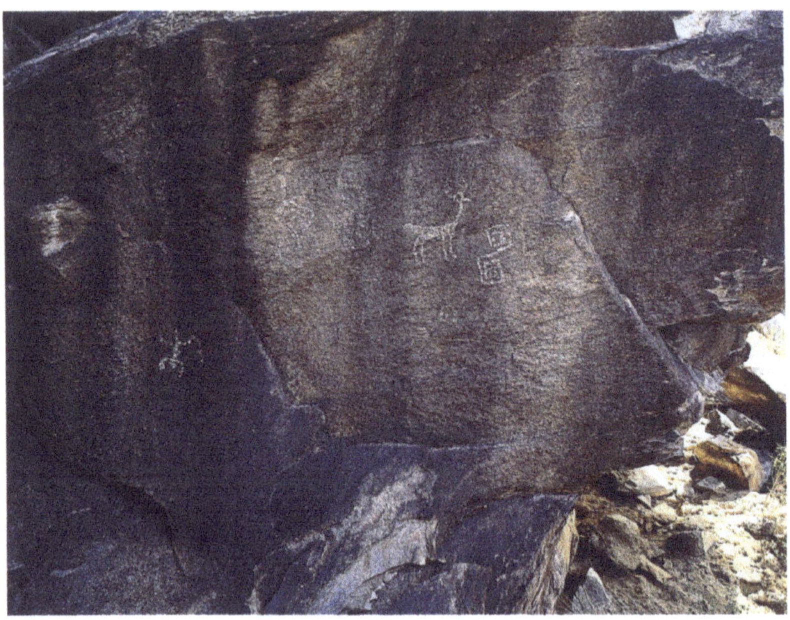

Rock art panel depicting a shaman and his spirit helpers. A lizard, a waterbird, a deer, and two geometric designs loom above an anthropomorph holding a cane. This panel is located in a rock alcove above a natural tunnel and next to a wash in upper Goodman Canyon.

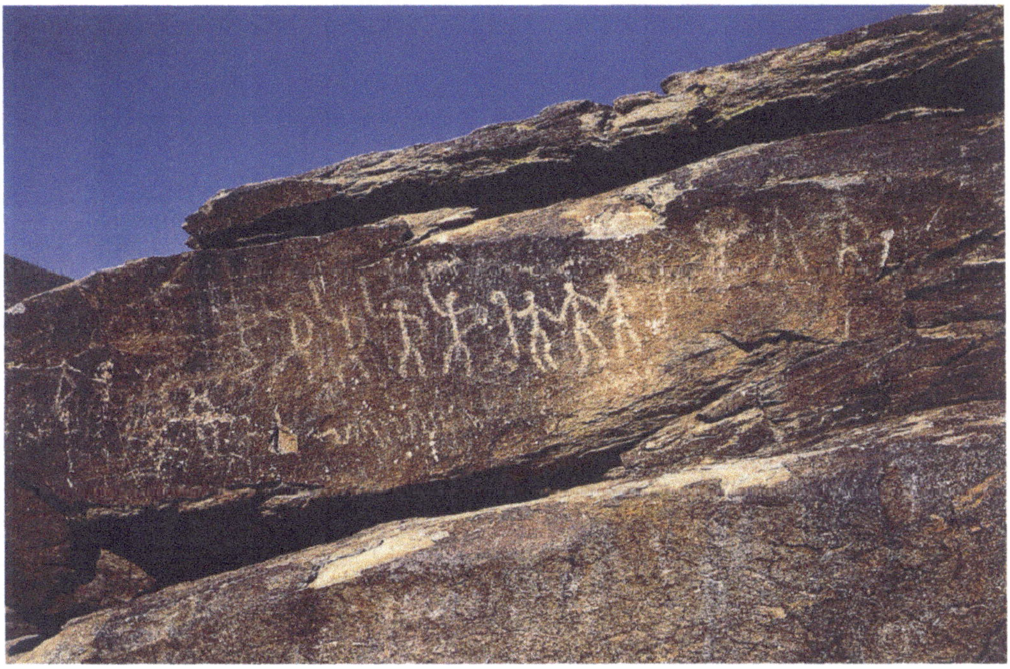

Dancers on a large boulder next to a wash in upper Pima Canyon. A sketch of this panel was published by anthropologist Frank Hamilton Cushing in 1890. One of the dancers in the middle of the panel appears to originally have been a cane that was later turned into a dancer.

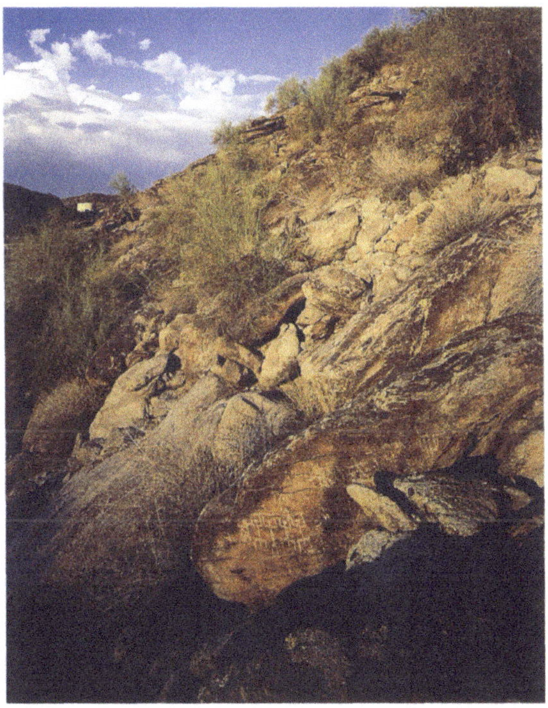

Dancers on an outcrop in Box Canyon. Five anthropomorphs are standing with their arms upraised and holding a string that is attached to the neck of another anthropomorph who is sitting or crouching. Petroglyphs that appear to be quadrupeds with segmented bodies also are present in this panel.

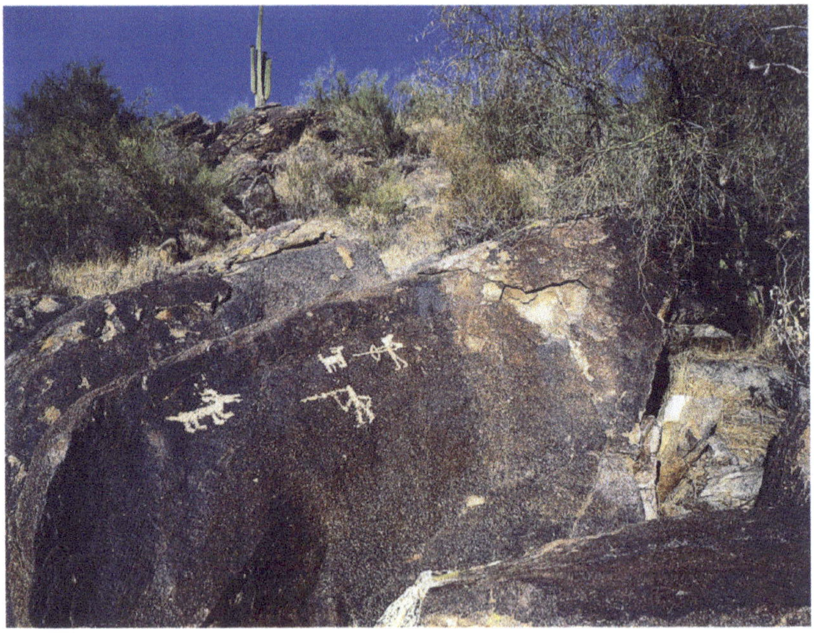

Hunter with a bow and arrow in the 12th Street Locality. The other anthropomorph in the panel may be playing a flute or shooting a blowgun.

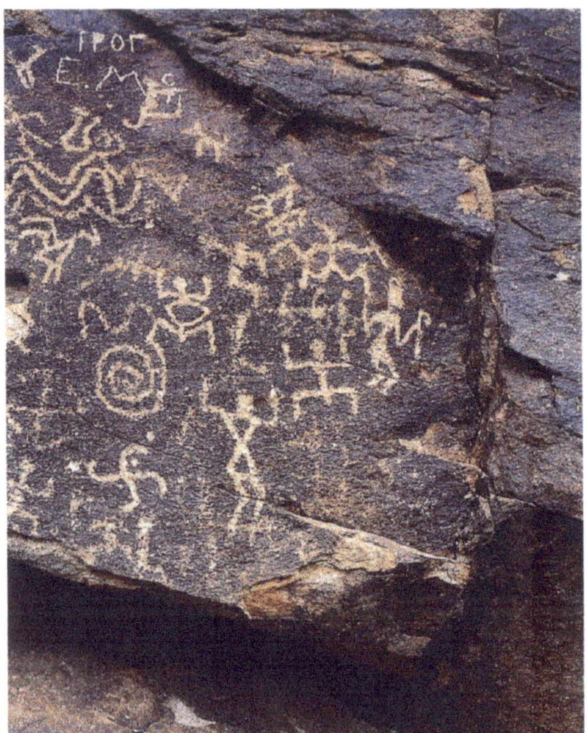

Rock art panel containing two anthropomorphs with unusual hourglass-shaped bodies, Box Canyon. One of the hourglass anthropomorphs holds a cane. The small boulder below this panel also contains rock art and has a natural hole that has been enlarged, perhaps for holding prayer sticks.

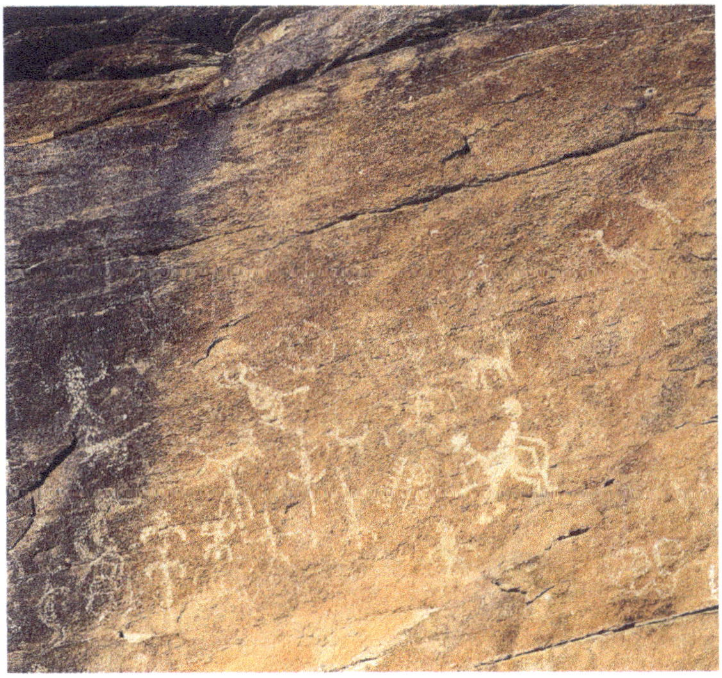

Complex rock art panel in Hieroglyphic Canyon. Some of the many interesting petroglyphs in this panel are singing birds (upper right) and an anthropomorph wearing a bird mask (lower left).

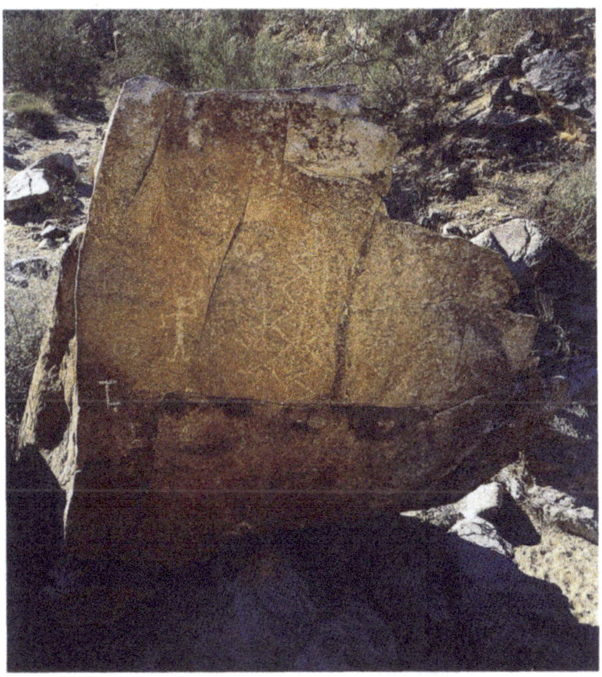

Boulder with rock art next to a wash in the Kiwanis Trail Locality. In the lower, left portion of the boulder is an anthropomorph wearing a bird mask. A large diamond chain also is present to the right of the masked figure.

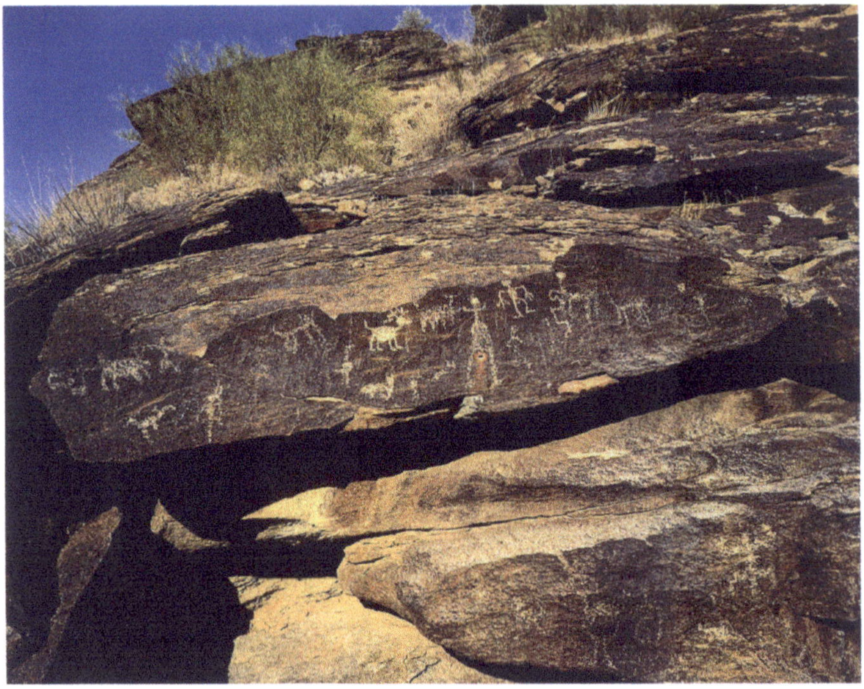

Complex rock art panel containing a female anthropomorph who has a natural red stain between her legs that appears to represent menstruation. This rare depiction of menstruation is located in front of a natural water tank in upper Goodman Canyon.

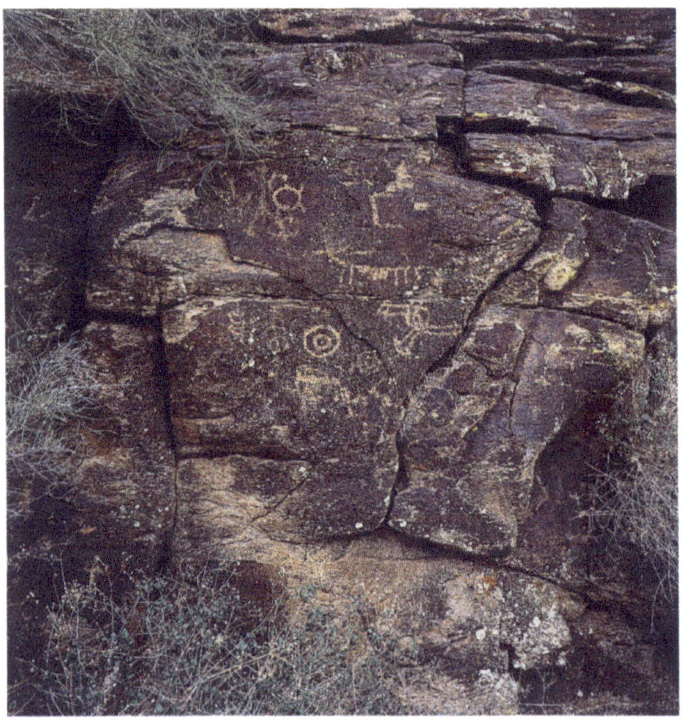

Complex set of petroglyphs with superpositioning of designs, upper 32nd Street Locality. Petroglyphs include anthropomorphs, quadrupeds, lizards, snakes, and geometric designs.

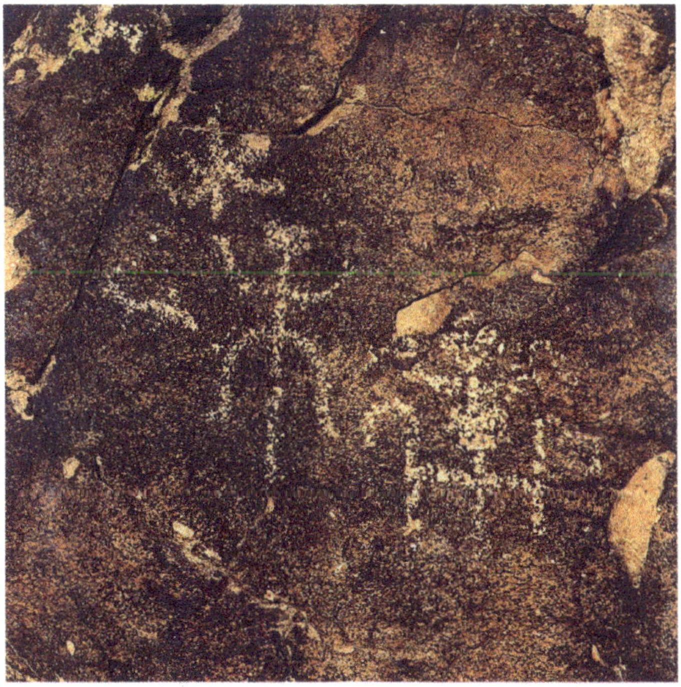

Anthropomorphs in San Juan North Locality. The anthropomorph on the lower right has crooks coming out of both knees and is holding an unknown object.

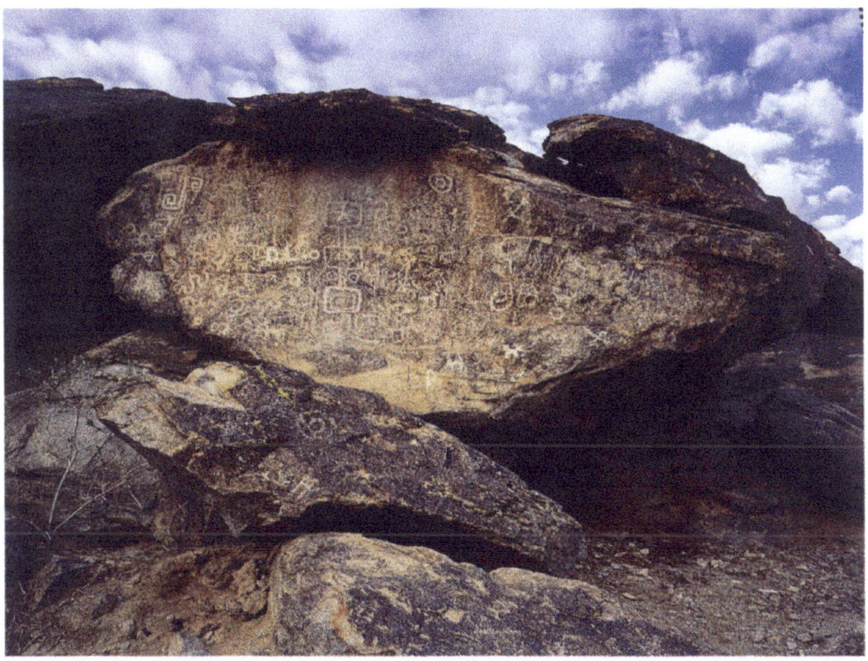

Boulder with a pipette design among numerous other petroglyphs, southeastern side of the South Mountains, near the entrance to Pima Canyon. Hohokam ceramics dating to the ninth and tenth centuries have been found next to this cluster of panels. This rock art is highly visible from a major trail that winds around the southeastern side of the mountains and connects with the route into Pima Canyon.

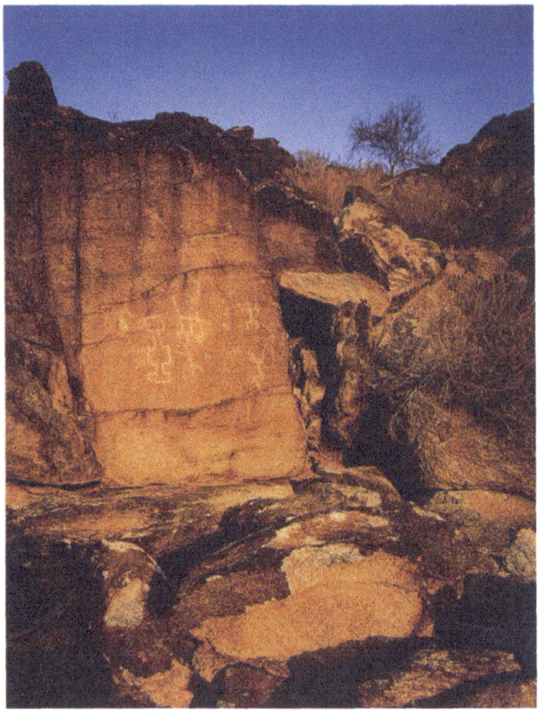

Rock art panel containing a pipette design in a rock alcove, Box Canyon. Other interesting petroglyphs in this panel include a tadpole, a mountain sheep with a segmented body, an anthropomorph attached to lightning, and an anthropomorph holding a snake.

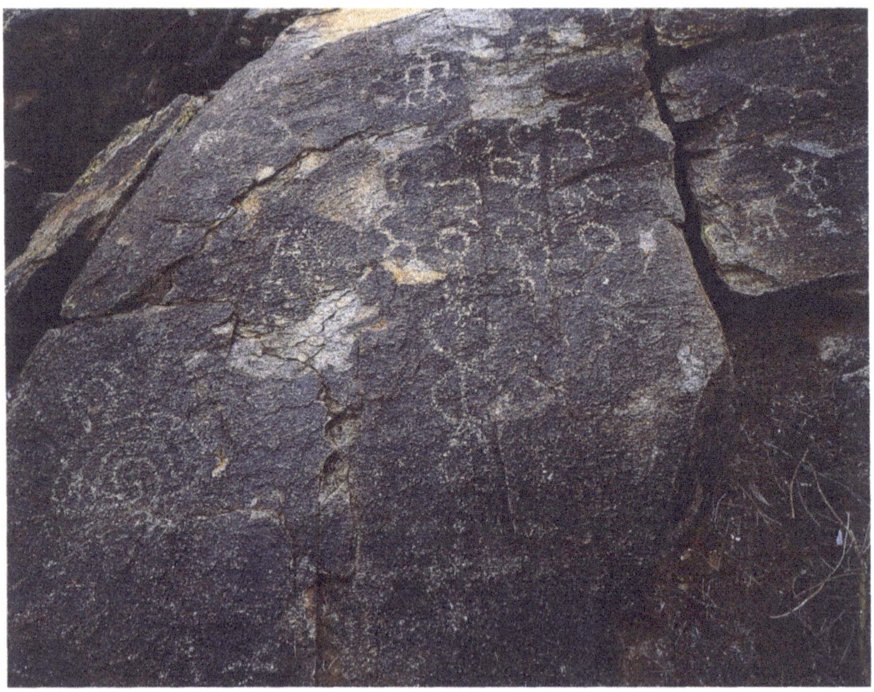

Rock art panel containing a pipette design at the entrance to lower Hieroglyphic Canyon. Anthropomorphs or lizards, turtles/tortoises, a circle chain, circles, and other petroglyphs also are present.

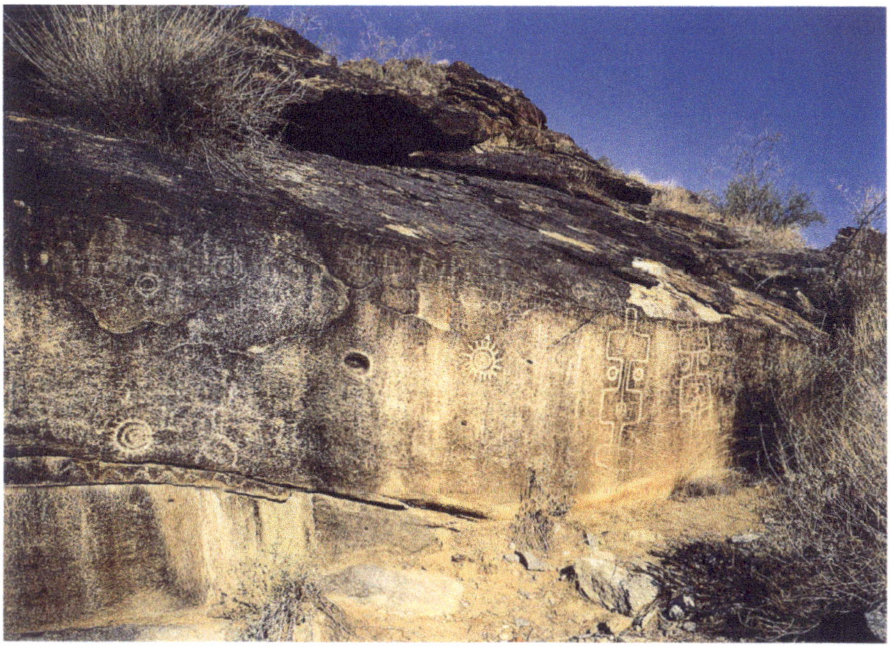

Rock art panels on the western side of the upper part of Hieroglyphic Canyon. Two large pipettes are present to the right. Most of the face of this outcrop has been rubbed with a stone, with older designs obliterated and later designs added over some of the rubbed areas. In addition, a natural hole in the outcrop has been outlined with pecking marks.

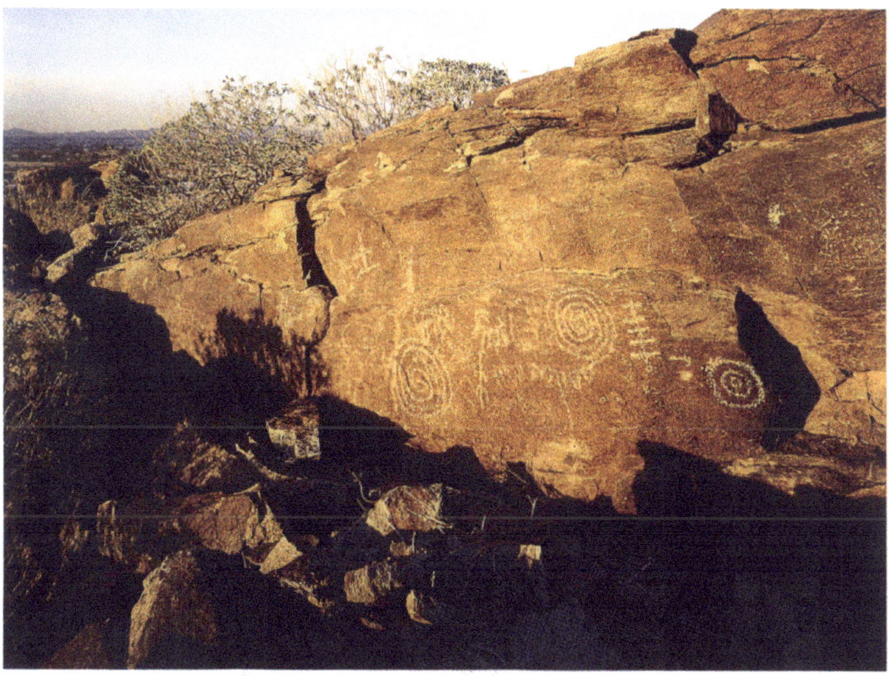

Complex rock art panel with two large spirals at the 36th Street Locality. One of the spirals has a series of triangles attached to it. Other petroglyphs include anthropomorphs, mountain sheep, concentric circles, and a centipede. This panel has been repatinated by "desert varnish" and may belong to the ancient Archaic tradition, which precedes the Hohokam.

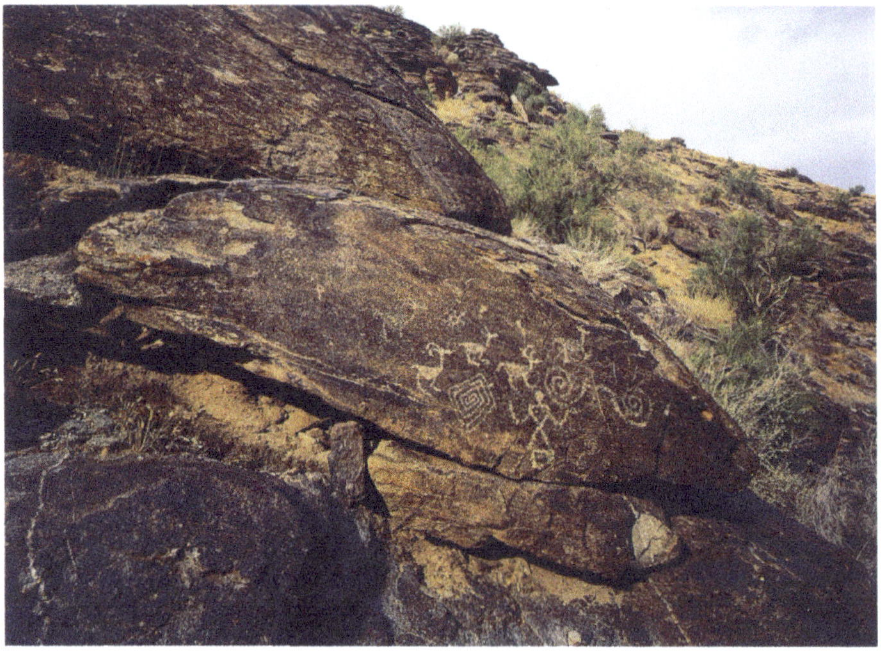

Rock art panel with an hourglass anthropomorph holding a line attached to a double spiral. Several mountain sheep are present, including one with unrealistic, forward-pointing horns. Panel faces to the northeast.

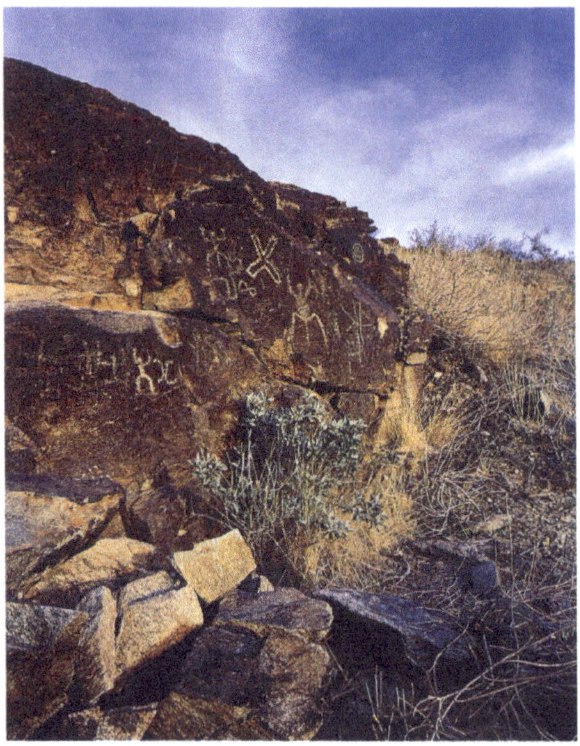

Rock art panel in which a large negative "X" is the central figure in the panel, 36th Street Locality. The anthropomorphs on the far left appear to be dancing.

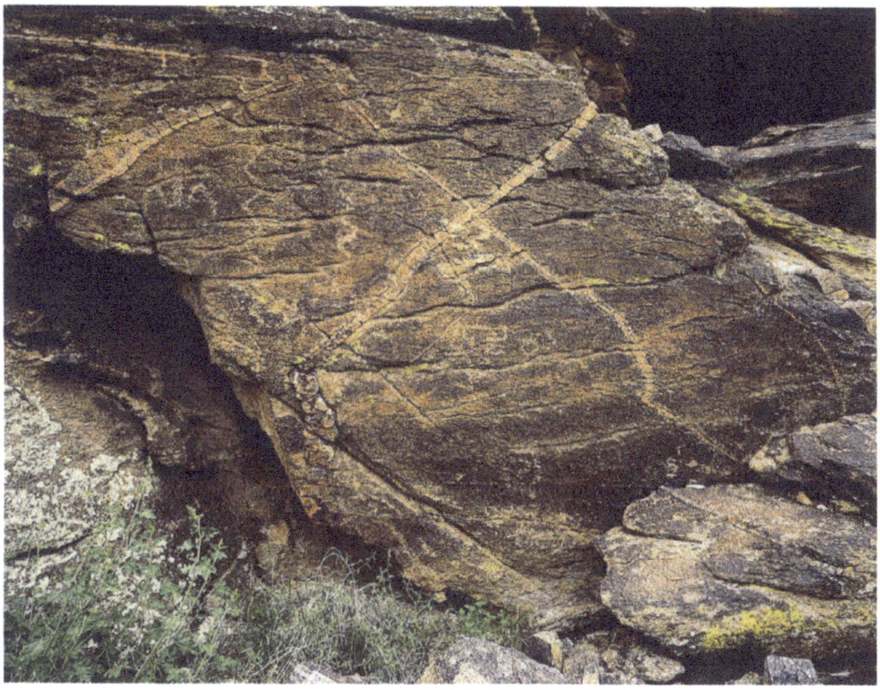

Rock art panel in which a natural "X" design created by a mineral vein in an outcrop has been outlined by pecking, Yellow Rock Site, 24th Street Locality. Other petroglyphs include anthropomorphs, snakes, spirals, a small "X," and other designs.

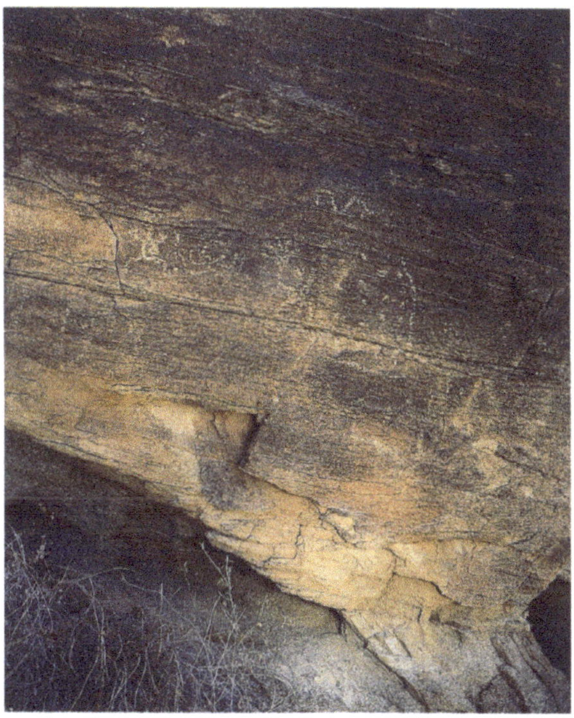

Box with multiple dots inside, Hieroglyphic Canyon. The anthropomorph with a large left hand is adjacent to the box and may be responsible for the content of the box.

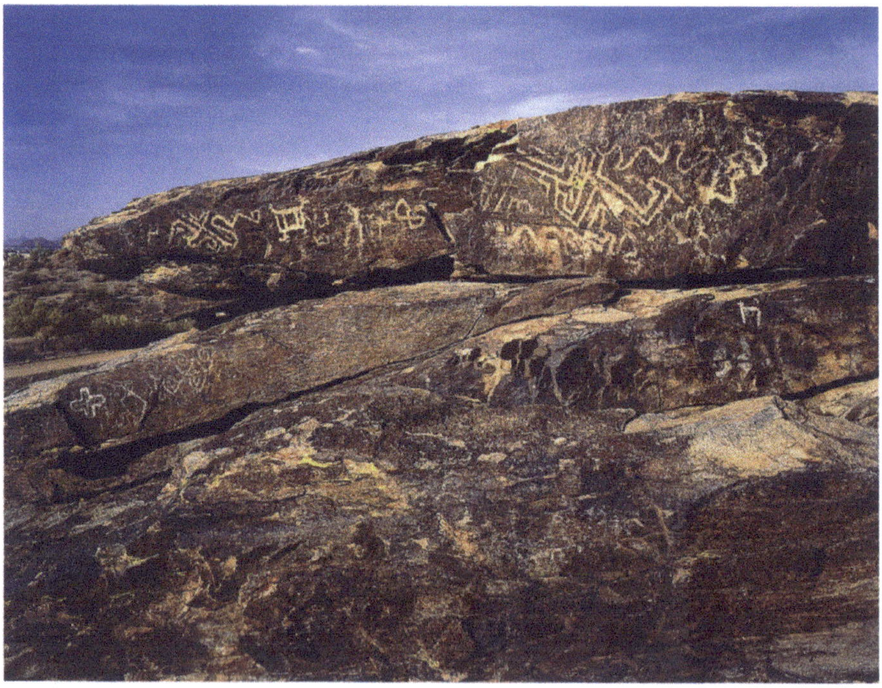

Rock art panels containing a reverse mirror-image quadruped (upper left), a maze design surrounded by snakes (upper right), and an anthropomorph holding an outlined cross and standing on the foot of a waterbird (lower left). This outstanding cluster of panels is located on a ridge at the 36th Street Locality.

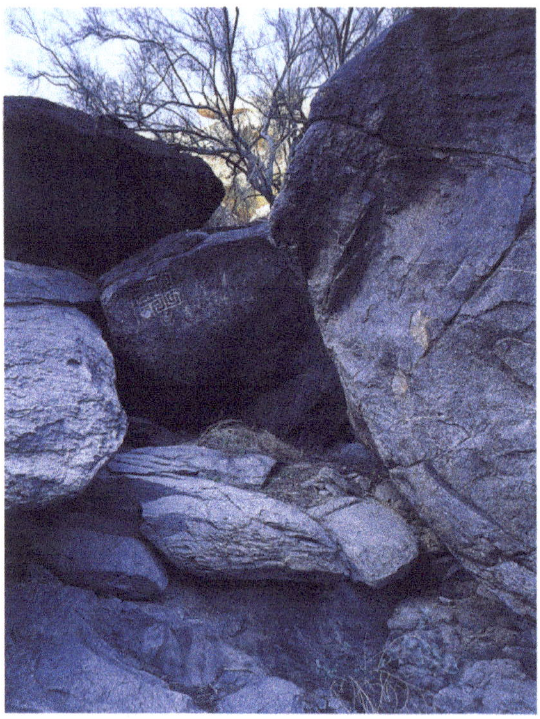

Boulder alcove with a rock art panel containing a maze design and a smaller lizard, Hieroglyphic Canyon. The alcove is located next to a bend in a wash.

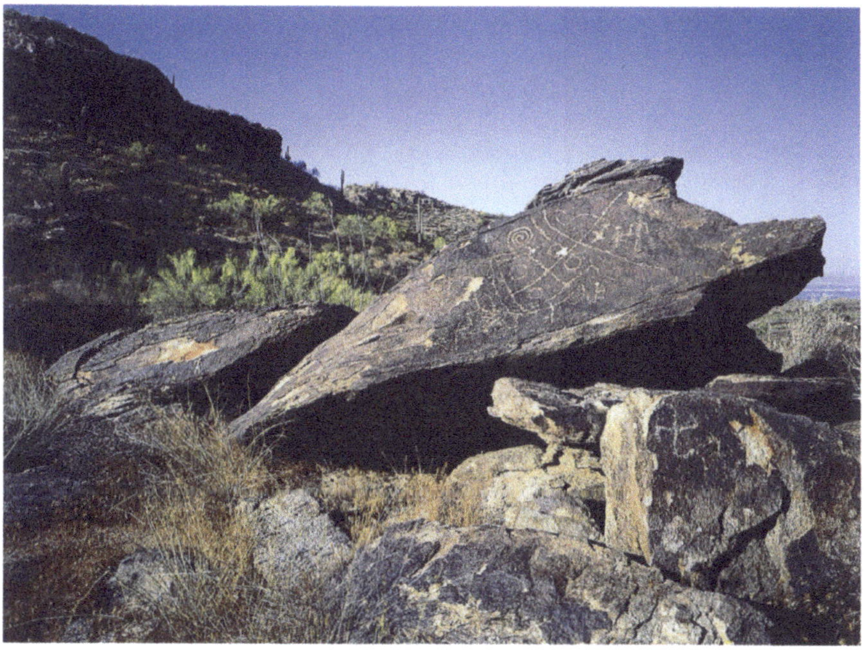

Four Pillars archaeoastronomy site, Twin Buttes Locality. The main panel on the large boulder in the background has four circles separated by lines into a quadrant pattern, an anthropomorph, a spiral, a cross, a snake, and quadrupeds. A whorl petroglyph is present on an upright slab in front of the main panel.

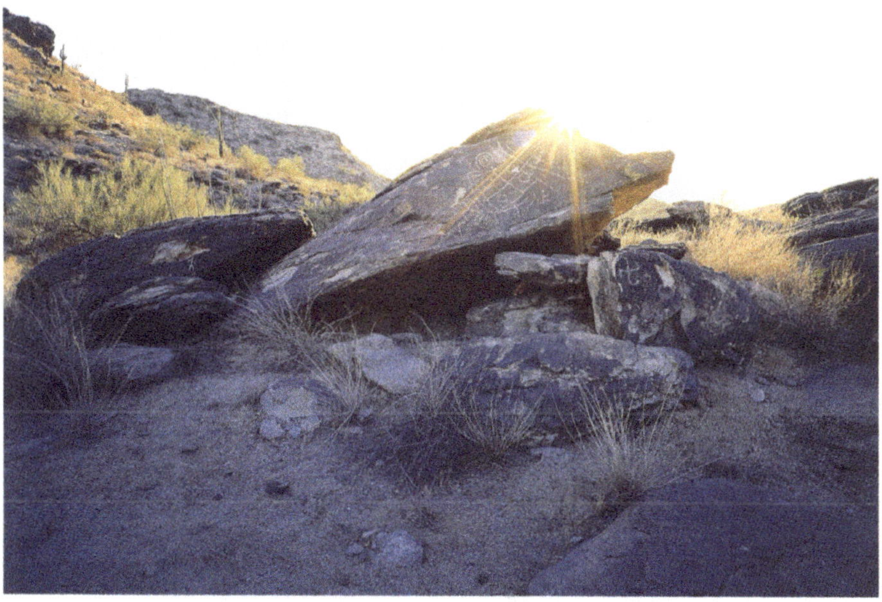

Summer solstice sunrise over the top of the main panel at the Four Pillars Site. The sunrise aligns perfectly with the pecked line that splits the panel in half when viewed from a small boulder located at the edge of a cleared area next to the main panel. In addition, the winter solstice sun rises over a sun disk petroglyph on the northwestern face of this boulder. Thus, the boulder marks the two extreme positions of the rising sun on the eastern horizon during a six-month period and could have been used by the Hohokam to create a solar calendar.

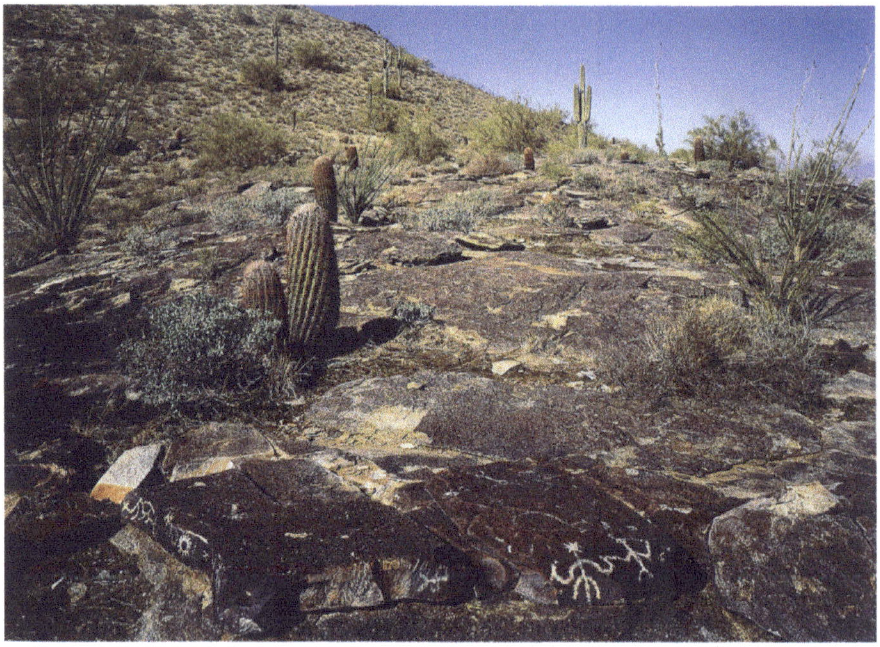

Rock art inside the cleared area at the Sungod Site. The main panel contains two anthropomorphs holding hands. One of these anthropomorphs has sun rays emanating from its head and is holding a crescent-shaped object. The panel faces to the northeast. Another panel to the left has a sun disk petroglyph.

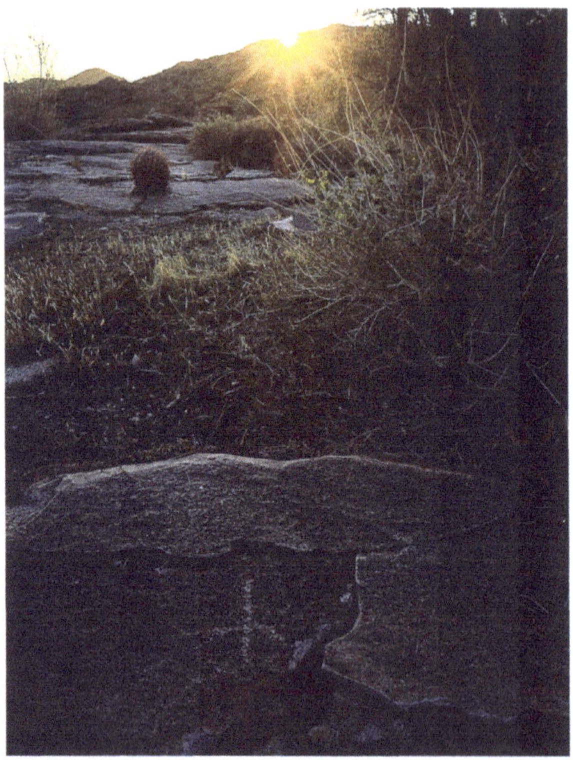

Winter solstice sunrise over a bird petroglyph at the Sungod Site.

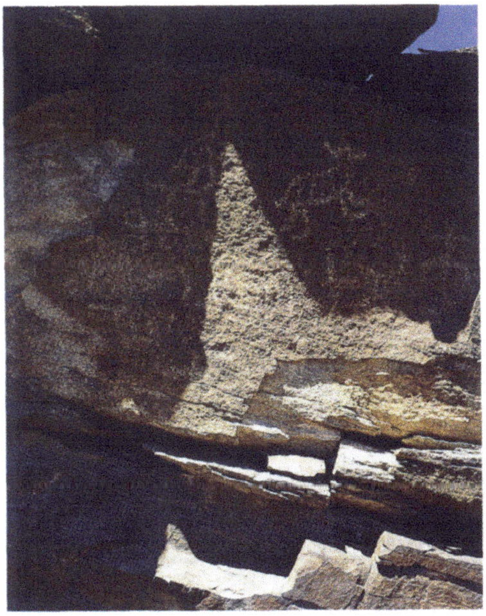

Light and shadow effect on a rock art panel during midday (zenith) on the summer solstice, 32nd Street Locality. Note the progression of the point of the ray of light in the following photographs.

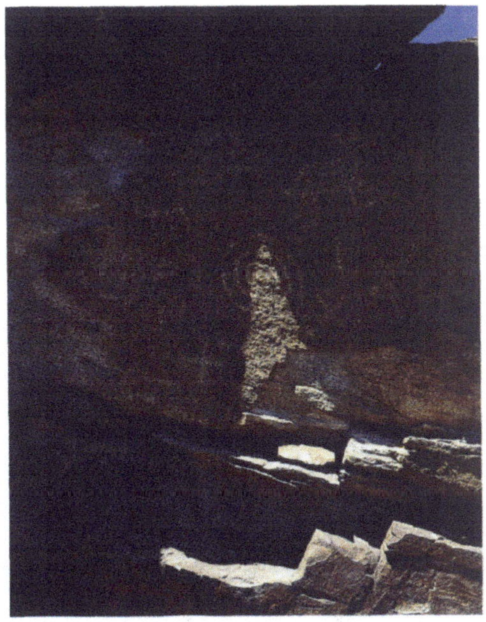

Light and shadow effect on rock art panel during midday (zenith) on the summer solstice, 32nd Street Locality.

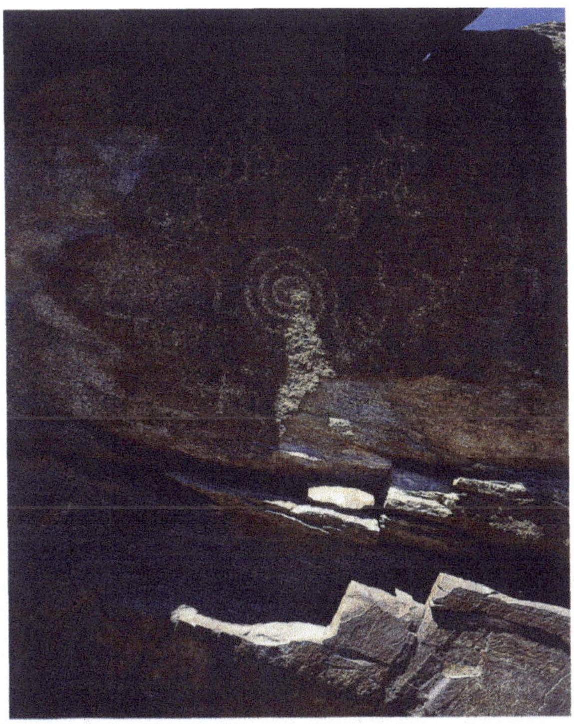

Light and shadow effect on rock art panel during midday (zenith) on the summer solstice, 32nd Street Locality. The point of the ray of light is at the center of the spiral.

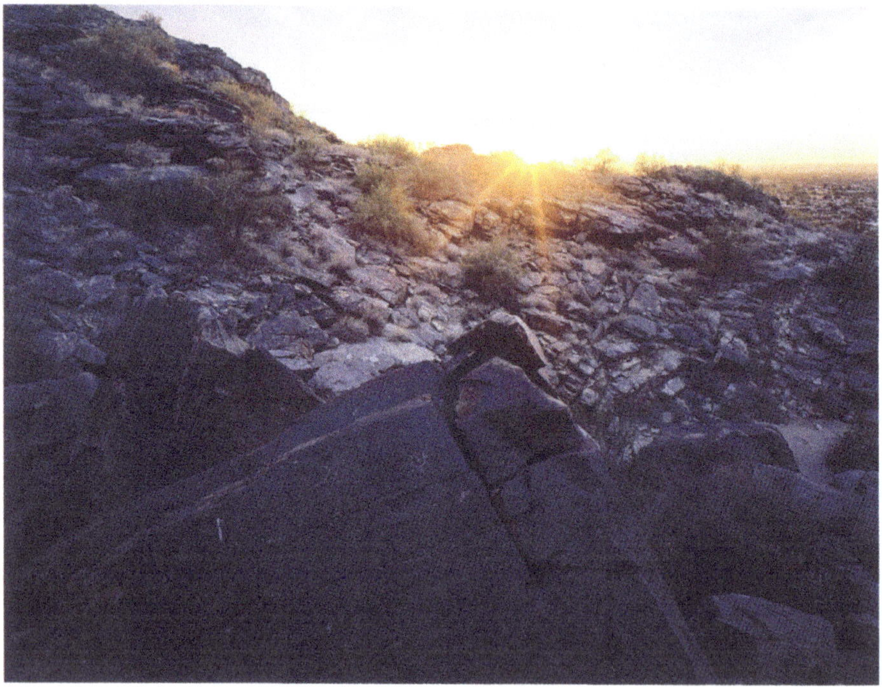

Winter solstice sunset over sun disk petroglyph, Hieroglyphic Canyon.

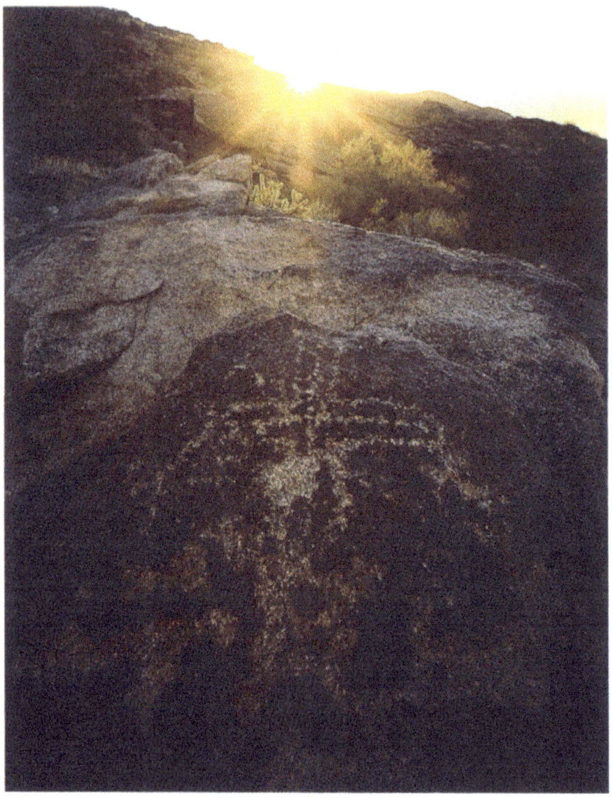

Winter solstice sunset over outlined cross, Goodman Canyon.

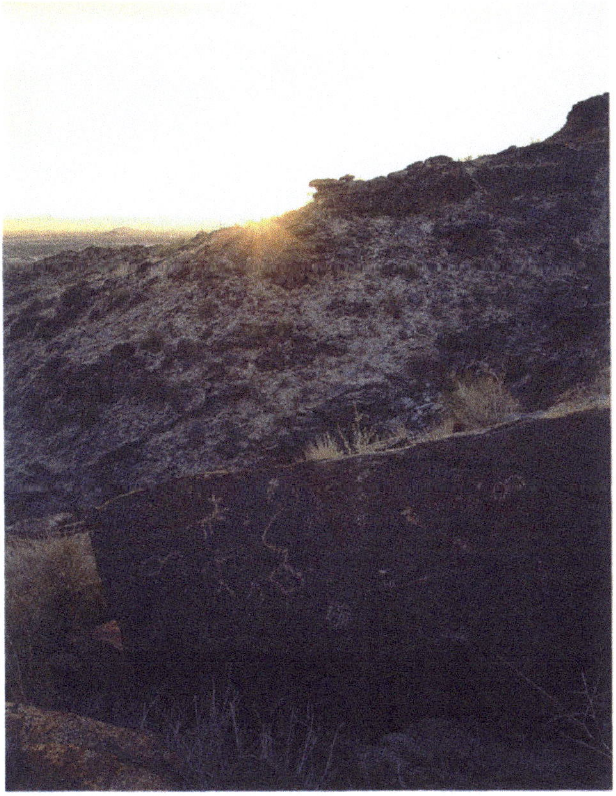

Summer solstice sunrise over snake petroglyph at the Morning Star Site, 24th Street Locality.

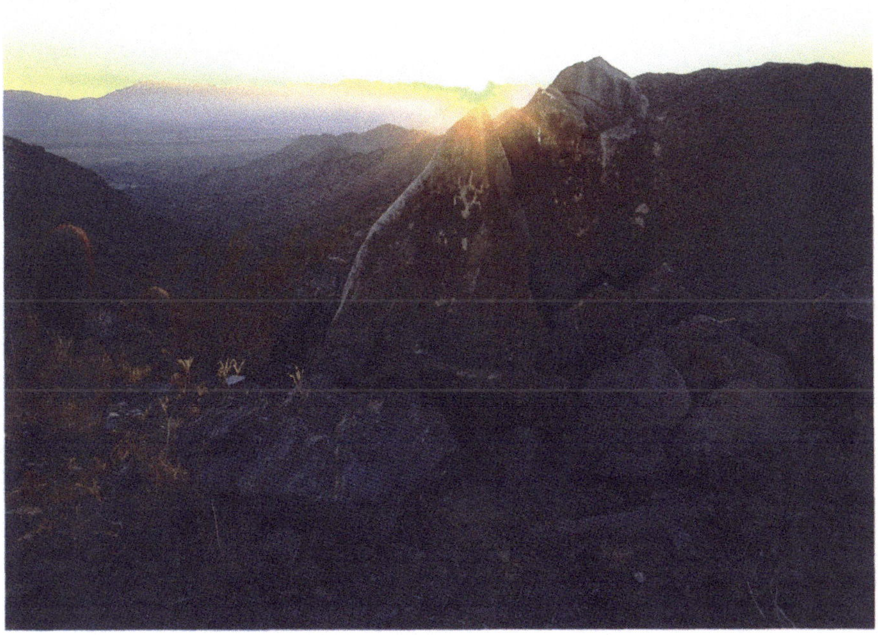

Winter solstice sunset over lizard petroglyph, Gila Vista Locality.

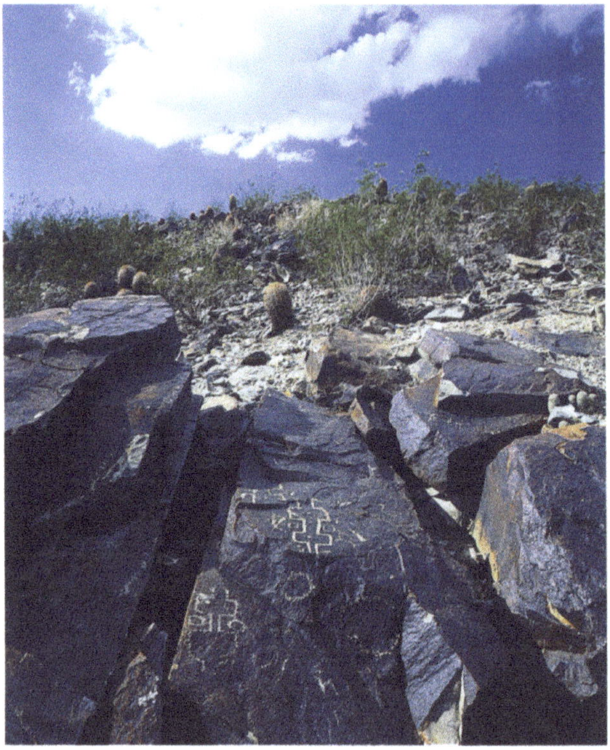

View of the sky over a pipette panel at the 28th Place Locality. Both of the pipettes at this location have a pair of centrally placed circles that give the pipette a masklike appearance.

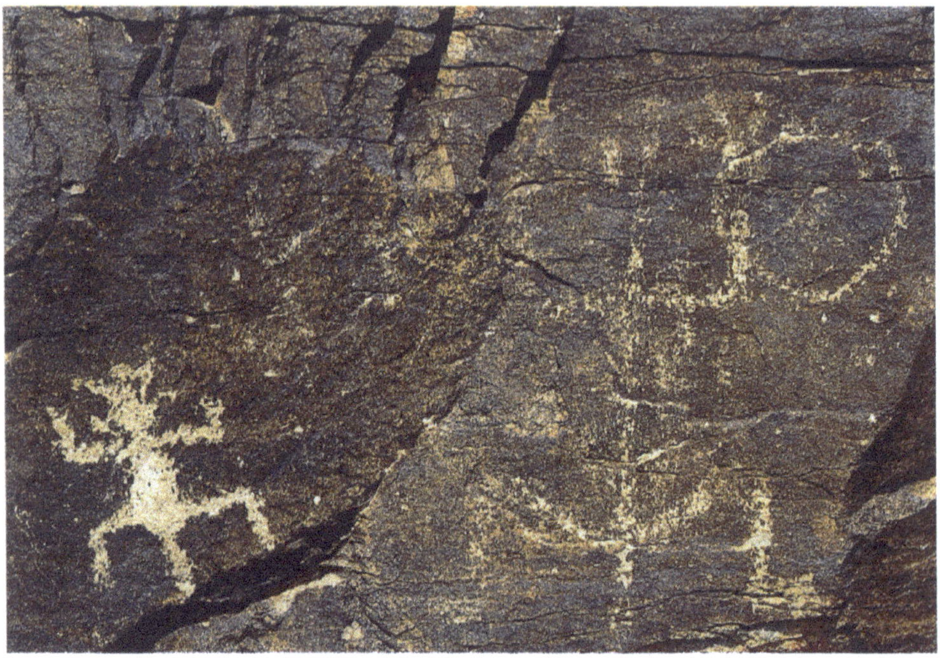

Panel located in the eastern portion of the 36th Street Locality with two lizardman images. Light and shadow patterns appear on this panel at midday on the spring and fall equinox. The middle torso of the smaller lizardman on the left has been repecked.

CHAPTER THREE

DATING ROCK ART IN THE SOUTH MOUNTAINS

Probably the most formidable task each rock art researcher must face is deriving a realistic chronology.

—HENRY WALLACE AND JAMES HOLMLUND (1986)

WHO MADE THE petroglyphs in the South Mountains? Scholars and other interested observers have long assumed that the answer is the Hohokam. Two factors support this premise: (1) the presence of Hohokam pottery at some of the rock art sites, and (2) the fact that the South Mountains are located in the Hohokam culture core area. Yet both of these indicators require some caveats. Although Hohokam pottery has been observed in the South Mountains, before this study it was never analyzed or even systematically collected from a range of locations. Ceramic specialists had not defined what types of Hohokam pottery occur in the South Mountains, much less established date ranges and place of manufacture for identified types. Nor had any study been conducted on pottery from other cultures (such as Patayan) present in the South Mountains.

Archaeologists have noted that the densest concentration of Hohokam villages and irrigated farms are along both sides of the Salt and Gila Rivers. The Salt River joins the Gila River west of the South Mountains. The desert basins created by these two broad valleys are the core area of the Hohokam culture, with the South Mountains in between. The presence of Hohokam pottery certainly indicates that they visited and possibly lived in these mountains (Snyder 1966). But what about the hunter-gatherer peoples who lived in the Sonoran Desert for thousands of years before the Hohokam? And what about the native people who occupied the desert after the Hohokam culture collapsed in the mid to late fifteenth century, about two hundred years before the first Europeans arrived in the area? The O'odham (a Piman-speaking people) were farming the desert in small rancheria-type villages along the Gila River, but not the Salt River, when the Spaniards first explored this part of the Sonoran Desert in the late seventeenth century.

Dating rock art remains one of the great challenges of American archaeology. The well-developed artistic tradition of the Hohokam spans hundreds of years, and, like changes in pottery designs, changes in rock art most likely occurred over time. Hence, to accomplish the challenging goal of dating rock art, one must associate particular Hohokam rock art sites and designs with specific time periods. Dating techniques include stylistic analysis, relative dating, and chronometric dating.

Stylistic Analysis

Early Hohokam pottery designs, such as parallel lines and rakelike forms, are typically geometric. Henry Wallace and others (1995) have noted that these designs are strongly associated with Archaic hunter-gatherer rock art of the Southwest and Great Basin (Schaafsma 1980). But Archaic people did not make pottery vessels. The earliest Hohokam designs on ceramic vessels appear in the beginning of the seventh century. Life-forms were not painted until the eighth century, when a creative explosion using an expanded design repertoire seems to have occurred. The use of these delightful images, including human figures in action, ended abruptly in the twelfth century. For the final three hundred years of the Hohokam red-on-buff pottery tradition, designs were restricted primarily to complex geometric designs.

Changes in designs on Hohokam pottery over time provide a comparative framework in which to examine changes in rock art elements. Perhaps the use of life-forms in rock art also is restricted to certain time periods. Because geometric designs occur throughout the ceramic art sequence, they are not likely to be a chronological indicator.

Relative Patination

Relative dating techniques include the observation of superpositioning of individual elements and the different amounts of weathering or desert varnish ("patina") on top of the design (called repatination). Henry Wallace and James

Holmlund (1986) used these relative techniques with great success in their study of Archaic and Hohokam rock art in the Picacho Mountains. The manufacture of rock art involves removing the existing rock surface to expose the lighter-colored rock underneath. The exposed rock surface then develops its own desert patina over time, with hundreds, even thousands, of years required to redarken the exposed surface. Different designs located next to each other, or on top of each other, with different amounts of patina obviously date to different time periods. The darker designs are older than the less patinated designs. The patination process is complex, however, and involves chemical reactions between microscopic organisms, various minerals in the rock, sunlight, and occasional moisture. Different rocks in different geographic environments repatinate at different rates. Nonetheless, variations in patination have the potential to provide relative chronological information.

Many panels in the South Mountains have patina, and some are darker than others. But variations in patina, as discussed above, can be related to the rock material type and other factors. Not all the rock art elements that are common to the Archaic period—those few that have been identified—appear to be significantly darker than some Hohokam panels. Some typical Hohokam designs appear light and more freshly exposed than other Hohokam elements, which most likely provides chronological significance. Superpositioning of different elements on some panels also indicates different time periods (see figures 11.1 and 11.2). In some cases, human figures were added to the middle of an existing panel, incorporating them as part of the scene after the panel was created. Because repatination may take thousands of years, it is difficult to determine when an element was pecked into a rock's surface based solely on degree of patination.

Chronometric Techniques

Chronometric dating techniques for rock art, including radiocarbon dating, are still not fully developed for petroglyphs (Beck et al. 1998). No South Mountains petroglyphs have thus far been successfully dated by the radiocarbon technique. The direct dating of pigments used to create painted designs (pictographs) has achieved success elsewhere (Farrell and Burton 1992; Hyman and Rowe 1997), but we have not found any pictographs in the South Mountains.

The South Mountains Ceramic Study

Until more accurate dating can be obtained, rock art in the South Mountains can be dated only by association with pottery designs that have been dated to specific time periods. With this in mind, we undertook a systematic collection of ceramic sherds during the recording of the rock art. We collected a sample of sherds whenever we found sherd scatters, ending up with 23 different localities represented.

David Abbott, a preeminent Hohokam ceramic specialist, conducted the analysis of 769 sherds. Almost all the sherds are Hohokam (none could be identified as Patayan); some yielded information about their source of origin and time of manufacture. Of the total, there are 502 plainware, 243 red-on-buff, 18 redware, and 6 polychrome sherds. The presence of jars, bowls, and scoops indicates that a variety of water vessels were taken into the mountains, as well as vessels used for eating or carrying offerings.

The earliest ceramics from the South Mountains are buffware types that date to the Gila Butte phase of the Colonial period (ca. A.D. 750–850). Ceramics also were recovered that date to the Santa Cruz phase of the Colonial period (ca. A.D. 850–950) and to the Sedentary period (ca. A.D. 950–1150). A much smaller number of Classic period (ca. A.D. 1150–1450) sherds were found, including polychromes, Casa Grande Red-on-buff, and redware. Seven centuries of art are represented in these sherds. Identifiable and thus datable red-on-buff sherds from the South Mountains consist of 4 Gila Butte Red-on-buff (Pima Canyon, Telegraph Pass, 36th Street); 18 Santa Cruz Red-on-buff (Hidden Valley; Mormon Trail, Twin Buttes); 31 Santa Cruz/Sacaton Red-on-buff (Box Canyon, Mormon Trail, Pima Canyon, Valle Bonita, 32nd Street, 36th Street, San Juan North, Telegraph Pass); 17 Sacaton Red-on-buff (Chandler Blvd./19th Way, Telegraph Pass, 24th Street, 27th Street); and 1 Casa Grande Red-on-buff (Southeast Side, 43rd Street). Painted designs on the red-on-buff sherds are mostly geometric patterns, but flying bird motifs also occur (figure 4).

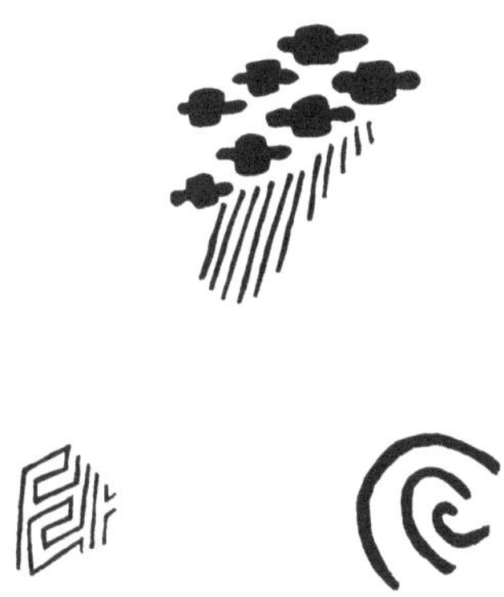

4. Painted ceramic designs from the South Mountains: **top,** stylized flying birds from the High Terrace Site; **bottom left,** from the 32nd Street Locality; **bottom right,** from Pima Canyon.

David Abbott also identified a variety of plainware types (table 1), primarily based on types of rock materials (temper) found in the clay. Most of the tempers were intentionally added to the clay by the potters to improve the workability of the clay and to give it greater strength when fired, but some tempers occur naturally in certain clays. The nine plainware types or varieties identified in the South Mountains collection are South Mountain granodiorite, Estrella gneiss, Squaw Peak schist, mica-schist with red sediment, mica-schist without red sediment, phyllite, arkosic sand, sherd tempered, and unidentified. South Mountain granodiorite and Estrella gneiss were both available from the South Mountains; Squaw Peak schist and phyllite temper were obtained from the Phoenix Mountains; the mica-schist with red sediment was acquired from the Queen Creek area; and the mica-schist without red sediment is from the middle

Gila River region. Each of the different plainware types was manufactured in a different ceramic production zone in the Salt River Valley (Abbott 2000).

The eighteen redware sherds from the South Mountains were identified as four different temper types: South Mountain granodiorite, South Mountain granodiorite with sherd temper, Estrella gneiss, and sherd temper with unidentifiable sand. The infrequent occurrence of redware does not necessarily reflect the absence of the

Table 1. Ceramic Types Collected from the South Mountains

	Red-on-buff-	**Redware and Gila Polychrome**	**Plainware**						
Locality	Pre-Classic R/b Sherds	Classic Sherds	Mica-Schist Red Sedimentary Plain	South Mt. Granodiorte Plain	Estrella Gneiss Plain	Mica-Schist Plain	Phyllite Plain	Squaw Peak Schist Plain	Arkosic Sand Plain
Beverly Canyon			1	1		2			
Box Canyon	6		2	125	61	3	1		2
Central Avenue					2				
Chandler/19th Way	2				4				
Goodman Canyon	2	1 Red	2	2	2	1			
Hieroglyphic Canyon				2	5		1		
Mormon Trail	15	2 Red		5	3			1	
National Trail						4			
Pima Canyon	4		2	40	11	3		3	
San Juan North					4	2	1		
San Juan East	1			1	2				1
Southeast side		3 Red 1 R/b*		8	8				
Southwest Side					2			1	
Telegraph Pass	5	1 PC			11		1		3
Twin Buttes	13			3	1				
Valle Bonita	1	1 Red 5 PC					1		
16th St.					1				
20th St.		1 Red		9					
24th St.	11	4 Red		5	6	2			2
27th St.	1			2	1				
32nd St.	8			86	4	2			
34th St.				1	1	1			
36th St.	3			23		1			
Totals:	72	19	7	313	129	21	5	5	8

Note: Totals do not include unidentifiable types and three sherds with sherd temper. Ceramic specialist David Abbott conducted the analysis.
Abbreviations: PC=Gila Polychrome; R/b=red-on-buff; R/b*=Classic period red-on-buff

Hohokam in the South Mountains during the Classic period, because redware vessels may have had specialized use in Hohokam society (Abbott 2000) and those functions may not have included journeys into the mountains.

Well over half of the plainware ceramics found in the South Mountains are the South Mountain granodiorite type. This plainware was manufactured in the ceramic production zone located 1 mile (1.5 km) northeast of the South Mountains, which includes the Hohokam village of Los Hornos (map 3). This finding is not unexpected, because Los Hornos is the closest major village to the South Mountains. Some of the granodiorite-tempered ceramics also may have come from Las Canopas, about 3 miles (5 km) west of Los Hornos (Abbott 1997).

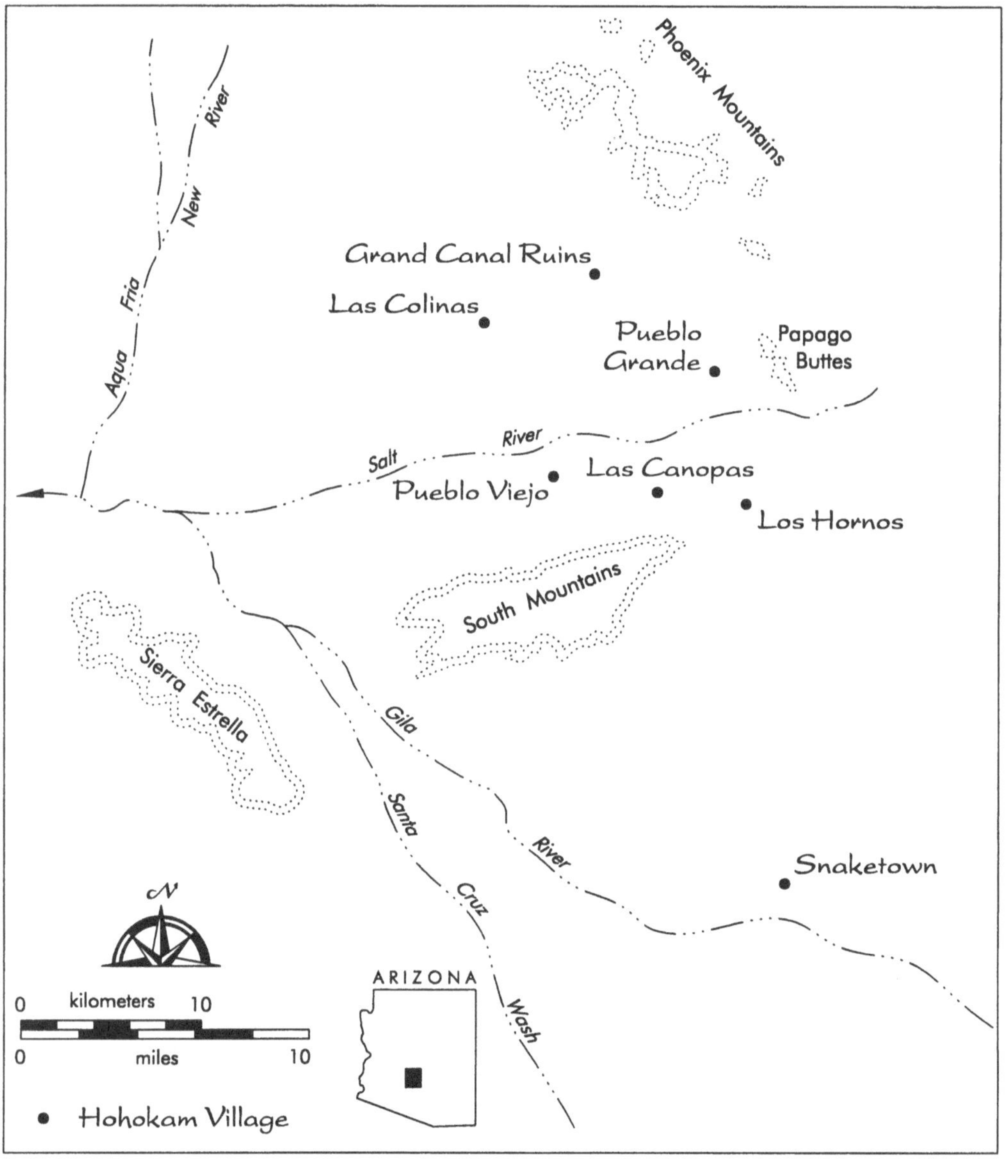

3. Locations of Hohokam villages mentioned in text

More than one-fourth of the plainware is the Estrella gneiss variety. These ceramics originated from production zones to the northwest of the South Mountains, on the south side of the Salt River. The village of Pueblo Viejo, located 2 miles (3 km) north of the South Mountains, contains a sizeable quantity of Estrella gneiss plainware ceramics (Abbott 1993).

The other plainware ceramic types, most of which originated from production zones on the north side of the Salt River (for example, the villages of Las Colinas, Grand Canal Ruins, and Pueblo Grande), occur in much smaller quantities. This indicates that people living on the north side of the river did visit the South Mountains, but perhaps less frequently than individuals from villages located closer to the mountains. In addition, the mica-tempered plainware and some of the red-on-buff ceramics probably originated from villages along the Gila River, to the south and east of the South Mountains (such as Snaketown). These ceramics, however, could have been traded into the Salt River Valley and then transported from there to the South Mountains. Our ceramic data suggest that individuals from several different Hohokam villages had access to the South Mountains but that Los Hornos villagers visited most often. Perhaps they even controlled access into the mountains from the east, where several major trails are located.

Hohokam ceramics dating to the earlier Pioneer period also were not recovered in our sample, but their absence does not preclude the presence of Pioneer period rock art in the South Mountains. Although the characteristics of Pioneer period rock art are currently not well understood, Henry Wallace and his colleagues (1995) have suggested that rock art from this early Hohokam period is dominated by geometric designs, because pottery designs from this period are primarily geometric. Furthermore, it is similar to rock art from the Archaic period that preceded the Pioneer period. On the basis of this argument, Wallace and others (1995) proposed that the Hohokam art styles of the Colonial period, with their prolific variety and quantity of life-forms, are such a drastic change from earlier rock art that the shift may represent a different people, culture, or ideology. The relationship of the Hohokam to the earlier Archaic people is a hotly debated topic among archaeologists. Even those archaeologists who believe that the Hohokam evolved from the Archaic people, stimulated by the introduction of agriculture from Mexico, cannot agree on when the Hohokam culture first appeared here. Unfortunately, evidence for Archaic people in the heart of the Salt River Valley remains elusive, although archaeological investigations in the McDowell Mountain region to the northeast have discovered numerous Archaic campsites and rock art (Schroeder 1999).

Archaic Rock Art

Our study found several panels that may have been created by hunter-gatherers from the Archaic period, as evidenced by their particular element types and relative repatination. However, Archaic panels are not very common in the South Mountains compared to the large number of Hohokam panels.

The identification of Archaic rock art in the Sonoran Desert is based primarily on the presence of several patinated geometric element types that are assigned to Archaic people elsewhere in the American Southwest and Great Basin. Henry Wallace and James Holmlund (1986) identified Archaic elements at the Picacho Mountains as atlatls, parallel lines, gridirons, ladders, rakes, centipedes, vulva forms, sectioned rectangles, and cupules. They noted that Archaic anthropomorphs are rare in the Picacho Mountains. In addition, J. Simon Bruder (1983) recorded a large number of squiggles, circle clusters, and other Archaic geometric designs at the Hedgpeth Hills petroglyph site in Deer Valley, 21 miles (34 km) north of the South Mountains.

A San Pedro projectile point fragment from the late Archaic period was found in the Hidden Valley Locality, indicating that Archaic people visited the South Mountains. Archaic designs identified in the South Mountains rock art sites include atlatls (Mormon Trail, 28th Place, 36th Street); circle clusters (Mormon Loop Trail, 34th Street); meanders (32nd Street); and rakes (Hieroglyphic Canyon, 32nd Street, 36th Street).

Several geometric designs in the South Mountains may represent atlatls, which are the throwing-board part of the weapon system Archaic hunters used to hurl spearlike darts (figures 5 and 6). Atlatl is an Aztec word, and although the Aztec used these weapons, the more efficient bow and arrow replaced the atlatl among most Native American groups around A.D. 400–500. Therefore, the presence of atlatl images at a rock art site in the American Southwest generally indicates an Archaic origin, preceding the development of pottery. The South Mountain examples (located in the lower part of the 36th Street Locality, at the 28th Place Locality, and possibly in a panel near the upper part of the Mormon Trail) are somewhat ambiguous but do fit into the range of forms called atlatl images elsewhere.

Other possible Archaic panels consist of a meander pattern at the 32nd Street Locality (figure 7), circle cluster elements at the Mormon Loop Trail and 34th Street Locality, and rake elements in three localities: Hieroglyphic Canyon (figure 8), 32nd Street, and 36th Street. Centipede images, discussed in chapter 4, are in some cases very similar to the rakes except that centipedes have distinct heads and rakes do not. Centipede images also occur in Archaic rock art.

The Mormon Loop Trail circle cluster panel (figure 9), located near a spring, resembles some of the Archaic elements at the Hedgpeth Hills rock art site (now called the Deer Valley Rock Art Center). The circle cluster in the 34th Street Locality is being held by an anthropomorph with a headdress (figure 10). A sun disk, a small spiral, a zigzag, and a lizard also are present on the panel, which is facing up and is very patinated. Perhaps circle cluster images represent nets, which could have been used to capture game at ambush locations, such as springs or other watering places.

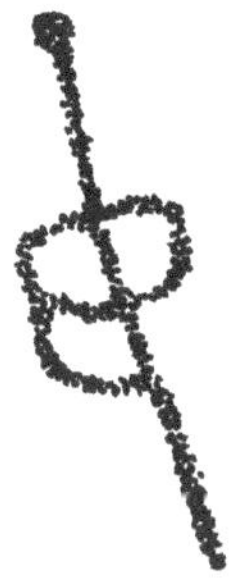

5. Possible atlatl at the Split Dome Site, Mormon Trail. Atlatl is 1.02 m in length.

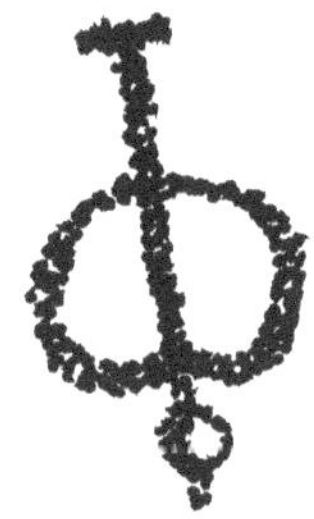

6. Possible atlatl, 36th Street Locality. Atlatl is 19 x 17 cm.

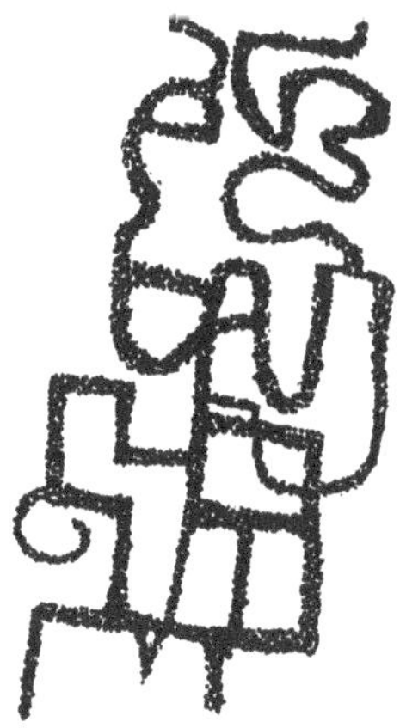

7. Archaic period meander pattern, 32nd Street Locality. Meander is 48 cm in length.

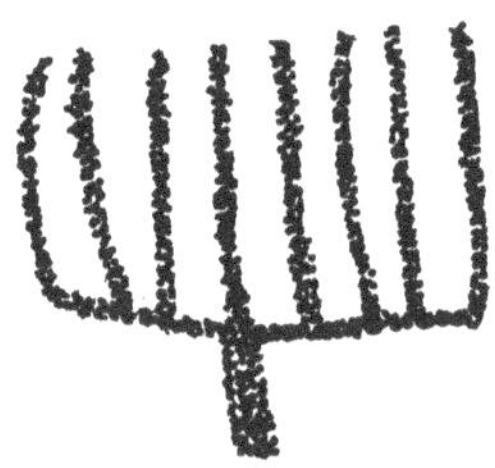

8. Rake design, Hieroglyphic Canyon. Rake is 23 x 20 cm.

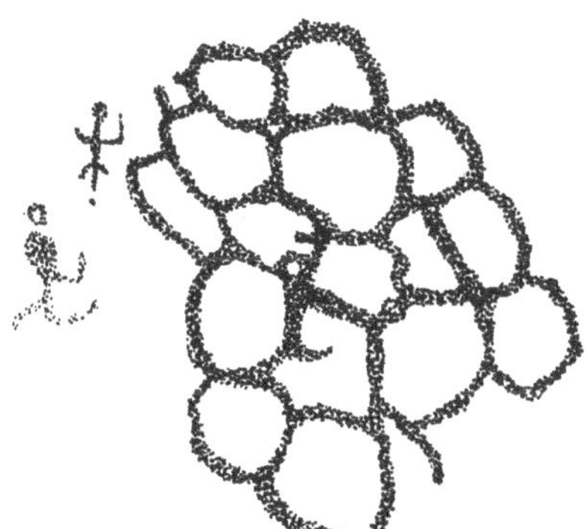

9. Circle cluster and faint anthropomorphs, Mormon Loop Trail. Anthropomorph is 9 cm in height.

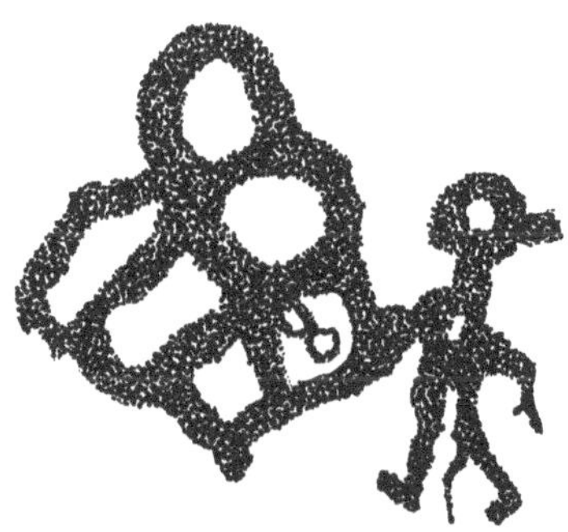

10. Circle cluster and anthropomorph, 34th Street Locality. Anthropomorph is 12 cm in height.

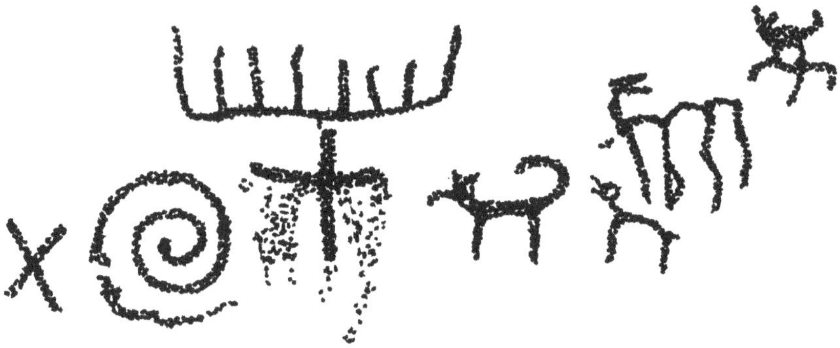

11. Rake design, 32nd Street Locality. Rake is 20 x 22 cm.

The rake image in the 32nd Street Locality is located high up in the mountains in a panel with other elements, including an "X," a spiral, a coyote, other four-legged animals, a crude circle, and a lizard/human (figure 11). The panel has been pecked into a rough surface and the elements are faint, possibly indicating it is well repatinated, but all of the elements besides the rake appear on the Hohokam rock art roster. Situated in a flat area with a commanding view of the Salt River Valley, the panel faces in the direction of the summer solstice sunrise. Rake designs have been interpreted as abstract symbols for shamanic flight (Hedges 1985:89) or as falling summer rain (Malotki 2000:22).

Protohistoric and Early Historic Rock Art

A small number of panels in the South Mountains have elements in a style that suggests they are neither Hohokam nor Archaic in origin but were made during the Protohistoric or early Historic period (ca. A.D. 1500–1900). Turn-of-the-century ethnographer Frank Russell (1975) found no evidence that the O'odham made rock art during the late nineteenth century. However, Jose Santos, an O'odham who was raised at Akchin (south of the South Mountains), told ethnographer E. W. Gifford (1940:59) that the O'odham did make petrogylphs (see also Martynec and Martynec 1995).

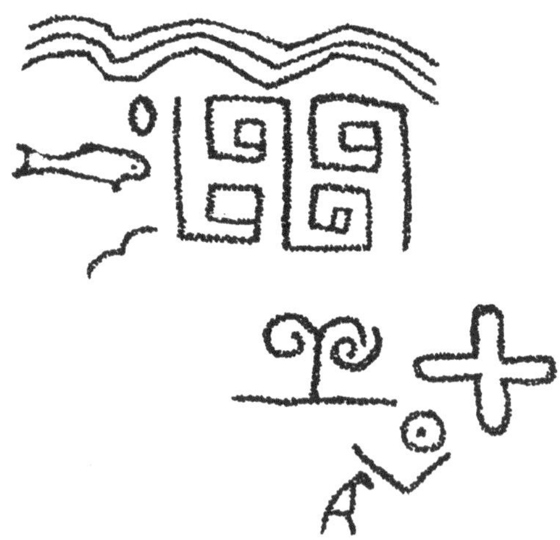

12. Post-Hohokam petroglyph panel, Southeast Side Locality. Fish is 19 cm in length. Some of the designs in this panel, such as the negative cross, also occur as Hohokam petroglyphs in the South Mountains. The panel faces southwest, toward the Gila River.

A panel in the Southeast Side Locality contains a scene that is more modern than nearby Hohokam panels. This panel shows no repatination and contains two birds, several zigzags, a fish, and other designs (figure 12). Although the outlined cross is in the Hohokam rock art repertoire, the birds are dissimilar from Hohokam birds, and fish rarely appear on Hohokam panels.

Half a dozen panels in the South Mountains either in whole or in part contain elements that are obviously of post-Hohokam design. These include human faces in profile, an arrow, and other designs (figure 13). For example, relatively few petroglyphs occur on the southwestern side of the South Mountains. However, a small cluster is present on an outcrop located next to an east-west trail where it turns into the Salt River Valley. Most of the panels—showing large spirals, anthropomorphs, and lizards—appear to be Hohokam. But one of the panels includes a pecked human face in profile. The head has a prominent nose, an eye, and a pointed headdress. The combined initials "AP" below and "ER" above the head confirm that it is not Hohokam.

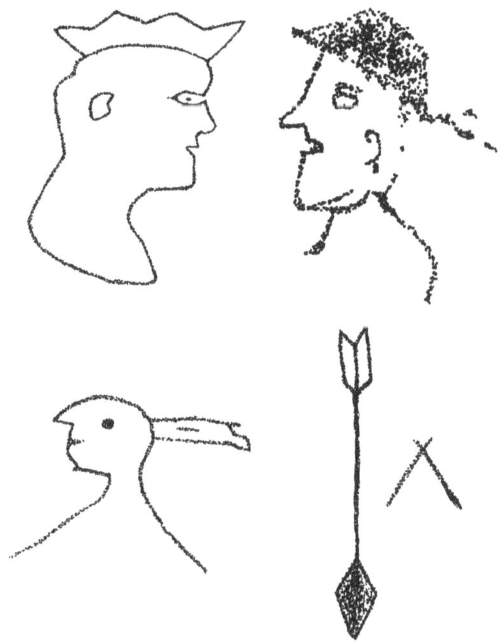

13. Post-Hohokam petroglyphs, **left to right:** person in profile (85 cm in height), Box Canyon; person in profile (27 cm in height), 28th Place Locality (the name "Lloyd" is pecked into a nearby boulder); person in profile (50 cm in height), Pima Canyon; arrow (36 cm in length) and crossed lines, Chandler Boulevard/32nd Street Locality.

Another petroglyph, located on the southeastern side of the South Mountains, appears to be more recent and resembles a javelina (figure 14). Current evidence indicates that javelina were not present in the northern Sonoran Desert during Hohokam times but migrated into Arizona sometime after the Hohokam abandoned the Salt River Valley. Consequently, the javelina petroglyph may be O'odham in origin. A cross petroglyph (with the dates "1900" and "1907" pecked next to it) also is present on the southern side of the South Mountains, suggesting that other petroglyphs in this area may have been created around the turn of the century by O'odham living in villages along the Gila River.

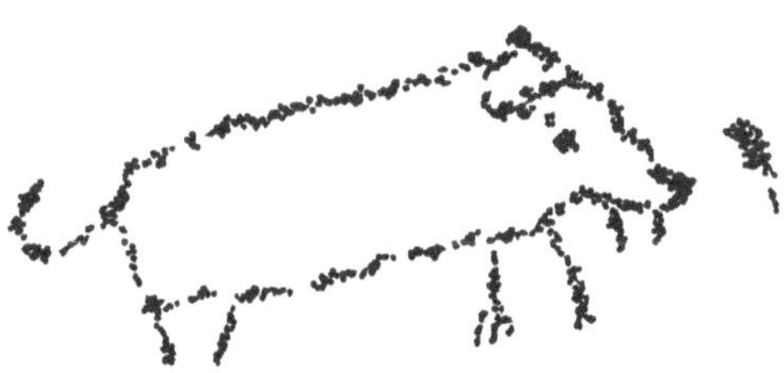

14. Javelina, 28th Place Locality. Javelina is 24 cm in length.

Among the many bird designs in the South Mountains, a few appear stylistically to be more recent than typical Hohokam birds. A Protohistoric example is a hollow bird head in profile in the Holbert Trail Locality (figure 15). Hohokam bird petroglyphs are discussed in chapter 7.

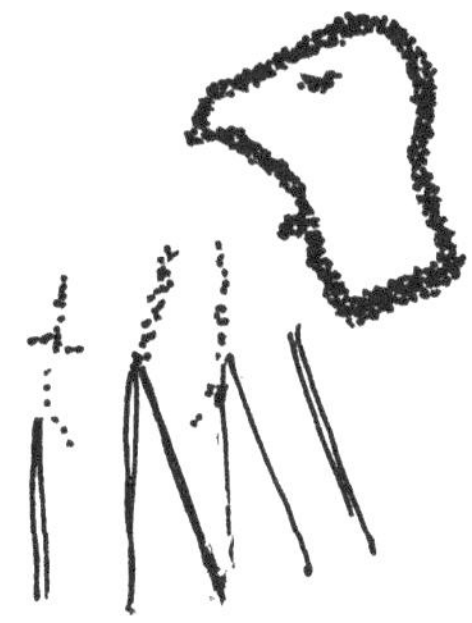

15. Bird profile, Holbert Trail. Bird head is 15 x 18 cm.

Several geometric petroglyphs located at the 28th Place Locality on the southeastern side of the South Mountains also may be from the Protohistoric or early Historic period.[1] These petroglyphs, while not heavily patinated, also are not freshly made. Interestingly, some look like cattle brands (figure 16). Near the border of Arizona and Mexico, archaeologists Rick and Sandy Martynec (1995) have recorded similar geometric petroglyphs that O'odham informants identified as cattle brands designating family or cooperative ownership of livestock.[2] The Martynecs date these petroglyphs to the 1800s or possibly as early as the 1700s. The first Spanish missionary in southern Arizona, Father Eusebio Francisco Kino, brought cattle with him when he established missions in the region in the 1690s.

At the east entrance to the South Mountains, in Pima Canyon, is a petroglyph panel with the name "Fray Marco de Niza," the date "1539," and the statement, "Coronoa todo el nuebo Mexico a su costa." Fray Marcos de Niza was a famous Spanish explorer who traveled through eastern Arizona in 1539. Two well-respected Southwestern scholars, Katherine Barlett and Harold Colton (1940), present a convincing argument that this rock art panel, first discovered in 1926, is not authentic. No evidence indicates that Fray Marcos traveled through the Salt River Valley, and the Spanish inscription is "so peculiar in its wording as to be practically senseless" (Bartlett and Colton 1940:58).

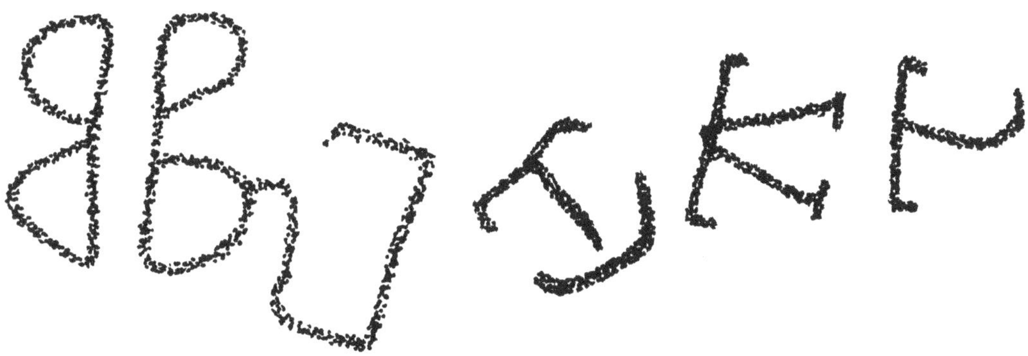

16. Possible Pima cattle brands, 28th Place Locality. Petroglyphs vary from 10 to 16 cm in height.

Scratched Style

A small number of petroglyphs were made in a scratched style, distinct from the pecked style typical for the Hohokam. It should be noted, however, that close inspection of Hohokam panels in the South Mountains reveals that scratching is not infrequently combined with pecking in the same elements. Furthermore, the completely scratched petroglyphs always occur with pecked petroglyphs, often in the same panel. Examples of scratched panels are present in the 12th Street Locality, the 36th Street Locality (figure 17), and Goodman Canyon. All of these scratched panels have parallel lines and grid forms.

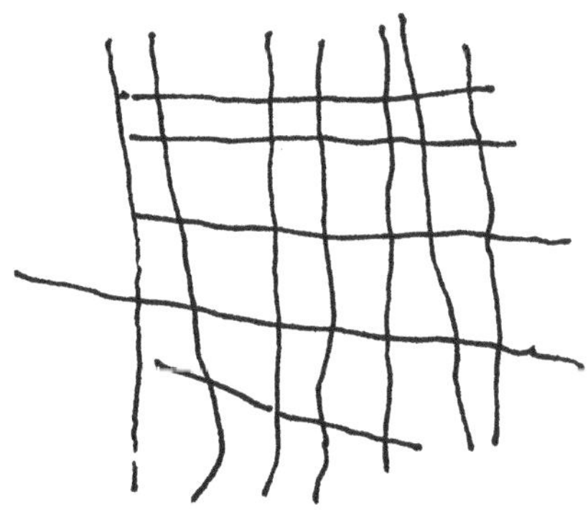

17. Scratched geometric design, 36th Street Locality. Scratch pattern is 10 x 11 cm. This scratched petroglyph is located among other pecked designs.

In the Tucson area, archaeologist Alan Ferg (1979) identified a scratched style, which he argued is Hohokam in origin. Ferg based his argument on the fact that the scratched elements do not appear to have been placed over the Hohokam elements at a later date but are in some cases under Hohokam pecked elements. According to the principle of superpositioning, the underlying scratched elements cannot postdate the overlying pecked elements.

CHAPTER FOUR

SMALL CRITTERS

INSECTS AND OTHER ARTHROPODS

Small animals can exploit habitats more fully than large ones. A single plant may be a meal to a vertebrate, but to arthropods it can be a universe.

—BARBARA TERKANIAN (2000)

DESPITE THE ARIDITY of the Sonoran Desert, insects and other arthropods are plentiful. They also are among the desert's most fascinating creatures. Some are predators, some have complex communal lifestyles, and some live solitary lives like other desert animals—they escape the heat of day in burrows or crevices and hunt for food in the evening (Werner and Olson 1994). Some, such as several species of scorpions, centipedes, and some ants, are even poisonous to humans.

Although rare compared to other elements, several insect and arthropod petroglyphs are present in the South Mountains. These include a scorpion, a few centipedes or millipedes, an unidentified insect,[1] and dragonflies.

SCORPION

THE SONORAN DESERT harbors several species of scorpions, all of which inject venom from their stinger tail. Scorpions have been called the denizens of the desert and rightfully so. They have an ancient history, from long before humans occupied this part of the world. Scorpions grow from 2 to 4 inches (5–10 cm) in length, with the largest, the giant hairy scorpion *(Hadrurus arizonensis),* actually having the mildest poison. The stripe-tailed or devil scorpion *(Vaejovis spinigerus)* is a common, medium-sized desert scorpion, and the slender, yellow bark scorpion *(Centruroides exilicauda)* has the most venomous poison. Scorpions are often sedentary, lying dormant under rocks or other moist, dark shelters for long periods of time. But when hunting they can be very athletic. The bark scorpion can climb vertical surfaces, and the fright one gets today when finding a scorpion on the ceiling of one's home was very likely experienced by the ancient people of the Sonoran Desert on a regular basis. Scorpions' mating courtships are fascinating: the male grasps his mate's pincers in his own, and as they are interlocked, the scorpions twist and circle each other in a mating dance that can last for hours.

Only a single petroglyph in the South Mountains appears to clearly represent a scorpion (figure 18). This scorpion image occurs by itself, in a lower area of the 32nd Street Locality with several other panels nearby. A well-pecked petroglyph, this scorpion image is depicted in profile. It has two pincerlike appendages and a long, curved tail. The pincers have three lines instead of two, perhaps to signify motion.

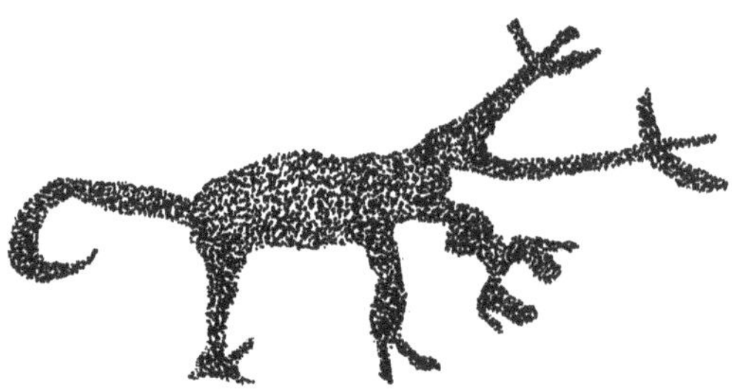

18. Scorpion, 32nd Street Locality. Scorpion is 45 cm in length.

Emil Haury (1976) reported that Hohokam pottery from the site of Snaketown contained painted scorpion designs in contexts dating to the Colonial period (ca. A.D. 750–950). He noted that scorpion designs did not look exactly like scorpions, many having only four legs. All, however, had tails that bend upward and forward.

Centipede and Millipede

Two of the more well known insects in the Sonoran Desert are centipedes (*Scolopendra* spp.) and millipedes *(Orthoperus ornatus).* The English name for centipede means "hundred legs," but centipedes do not have that many legs. They grow up to 6 inches (15 cm) long and have a pair of legs for each body segment. Centipedes spend the day under rocks or down other creatures' holes. At night they actively hunt their prey, which they inject with venom via fangs at the end of a pair of legs. Millipedes not only have more legs than centipedes, but they also have a cylindrical body in contrast to the flatter centipede. Millipedes obviously do not have a thousand legs; having two pairs of legs on each of most of the body segments makes them appear to have more legs than they actually do. Millipedes eat living and dead plant material and defend themselves by exuding a bad-smelling fluid from glands on each side of their body segments. Entomologists Floyd Werner and Carl Olson (1994) have noted that the only enemy of the millipede is an unusual larva of the zarrhipis beetle. This yellow-and-black-banded larva bites the millipede, injects it with poison, then slowly eats it. What makes the larva so unusual is that it is luminescent and can be seen against the ground on moonlit nights.

Millipedes thrive in the lower canyons of the South Mountains. They are especially noticeable because they spend most of their life underground, but emerge in large numbers after summer storms. Leaving behind the bodies of numerous dead relatives on the ground's surface, they soon return to their underground homes.

The petroglyphs identified as centipede/millipede images have linear bodies, multiple legs, and heads. Several similar rake or ladderlike designs have been recorded, but these do not have well-defined heads and legs that would identify them as insects. The most convincing examples of centipedes are present in the upper reaches of the east side of Box Canyon (figure 19) and on a large panel in the 36th Street Locality (figure 20). Both of these creatures have ten legs and are oriented with their heads down. An anthropomorph is present next to the centipede/millipede in Box Canyon.

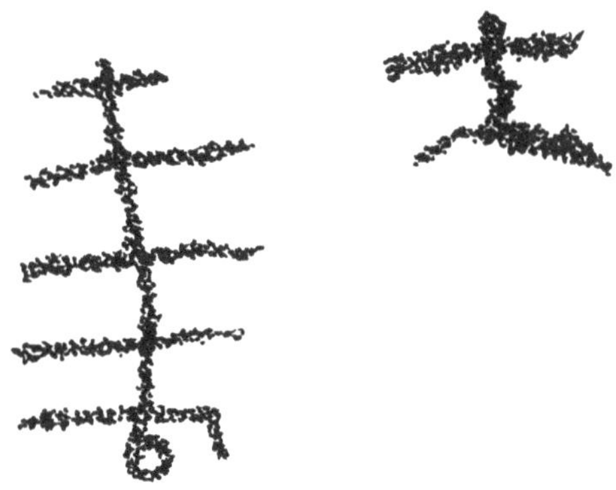

19. Centipede with anthropomorph, Box Canyon. Centipede is 25 cm in length.

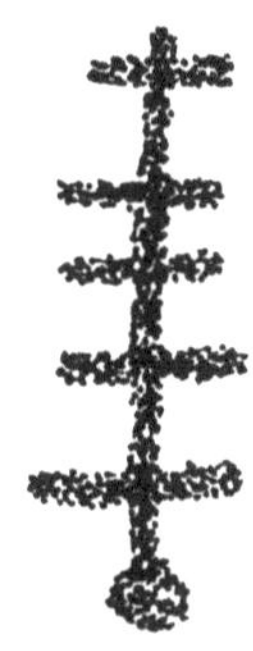

20. Centipede, 36th Street Locality. Centipede is 21 cm in length.

Two unusual multilegged creatures are present in a large panel in the 32nd Street Locality (figure 21). One of these has twenty-four legs, all pointing backward, and a round head. The other centipede/millipede on this same panel has eight legs, a long tail, and a round head. It is located right below an anthropomorphlike figure with six legs. Other elements on this panel include a number of quadrupeds with sectioned bodies and various geometric designs, including two negative crosses on opposite sides of the panel.

Centipedes are associated with the underworld among some native people of the American Southwest. They occur as Anasazi petroglyphs (Colton 1946) and occasionally are painted on black-on-white ceramic vessels. Their multiple legs have been equated with different levels of emergence from the underworld or different ages of human existence. Anthropomorphs with upraised arms, similar to the South Mountain examples, also are associated with centipede images in some Anasazi rock art panels in the Colorado Plateau region.

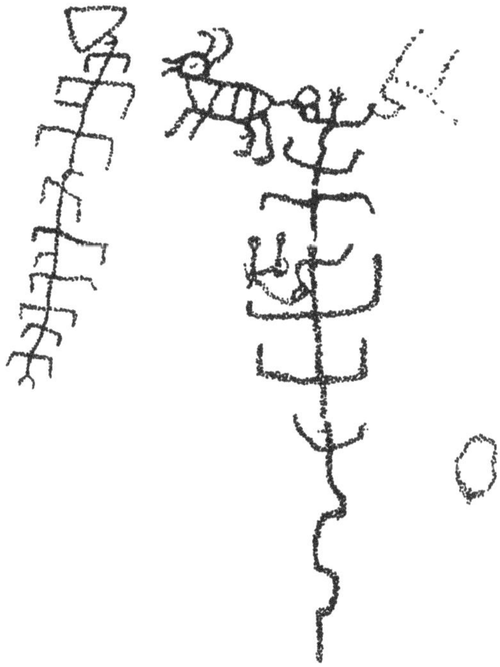

21. Multilegged creatures, central portion of panel, 32nd Street Locality. Mountain sheep is 34 cm in length.

Unidentified Insect

High up in the 32nd Street Locality is a large rock art panel that includes what appears to be an insect petroglyph of some kind (figure 22). This insect, perhaps a tick, has multiple legs and possible antennae or pinchers. It is being held by a smaller anthropomorph.

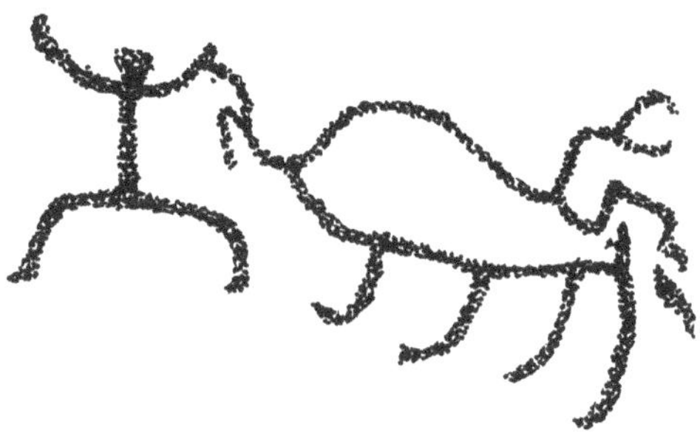

22. Anthropomorph holding tail of unidentified insect, 32nd Street Locality. Anthropomorph is 15 cm in height.

Dragonfly

Three petroglyphs found in the South Mountains appear to be dragonflies. These images consist of a straight line crossed by two perpendicular lines. One is located in Box Canyon, and another is in Hieroglyphic Canyon. A third dragonfly petroglyph is in a remote canyon in the upper reaches on the southern side of the South Mountains, where several rock art panels occur in association with a series of natural water tanks. This beautiful canyon has been called Valle Bonita. One of the panels in a cluster of petroglyphs is a large dragonfly image (figure 23). Nearby is a partial pipette petroglyph.

Dragonflies are predacious insects, during both adult and nymph stages. According to Tom Dudley (2000:360–361), Sonoran Desert dragonfly nymphs "have spiny posteriors that suck oxygenated water into their rectums where the oxygen is absorbed. Many nymphs dart through water by rapidly forcing the water out

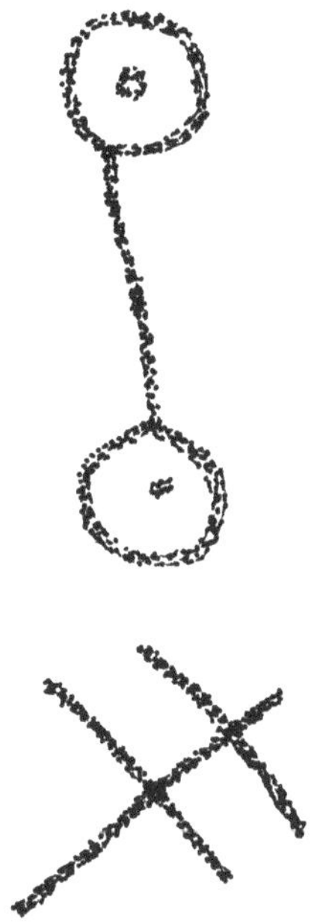

23. Dragonfly and geometric design, adjacent to a wash in Valle Bonita Locality. Circles are 10 cm in diameter.

of their rectums—jet propulsion!" Dragonfly nymphs also appear to be covered by a toothed mask, which is actually a retractable set of mouthparts used to capture their prey. Adult dragonflies patrol their territories and cruise streams in search of other flying insects, which they capture in the air. Some female dragonflies release their eggs on the wing by touching their abdomen to a water source while flying.

In the late nineteenth century, Frank Hamilton Cushing (1890) recorded a dragonfly petroglyph on Tempe Butte, 5 miles (8 km) north of the South Mountains. He noted that the dragonfly was a symbol of summer rains. An O'odham circling dance song celebrates a dragonfly skimming the surface of a pool of water, touching only his tail while flapping and rustling his wings. Dragonflies are also common images on Pueblo masks and pottery and occur on prehistoric kiva murals and altars in northern Arizona (Fewkes 1919). Among the Hopi, dragonflies are associated with springs, rain, and fertility. It is taboo for San Juan Pueblo Indians to kill a dragonfly because it has supernatural power and is a shamanistic creature.

Conclusions

A variety of insects and arthropods live in the deserts of the American Southwest, although only a select few are important in oral traditions and religions of the native people. Insects were occasionally spirit helpers for shamans of the Yuman-speaking Maricopa of western Arizona (Spier 1933), and water insects such as the dragonfly had religious significance to some Pueblo groups (Parsons 1939). Only a small number of rock art designs in the South Mountains represent insects and arthropods.

CHAPTER FIVE

CREATURES OF THE UNDERWORLD

AMPHIBIANS, REPTILES, AND FISH

Fear of reptiles and their kin is a learned, not instinctive, behavior—an infant watching a snake will giggle with delight, not recoil in horror. So the more we learn about reptiles and amphibians, the closer we can come to understanding and then enjoying them.

—JONATHAN HANSON AND ROSEANN B. HANSON (1997)

WE IDENTIFIED SEVERAL amphibians and reptiles in the rock art of the South Mountains. These include tadpoles and frogs, a salamander, turtles or tortoises, Gila monsters and other lizards, and snakes. We also found three fish petroglyphs. Amphibians and reptiles are well adapted to the Sonoran Desert and its large stretches of arid landscapes that are interspersed with occasional springs, washes that flow intermittently, and other small oases. An interesting variety of these creatures live within the South Mountains and the surrounding area.

TADPOLES

THE EXISTENCE OF amphibians in the arid desert may seem odd, but life finds clever ways to adapt. Tadpoles are hatched from eggs laid in seasonal water sources. In a short period of time, before the water evaporates, they undergo an amazing transformation, developing legs and emerging as adult frogs. Once the water is gone, the frogs dig into the ground, where they remain until water returns to their world. Tadpoles are often observed in temporary, natural water tanks after summer rains.

We identified about a dozen tadpole images in the South Mountains: nine in Box Canyon and one each in the 12th Street and 28th Place Localities (figure 24). They look like a large comma, with a small rounded head and a short, tapering tail. Most face to the right, although one faces to the left and two face down. None of the tadpoles appears as a single element, although one panel has only two tadpoles, each facing in a different direction. Most tadpole petroglyphs are relatively small, although a very large one in Box Canyon has been interpreted by some as a whale. We prefer to classify it as a large tadpole. This image dominates the panel in which it is located, being about twice the size of a human figure in the same panel. It is worth noting that some rock art researchers have identified similar comma designs as corn or bean sprouts, which also would have been important life symbols to desert farmers.

24. Tadpoles from two rock art localities in the South Mountains: **left,** 12th Street Locality (11 cm in length); **right,** Box Canyon (18 cm in length).

According to Frank Russell (1975:294), a Pima song mentions "tadpoles singing." Pueblo ethnographer Jesse Walter Fewkes (1919) recorded numerous tadpole designs on Hopi pottery. These had solid, circular heads and wavy or zigzag bodies. They were colored black as they are in nature. Fewkes noted that tadpoles among the Hopi were associated with rain and were painted on terraced medicine bowls used in rain-making ceremonies.

Frogs and Toads

Several species of frogs and toads make their homes at Sonoran Desert water sources. They are primarily creatures of the night who announce their presence with loud singing. The more common ones are the canyon treefrog *(Hyla arenicolor),* Couch's spadefoot *(Scaphiopus couchi),* Sonoran Desert toad *(Bufo alvarius),* Sonoran green toad *(Bufo retiformis),* and the very distinctive red-spotted toad *(Bufo punctatus).* The red-spotted toad is active at twilight, with males sitting at the water's edge singing a high-pitched musical trill. Tadpoles of this species develop remarkably quickly and often seek refuge in rodent burrows. The spadefoot and Sonoran Desert toad produce a secretion that can cause skin irritation when handled.

The life cycle of Couch's spadefoot exhibits one of the most remarkable processes in the Sonoran Desert. These tiny creatures with stout bodies (not true toads, although often called such) have a "spade" of bonelike material on the underside of each hind foot to help them dig as much as 2 feet (0.75 m) underground, where they retreat for up to nine months. With the arrival of summer thunderstorms, hundreds of spadefoots emerge from their underground homes and gather where rainwater has collected. Biologist John Alcock has claimed that the frogs cannot see or feel the rain but in fact hear the thunder. At night, a chorus of males attempts to attract females, and their loud broadcasts reflect the urgency with which they must mate. The sight of spadefoots emerging from desert sands as though summoned by the rain clouds is an unforgettable experience. It is easy to imagine why frogs were sacred animals to many Native American groups.

Sonoran Desert toads, also called Colorado River toads, can grow up to 7 inches (18 cm) long, much larger than any other toad in Arizona or California. Slow-moving, these toads have developed a chemical toxin secreted from glands all over their skin. This poison can disrupt nerve and muscle functions in any mammal that tries to eat it. The toxins have killed dogs that put the toads in their mouth. Curiously, humans have found that smoking the dried secretions of this toad causes powerful hallucinations.

Possibly three or four rock art elements could be identified as frogs, and they are all located at intermittent springs. On a large outcrop at Johnson Camp in upper Pima Canyon, a frog is stretched out horizontally next to several human figures (figure 25). The physical details of this frog are depicted with relative accuracy. Another possible frog may be present in a complex but faded panel in Hidden Canyon (figure 26). Located on a massive boulder next to a natural water tank, this large rock art panel has a possible frog image with a vestigial tail between two quadruped images. Another panel at a different site in the same locality has a strange-looking creature that may also be a frog (figure 27).

The O'odham have several songs about frogs and their association with water and rain. Anna Shaw (1968:79–81) tells a story about how a frog shaman was eaten by Coyote, which caused a flood. In a medicine song recorded by Frank Russell (1975:304), blue frog woman carried a person "to the cloud land in the east . . . where the clouds are standing." O'odham oral traditions record that at a Hohokam village called Casa Blanca, a shaman had a pet frog as his assistant. In Hopi stories,

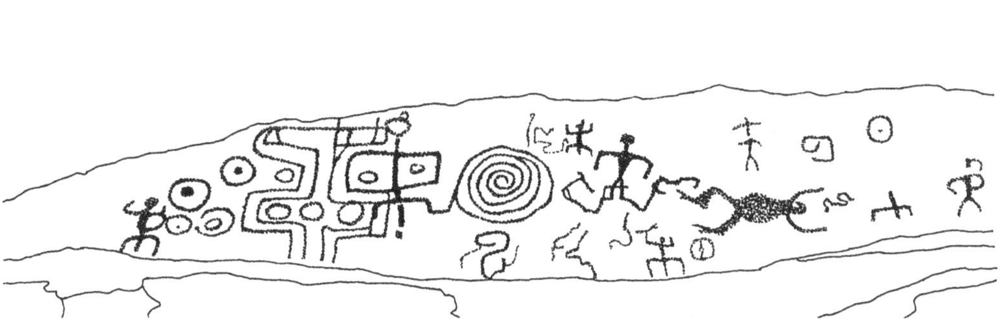

25. Frog stretched out horizontally in the upper right portion of a large and complex panel located near a natural water tank in upper Pima Canyon. A pipette and spiral are located to the left of the frog. Spiral is 28 cm in diameter.

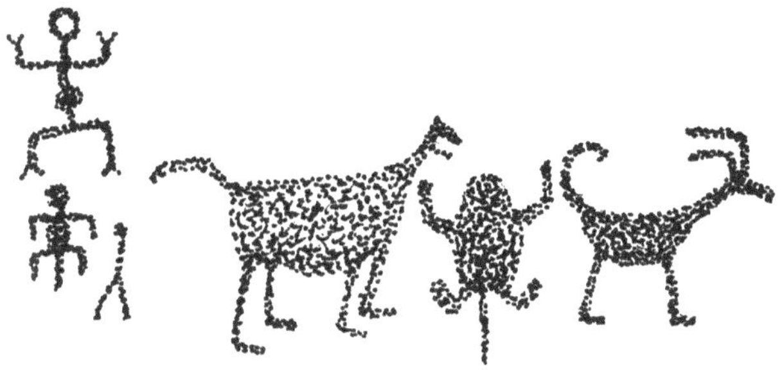

26. Possible frog in a panel located next to a large wash in Hidden Valley. Frog is 36 cm in length.

the frog is a pet of the horned water serpent. Frogs and toads are affiliated with the Aztec rain and storm god, Tlaloc, and are the musicians or voice of the Maya rain god, Chac (Benson 1997). Frogs and toads also appear in Mesoamerican myths about man's acquisition of fire.

Salamander

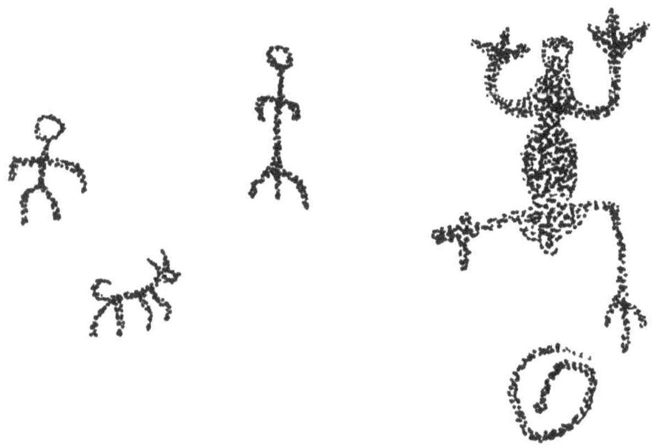

27. Possible frog, Hidden Valley. Panel is located adjacent to a rock shelter and a wash. Froglike creature is 47 cm in length.

Three species of salamanders live in the American Southwest, the largest and most common being the tiger salamander *(Ambystoma tigrinum).* Salamanders, also known as "mud puppies," look somewhat like lizards but have a larger head and small eyes. These creatures live underground, usually in burrows dug by other animals such as ground squirrels and badgers. They also live among rocks or in logs. Salamanders can be seen at night, when they hunt earthworms, insects, mice, and other amphibians. During the breeding season, usually in the spring or summer, the males and females congregate at pools of water. When the water dries up, some salamanders dig themselves into a bank of mud and enter a state of dormancy called estivation, emerging only after a solid rain.

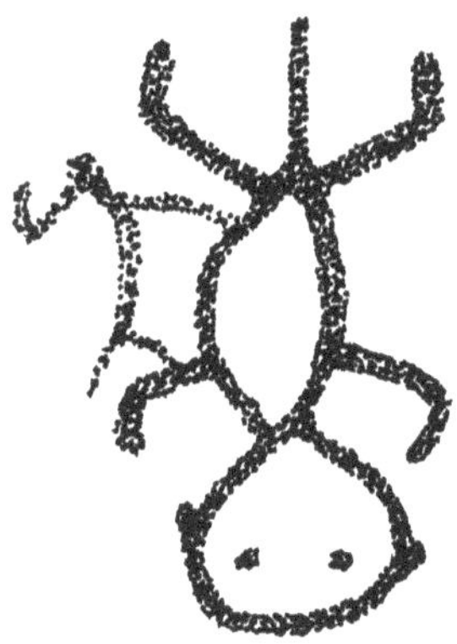

28. Salamander and anthropomorph located near a spring in Hieroglyphic Canyon. Salamander is 40 cm in length.

A single petroglyph in the upper portion of Hieroglyphic Canyon looks like a salamander (figure 28). This four-legged creature has a stout body, a big head, small eyes, and a tail. It is located adjacent to a spring and is pointing downward, as though climbing down into the wash, which is fed by seep after seasonal rains. A small human figure is holding the side of the salamander. The panel appears a little less patinated than some of the other petroglyphs at this location and, therefore, may be more recent.

Tortoises and Turtles

One of the oddest sights in the Sonoran Desert is a desert tortoise *(Gopherus agassizii)* slowly lumbering across a sandy stretch of arid land. These land-based reptiles have domed shells and thick, stumpy legs with webless toes. Their heads are small and roundish. They feed on grasses and forbs in the early morning and late afternoon, spending much of the day in their burrows, some of which have long, horizontal tunnels. Although their habitat is in arid, sandy locales, they also live near washes, canyon bottoms, and oases. In the spring, opposing males engage in strange mating bouts. They bob their heads, grunt and hiss, circle each other, bite their rival's head and legs, and ram each other with the lower plate of their shell. Tortoises can live up to forty years, spending that long life within a few miles of where they were born.

Water turtles also make the Sonoran Desert their home wherever springs, creeks, ponds, or even intermittent streams occur. The most common species is the Sonoran mud turtle *(Kinosternon sonoriense)*. This small turtle has a smooth, elongated shell. Its habitat ranges from springs, water holes, ponds, and creeks in low deserts, to high mountains. During dry periods they sometimes congregate at water holes.

Tortoise or turtle rock art images are much more frequent than frog petroglyphs in the South Mountains. We recorded at least two dozen tortoise or turtle petroglyphs at eleven different locations. The largest concentrations are in Box Canyon, with seven, and Hieroglyphic Canyon and 32nd Street, each with four. Tortoise/turtle images are mostly outline forms (figure 29), with only four examples having solidly pecked bodies. Three with the outlined bodies have a small dot inside the body. Tortoise/turtle images usually have a distinct head that is often a solidly pecked triangular form, although some are circular or simply a thick, straight line (figure 30). Almost all of the tortoise/turtle petroglyphs are oriented vertically. A few are tilted to the right, and one is titled to the left. The most dramatic example of this motif is a panel that contains two tortoise or turtle images on a large boulder located along the northeast side of Box Canyon (figure 31).

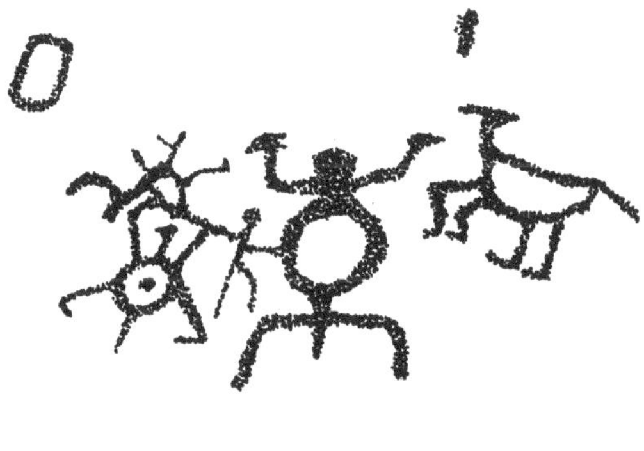

29. Panel with a tortoise/turtle petroglyph along a trail in Box Canyon. Tortoise/turtle on lower left has a dot in the center of its body. The large central figure, which looks like an anthropomorph with a tortoise/turtle body, is 44 cm in height.

Turtle stories are part of O'odham oral traditions. Anna Shaw (1968) relates a story about how Turtle feeds his children. In this story, two antelopes tried to stomp Turtle to death but slipped and broke their necks. Coyote and Turtle cut up the antelope meat, but Coyote hung Turtle on a rope from a tree branch and took the best meat. Because of Turtle's magic, the meat became full of ants and scorpions. Coyote then jumped into the water to bite Turtle but drowned instead.

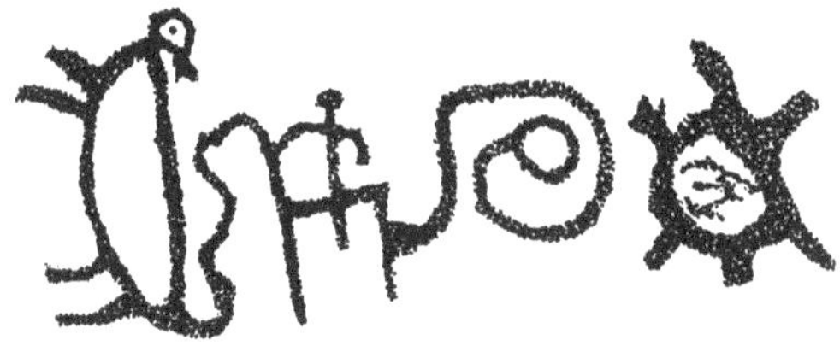

30. Tortoise/turtle next to an anthropomorph attached to a snake and a vertical mountain sheep, 16th Street Locality. Mountain sheep is 29 cm in length. This panel may be a shaman scene.

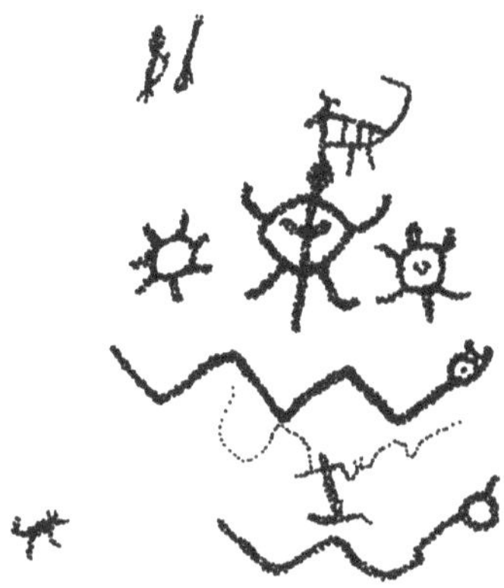

31. Panel with two tortoise/turtle petroglyphs associated with two snakes, a sun symbol (to left of large tortoise/turtle), quadrupeds, and an anthropomorph connected to wavy lines, Box Canyon. Large, central tortoise/turtle is 37 cm in length. One of the snakes has two horns and a face.

In another O'odham story, Turtle is a powerful shaman who brags too much about his powers (Saxton and Saxton 1973). The telling of his feats was so loud that his boasts reached the sky. Spider was offended and challenged Turtle to a contest to see which could go the longest without eating or drinking water. For four months, they lay side by side singing songs of defiance at each other. Finally, Spider gave in. Turtle then challenged Spider to another contest, but Turtle smoked too much sleeping-tobacco and Spider tied him up and hung him from the ceiling in his house. Turtle escaped but lost his wife. When he searched for her on top of Baboquivari Peak, Spider sang a song that was so powerful it made Turtle fall to his death. Thus ended the life of a mighty medicine man.

Among the Maya, turtles are symbols of the earth and water, but they also represent a constellation, perhaps Orion. Turtles are sometimes associated with fire, and, according to the Mayan book of Popol Vuh, Orion is where the Three Hearthstones of the original kitchen fireplace are located. An O'odham shaman's song has an interesting stanza: "The black turtle now approaches us, wearing and shaking his belt of night" (Russell 1975:306).

GILA MONSTER

FEW NORTH AMERICAN animals have been the subject of more legends and exaggerated claims than the Gila monster *(Heloderma suspectum)* (Brown and Carmony 1991). This strange, slow-moving creature of the Sonoran Desert is America's largest and only poisonous lizard. It is also the only American lizard with an armored hide and a forked snakelike tongue. Its beaded hide is typically patterned with black or brown blotches against a background color of yellow, cream, or salmon. Gila monsters raid nests and eat the eggs of ground-dwelling birds, desert tortoise eggs, and young mammals. The fat they store in their swollen tails allows them to hibernate for nine or more months. So much of the life of this lizard is spent underground that few humans have observed a Gila monster hatching in the wild. Little wonder they are so mysterious.

Only one panel in the South Mountains has a Gila monster image, but it is a special panel containing two of these unusual creatures (figure 32). It is located in the northeastern end of Box Canyon, near the Holbert Trail. Clearly visible from a distance, the panel consists of a well-pecked Gila monster holding the front foot of another Gila monster, who is holding a large spiral. Several small human figures are located at the bottom of the panel. The Gila monster holding the spiral is larger but more lightly pecked than the other, creating a ghostlike image.

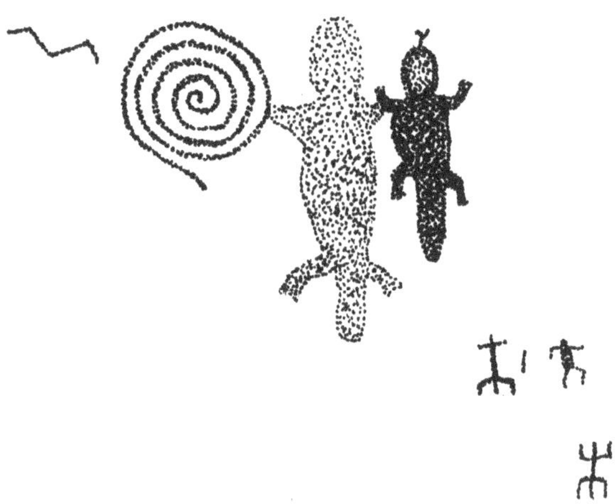

32. Two Gila monsters, Holbert Trail. Smaller, more densely pecked Gila monster is 56 cm in length. Spiral is 35 cm in diameter. Much smaller anthropomorphs are present at the bottom of the panel.

This panel has the appearance of shamanistic art (see discussion in chapter 11). The humans are puny creatures compared to the powerful Gila monsters and are placed below and to the right. The large spiral held by the ghostlike lizard could represent a portal into another world, and the Gila monster is a powerful spirit helper. The O'odham have a shaman song about the Gila monster as a "pitiable harlot," but one "whose heart glows with the singing" (Russell 1975:307).

Other Lizards

Lizards can be seen everywhere in the Sonoran Desert and occur in large numbers in the South Mountains. They love to sun themselves during early morning hours, have amusing mating habits, and live underground (Hanson and Hanson 1997). Upon close observation, one cannot help but notice their extremely long, back-toed feet. The more common lizards living in the South Mountains include the chuckwalla *(Sauromalus obesus),* desert iguana *(Dipsosaurus dorsalis),* zebra-tailed lizard *(Callisaurus draconoides),* desert spiny lizard *(Sceloporus magister),* collared lizard *(Crotaphytus collaris),* tree lizard *(Urosaurus ornatus),* longnose leopard lizard *(Gambelia wislizenii),* western whiptail *(Cnemidophorus tigris),* short-horned lizard *(Phrynosoma douglassii),* and western banded gecko *(Coleonyx variegatus).*

Chuckwallas are easily identifiable because of their large size—up to 16.5 inches (42 cm) in length. Their scientific name means fat, ugly lizard. They have a distinctive colored tail, a large potbelly, and loose folds of skin around their neck and shoulders. At the first sign of a threat, they wedge themselves deep inside cracks in boulders and fill themselves with air.

Desert spiny lizards also are large, but they are characterized by their rough scales. Collared lizards have distinctive black and blue-green or orange markings around their neck. Leopard lizards have patterned spots on a yellow background. Zebra-tailed lizards are impressive for their speed, up to 18 miles (29 km) per hour.

The western whiptail is another easily recognizable desert lizard because of its noticeable behavior. This striped and spotted lizard is very active within a clearly defined territory, racing around and digging up stones and earth in search of food, which includes other lizards. When two males meet, they put on quite a show. They usually run wildly around each other, playing a game of tag, the leader zigzagging and the other in hot pursuit. Occasionally, two males will meet one another belly to belly and their arms flail in a wild wrestling match that typically ends suddenly with the departure of one of the combatants.

The horned lizard has a flat, round body and daggerlike spikes crowning its head. Although it is a true lizard, it is often called a horned toad because of its toadlike body. Horned lizards are friendly and love to bask in the sun, sometimes digging into the sand as though they are swimming. Their armor of sharp, spikelike scales discourages other creatures from swallowing them, and they can inflate themselves by gulping air. One species of horned lizard can squirt a stream of blood up to 6 feet (1.8 m) from a pore in its eyelids, startling would-be predators. A horned lizard's main food is ants, and they have even developed an antitoxin specifically for the poison of harvester ants.

Geckos are medium-sized, nocturnal lizards with cross-band coloring and protruding eyelids. They hide during the day and hunt insects at night. When caught by a predator, they make a chirping sound. Their tails are easily detachable, which serves as an escape mechanism for them and a disappointing but tasty morsel for predators.

Lizards are frequent rock art images in the South Mountains, taking many forms. Variability in form may reflect different species, but, if so, identification is problematic. Larger images may be chuckwallas, while those with crowns may be horned lizards. Some lizard petroglyphs appear humanlike, as Henry Wallace (1989) noted during his study of Hohokam rock art near Tucson. He suggested that anthropomorphs with middle appendages longer than their legs should be called lizards. If a figure with a long middle appendage is obviously human or has a humanlike face, it should then be called a lizardman.

Lizard elements occur as both outlined and solidly pecked forms. Their torsos are naturally shaped, diamond shaped, or circular. One of the better naturally shaped lizard petroglyphs occurs next to a wash along the Holbert Trail. Examples of lizards with diamond-shaped bodies are present at sites in Goodman Canyon, Box Canyon, and the upper 32nd Street Locality. The latter rock art panel has a very large lizard being held by an anthropomorph (figure 33). The circular form of lizard body has two variations, one being the equivalent of concentric circles (figure 34). Excellent examples of this type can be found at the Desert Foothills Locality on the southern

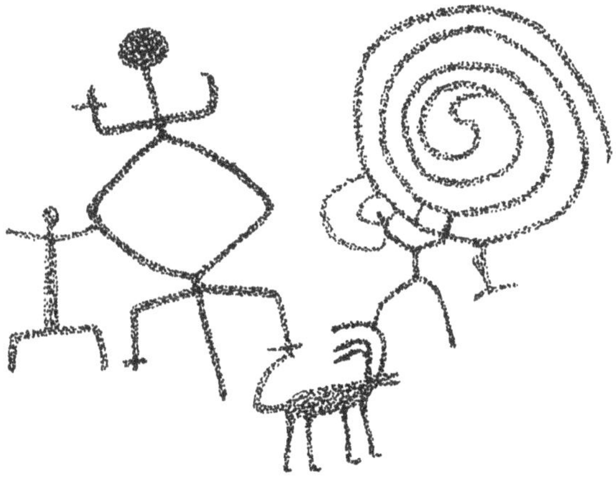

33. Large diamond-bodied lizard, upper 32nd Street Locality. Lizard is 47 cm in length. Panel faces southeast.

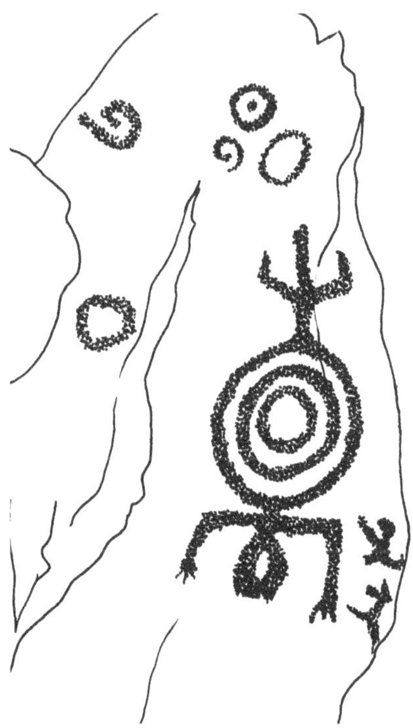

34. Large lizard with concentric circle body form, 28th Place Locality. Lizard is 46 cm in length.

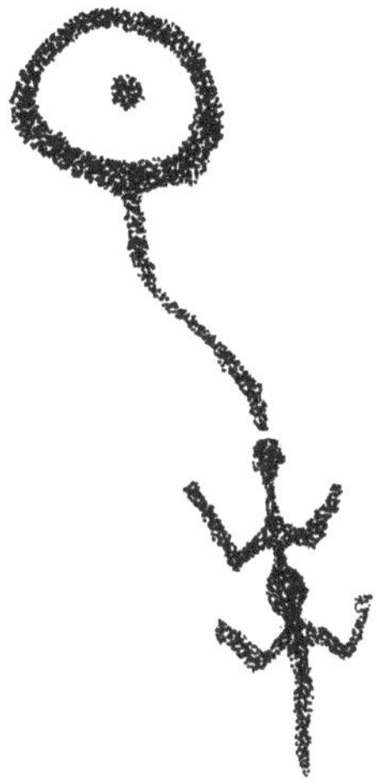

35. Lizard connected to circle/dot in alcove with seasonal water seep, Box Canyon. Lizard is 38 cm in length.

side of the mountains and in Hieroglyphic Canyon. The other is a stick-body lizard with a small, solid circle located along the mid axis of the torso (figure 35). This latter variation also appears on many human figures and contributes to the confusion concerning lizards versus humans. A dramatic example of this type of lizard is present in a panel in lower Pima Canyon (figure 36). This exceptional lizard, more than 2 feet (0.73 m) in length, occurs in the same panel with much smaller human figures, a large snake, and some geometric elements. A lizardman on the left side of the lizard is upside-down and appears to be dead. A human on the right side of the lizard holds his arms upward, as though saluting the lizard.

Lizard head shapes vary. Some are solid or outline circular shapes, some are triangular, and some are natural looking. The four legs of lizards are portrayed both forward and backward, but the front feet are predomi-

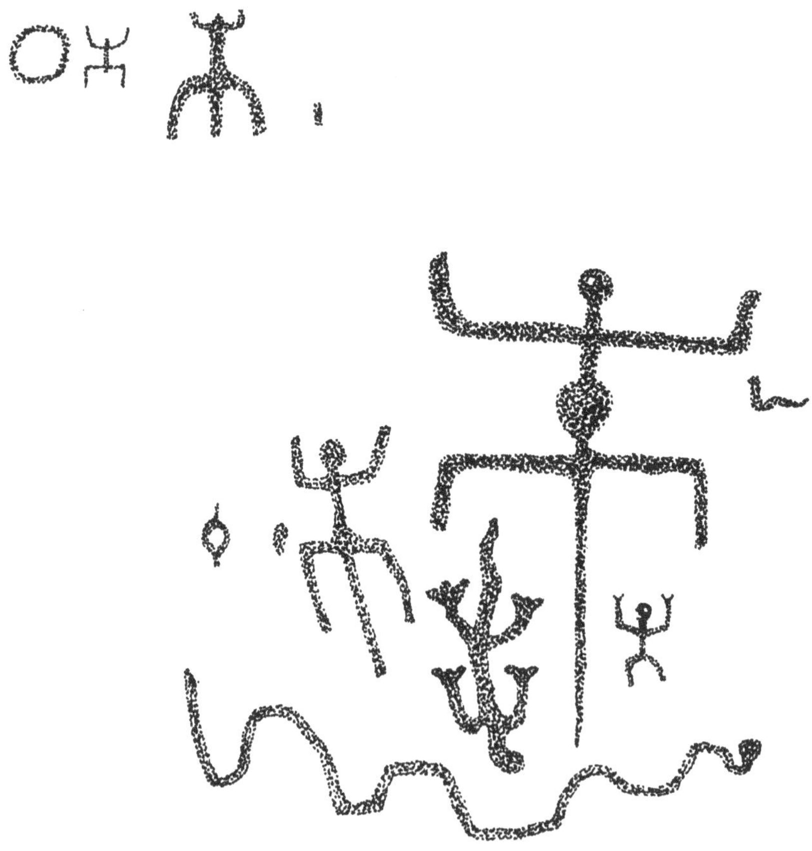

36. Large lizard, lower Pima Canyon. Lizard is 73 cm in length.

nantly oriented forward. Lizard feet are generally not well defined, although it is not uncommon to have three toes on all four feet depicted. Nowhere in the South Mountains were completely natural-appearing feet represented on the rock art elements identified as lizards. Lizard tails may be short or long; most tails are straight, but slightly bent tails are also present (figure 37).

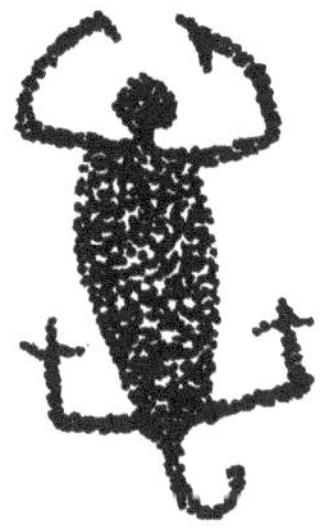

37. Lizard with curved tail, Hieroglyphic Canyon. Lizard is 19 cm in length.

Lizards are common shamanic symbols, representing messengers between worlds. Their behavior is considered highly symbolic. An O'odham shaman song about the Black Lizard recalls the lizard's association with the sun and water (Russell 1975:308):

> *We first sing at the magician's,*
> *the round disk of the sun arose,*
> *accompanied with its rays.*
> *Black Lizard found the trail where Elder Brother had been running,*
> *and he came out from the clouds,*
> *with water upon his arms.*

Horned lizards also were important in O'odham oral traditions (Russell 1975; Shaw 1968). One story recalls the Horned Toad people who were led to safety after the conquest of the Hohokam. Another O'odham song describes a little gray horned toad (lizard) medicine man, associating horned lizards with shamanism. For the Zuni, lizard petroglyphs have different levels of meaning and are metaphors of power (Young 1988). Some lizards represent the Zuni people "at the time of beginning." They are the Zuni's ancestors, people who had webbed toes and lived in the fourth underworld.

Snakes and Serpents

Snakes are abundant in the Sonoran Desert. Several species live in the South Mountains, although most are nocturnal and thus rarely seen by humans. Many of these snakes have brightly colored markings or unusual scale patterns. Most are harmless, but some of the more common snakes are very poisonous. Nonpoisonous snakes include the garter snake (*Thamnophis* spp.), common or desert kingsnake *(Lampropeltis getulas),* ground snake *(Sonora semiannulata),* longnose snake *(Rhinocheilus lecontei),* gopher snake *(Pituophis melanoleucus),* and coachwhip or red racer *(Masticophis flagellum).* The tricolored longnose snake is nonpoisonous but has developed the defensive technique of coiling, hissing, and striking like a rattlesnake and discharging a foul-smelling musk. It eats lizards and other snakes.

Poisonous snakes include the Arizona coral snake *(Micruroides euryxanthus),* western diamondback rattlesnake *(Crotalus atrox),* western rattlesnake *(Crotalus viridis),* blacktail rattlesnake *(Crotalus molossus),* Mohave rattlesnake *(Crotalus scutulatus),* and desert sidewinder *(Crotalus cerastes).* The red-black-and-yellow banded coral snake is extremely poisonous but tends not to be aggressive, usually emerging from its hole only at night or following a warm rain shower.

Rattlesnakes are especially noticeable in spring, when they spend early-morning hours sunning themselves. Although they are adapted to lying in wait and capturing small mammals along desert trails, rattlesnakes also hunt by day, and some eat lizards, frogs, and toads. They can detect an animal's body heat from at least twelve inches (30 cm) away. Rattlesnakes swallow their prey whole and patiently wait for the enzymes in their poison to digest the victim. The sidewinder has prominent triangular projections over each eye that make the snake look like it has horns. It moves in a slithering, looping, sideways motion over sandy areas, leaving a series of linear tracks. The western diamondback is the largest of the rattlesnakes, growing to over 6 feet (2 m) in length, and is distinguished by its diamond-shaped scale patterns and its head having a shape distinct from its neck. It eats rodents and birds and can live up to 25 years. One of the unusual characteristics of the rattlesnake is its ability to regulate the amount of poison injected through each of its hypodermiclike fangs, even discharging no venom into its prey if it so chooses.

Snake images are very common in the South Mountains, occurring in the majority of localities in a wide variety of forms that perhaps represent different snake species. Snake petroglyphs are coiled and extended, as well as combinations of both. Extended snakes almost always are wavy in form (figure 38), usually with curvilinear bends in their bodies but occasionally with crenulated body forms (figure 39). The number of bends in the snake's body ranges from one to as many as thirteen (figure 40). Snakes usually have a recognizable head, but that too varies from small to large, may be circular or triangular, and occurs in both outline and solidly pecked forms (figure 41). Some snakes have horns or headdresses (figure 42). With only a few interesting exceptions, snake images in the South Mountains do not have tongues or fangs (figure 43). In Hieroglyphic Canyon, a large horned snake has what appears to be a stylized fang hanging out of its mouth (figure 44). An elaborate maze is located above the horned snake, and various anthropomorphs in different postures are also present in the panel.

Snake images occur alone in the South Mountains, but they are most often associated with anthropomorphs (see figures 125–129) and other life-forms in multiple-element panels (figure 45). In a panel overlooking a wash in upper Pima Canyon, a human (perhaps a shaman or religious leader) holds a snake in one hand and a staff in the other (see figure 116). In a panel in the 16th Street Locality, a partly extended

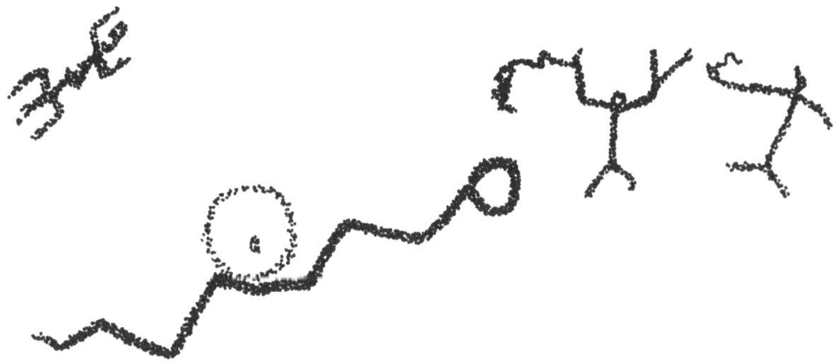

38. Extended snake facing anthropomorphs holding possible snakes, San Juan East Locality. Snake is 62 cm in length.

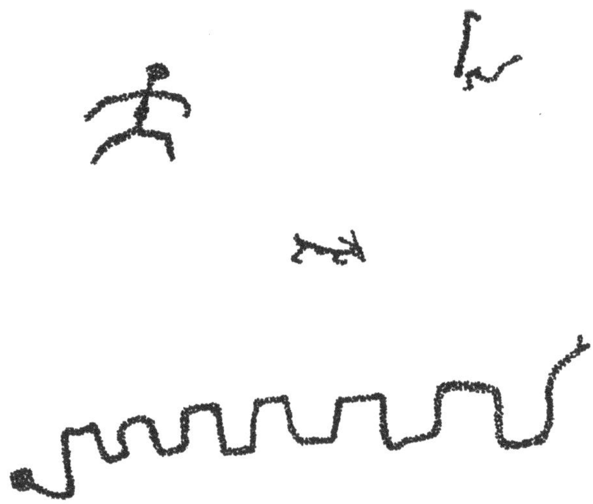

39. Snake, anthropomorph, and coyote/dog petroglyphs, 32nd Street Locality. Snake is 78 cm in length.

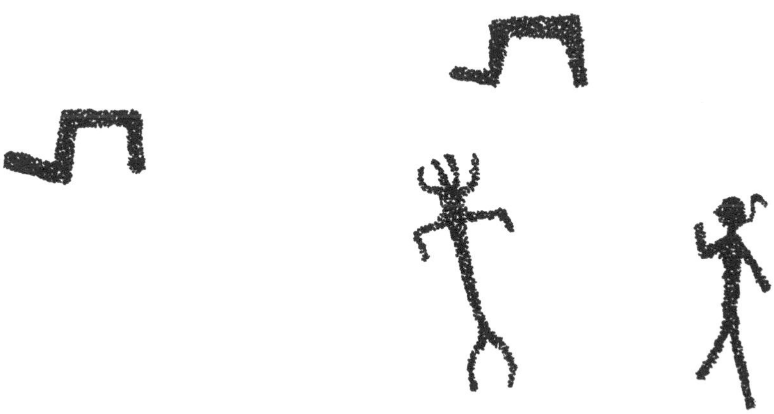

40. Single-bend rectilinear snakes above two anthropomorphs, 24th Street Locality. Anthropomorph on left is 42 cm in height.

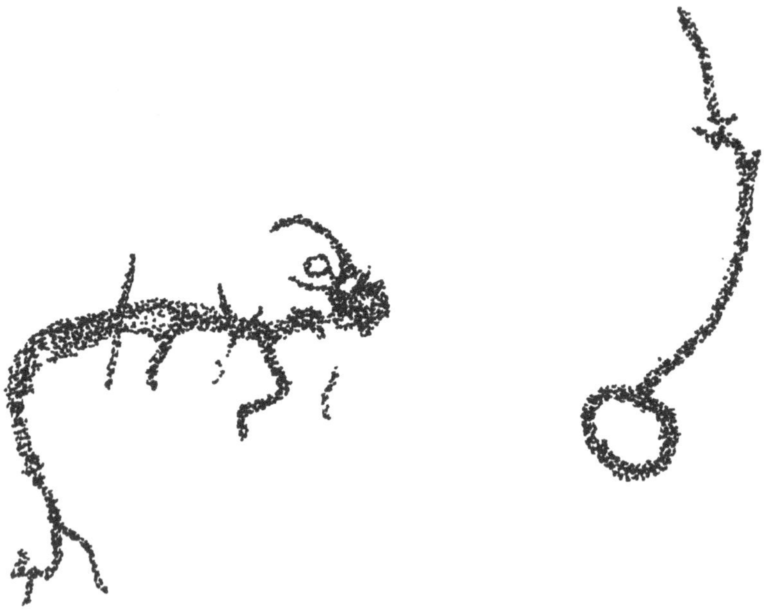

41. Serpent/snake petroglyphs located in front of a small rock shelter in Box Canyon. Figure on right is 40 cm in length. Serpent on left may be a spirit being or a shaman transforming into a snake.

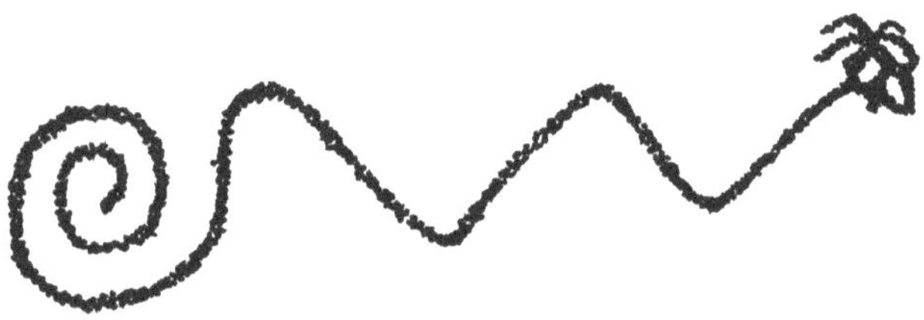

42. Snake with face and headdress, 32nd Street Locality. Snake is 35 cm in length.

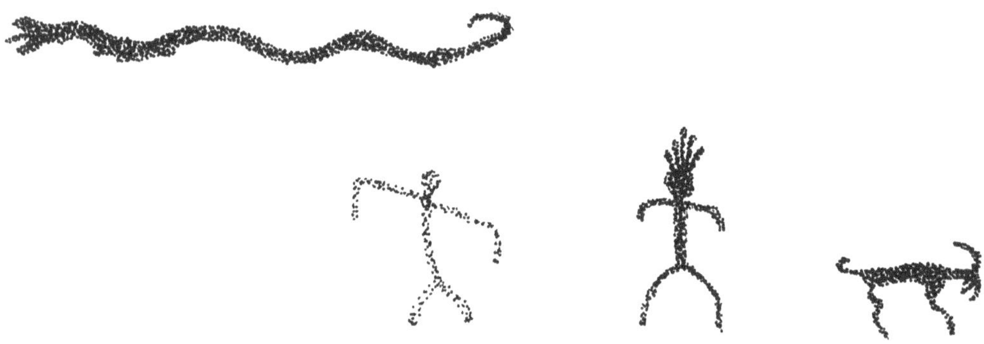

43. Snake, anthropomorphs, and mountain sheep on a panel in Box Canyon. Snake is 73 cm in length. These petroglyphs appear less repatinated compared to others in Box Canyon, suggesting a more recent origin.

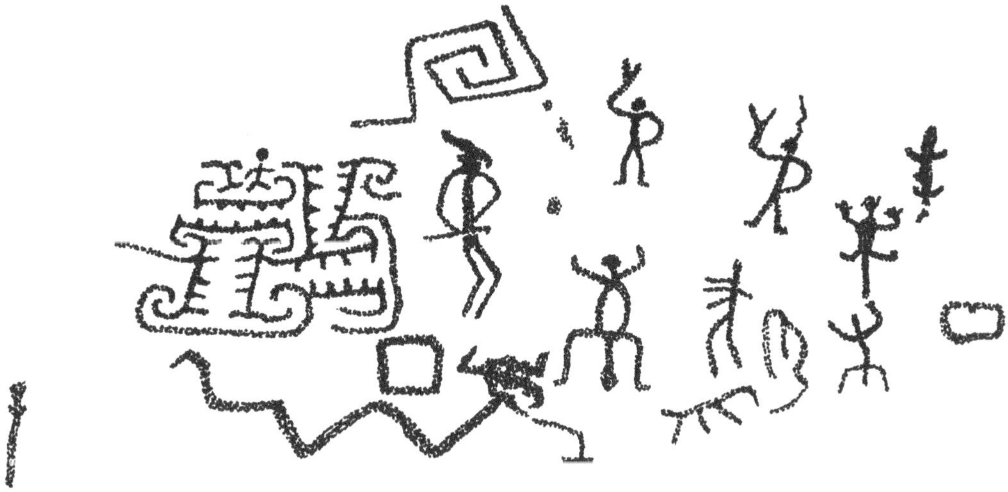

44. Horned snake in elaborate panel that includes a mazelike design, Hieroglyphic Canyon. Horned snake is 58 cm in length.

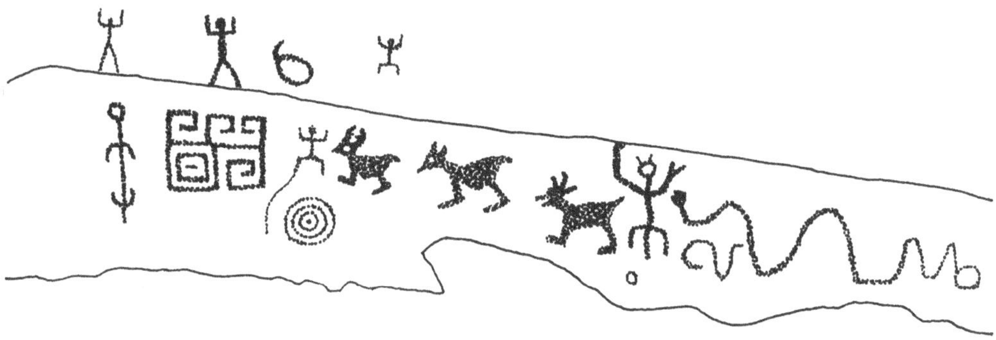

45. Snake images and other petroglyphs, 32nd Street Locality. Panel sits in front of a level area with an elevated view of the Salt River Valley.

and partly coiled snake is next to a bent-over human holding a cane (see figure 139). Two coiled snakes are situated on each side of an anthropomorph in a panel in Box Canyon. In Goodman Canyon, an elaborate rock art scene includes two snakes, one of which has horns or plumes and is staring at a mountain sheep (see figure 52). The other snake is very long and located behind the mountain sheep.

A snake petroglyph panel at the 48th Street Locality is partly rectilinear and partly curvilinear, with several circles spaced between each of the bends in the snake's body (figure 46). A small quadruped is located to the left of the snake. A panel in the Southeast Side Locality has a coiled snake adjacent to a double spiral that somewhat mimics the snake form. Another panel in the same locality has a group of at least five extended snakes with partly coiled tails (figure 47). Two of these snakes have small dots inside their coils. To the left of the snakes are a lizard and a small spiral.

Another panel in the same locality has a well-executed snake coiled into an outlined cross form, sometimes called a Venus or morning star shape, with the snake's head (facing west) at the interior of the cross (figure 48). A lizard, with its tail hooked right, is present below this unusual snake image.

It may be impossible to identify different species of snakes in the South Mountains rock art. However, some examples do appear to be rattlesnakes because the ends of their tails look somewhat like rattles. The characteristic triangular head of rattlesnakes also appears in some of the South Mountains petroglyphs.

In addition to snake images, snake symbols may be visible in other petroglyphs.

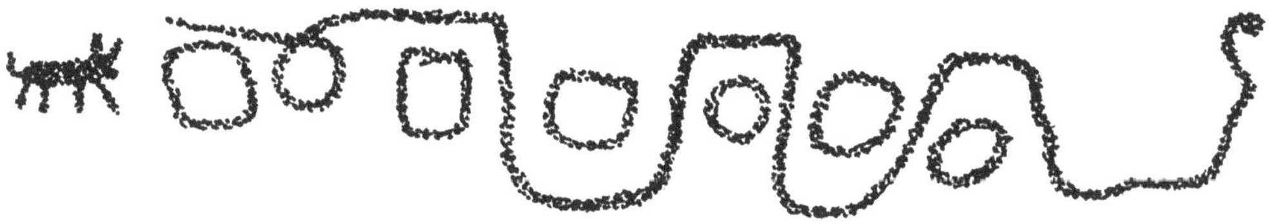

46. Unusual crenulated snake design, 48th Street Locality. Snake is 1.3 m in length.

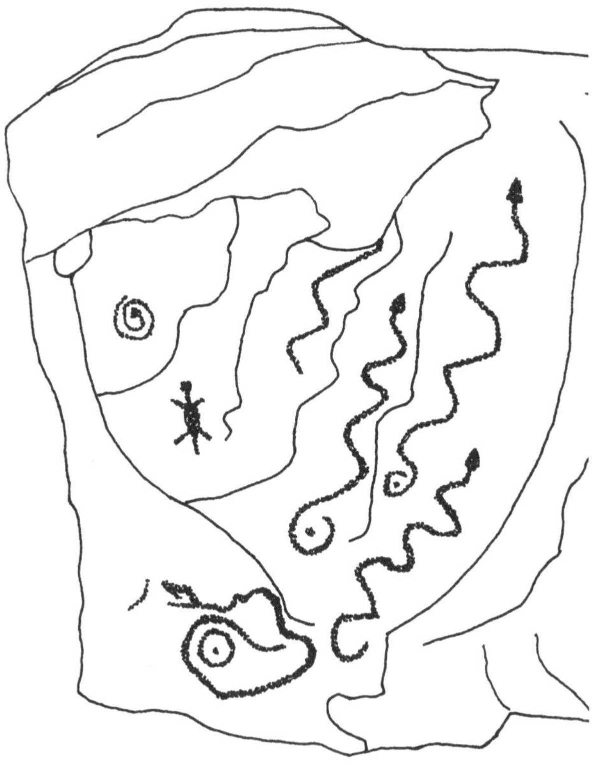

47. Six snakes in the same panel, Southeast Side Locality. Lower right snake is 36 cm in length. Lower left snake has fangs depicted. Upper left snake has been partially eroded.

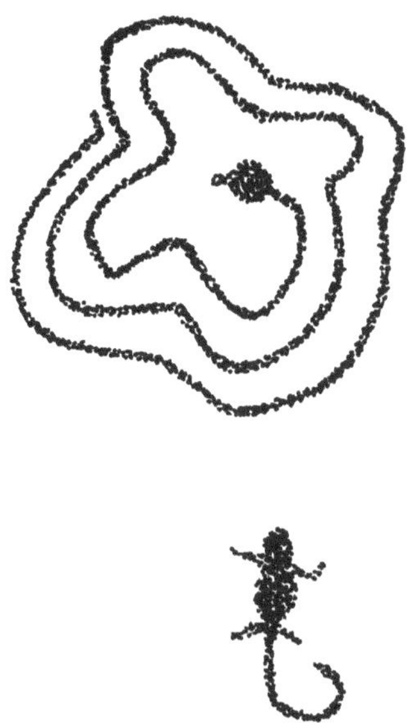

48. Snake coiled into star pattern above lizard, Southeast Side Locality. Snake is 26 x 26 cm.

A geometric design, composed of several S-curves in a row, in Box Canyon may represent the tracks of a sidewinder.

O'odham people, as well as several Native American groups in California, associate rattlesnakes with shamans because of their powerful poisonous bite. Archaeologists have long known that, in days past, anyone who recovered from the bite of a rattlesnake could become a shaman. Rattlesnakes possess magic power and have the wisdom to find the best mesquite beans. In an old O'odham story, Rattlesnake once was not able to protect himself and was abused. He liked to sing and attend gatherings but was tied in a knot and passed over the fire by Rabbit. The Sun god then gave the rattlesnake two rays for fangs so that it could defend itself. Folklorist Jim Griffith (1992) also has documented several O'odham stories about dangerous serpents that live in springs. This serpent is called "La Corua," or "Nehbig."

In Pueblo culture, snakes and serpents play important roles in religious ceremonies and imagery. Horned and plumed serpents are said to live in water sources such as springs and streams. The Zuni call the plumed serpent "Ko'lowisi" (Bunzel 1992). Among these people, encountering a snake on the way back to a village from a spring was considered a good omen, and the patron of the Antelope society is the rattlesnake. The famous Hopi snake ceremony is held in late summer for two weeks: after using live rattlesnakes in their ritual dance, Hopi priests deposit the snakes at shrines located in the four cardinal directions so that the snakes will carry the people's prayers for rain to the rain deities (Bourke 1984; Fewkes 1986; Hodge 1896; Parsons 1939). In New Mexico, priests in charge of Santa Ana Pueblo's irrigation ditches make offerings to water serpents. Considering that the Hohokam relied heavily on crops watered by a vast irrigation system, Hohokam priests and shamans may very well have venerated water serpents in ways similar to those of the Puebloans.

On the Colorado Plateau and in the upper Rio Grande region, petroglyph snake images are often associated with scenes of copulation and birth (Slifer 2000). They are also commonly associated with flute-player images. In some Pueblo fertility rituals, snakes are considered lightning symbols that bring summer rain, appearing as celestial serpents that can be either good or bad.

Snakes in Mesoamerica have served as metaphors for the cosmos and guardians of sacred space and may have been the most important fauna in Mesoamerican religion (Benson 1997). They stand for regeneration because they shed their skins and also represent the life-giving energy of the earth. Capable of moving between different worlds, they were often used as symbols of the supernatural. Their movement looks like water, and they have been associated with moving water, caves, and serpentlike lightning "strikes" between rain clouds in the sky. The Maya equate the serpent with the sky, as well as the earth, and a double-headed serpent was sometimes used to define the sky phenomenon known as the Milky Way (Miller and Taube 1993). The feathered or horned serpent also is associated with Quetzalcoatl and Venus/morning star imagery in Mesoamerica.

Fish

We found only three examples of fish petroglyphs in the South Mountains. A small fish design may be present in a rock art panel in the 36th Street Locality. This crudely made glyph has a dorsal fin and is oriented vertically. The other two fish images probably are not Hohokam in origin but more likely were made in the Protohistoric or early Historic period. Fish are not a common design in Hohokam art. Nor are they present in large numbers in Hohokam trash deposits, although they clearly were eaten, especially during the Classic period (ca. A.D. 1150–1450). A fish image on a panel in the Southeast Side Locality is in profile, with dorsal and ventral fins depicted (see figure 12). Two bird images in this panel appear more modern than the Hohokam bird style. Another fish petroglyph is present near an hourglass petroglyph at Johnson Camp in the Upper Pima Canyon Locality (figure 49). This long, slender fish image is in profile, with dorsal and ventral fins depicted, and has a small eye on the side of its head.

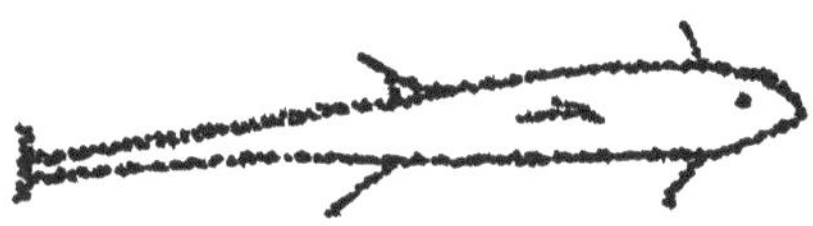

49. Fish, Upper Pima Canyon Locality. Fish is 38 cm in length and probably postdates Hohokam.

Emil Haury (1976:235–236) noted that the fish was "seldom delineated by the painter's brush" on Hohokam painted ceramics. Fish designs on Snaketown ceramics are simple and abstract in design.

Conclusions

Lizards and snakes are common petroglyph designs in the South Mountains, occurring in a wide variety of forms. Less common designs include turtles or tortoises and Gila monsters, while only very few amphibians are present. Ethnographic data for the O'odham and Pueblo Indians indicate that many of these land and water animals had symbolic and ceremonial importance.

We were surprised by the large number and variety of snake designs in the South Mountains. We identified more than five hundred snake petroglyphs at more than three-quarters of the total rock art localities, thus representing the fourth most frequent petroglyph type (after anthropomorphs, various circle designs, and quadrupeds).

Snakes are often depicted with anthropomorphs—surrounding some humanlike petroglyphs, being held in their hands, and even as parts of their bodies. This frequent visual connection of anthropomorphs and snakes suggests that snakes had ceremonial significance for the Hohokam artists who pecked these intriguing designs (see chapters 8 and 11). Studies of ceramic designs from the Mimbres Culture, which was contemporaneous with the Hohokam, indicate that snake ceremonies may date back to the eleventh century in some parts of the American Southwest (Shaffer et al. 1995). The Hohokam also may have had such ceremonies.

CHAPTER SIX

OUR FOUR-LEGGED BROTHERS

MAMMALS

It is true that man kills the animals for his food and clothing, but this is only with their own consent. They are willing to offer their bodies for death—which is not real death, because after it they go back to their secret kingdom and take bodies again.

—RUTH UNDERHILL (1938)

THE SONORAN DESERT is home to several animals that were hunted, revered and even kept as pets by ancient and historic Native Americans. These include mountain sheep, deer, pronghorn, mountain lions, badgers, and the coyote or dog. All of these mammals had symbolic importance, and most are represented in Hohokam rock art. Archaeologists call four-legged animals in rock art by the generic term "quadrupeds" because distinguishing which species is represented is sometimes difficult.

Some desert animals were obviously important to the Hohokam as a source of food and can be recognized in Hohokam art, including petroglyphs, painted pottery, carved stone, and shell jewelry. Animal figurines that depict dogs or female deer have been discovered at some Hohokam sites. Bones that are excavated from buried deposits provide one means of studying the relationship between the Hohokam and desert animals. Paleozoologist Christine Szuter (1991) compiled a large data base on faunal remains from Hohokam sites. These include four main categories of small to large mammals: (1) lagomorphs (jackrabbit and cottontail); (2) rodents (squirrel, mice, and rats); (3) carnivores (dog, fox, badger, mountain lion, jaguar, bobcat, skunk); and (4) artiodactyls (deer, pronghorn, bighorn sheep, elk, bison).

Faunal remains clearly indicate that the Hohokam used many of the common desert mammals for food, tools, and raw materials. Ethnographic information indicates that the procurement and preparation of animal food was likely associated with certain hunting methods and strategies, as well as with special acts and proscriptions. Large game hunting in the American Southwest required elaborate ceremonies and rituals, song magic, dances, and purification acts and was restricted by taboos (Szuter 1991). The success of the hunt depended on certain types of plants. Even the butchering and disposal of mountain sheep and deer bone during certain ceremonies were regulated by rituals reflecting respect for the animal's spirit.

Christine Szuter (1991) noted a scarcity of water animals such as muskrat and beaver in Hohokam deposits. Historic travelers observed many water animals in the desert streams and waterholes, so these animals most likely were present during Hohokam times as well. Szuter suggests that water animals may have been considered too important symbolically by the Hohokam to have been killed for food. This symbolic importance may have changed during the twelfth century; paleozoologist Steven James's (1994) analysis of faunal assemblages from several Classic period sites indicates that the Hohokam of that time were eating a number of water-related mammals and fish that previously had not been exploited. A shortage of protein in a corn-dominant diet may have forced the Hohokam to eat animals that were taboo in earlier times.

Mountain Sheep

One of the more majestic animals of the Sonoran Desert is the mountain sheep *(Ovis canadensis),* also called bighorn or desert bighorn sheep. These large native sheep have heavy curving horns in the males and more slender and less curved horns in the females (Cockrum and Petryszyn 1992). The average ram weighs 250 to 300 lbs (140 kg). Even from a distance, an observer often can see their characteristic small black tails with a large, white rump patch. They live in bands of a few individuals to as many as a dozen or more and were once common in most mountain ranges and foothills throughout the desert.

Mountain sheep eat a variety of plants, especially grasses and leafy bushes. Their horns are used for digging up plant bulbs and roots, and thus the tips are often broken. They have been observed ripping open barrel cactus with their horns to get at the succulent pulp inside. Blessed with incredible athletic ability, mountain sheep can easily scale the most rugged rocky crags at the highest elevations in the most desolate desert mountains. They also can go long periods without drinking water, except during the hottest times of the year. During the summer, their movements are typically restricted to a particular mountain home, but males will travel from mountain to mountain during winter months.

One of the more dramatic scenes to be witnessed in the desert is the sight of two rival mountain sheep males battling during the rutting season. Using their horns as battering rams, the males charge each other at full speed, with the impact creating a thunderous sound. Some males get so excited that they even run into the trunks of trees with their horns. Rarely are they seriously injured during these battles.

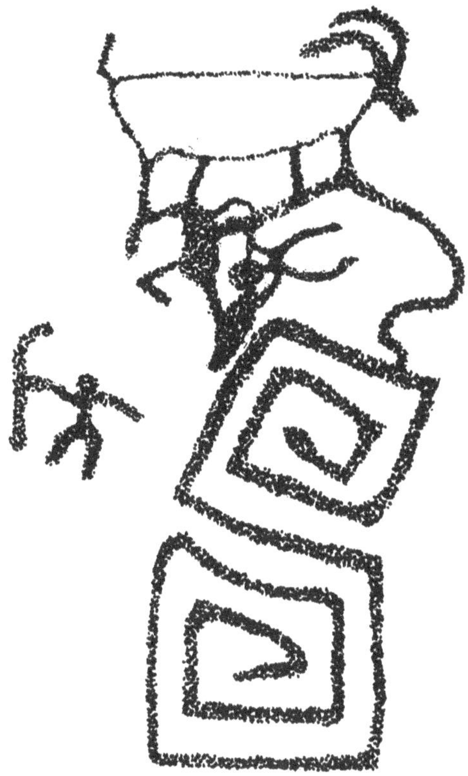

50. Mountain sheep, anthropomorph with cane, and geometric designs, Box Canyon. Rectilinear scroll is 55 x 30 cm.

Mountain sheep are a common image in the rock art of the South Mountains, taking on a wide range of forms and styles (figures 50 and 51). Variations in Hohokam mountain sheep art designs have long been recognized. Archaeologist Gayle Hartmann (1985) compiled published data on Hohokam mountain sheep rock art in the Tucson, Rincon, Painted Rocks, and South Mountains, on Tumamoc Hill, and in the Sierra Estrella to create the following set of characteristics.

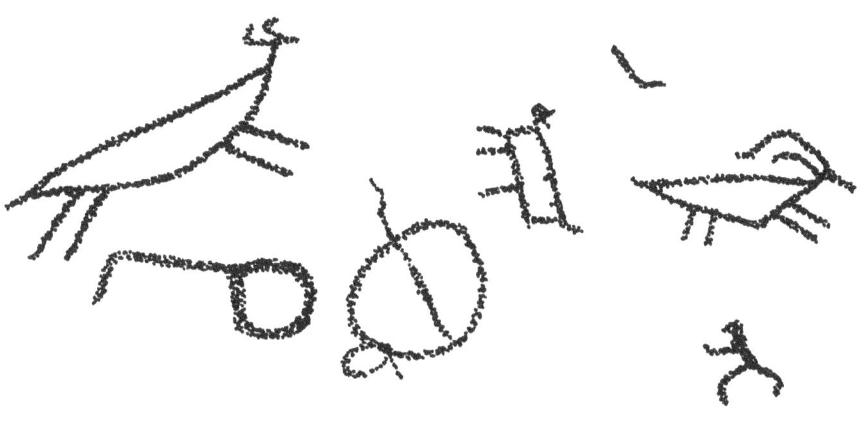

51. Mountain sheep, San Juan North Locality. Mountain sheep on left is 43 cm in length.

- **Execution:** Usually simple, sometimes as stick figures but usually as solid forms
- **Body shape:** Modified boat shape, occasionally with a protruding abdomen and occasionally with a curving back suggesting an attempt to represent haunches and shoulders
- **Head:** Long and thin; mouths usually not depicted but occasionally shown open; eyes not present
- **Legs:** Usually straight, frequently with feet facing forward; sometimes have a tendency toward thickness; four legs nearly always shown
- **Horns:** Thick, backward-curving, seldom recurving toward the head; usually shown in profile, one above the other
- **Tails:** Nearly always present and usually thick; most are short and stubby, but a few are unrealistically long; tend to point backward or upward but occasionally hang down

Our study reveals that an even greater variety of depictions can be added to this list when a more thorough examination of the mountain sheep images from the South Mountains is included. These designs were pecked in both solid and outline form, as stick figures and as full-bodied animals. The modified boat shape mentioned by Hartmann is present (figure 52), but so are various other shapes, including triangular bodies, square bodies, rectangular bodies with segments, linear bodies with bulging bellies, linear bodies without bellies, and more naturalistic body shapes (figures 53 and 54). The mountain sheep with segmented bodies have between four and six segments (figure 55). Hohokam rock artists appear to have had no standardized convention for depicting mountain sheep in the South Mountains.

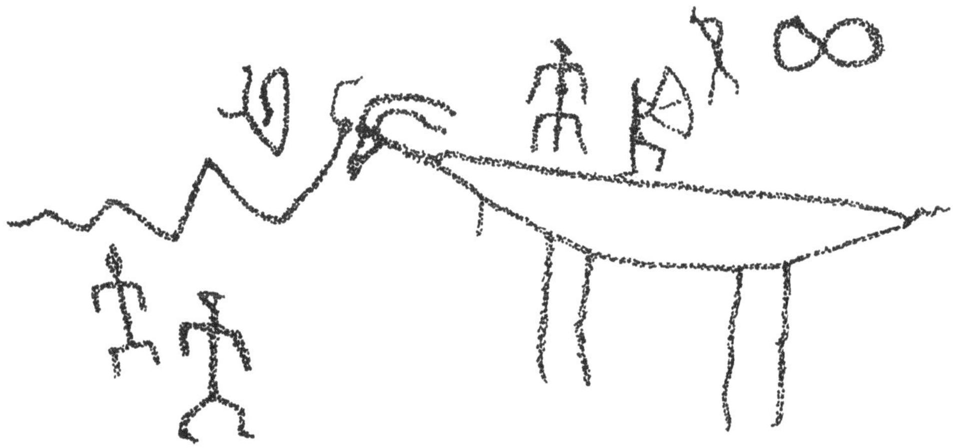

52. Mountain sheep staring at a plumed snake and surrounded by anthropomorphs, entrance to Goodman Canyon. Mountain sheep is 85 cm in length. A long snake, not shown here, is present in the same panel to the right of the mountain sheep.

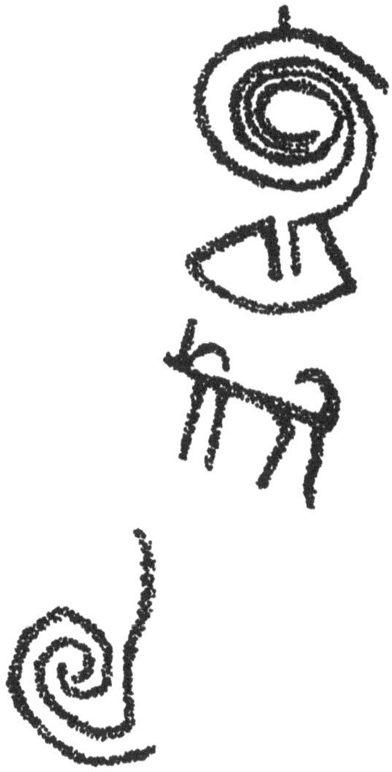

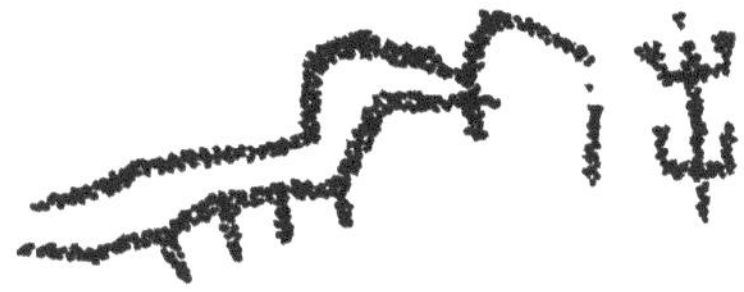

54. Mountain sheep with exaggerated horns, Goodman Canyon. Mountain sheep is 52 cm in length.

53. Mountain sheep between two elaborate spirals, Box Canyon. Mountain sheep is 15 cm in length.

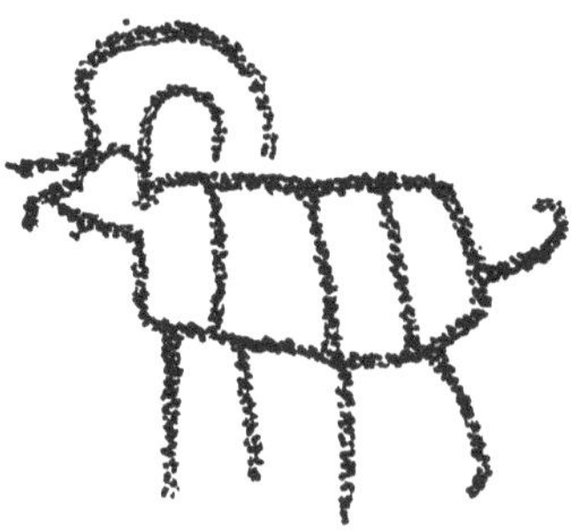

55. Mountain sheep with segmented body form, eastern side of Box Canyon. Mountain sheep is 55 x 43 cm.

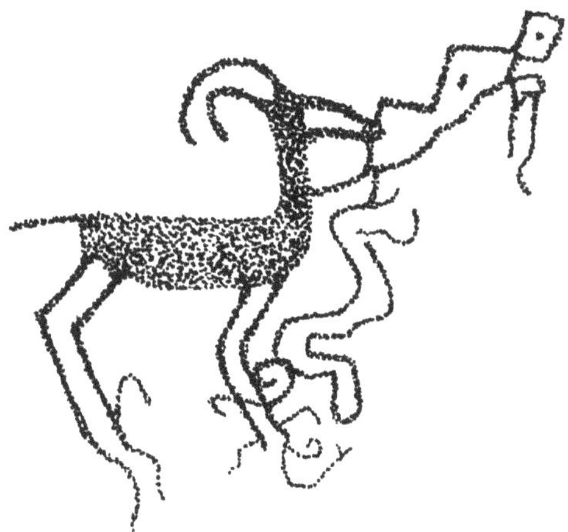

56. Mountain sheep holding snake, along north-south trail into Telegraph Pass. Mountain sheep is 47 x 49 cm.

The heads of mountain sheep images in the South Mountains are generally long and thin, as Hartmann noted, but some are round. The mouths of mountain sheep images often are closed, but many are open. A large mountain sheep design with a natural body form at the Telegraph Pass Locality has a long, partially open mouth holding a snake (figure 56). Meandering lines swirl around the mountain sheep and appear to come out of its legs. Eyes are rarely depicted in the petroglyphs of the South Mountains bighorn sheep, but they do occur in a few examples. Curiously, the heads of those mountain sheep are more birdlike than sheeplike. An example of this composite creature occurs in the 36th Street Locality (see figure 275).

Legs are generally not well defined for the mountain sheep petroglyphs in the South Mountains. They may be either straight or bent at the knees or feet. When present, feet may point forward or backward. In a few instances, such as in the upper right portion of a panel at the 16th Street Locality, the feet on the same sheep point in opposite directions (see figure 265). A few mountain sheep images have cloven hooves for feet: the best example is a mountain sheep with a boat-shaped body in Hieroglyphic Canyon (see figure 60).

Mountain sheep horns in the South Mountains also show considerable variability. Usually they are curved and in profile, but some that point backward are straight (figure 57). Horns may be short or long and may point either forward or backward (figure 58).

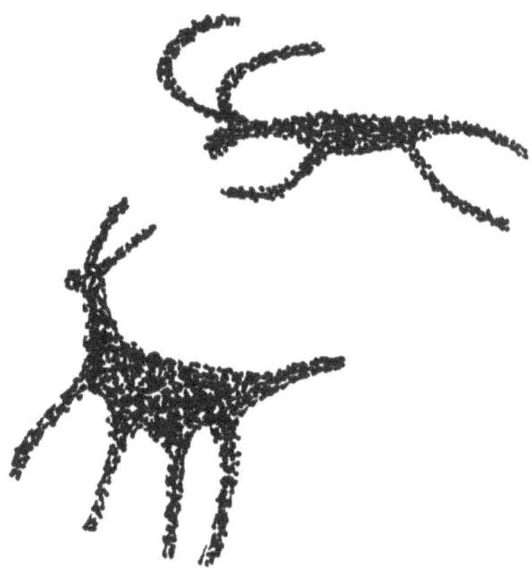

57. Two unusual quadrupeds possibly representing stylized mountain sheep, Central Avenue Locality. Upper mountain sheep is 24 cm in length.

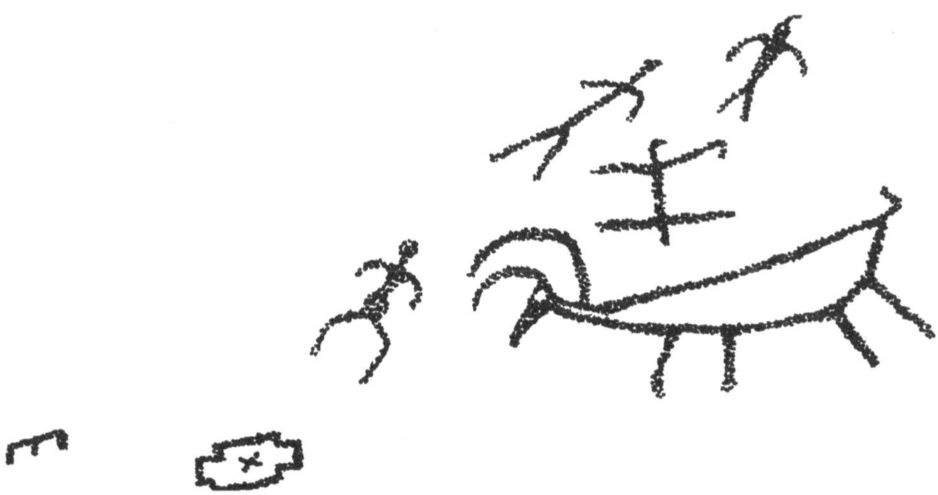

58. Mountain sheep with horns pointing forward, Goodman Canyon. Mountain sheep is 52 cm in length.

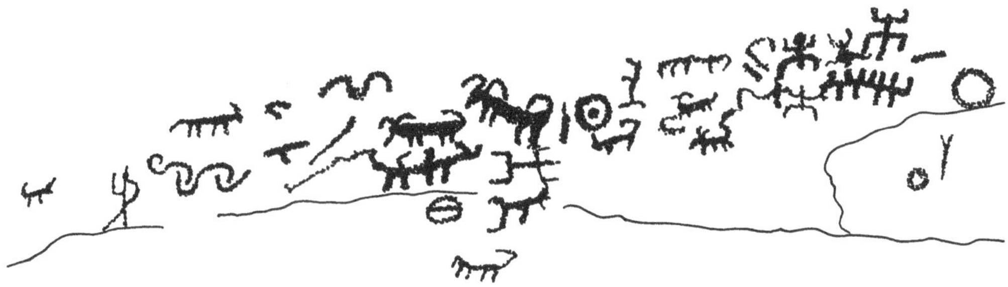

59. Mountain sheep with horns pointing in opposite directions, upper Goodman Canyon. Central mountain sheep left of the circle/dot is 26 cm in length.

Those that point backward rarely recurve toward the face as the horns of adult male mountain sheep do. A mountain sheep with a boat-shaped body at the 16th Street Locality has a pair of horns that point inward (this sheep also has opposite-pointing feet). In a few examples, the horns curve in opposite directions, such as those in Pima Canyon, Goodman Canyon, Hidden Valley, and the 16th Street Locality (figure 59).

Tails on most mountain sheep designs are short, as are the tails of actual mountain sheep, and depicted as straight or curved upward, with a few that curve downward. The vast majority are oriented horizontally as they would be viewed under natural conditions. Mountain sheep images face both to the right and to the left, although some are oriented vertically, mostly with the head up. A panel in the 16th Street Locality shows a mountain sheep with a boat-shaped body oriented vertically next to a human, a concentric circle, and a turtle or tortoise. Another sheep with a boat-shaped body in Hieroglyphic Canyon is upside-down, as though floating or dead (figure 60). An apparently unfinished mountain sheep in the San Juan North

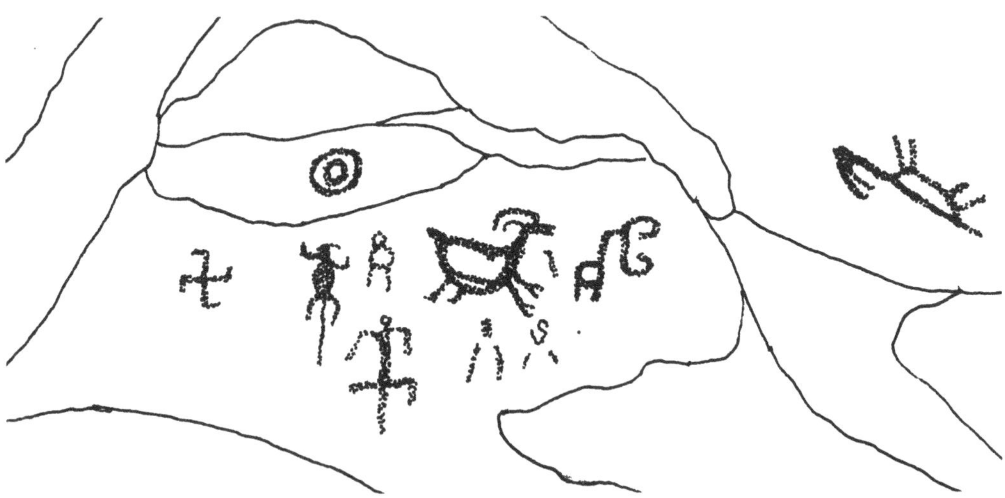

60. Two mountain sheep (one upside-down), Hieroglyphic Canyon. Upside-down mountain sheep is 35 cm in length.

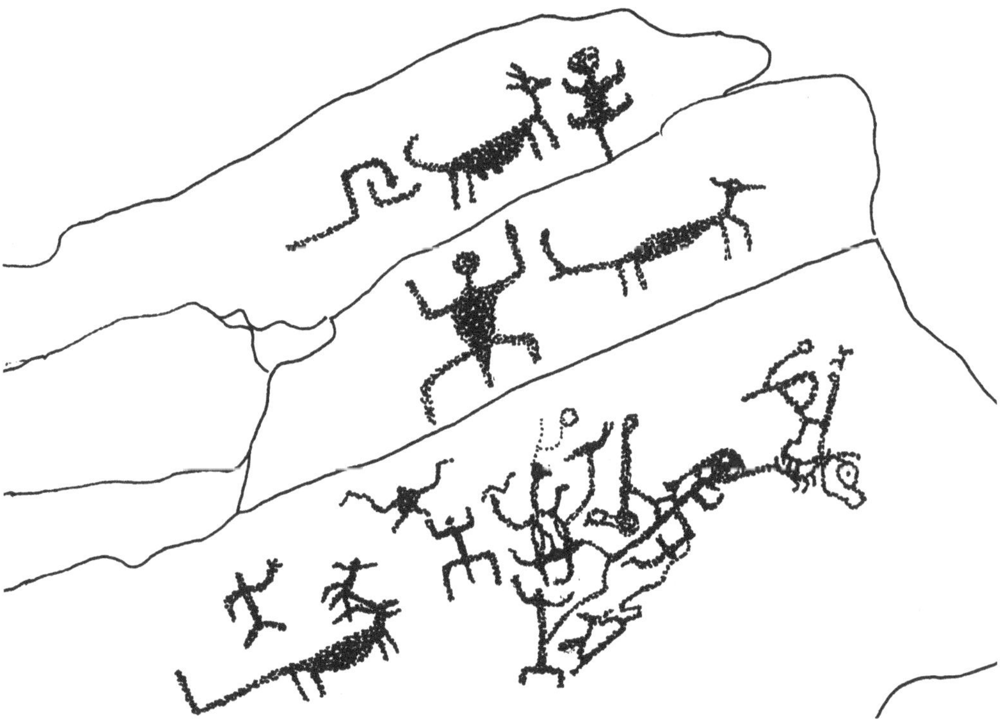

61. Mountain sheep with very long tail and other quadrupeds, Hidden Valley. Upper quadruped appears to be pregnant. Upper, central quadruped is 28 cm in length.

Locality is oriented upside-down at an angle. This image was placed near another finished sheep image depicted in a natural orientation. Both of these mountain sheep have similar oblong bodies.

Some mountain sheep have extended bellies that suggest they are pregnant. A quadruped that may represent a mountain sheep at the Hidden Valley Locality has two nipples at the base of its extended belly, suggesting a female animal (figure 61). A few mountain sheep petroglyphs have been depicted with a penis.

A number of rock art sites in the South Mountains combine mountain sheep and humans with weapons in the same panel, suggesting hunting or a spiritual quest (see chapter 8). Those panels include several at the 7th Street and 16th Street Localities. In addition, several other panels in the 32nd Street Locality contain images of sheep with humans that appear to be associated with natural solstice events (see chapter 10).

A few other mountain sheep panels merit special attention here. A well-executed mountain sheep petroglyph on top of Bird Hill in Box Canyon has a long, linear body with its tail connected to a large concentric circle as though emerging from a portal (figure 62). A person sitting behind this panel has a view of the eastern horizon.

A simple panel with a sheep image is located on a low hill in the San Juan East Locality overlooking the Salt River Valley to the north. This image is surrounded by

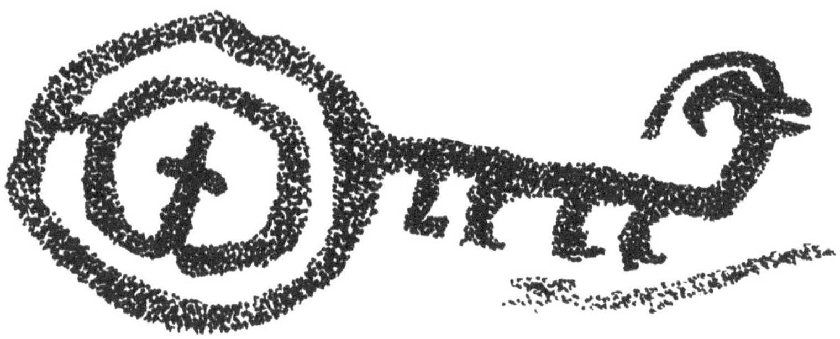

62. Mountain sheep with concentric circle attached to its tail, Box Canyon. Concentric circle is 24 cm in diameter.

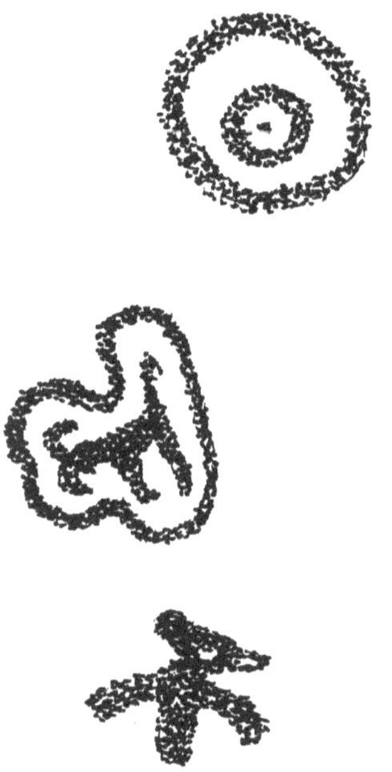

63. Outlined mountain sheep, San Juan East Locality. Concentric circle is 10 cm in diameter.

a thick, continuous outline (figure 63). Another petroglyph is present below the outlined mountain sheep, with small concentric circles above it.

At the 12th Street Locality, mountain sheep and other designs appear on a special panel situated in a natural, shrinelike boulder arrangement (figure 64). The panel is on the southwestern face of a huge boulder. An open area in front of the boulder provides a perfect view of the panel. Some unknown artist delicately pecked a naturalistic mountain sheep and other images at this secluded location.

In the upper reaches of Goodman Canyon, in an area of numerous rock art panels, there is a rock shelter. To some Native Americans, such shelters and eaves are womblike portals to Mother Earth. Within this rock shelter, which is big enough to hold several people, is a panel with a large mountain sheep (figure 65). This petroglyph can be seen only from inside. It is one of a very few petroglyphs located inside rock shelters in the South Mountains, although many are located outside rock shelters.

Ethnographer Amadeo Rea (1998) has noted that no other animal was treated with such awe and reverence by the O'odham as the mountain sheep. Called "Cheson" by the Northern Pima, the bighorn sheep was closely associated with the wind. Some villages had shrines dedicated to the wind and Cheson. Parts of the mountain sheep are very powerful; both the hide and the horns must be kept in a safe, respected location to avoid insulting the wind and bringing on violent storms. Hunters would usually not bring back horns to the village but instead had a special place to deposit the horns of animals that had been killed. Spanish explorers in the

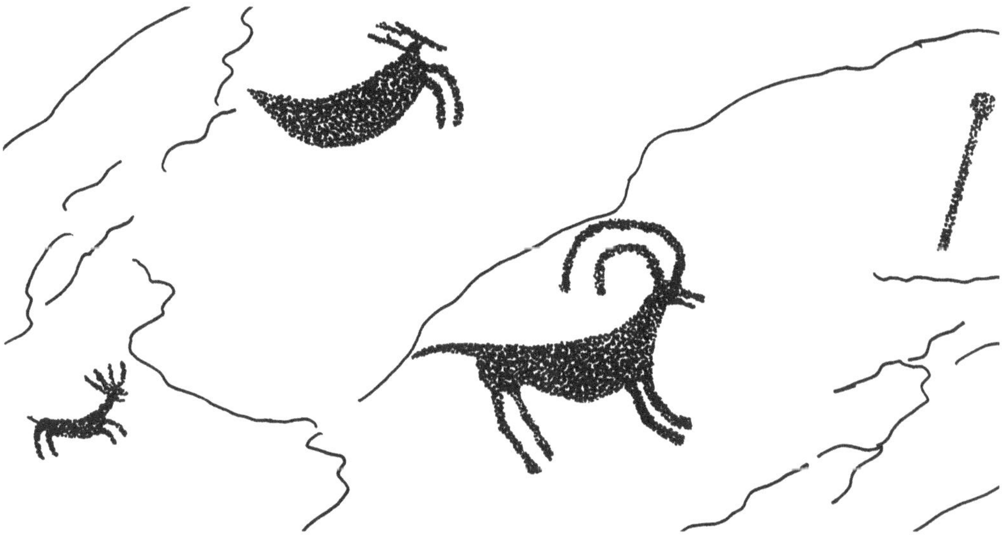

64. Mountain sheep panel situated in boulder alcove in lower 12th Street Locality. Lower right naturalistic mountain sheep is 39 x 47 cm. Lower left quadruped may be a stylized deer.

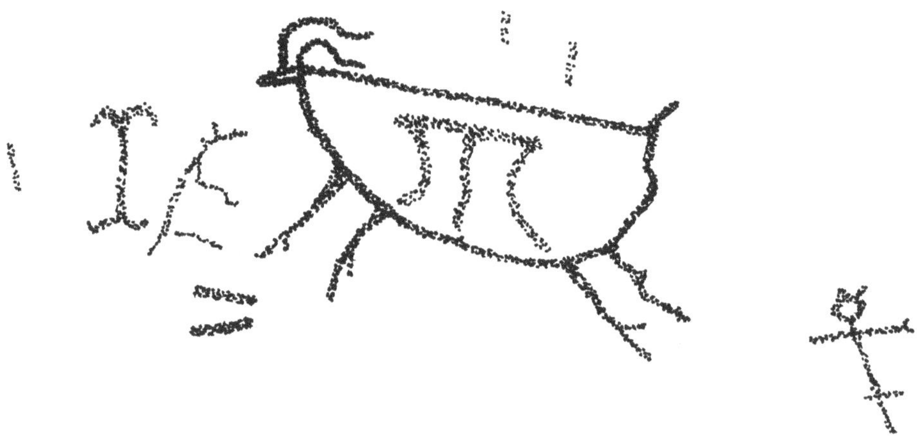

65. Mountain sheep inside large rock shelter, upper Goodman Canyon. Mountain sheep is 52 cm in length and faces east.

eighteenth century described huge piles of mountain sheep horns in the Sonoran Desert, some containing thousand of horns. Archaeologist Julian Hayden (1985) has discovered similar horn piles in the Sierra Pinacate region of northwestern Mexico. Anthropologist P. Drucker (1941) reported that the O'odham only occasionally hunted the mountain sheep because it was considered a supernatural being; on those occasions, dogs assisted in the hunt. On the northeastern side of the South Mountains, a rock art panel has a quadruped (perhaps a mountain sheep) depicted in a lively, upright pose; this may be a human impersonating a mountain sheep for the purposes of hunting or other ceremonial reasons (figure 66).

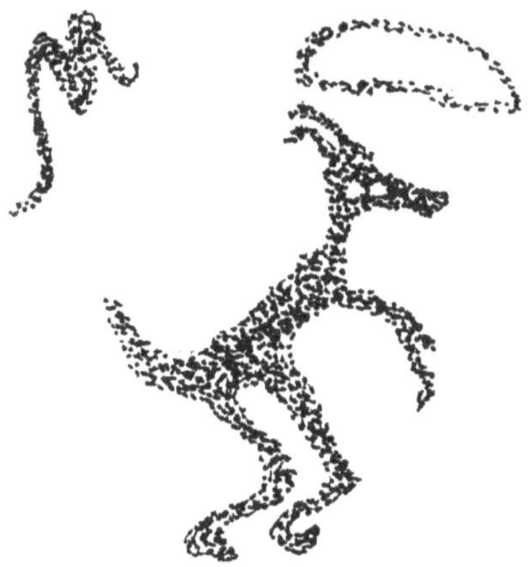

66. Mountain sheep in a pose suggesting it may be a human in a mountain sheep costume, 48th Street Locality. Mountain sheep is 24 cm in height.

Bighorn sheep were clearly important to the Hohokam. Their images were frequently painted on Hohokam pottery, as well as sculpted in stone, modeled in clay, and carved in bone. Cremated mountain sheep horn cores have been found at the Grewe Site along the Gila River and at Pueblo Grande along the Salt River. The mountain sheep horn cores at Pueblo Grande lay within a room on top of the Classic period (ca. A.D. 1150–1450) platform mound and in a niche burial with a variety of ritual objects that date to the Colonial period (ca. A.D. 750–950). Among these objects were several arrow points, as well as stone bowls carved into the shape of a mountain sheep, a rattlesnake, a human and a bird (Bostwick and Downum 1994). At least four sets of cremated horn cores were associated with the objects. This unusual ritual offering may have been an attempt by Hohokam priests or shamans to use the bighorn's supernatural power to control the weather or bring rain.

Deer

Deer are amazing animals to watch because they bound gracefully when they run. They also shed their antlers every winter in an annual renewal process. The Sonoran Desert is home to two species of deer: the mule deer *(Odocoileus hemionus)* and the white-tailed deer *(Odocoileus virginianus).* The white-tailed deer prefer higher elevations, while mule deer are common to the lower deserts. The two deer species exhibit noticeable differences. Mule deer have large ears, a narrow white tail with a black tip, and equally branched antlers with up to ten points. The white-tailed deer has narrower ears, a brown tail with a white tip, and antlers with small branches growing from a main beam. In addition, the male mule deer is considerably larger than the white-tail. Both species forage for brush and other plant food in the morning and evening and on moonlit nights. Typically they hide in desert washes and canyons during the day and drink nightly at a nearby water source. Herds generally stay in restricted territories.

Deer images are not as common as those of mountain sheep in the South Mountains, although more deer may be depicted than we were able to definitively identify; without their characteristic antlers, they would be ambiguous quadrupeds (figures 67 and 68). Identifiable deer images are present in less than a dozen localities. Similar to the mountain sheep designs, the deer are depicted in profile. Body shapes, most being solidly pecked, vary from somewhat naturalistic shapes (figure 69) to linear shapes with or without a bulging belly. Some are outlined and have a segmented body (figure 70). A single example at Johnson Camp in upper Pima Canyon has a triangular body with four segments. Antlers also vary, most having four to nine points (figure 71). Legs are simple, being bent or straight, and may point either forward or backward (figure 72). Examples of deer with cloven hooves occur in Pima Canyon, Hidden Valley, and the 32nd Street Locality.

Deer occur alone and in panels with humans and other designs. Only one of these panels, however, appears to be a hunt scene or a spirit quest. This unusual panel, in the 36th Street Locality, has three humans and four deer. Each of the deer has a long trail of tracks behind it (figure 73). One of the humans is aiming a bow and arrow at the largest deer. Another human, at the opposite side of the panel, is wrestling with the antlers of a smaller deer. A large circle element is present near the bottom of the boulder.

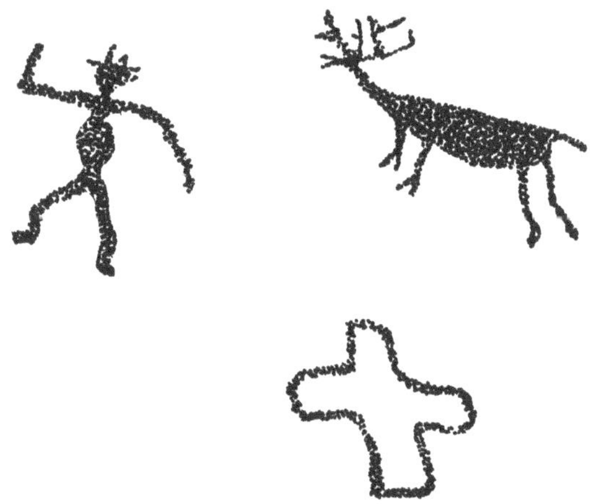

67. Deer, anthropomorph, and negative cross on large boulder, Holbert Trail. Deer is 37 cm in length. Panel is located adjacent to a trail, indicating that portions of the Holbert Trail are prehistoric.

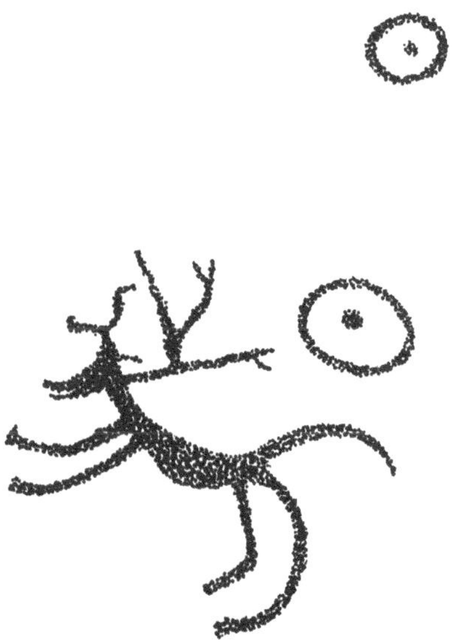

68. Deer beneath circles with dots, 32nd Street Locality. Deer is 60 cm in length.

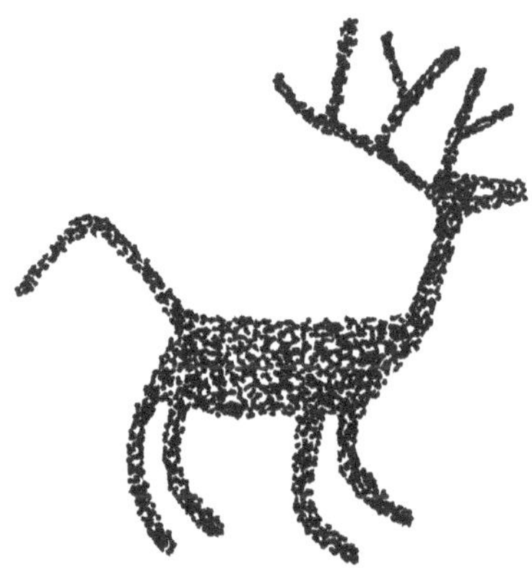

69. Deer, 32nd Street Locality. Panel is located on a rock face that is difficult to reach.

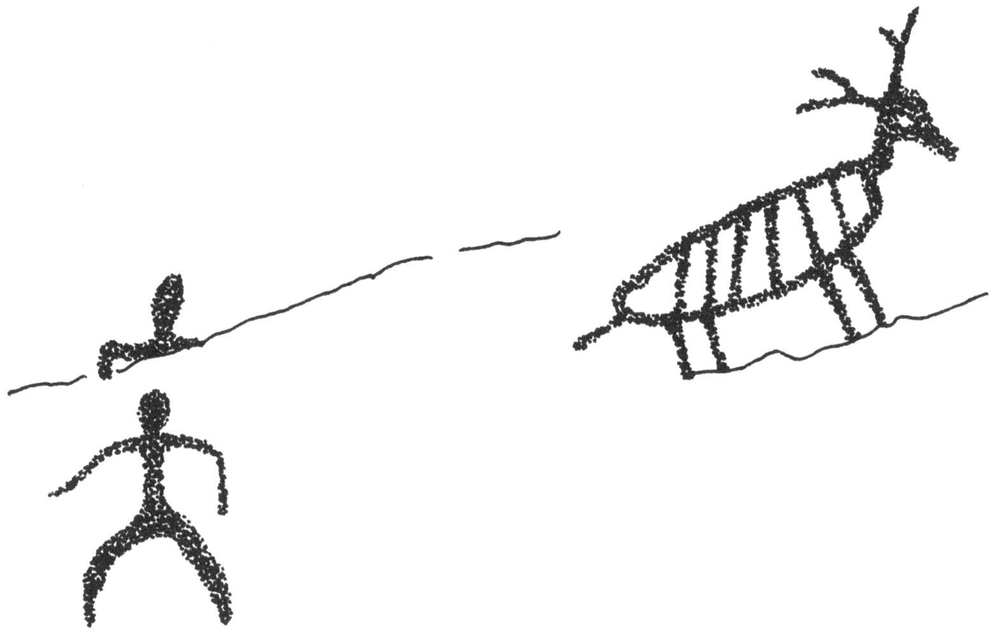

70. Deer and anthropomorphs, 24th Street Locality. Upper anthropomorph appears to be emerging from the rock. Deer is 49 cm in length.

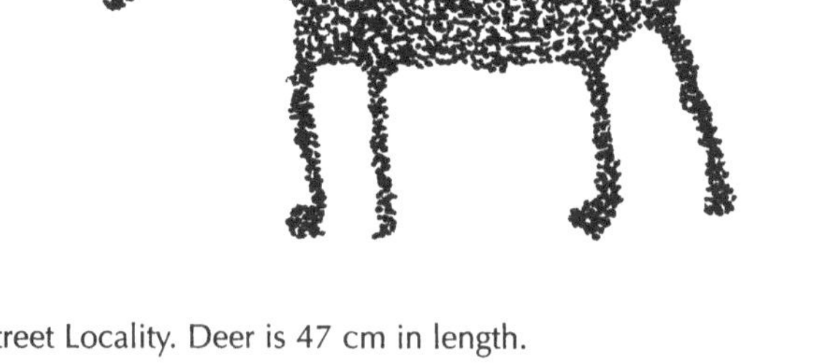

71. Deer, 32nd Street Locality. Deer is 47 cm in length.

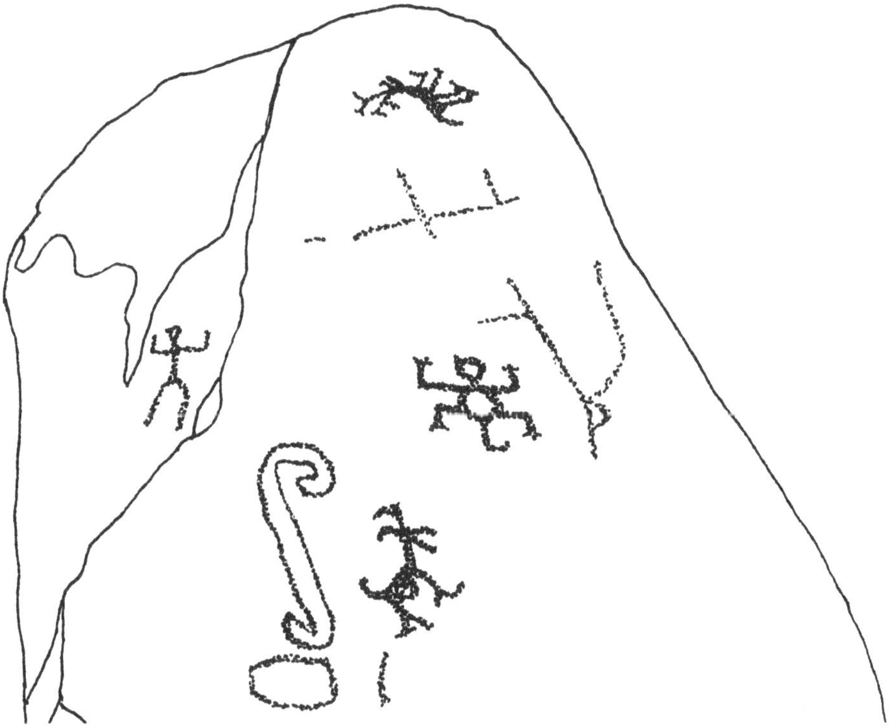

72. Upside-down deer, mountain sheep, lizard, anthropomorph, and geometric designs on a boulder in a wash along Mormon Loop Trail. Lizard is 18 cm in length.

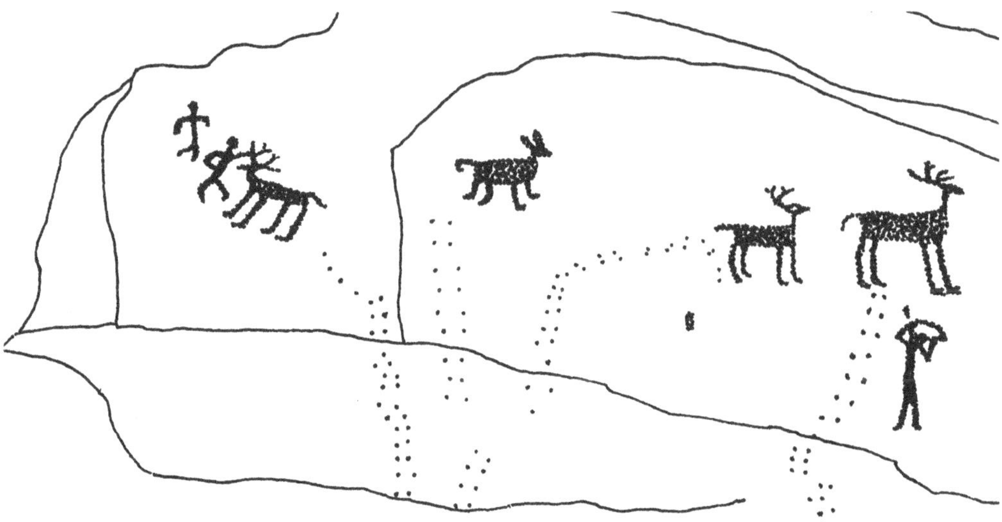

73. Deer with tracks, being hunted by anthropomorphs, 36th Street Locality. Anthropomorph to the right is using a bow and arrow, while one of the anthropomorphs in the upper left is wrestling with a deer's antlers. Upper right deer is 15 cm in length.

Mule deer were the focus of myth and religion among the O'odham, appearing frequently in their creation stories. The O'odham culture hero, Elder Brother (I'itoi), gave deer the wind as a friend to tell it of human approach but also caused the deer to know when to submit itself willingly to the hunter. However, hunting deer still required the use of hunting magic, and each settlement in historic times contained only a few deer hunters. Deer are frequently shaman spirit helpers among O'odham shamans. The O'odham believe that deer are very powerful and have the ability to give humans diseases. Deer tails are especially dangerous.

For an O'odham cleansing ceremony, usually held at the end of the summer rainy season, a mule deer was killed in a special manner (Underhill 1946). This deer had to be run down on foot and strangled, then butchered in a special way with the bones carefully gathered. Dancers in the deer ceremony had to undergo four days of fasting and seclusion at the end of the ceremony, similar to the ritual cleansing practiced after killing or capturing an eagle.

Shamans view deer as mediators between heaven and earth. In some shamanistic art, tracks of their spirit helpers depict paths to the underworld. Deer antlers are also associated with the sacred tree that allows movement between the three worlds (below, present, and above) or shamanic realms. Also, deer flesh was thought to have curative powers.

In Mesoamerica, the deer takes many forms in the calendar systems (Miller and Taube 1993). The name of the seventh day is a deer. Deer were venerated as well as sacrificed, and deer meat was an esteemed food offering. Deer were once symbols of rulership and had agricultural symbolism (Benson 1997). The stag of the white-tailed deer, often depicted in Mesoamerican art, has branching antlers that may be seen growing along with the seasonal growth of crops.

Pronghorn

Another very graceful desert mammal is the pronghorn antelope *(Antilocapra americana)*, a picturesque animal with distinctive color markings. Pronghorns are about the size of small deer but have more delicate legs. They are a soft buff color, with white splotches on the body and two white stripes on the neck. Large, protruding black eyes combine with black markings on the nose and forehead to create a masklike face. When alarmed, its glistening white rump patch is spread at will and can be seen for some distance. Both males and females have black, flattened horns that curve backward and inward. Pronghorns are curious but also timid. When a band is lying down, individuals face in different directions to keep close watch on their surroundings. They use their great speed to escape predators, being capable of running up to 40 miles (64 km) per hour for long distances. Bands generally migrate to seek out seasonally available grass and weeds. Amadeo Rea (1998) has stated that pronghorn antelope were recorded in the early twentieth century in the Sierra Estrella, only 5 miles (8 km) west of the South Mountains.

We found no rock art images clearly identifiable as pronghorn in the South Mountains, but some of the unidentified quadrupeds may be pronghorn (see especially figure 57). Pronghorns were sought by ancient and historic hunters of the Sonoran Desert. Their bones and horns have been found in Hohokam sites, indicating that they served as an occasional food source. The pronghorn's dark, forked antlers and snowy white rump patches make them easily identifiable in the wild. In the late 1880s, Frank Hamilton Cushing (1890) found an antelope mask and beads and feathers in a stone cache at the Papago Buttes, 5 miles (8 km) north of the South Mountains. Interestingly, although Antelope Katchina do appear in Hopi ceremonies, antelopes do not figure prominently in the O'odham oral traditions, although they are mentioned in a few stories. An O'odham story mentioned in chapter 5 describes the unpleasant interaction between Turtle and an antelope.

Coyotes and Dogs

Perhaps the best-known animal of the North American desert is the coyote *(Canis latrans),* an extremely intelligent carnivore that is celebrated and ridiculed in many Native American stories. Many a desert dweller and visitor has experienced the high-pitched serenades of this native canid during early-morning hours or after dusk. Because of their ability to adapt to different environmental conditions, coyotes today can be found from high mountains to low deserts, as well as in the suburbs of most major cities. Evidence of coyotes can be seen along the trails they regularly travel, especially ridges where they can have good views, as well as along scent-post trails they establish with an accumulation of feces and urine stains.

The name coyote is borrowed from the Aztec word "coyotl." These relatives of the wolf grow to about the size of a small German shepherd dog, weigh up to 23 pounds (10.5 kg), and have tails more than 12 inches (30 cm) in length. They are most active in early morning and late afternoon, although some hunt for food at night and on cooler overcast days. Coyotes often talk to each other at long distances shortly after sunset, with a series of short yaps followed by high-pitched barks or cries. During the day, they stay in their hideouts in rock shelters, in underground dens, or under bushes. The coyotes' great speed, up to 40 miles (64 km) per hour, allows them to catch rodents and rabbits, but they also eat insects, seeds, berries, and cactus fruit. There are reports of deer being killed by coyotes, but most of those deer probably died by other causes. The coyote is involved in one of the great ironies of the desert. They are known to dig wells in dry washes, bringing hidden water to the surface so other animals can drink. However, the coyote then lies in wait and eats many unsuspecting visitors to the new water hole.

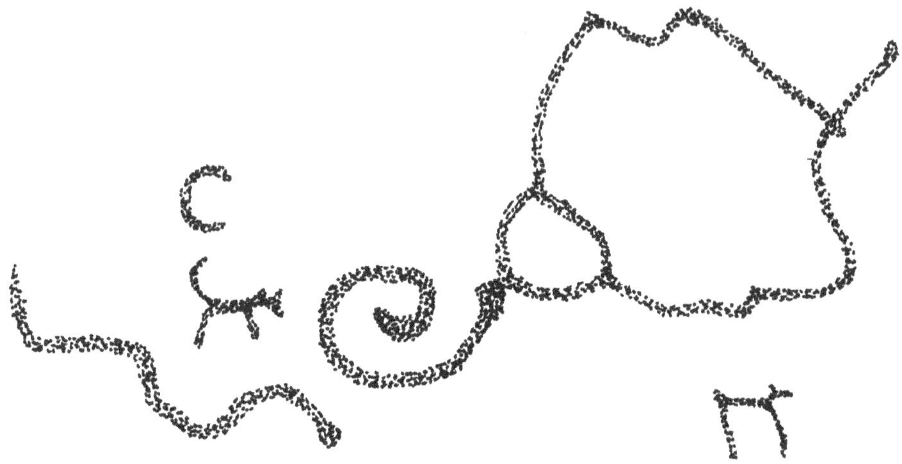

74. Coyote/dog, snakes, and other designs. Panel is located at one of the entrances to a natural tunnel in Box Canyon. Coyote/dog on left is 10 cm in length. A crescent moon is present above this animal.

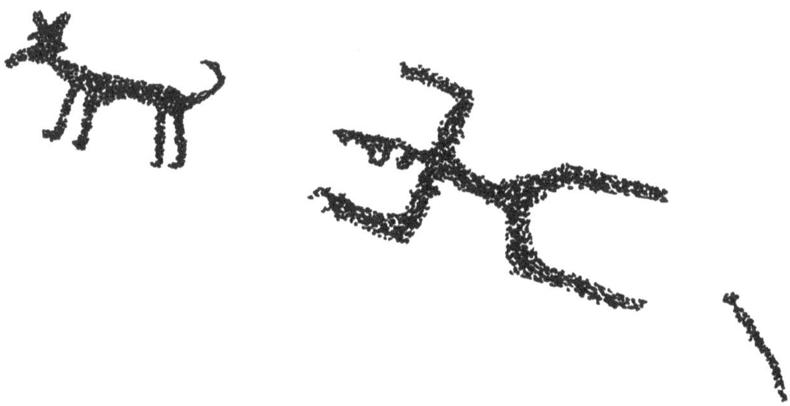

75. Coyote/dog and anthropomorph, Hieroglyphic Canyon. Anthropomorph is 23 cm in height.

Petroglyph images of small, four-legged mammals without horns that may represent coyotes or dogs are scattered throughout the South Mountains (figures 74–76). A panel in the upper portion of Goodman Canyon has four animals, two of which appear to be dogs or coyotes (figure 77). They have long tails, with one bent upward and the other straight. The largest of these two animals has a bulging stomach, possibly suggesting that the animal is pregnant. A rock art panel in Hidden Valley has two four-legged mammals (figure 78): one is a mountain sheep oriented at an angle as though climbing uphill; the other has a very different shape and may be a coyote or dog chasing the sheep—but the coyote/dog has cloven hoofs!

The trickster Coyote occurs frequently in O'odham oral traditions, in which he is called "Ban." Amadeo Rea (1998) states that Coyote is the archetype of several human character traits for the O'odham. In different stories he is a braggart, a liar, mischievous, bumbling, deceitful, lazy, and lecherous, but also occasionally thought-

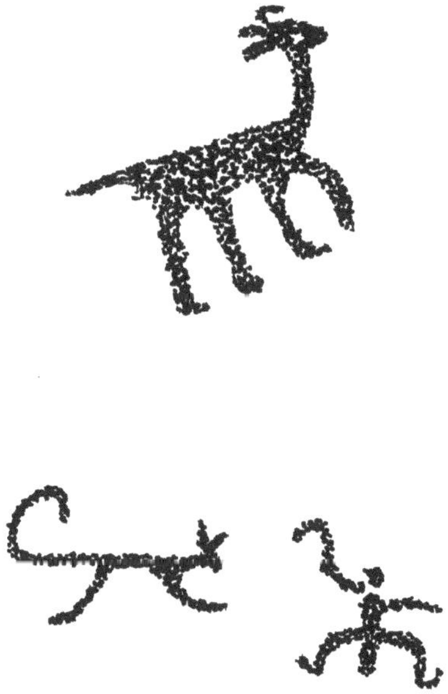

76. Coyote/dog, horned quadruped, and anthropomorph, San Juan East Locality. Coyote/dog is 19 cm in length.

ful and cooperative. Often he is duped by his fellow creatures. In one story, Coyote stole a bag of seeds that broke as he escaped, scattering them across the sky; they became the Milky Way. Coyote also is one of four O'odham primordial creatures, along with Earth Doctor, Vulture, and Elder Brother. After escaping the flood in the creation story by floating on a log, Coyote helped repeople the earth. But Coyote's people were web-footed, and Elder Brother threw them into the water, where they became ducks and beavers. In addition, Coyote is one of the O'odham moiety mascots or symbols (the other is Vulture). Coyotes also were spirit helpers for some shamans and served as spies to determine the location of an enemy. They were not a food source for the Hohokam.

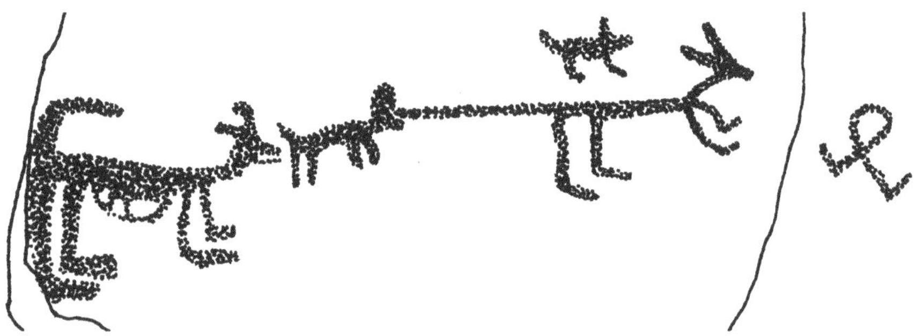

77. Coyote/dog petroglyphs, upper Goodman Canyon. Coyote/dog on right is 39 cm in length.

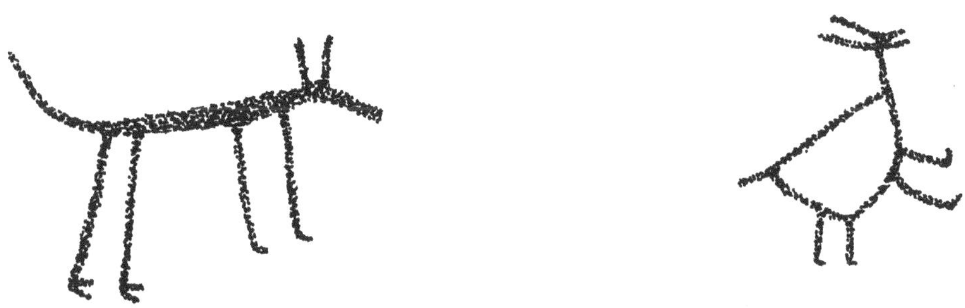

78. Quadrupeds possibly representing a coyote/dog and a mountain sheep, Hidden Valley. The coyote/dog appears to have cloven hind feet. Quadruped on left is 40 cm in length. Panel is located at the entrance to a natural tunnel high up in the mountains.

The Hohokam had the domesticated dog and apparently represented this companion animal in their art. Small, four-legged mammals are commonly depicted in Hohokam painted pottery designs. O'odham dogs were used to warn of an approaching enemy and sometimes in hunting. Because of their status in the creation story, dogs were given special treatment at death. Several examples of child burials accompanied by dogs occur at Hohokam village sites, suggesting special treatment of the dogs (Hill 2000). Dog burials by themselves also have been identified at Hohokam sites. No evidence indicates that the Hohokam sacrificed or ate their dogs, as has been recorded for Mesoamerican cultures.

In Mesoamerica, dogs are connected with water because they are natural swimmers. Among the Aztecs, unlike the Hohokam, the close association between dogs and humans led to the offering of dogs to various deities as sacrifices. In addition, dogs were cared for as pets because they were believed to have served as guides to enable the recently dead to cross a body of water to the underworld. Elizabeth Benson (1997) argues that this is probably because dogs dig in the earth and bury bones, have good night vision, howl at night, and can sense things moving in the dark. Therefore, it seems they have esoteric knowledge and special connections with the underworld. The Aztec god Xolotl was a skeletal dog-faced god who was an avatar of the planet Venus as the evening star (Miller and Taube 1993).

Mountain Lion

One of the four-legged mammal petroglyphs in the South Mountains (36th Street Locality) may represent a mountain lion *(Felis concolor),* although this identification is tentative (figure 79). This animal has a long, upwardly curving tail but does not have the ball-shaped or clawed feet typical of mountain lion rock art elsewhere, although the Zuni identify the long, curved tail as the most important attribute (Young 1988:156). Curiously, the South Mountain petroglyph has two tails, perhaps suggesting a tail in motion.

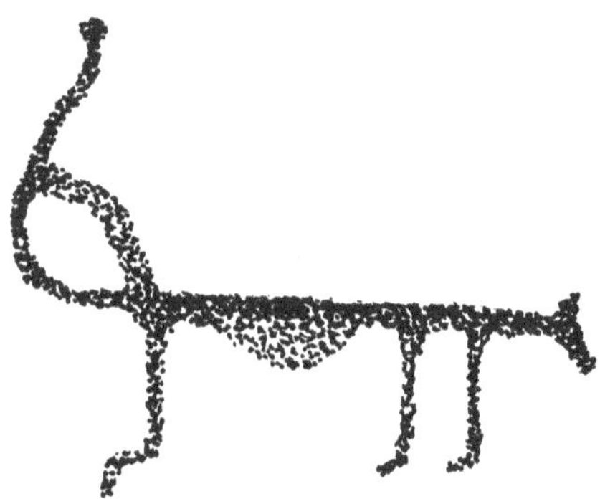

79. Possible mountain lion apparently having two tails (maybe representing motion), 36th Street Locality. This petroglyph is located on a knoll at the southern base of the South Mountains. Mountain lion is 35 cm in length.

Mountain lions, considered to be powerful animals by Southwestern peoples, are excellent hunters. Frank Russell (1975) noted that the mountain lion, also called puma, was once abundant in the mountains of Arizona. The O'odham occasionally hunted the mountain lion, whom they called "Mavid." O'odham shamans were visited by mountain lions in their dreams, which gave them major hunting or other powers. According to Alexander Stephen in his *Hopi Journal* (1936), the mountain lion was one of the "pets" of the spirits. At the Hopi villages of Walpi and Hano, the mountain lion was associated with the war society and appeared at or after the winter solstice observance (Stephen 1936).

Other Quadrupeds

Some four-legged animal petroglyphs in the South Mountains are not clearly identifiable. These quadrupeds may be mountain sheep without horns or deer without antlers, although they sometimes have exaggerated body shapes or horns, suggesting that they may instead represent animal spirits (figures 80–84).

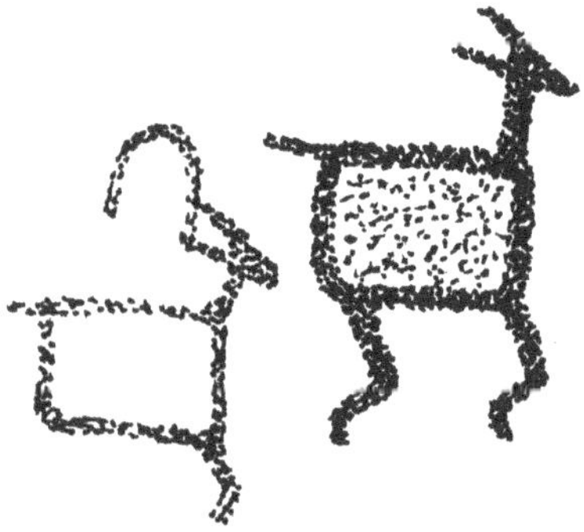

80. Quadrupeds, San Juan North Locality. Quadruped on right is 18 x 26 cm. Quadruped on left is pecked more lightly, suggesting a ghostlike image.

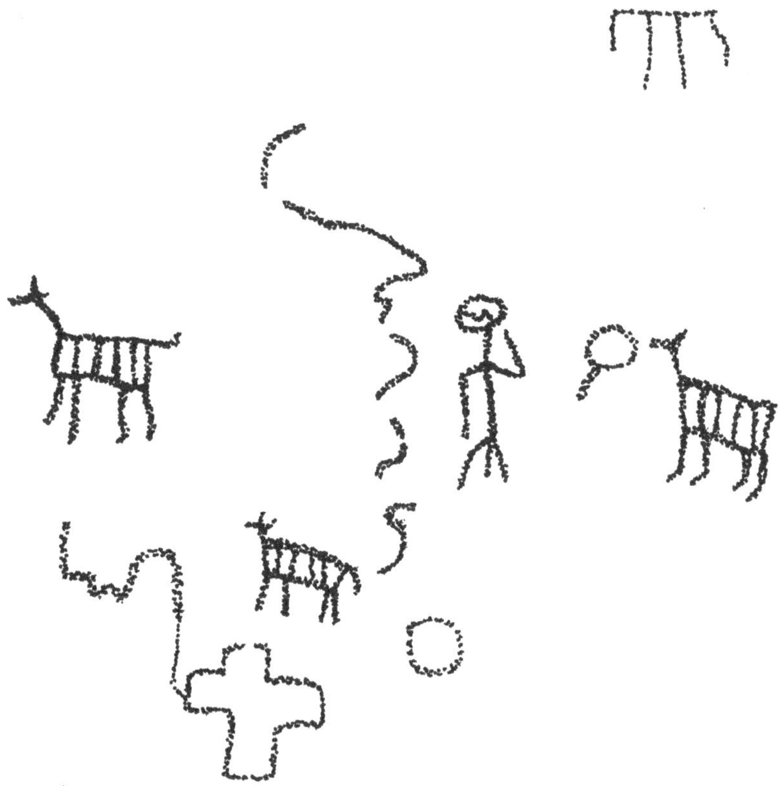

81. Quadrupeds with segmented body forms, 32nd Street Locality. Upper mountain sheep is 32 cm in length.

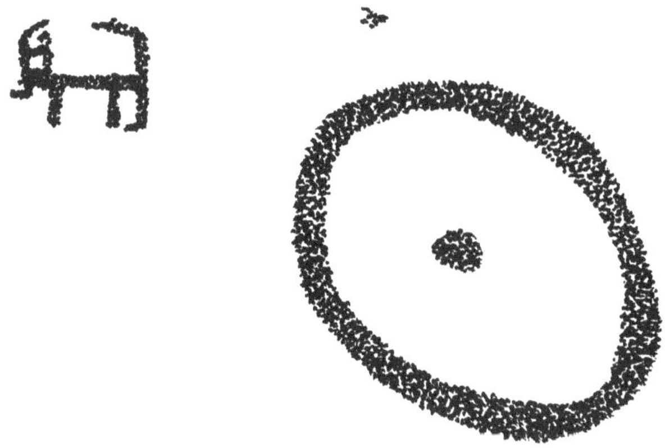

82. Small quadruped and large circle with dot, Box Canyon. Quadruped is 17 cm in length.

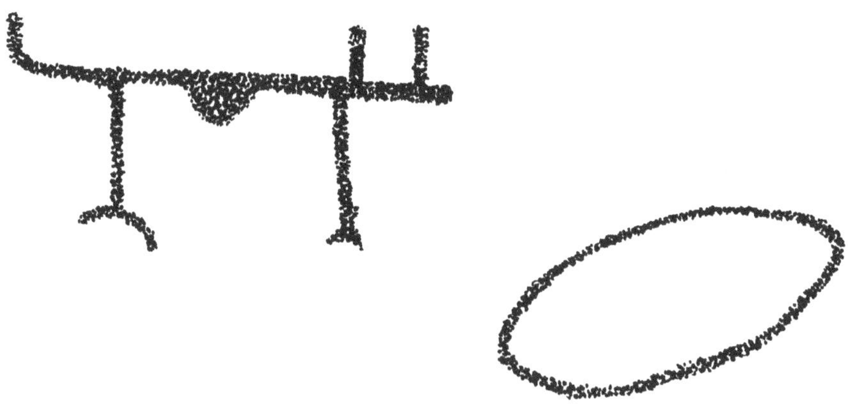

83. Quadruped with circle, Box Canyon. Panel is located on an outcrop that is difficult to access.

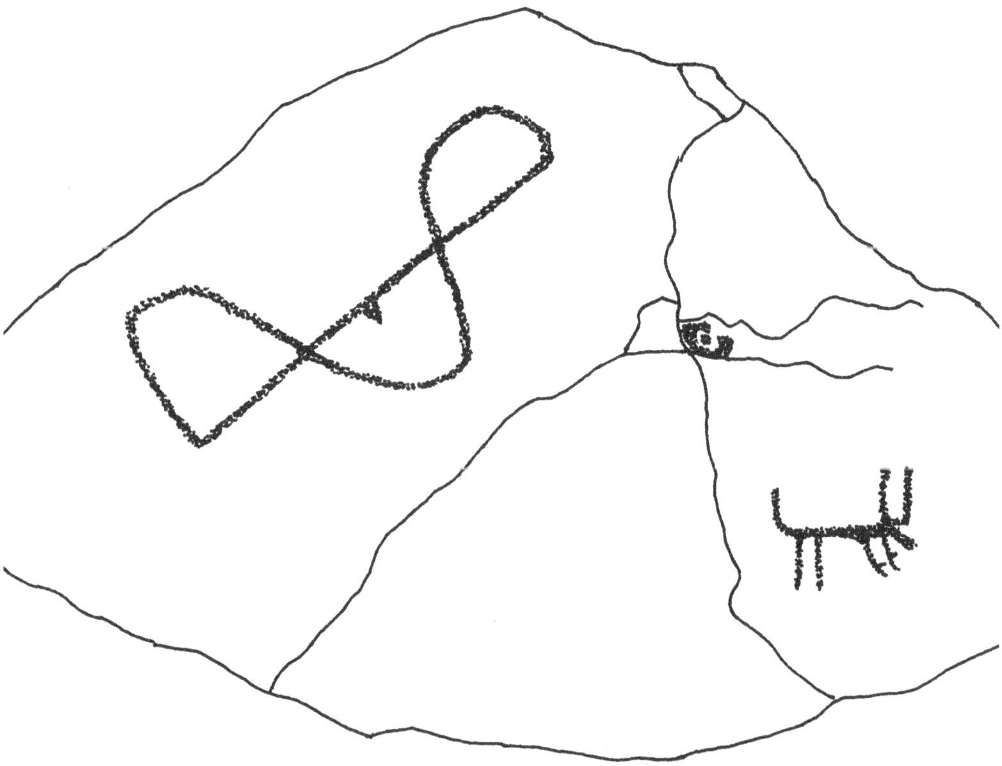

84. Quadruped with long ears and cloven front feet, San Juan East Locality. Quadruped is 15 cm in length.

Conclusions

The Hohokam depicted a variety of four-legged mammals in the rock art of the South Mountains; indeed, quadrupeds represent the third most frequent petroglyph type. All of these mammals currently live in the Sonoran Desert, and most once roamed the South Mountains. Faunal remains at Hohokam villages indicate that many of these large mammals were hunted by the Hohokam. Their frequent depiction in Hohokam art may include hunting magic. Their importance also may have extended to possible use as spiritual metaphors, as characters in oral traditions, or as records of vision quests in which mammals taught songs or extended spiritual powers in other ways to the individuals who dreamed about them.

CHAPTER SEVEN

FRIENDS OF THE UPPER WORLD

BIRDS

Wherever there is water in arid country there will be a concentration of birds; often these will include some true waterbirds, seemingly quite out of place in the desert.

—KENN KAUFMAN (2000)

THE SOUND OF birdsongs fills the desert air. Indeed, a surprising number and variety of birds live in the Sonoran Desert (Monson and Phillips 1981; Peterson 1961; Phillips et al. 1964). Common small birds include sparrows, wrens, gnatcatchers, verdin, bluebirds, thrashers, doves, woodpeckers, quail, hummingbirds, and many others. Larger birds consist of roadrunners, ravens, owls, hawks, falcons, eagles, vultures, cranes, and herons. More than seventy different kinds of birds are recognized in the O'odham (Piman) language, and birds are frequently mentioned in O'odham oral traditions (Rea 1983). Some of the birds played central roles in their creation and flood stories. Buzzard (Nooee or Nui), for example, created the mountains and valleys of the desert to help keep humans from getting lost during their journeys (Bahr et al. 1994). Close observation of desert birds reveals fascinating patterns of behavior, some seeming very humanlike.

Birds are highly symbolic to native peoples of the American Southwest. Many groups use feathers as offerings to the spirit world for precious rain or other benevolent wishes (Parsons 1939; Russell 1975; Stoller 1991). Birds also symbolize "flight" into the spirit world and transformations undergone by religious specialists, especially shamans (Eliade 1964; Hedges 1985; Turpin 1994; Wellmann 1976). Rock art bird images appear in various parts of the Southwest (Schaafsma 1980). In Canyon de Chelly, some anthropomorphs have bird heads (Grant 1978).

In the Sonoran Desert, however, bird images are not as common in rock art designs. This makes their frequent occurrence in the South Mountains all the more intriguing. We identified more than sixty individual bird images, representing a variety of birds. Most frequent are waterbirds and thunderbirds, but other types include songbirds, a possible roadrunner, a hummingbird, bluebirds, unidentifiable birds, mammals with birdlike heads, and people impersonating or transforming into birds. Bird designs occur in twenty-one different localities, although nearly half of these elements are in Box Canyon.

Waterbirds

The most common type of bird image probably represents waterbirds, characterized by long, bent legs; a long, crooked neck; and a long beak (figure 85). These birds are almost always depicted in profile, most with outlined bodies, and most have hollow heads without eyes. Some have short crests; many have triangular tails and two to four stylized wing feathers (figure 86). The majority of these birds are standing, not flying. Some have triangular bodies that are sectioned into two, three, or four parts. Beaks are most often closed. A

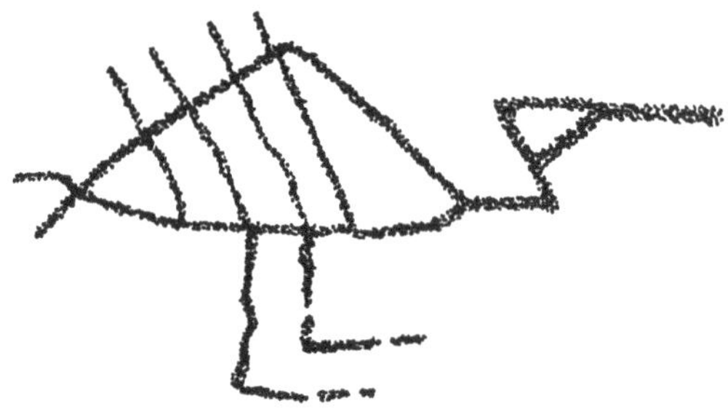

85. Waterbird, 36th Street Locality. Bird is 50 x 39 cm.

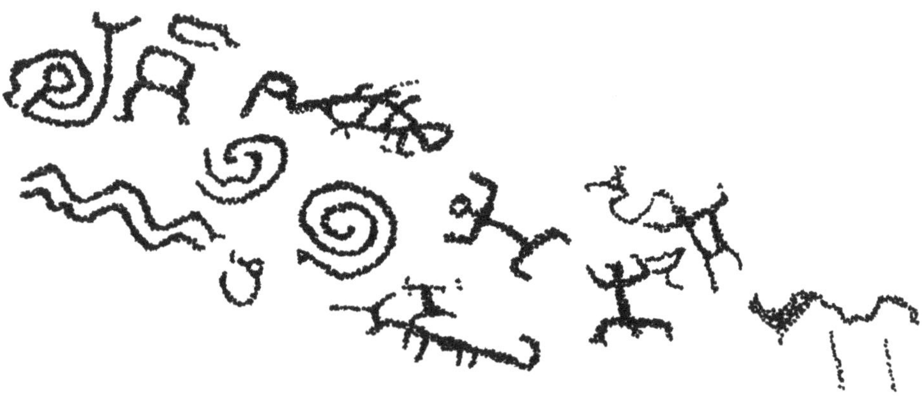

86. Waterbird with other petroglyphs including another possible bird at far right, 32nd Street Locality. Waterbird is 23 cm in length.

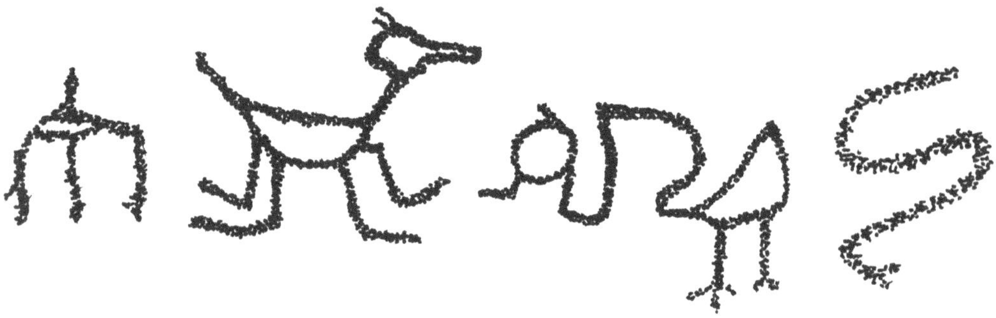

87. Stylized bird with other petroglyphs, 36th Street Locality. Bird is 22 cm in length.

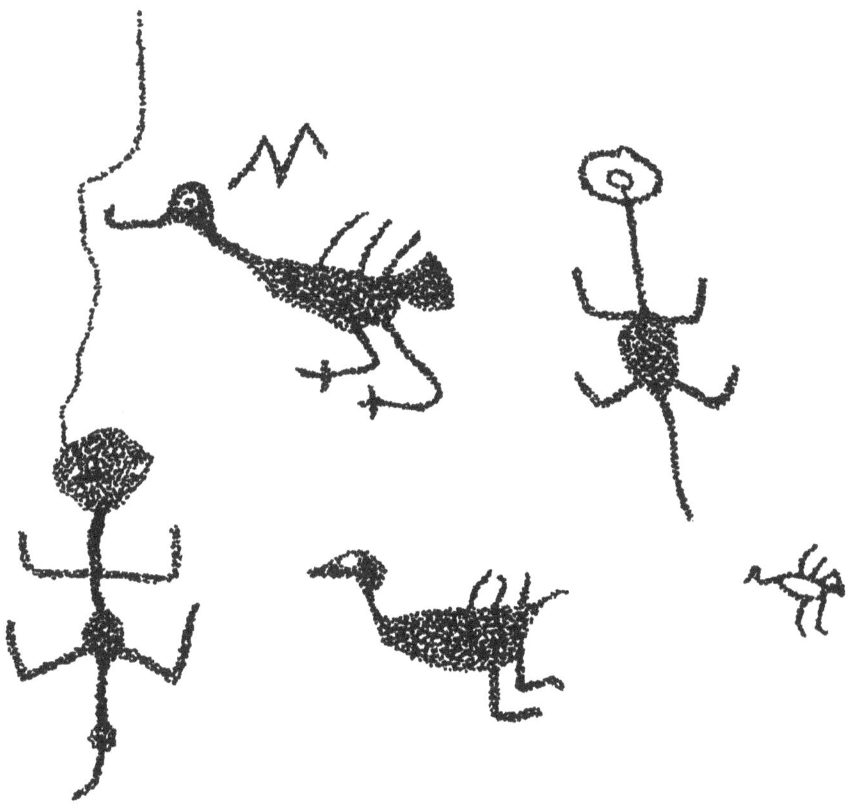

88. Waterbird petroglyphs that may represent flying ducks, Summit Locality. Two unusual four-legged life-forms also are present. Upper left bird is 46 cm in length.

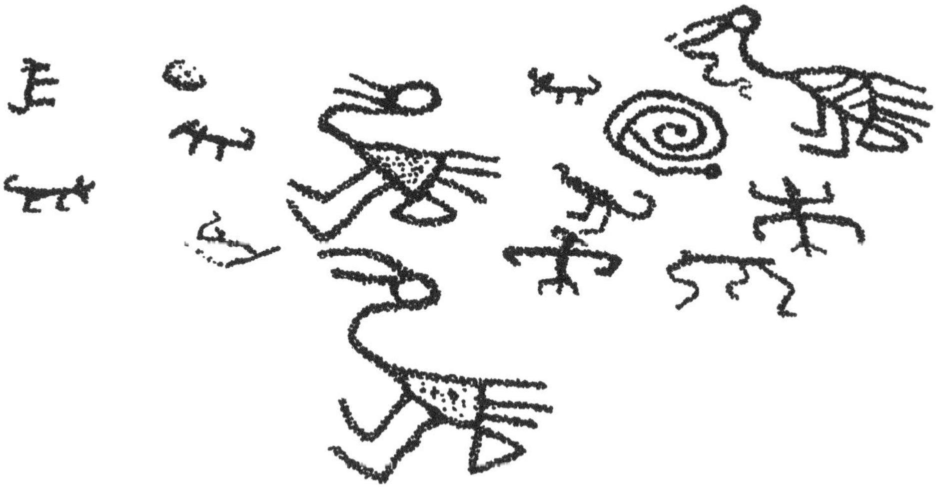

89. Waterbirds, Box Canyon. Lower bird is 50 cm in length.

few are three-toed birds, but many have poorly defined feet without toes. Some waterbirds are highly stylized (figure 87) or are depicted differently than most of the others (figure 88).

We identified more than two dozen waterbird images at eleven different locations. They occur broadly across the northeastern face of the mountains but are most common in Box Canyon, particularly on a distinctive knoll we named Bird Hill.

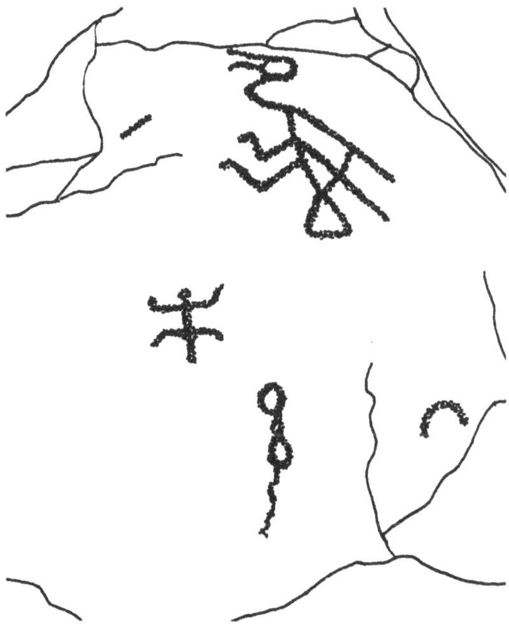

90. Waterbird, Box Canyon. Bird is 48 cm in length.

Bird Hill, on the western side of Box Canyon, has a rather dramatic waterbird scene (figure 89). A panel high up on the hill, yet visible from below, has a triangular arrangement of three large waterbirds surrounded by quadrupeds (coyotes or dogs), a lightning design, and other elements. One of the waterbirds has a snake in its beak, and in the middle of the group is a birdlike anthropomorph, perhaps representing a shaman, that is half the size of the waterbirds. Two other panels on the western side of Box Canyon have nearly identical, large waterbird depictions (figures 90 and 91). In addition, a complex panel on the eastern side of Bird Hill has two small waterbirds in association with humans holding canes and a variety of other designs (see figure 267). A

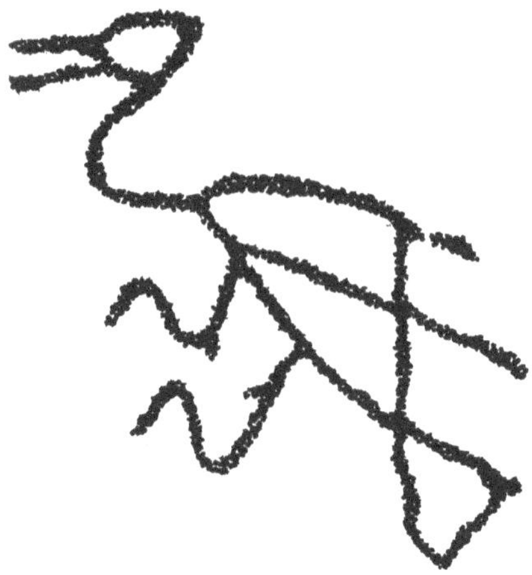

91. Waterbird, Box Canyon. Bird is 54 cm in length.

large rock below this panel has petroglyphs adjacent to a small circular hole that appears to have been drilled into the rock, perhaps to hold special objects such as prayer sticks, or perhaps representing a portal into the spirit world.

Interesting bird images occur outside Box Canyon as well. A boulder alcove midway up Goodman Canyon has a panel with a waterbird next to a lizard, a deer, and a rectilinear scroll. Below these large figures, in the same panel, is a smaller human with a staff, possibly representing a shaman and his group of spirit helpers (see figure 276).

In Hieroglyphic Canyon, a waterbird 3 feet (1 m) long is depicted next to a dramatic lightning zigzag design and two anthropomorphs (figure 92). Meandering lines connect the large bird to the smaller humans and the lightning, giving the scene a sense of extreme power.

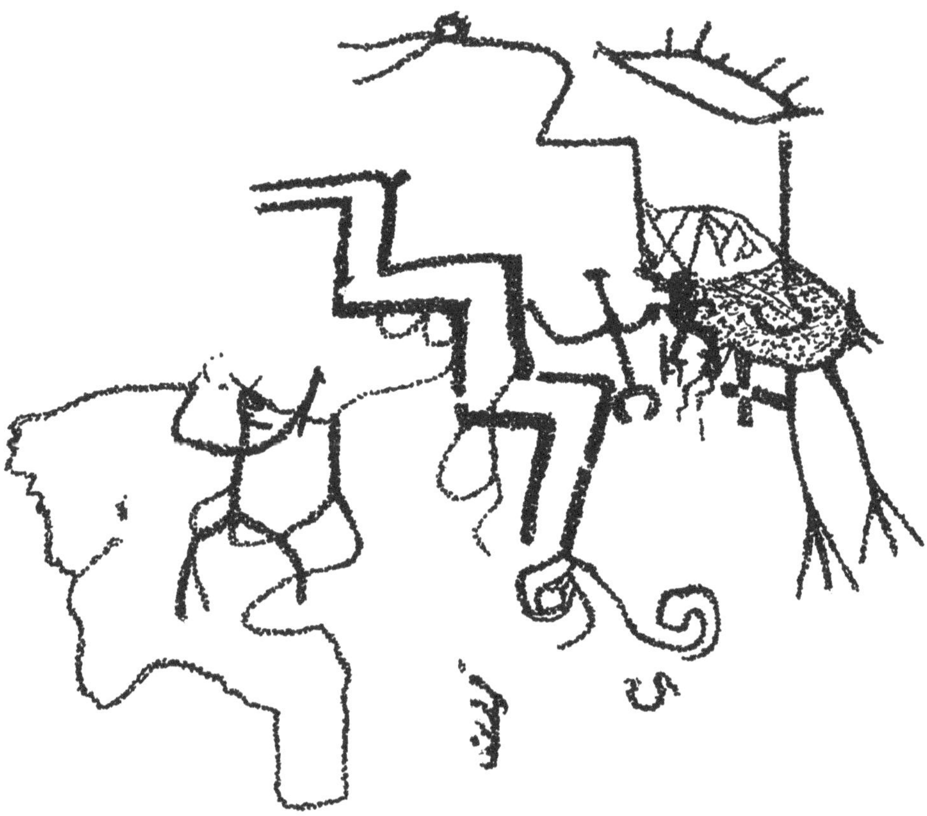

92. Waterbird, lightning, and anthropomorphs, Hieroglyphic Canyon. Bird is 1.03 m in length.

A prominent ridge at the base of the mountains in the 36th Street Locality has a panel with a human holding an outlined cross in its right hand while standing on the foot of a large waterbird with an elaborate headdress. The anthropomorph is smaller than both the outlined cross and the bird, but its position between these two images suggests it has control of two powerful forces (see figure 287).

Adjacent to the upper reaches of the Mormon Trail is a waterbird with quadrupeds to its right and left. A panel high up in the 32nd Street Locality has an anthropomorph that is connected by a line to a large waterbird. A small pipette is present next to the waterbird, and two small anthropomorphs and a figure-eight design are located above the larger anthropomorph (figure 93). Waterbirds are also present in two different panels in the South Mountains that contain pipette designs.

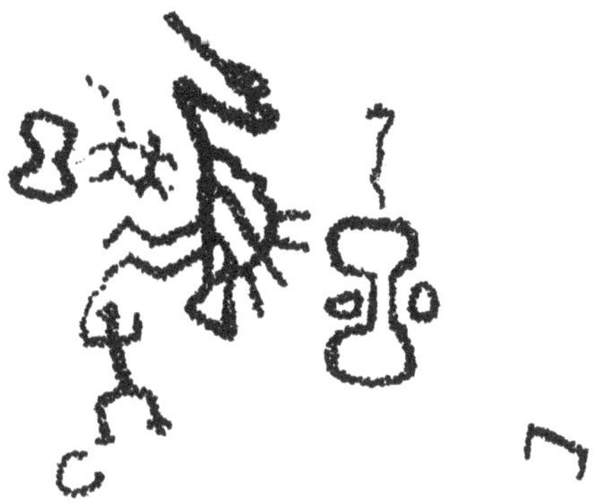

93. Waterbird, anthropomorphs, and pipette design, upper 32nd Street Locality. Bird is 16 cm in length.

Many waterbird images probably represent great blue herons *(Ardea herodia),* great or common egrets *(Ardea alba),* or sandhill cranes *(Grus canadensis).* Herons and egrets commonly nest in Arizona, and the crane is a winter visitor (Perkins and Brown 1981). Large numbers of cranes are reported wintering annually at Willcox Playa in southeastern Arizona, as well as smaller flocks along the lower Colorado and Gila Rivers. The great blue heron, which stands about 3 feet (1 m) tall, is the most frequently observed large waterbird in Arizona and is present wherever there is open water. The common egret may also be found in central Arizona all summer; in spring it develops long, delicate plumes. Herons typically curl their necks and pull in their heads when in flight, forming an S shape, similar to the crooked necks of the waterbirds depicted in South Mountains petroglyphs. Cranes, often confused with herons, fly with a straight neck but curve it into an S shape when fishing. Cranes have a stout, bayonet-shaped beak and a wingspan of 6 feet (2 m) or more. They are well known for their frenzied, leaping courtship dance and their loud trumpet call. Neither herons nor cranes have webbed toes.

Archaeologist Henry Wallace (1989) has suggested that some of the Hohokam waterbird designs represent pelicans (*Pelecanus* spp.). Small numbers of pelicans are transient visitors to Arizona during both winter and summer months along the lower Colorado River. They have long, thick bills and curve their necks when in flight, but they also have relatively short legs with webbed toes. It is possible that some of the short-legged waterbirds in South Mountains petroglyphs (as in figure 159) could represent pelicans.

Herons do not appear to have been mentioned specifically in O'odham oral traditions. However, in one story a crane ("Kohkod" in Piman) tricked Coyote into jumping into some floodwater, then saved Coyote's life by pulling him out again (Saxton and Saxton 1973). Amadeo Rea (1983) has noted that Piman speakers distinguish cranes from herons and other waterbirds. The root word "vakain" is used for herons, egrets, pelicans, and ospreys but not for cranes. A sandhill crane, for example, is called "hain julshap."

The crane was an important element in the Tohono O'odham skipping dance. The skipping dance is an intervillage musical ceremony, which anthropologist Ruth Underhill (1946) called a form of opera. It was performed to bring luck and rain to a village that had challenged another village to a race. After a singer dreamed a series of visionary songs, the singer trained several children to perform dance evolutions, carrying effigies that referred to the dream. Effigies carried during the dance included rainbowlike designs and cranes made of raw cotton and mounted on sticks, which were waved as though the birds were flying while crane songs were sung. Tohono O'odham runners involved in the sacred salt pilgrimage to the Gulf of California are reported to have seen flocks of white cranes, which served as omens for the runner's future, while at the ocean (Underhill et al. 1979).

A burnt heron bone and two crane bones were found at the Hohokam site of Snaketown (McKusick 1976). In addition, an unidentified Ardeidae bone was recovered from the Gecko Site, a small Hohokam village south of the Gila River (Strand 1993). The Gila and Salt Rivers, as well as the extensive canal systems associated with them, would have been ideal breeding grounds. In historic times, herons and cranes are known to have lived along and fed from irrigation ditches, and certainly prehistoric farmers would have been familiar with these elegant birds.

Roadrunner

One of the bird designs in Box Canyon may represent a roadrunner[1] (figure 94). Located on the eastern side of Bird Hill, this element is in a panel that includes several other life-forms including humans and a turtle or tortoise. The bird is similar in style to South Mountain waterbird petroglyphs but exhibits a few important differences, especially its long tail, a trait typical of roadrunners. Furthermore, the design has long legs and a noticeable crest, also typical roadrunner traits. The bird's bent legs, however, are not a roadrunner trait, suggesting that this image could be an individual impersonating a roadrunner.

Roadrunners *(Geococcyx californianus)* have interesting behavior patterns that, combined with their unusual appearance, make them easily recognizable. A ground-loving bird that prefers running to flying, the roadrunner has mischievous and comical manners. They have a reptilelike face and can raise or lower their bristle-tipped topknot at will. They pursue small to medium-sized birds with amazing success and

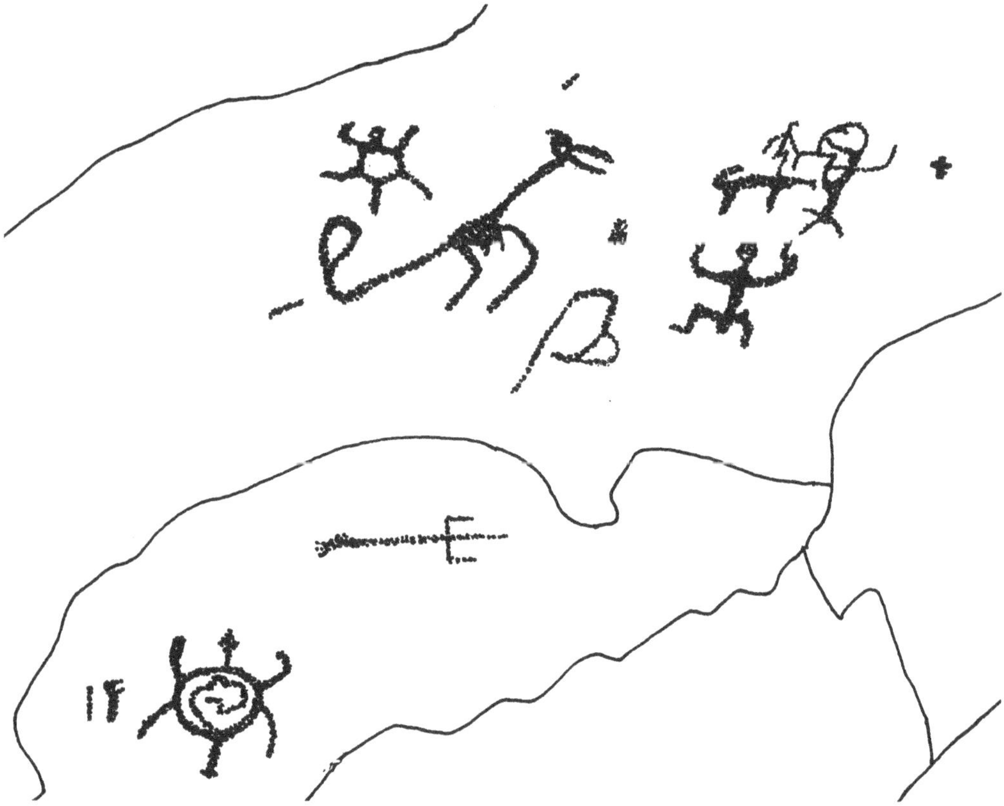

94. Roadrunner, Box Canyon. Lower left petroglyph is a turtle or tortoise. Roadrunner is 49 cm in length.

also eat crickets, grasshoppers, scorpions, cicadas, lizards, and snakes. Roadrunners often hunt in the early morning and develop predictable travel patterns. Although not a bird that talks much, the roadrunner occasionally makes a chickenlike clucking sound and a distinctive whistle that ends in a clatter.

Roadrunner was one of the first birds created, after quail, by the O'odham creator gods Earth Doctor and Siuuhu (or Se'ehe, also called I'itoi or Elder Brother). Roadrunner was sent to the east to determine how far water had "gone that way" and was then to return and meet Quail, who had gone west, at the center of the earth (Bahr et al. 1994). In another roadrunner story (Curtin 1949), Roadrunner was sent by the O'odham to get fire from the lightning god. Roadrunner was able to steal a fire-stick and escape, but a flaming arrow from the god singed the plumes on the roadrunner's head and turned his eyes red from the smoke.

Hummingbird

Another bird design on the eastern side of Box Canyon may represent a hummingbird (figure 95). This bird occurs in a panel with a coyote or dog, two humans, and some geometric designs. Although this image is similar in style to waterbird petroglyphs in the South Mountains, it has short legs. In addition, the bird has a long, thin beak as do all hummingbirds.

Hummingbirds are easily recognizable visitors and inhabitants of the Sonoran Desert. Biologist Kenn Kaufman (2000:404) praised hummingbirds when he wrote, "Describing hummingbirds without resorting to superlatives would be difficult, and hardly fair. This family includes the world's smallest birds, with the most brilliant iridescent colors, the fastest wing beats, and the most amazing ability to fly up, down, sideways and backwards." Arizona is host to more than a dozen species of hummingbirds; a few of these live in the state, but most are seasonal visitors (Kaufman 2000). Costa's hummingbird *(Calypte costae)* is a true desert inhabitant. Other common types include the broad-billed *(Cynanthus latirostris),* black-chinned *(Archilochus alexandri),* rufous *(Selasphorus rufus),* and Anna's *(Calypte anna)* hummingbirds. The males of the various species have bright, beautiful colors that sparkle in sunlight. Their small size and constant wing movement make them attractive to bird watchers. They feed on flower nectar and insects, and they are strongly territorial.

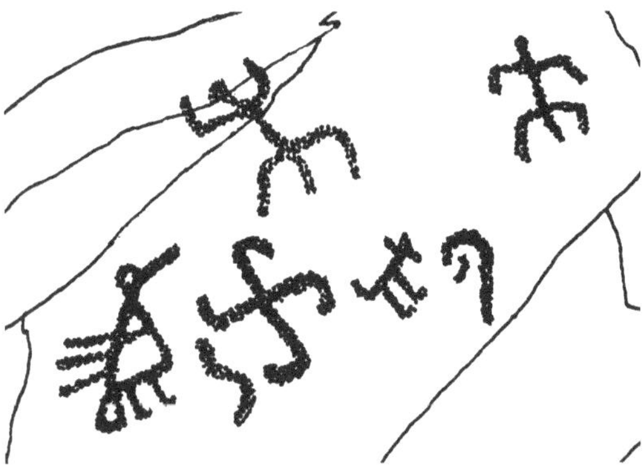

95. Hummingbird, Box Canyon. Bird is 25 cm in length.

Hummingbirds are mentioned in a few O'odham oral traditions (Bahr et al. 1994; Saxton and Saxton 1973; Shaw 1968). A "Singing Up the Corn" song describes Hummingbird finding Tobacco's flowers. In a story about the "Drinker Man," Hummingbird was sent with Coyote to get mud from which to make humans. Drinker Man then made various men, some of whom turned out good and others not so good. These men spread over the land and along the rivers. Because they learned to speak before they were told to do so, Drinker Man turned them into saguaros.

Bird images have been created in the ceramic, textile, and stone art of Mesoamerica from the earliest times (Benson 1997). Both bird images and bird attributes such as beaks, wings, crests, and claws were depicted. Hummingbirds—along with eagles, hawks, and owls—represented military power. They are aggressive and will even attack owls and hawks, and their long, sharp beaks resemble weapons or sacrificial implements. In addition, hummingbirds look like glints of sunlight and thus are creatures of the sun. The Aztec god Huitzilopochtli was a warrior and sun god who wore a hummingbird helmet; his name means "hummingbird on the left of the sun's path." Because some hummingbirds hibernate or go into a torpor when it is cold, the great Aztec chronicler Bernardino de Sahagún noted that the hummingbird appears to rejuvenate itself. After the Spanish conquest, the hummingbird became a symbol of resurrection.

Thunderbird

ANOTHER BIRD TYPE found in the South Mountains, in at least eight different locations, has been called a "thunderbird." It has spread wings, a straight or flaring body, and a small, sometimes indistinguishable head. The form varies from images that clearly look like birds (figure 96) to some that appear somewhat ghostlike (figure 97). We recorded more than a dozen of these motifs in the South Mountains, and others are likely to be discovered.

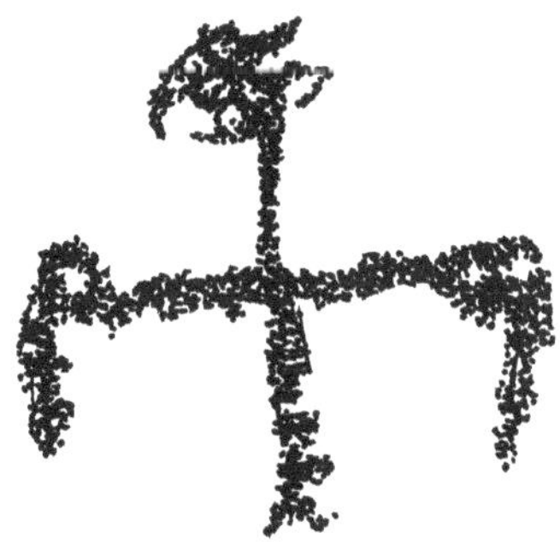

96. Thunderbird, 32nd Street Locality. Bird is 20 x 22 cm.

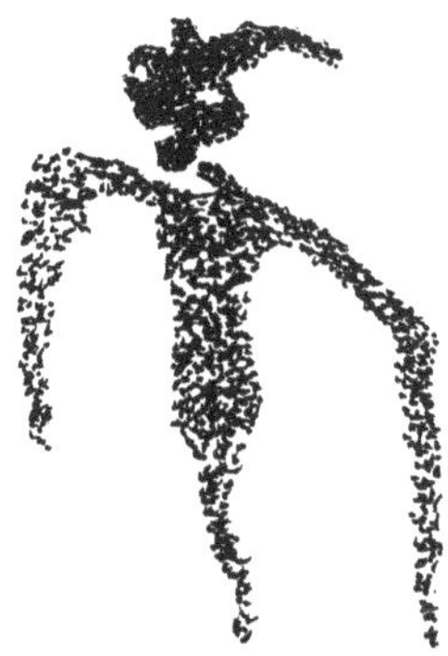

97. Ghostlike thunderbird, Box Canyon. Bird is 27 cm in height.

Which species are represented by the thunderbird is unknown. Some thunderbird images may symbolize eagles or other soaring birds. Eagle breast feathers have great power among the O'odham and are associated with rain magic, being so much like clouds that the feathers are thought to be able to summon clouds. O'odham shamans used eagle wing feathers as divining plumes. Anyone who killed an eagle had to undergo strict fasting and cleansing ceremonies and often received powerful dreams as a result of their experience. In addition, eagles are often mentioned in O'odham oral traditions (Bahr et al. 1994; Shaw 1968). One such story, the "Legend of Eagleman," is about a creature—part human and part eagle—who killed people and kidnapped the maiden Tall Flower. The people enlisted the Pima cultural hero, Elder Brother, to save Tall Flower. Elder Brother managed to kill Eagleman and relayed the good news to the people by having them watch for white clouds over Greasy Mountain (the South Mountains).

Both the Hopi and the Zuni have stories about a legendary bird with spread wings, called Knifewing by the Zuni; this bird also is painted on pottery and depicted in rock art (Schaafsma 1992).

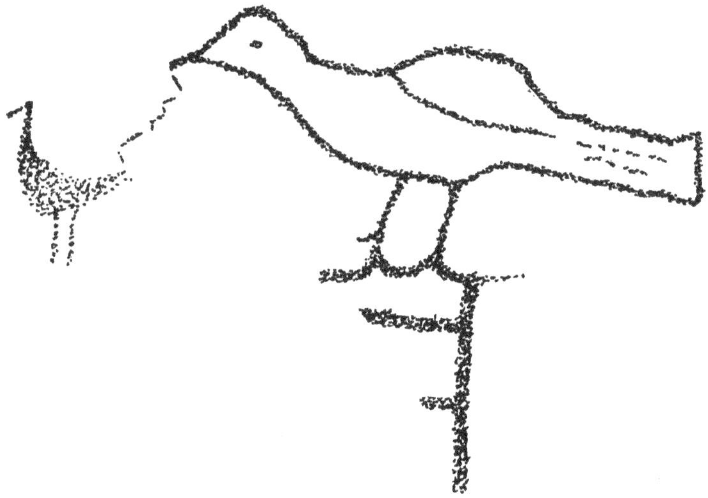

98. Songbird, Hieroglyphic Canyon. Large bird is 42 cm in length.

Bluebird

It is possible that the bluebird *(Sialia mexicana)* is represented in the rock art of the South Mountains. Two designs in particular are in a style different from the waterbirds. One is a naturalistic-looking bird in Hieroglyphic Canyon, occurring with a smaller bird that may be a waterbird (figure 98). The naturalistic bird is in profile and depicted as though perched on a stick. Although this image could represent several of the small bird species that live in the Sonoran Desert, the bluebird figures prominently in O'odham oral traditions.

Another more abstract design near the Holbert Trail, at the northeastern end of Box Canyon, also may represent the bluebird. Unlike any other bird petroglyph (and thus being possibly historic rather than Hohokam), it is the profile of a bird head and shoulders (see figure 15). O'odham ethnographer Frank Russell (1975) discussed a similar bird design found on a calendar stick, recording a time when bluebird songs were once sung; this image may be historic.

Bluebirds were considered powerful medicine helpers for O'odham shamans (Bahr et al. 1994). In O'odham oral traditions, bluebirds frequently are associated with desert clouds, wind, and precious rain. A story about the overthrow of the evil Hohokam chiefs by the O'odham tells how a Bluebird shaman used his power of thunder to destroy the Hohokam platform mound village of Pueblo Grande.

Songbirds

Three rock art panels in two locations have bird images that appear to be singing or speaking. These birds have pecked and scratched marks radiating from

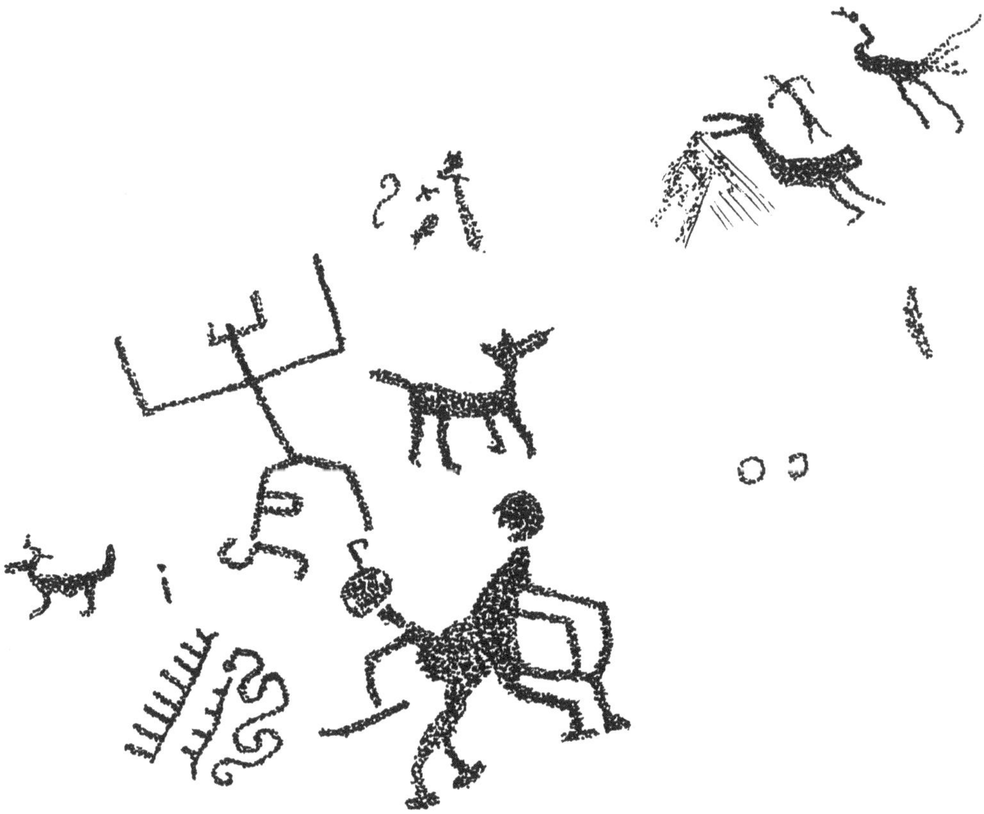

99. Songbird with lines from beak suggesting song, Hieroglyphic Canyon. Bird on lower left is 22 cm in length.

their beaks. A complex, multielement panel in Hieroglyphic Canyon has two birds standing above a scene that includes quadrupeds, geometric designs, and two interacting humans (figure 99). Both birds have long, bent legs, and the lower bird in this panel has lines coming out of its beak. Another panel in this canyon, discussed in the preceding section, has a large bird in outline form (possibly a bluebird) perched upon a stick and apparently singing to a smaller bird nearby (see figure 98). The third panel is situated in upper Pima Canyon on a massive boulder above a spring (figure 100). This bird has long legs, a short tail, and a long beak. Coming from the bird's beak is a beautiful curvilinear, meandering line, while above it is a lizard and to the right a triangular anthropomorph missing its left arm.

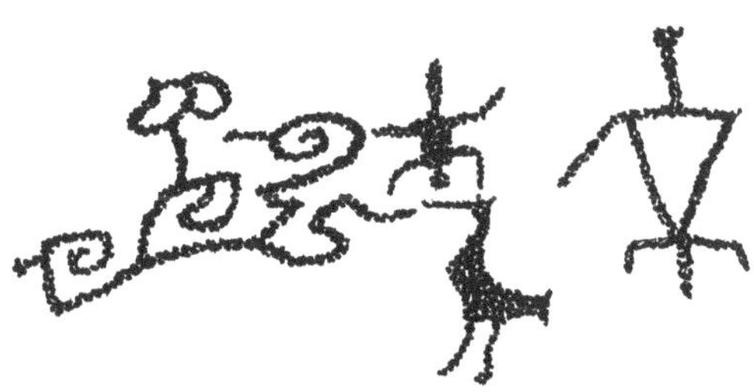

100. Songbird with elaborate song scroll, near a spring in upper Pima Canyon. Bird is 23 cm in length.

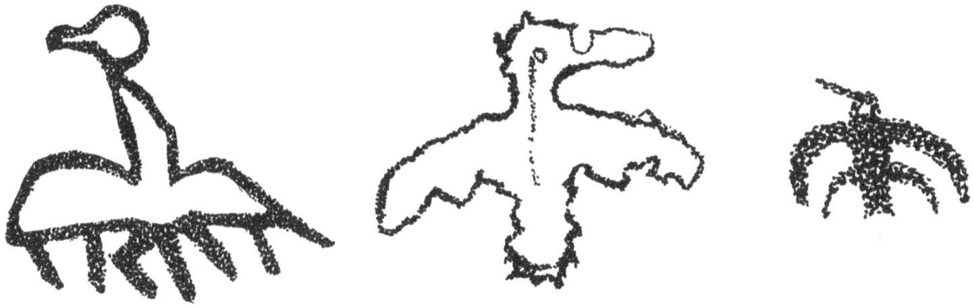

101. Flying birds: **left,** Box Canyon (33 cm in length); **center,** Pima Canyon (17 x 22 cm); **right,** possible four-winged bird, Box Canyon (18 cm in length).

Miscellaneous Birds

Several bird images do not fit into previously described categories. Some of these birds are in outline form and appear to be in flight, such as an unusual one on the eastern side of Box Canyon (figure 101, *left*). Some are simple outline figures (figure 101, *center*), while others are solidly pecked (figure 101, *right*). A panel in the Southeast Side Locality, easily visible to passers-by, contains two birds in a scene with other elements including a fish (see figure 12). One of the birds is in profile and may be a parrot. The other may represent a sea gull, but this panel is most likely from the early Historic period.

People in Bird Costumes

At least four panels contain figures that appear to be humans wearing bird costumes or perhaps shamans undergoing transformation into birds. All of these figures have four legs or are wearing birdlike masks. A panel in Box Canyon inside the entrance to a natural grotto is a scene with a bird, a quadruped, and another element (figure 102). The bird has a long neck, closed bill, sectioned body, triangular tail, two bent wing feathers, and four legs. Next to this figure is a circle with two short appendages that may represent a baby bird's head with its beak open, as if asking for food. Farther inside the grotto is another panel with a bird that has a quadrupedlike head (figure 103).

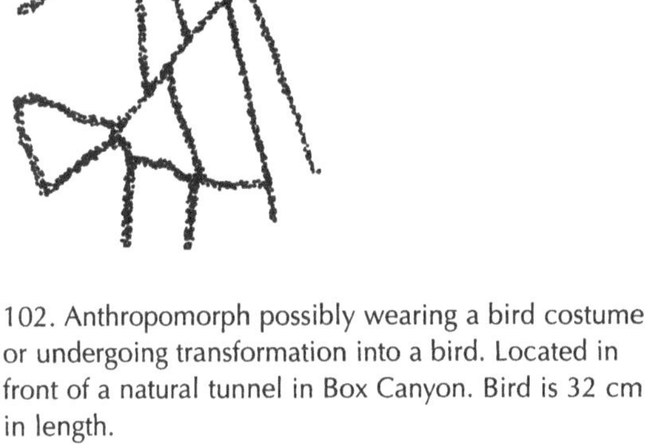

102. Anthropomorph possibly wearing a bird costume or undergoing transformation into a bird. Located in front of a natural tunnel in Box Canyon. Bird is 32 cm in length.

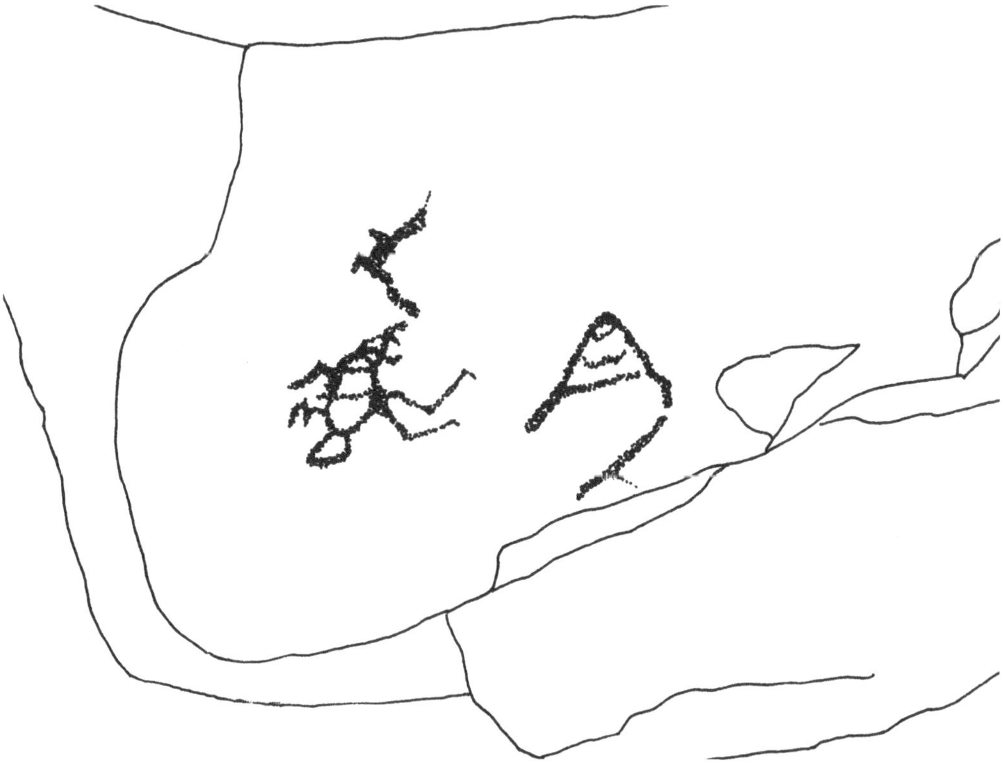

103. Bird and flute-player petroglyphs inside a natural tunnel in Box Canyon. Bird on left has a quadrupedlike head and is 28 cm in length. The bent-over flute-player is similar to another one located on the same hill (figure 112).

Another petroglyph element next to this composite creature may be a bird's head above a natural rock formation that appears to serve as the bird's body.

Two rock art panels have figures that appear to be wearing bird masks (see figures 164 and 165). Located in Hieroglyphic Canyon and along Kiwanis Trail, these panels are described in chapter 8 in the section on masks and masked faces.

Interpreting Prehistoric Bird Images

Bird images were obviously important to the Hohokam, and several possible meanings can be proposed. They may have represented Hohokam clan symbols, although archaeologists do not know whether the Hohokam had clans. Zuni petroglyph designs that appear to be three-toed tracks, for example, have been identified with cranes and may be Zuni clan symbols (Young 1988). Crane or heron petroglyphs also occur in Canyon de Chelly (Grant 1978) and the Petrified Forest region (McCreery and Malotki 1994). Crane clans were once present among the Hopi, and crane petroglyphs also have been recorded along the lower Gila River in prehistoric Patayan country.

Hohokam bird designs probably had ritual importance beyond group identity. Birds are often associated with clouds and rain. For both the O'odham and the Pueblo Indians, birds have magical properties that can be put to human use. For example, birds serve as messengers to the gods, and their feathers, when smoked over or breathed on, carry prayers to the spirit realm. Birds are very significant in Hopi ceremonies and are among the first of the sacred katsinas to appear during the annual Hopi ceremonial season. The Zuni Salako, covered with eagle feathers, is a tall birdlike katsina with a long, two-part beak that makes clacking noises. Cranes are specifically mentioned in several Pueblo stories and are identified as waterbirds that eat other water symbols such as fish and frogs, as well as plant seeds (Tyler 1979). Because of the crane's habit of posting guards while eating in a group, Puebloans considered cranes to be guardians of the katsina dancers and clowns.

In prehistoric Mexico, heron feathers were important parts of certain deities' costumes. The Aztec god Tezcatlipoca, or Smoking Mirror, wore double heron feathers in his hair; this deity was a powerful sorcerer who was worshiped with a festival during the dry season. In addition, the rain god Tlaloc was crowned with heron feathers in his unmasked form.

Birds are especially important symbolic figures in shamanistic practice because they can also symbolically represent the transformation that occurs when a shaman journeys into the supernatural realm on transcendent, magical flights (Eliade 1964; Hedges 1985; Turpin 1994). The large waterbird seemingly attached by strings to an anthropomorph in Hieroglyphic Canyon (see figure 92) is suggestive of a metaphorical connection between bird and human. The bird design at the entrance to the rock shelter on Bird Hill and the individuals with a birdlike mask (or head) in Hieroglyphic Canyon and Kiwanis Trail may represent humans in bird costumes (see figures 102, 164, and 165). Archaeologist David Whitley (1994) has noted that a cave in south-central California has a painted bird design identified by Yokuts Indians as a shaman dancer wearing a blue heron costume.

Conclusions

A variety of different types of birds are present in rock art elements of the South Mountains. All of the bird petroglyphs probably represent birds that the Hohokam would have observed in the Salt River Valley. A curious absence, however, is notable: we recorded no quail petroglyphs in the South Mountains. This contrasts with Hohokam red-on-buff pottery, in which the quail was a frequently painted image. Some of the anthropomorph petroglyphs, however, have headdresses that are similar to quail topknot feathers and perhaps represent quail people. Perhaps these anthropomorphs represent membership in a Quail clan or symbolize an important relationship with quail as spirit helpers.

CHAPTER EIGHT

HUMANS AND SPIRIT BEINGS

ANTHROPOMORPHS

While the people were dancing several shamans took their places in the center of the circle, each holding eagle plumes or a tuft of eagle down. Sometimes they also held the crystals used for divining. It was their function to foresee the coming of the rain and to announce when it might be expected. They walked up and down, holding their eagle plumes to catch the breeze. The Liquor Maker sometimes addressed them during the singing, to make sure that they were helping with the rainmaking, not mysteriously hindering.

—RUTH UNDERHILL (1946)

HUMANLIKE FIGURES WITH stick bodies are a common motif of Hohokam rock art and frequently occur as petroglyphs in the South Mountains. Archaeologists use the term "anthropomorphs" to denote such elements, partly because they may represent humans, spirit beings with humanlike shapes, or even an abstract concept. With some notable exceptions, Hohokam rock art sites typically have anthropomorphs depicted among other rock art elements, although the quantity and variety may vary. The details of stick figure anthropomorphs are diverse, depicting a range of different headdresses, facial features, hands, and postures.

Anthropomorph images also are seen as painted designs on Hohokam red-on-buff pottery. At Snaketown, Emil Haury (1976) identified hand-holding figures in dance postures, individuals carrying burden baskets, hunters, and flute-players. Human figures painted on pottery typically have full torsos and are slightly bent, either forward or backward, suggesting a body in motion. Headdresses are common, and occasionally humans are holding rakelike objects, wands, or gourd rattles.

An examination of rock art anthropomorphs can potentially reveal detailed information about the humans who made the rock art. Polly Schaafsma has suggested that few of the rock art panels in the American Southwest depict everyday human events. Anthropomorphic figures in rock art occasionally represent ordinary people, but Schaafsma (1992:3) argues, "more often the human form denotes anthropomorphized supernaturals, shamans, mythic heroes, or human ceremonial participants."

Henry Wallace and James Holmlund's (1986:144) study of Hohokam anthropomorphs in the Picacho Mountains identified scenes that were "almost certainly indicative of ceremonial functions." These anthropomorphs held spears, canes, bows and arrows, and flutes. They were depicted in curing scenes, birth scenes, and hunting scenes and as part of an apparent map. Other panels had multiple elements, but they appeared in haphazard arrangements, as is typical at many Hohokam rock art sites.

The rock art inventory of the South Mountains has a wide range of anthropomorph types, including a small but significant collection of Hohokam hourglass human figures. Ernest Snyder (1966) recorded 351 stick-figure anthropomorphs and noted that they were the most common element among all life-forms. Our study confirms his results. We have recorded more than two thousand humanlike elements, representing more than one-quarter of the total number of elements recorded. The ubiquitous nature of these figures is indicated by their presence in almost every locality. About two-thirds of the localities have at least ten anthropomorphs, and five localities each contain more than 150 anthropomorphs (Box Canyon, 32nd Street, 36th Street, Hieroglyphic Canyon, and Goodman Canyon). The frequent appearance of anthropomorphs in the South Mountains contrasts with Hohokam rock art recorded on Tempe Butte, where anthropomorphs make up less than 10 percent of the total inventory (Loendorf and Loendorf 1995). Anthropomorph petroglyphs account for 5 to 41 percent of the total rock art elements at Hohokam rock art sites in the northern Salt River Valley (Rodgers 1985:table 6.7).

Stick-Figure Anthropomorphs

The stick-figure form dominates the South Mountains anthropomorph inventory and is depicted in various ways (figure 104). These figures usually are small, generally 4 to 7 inches (10 to 18 cm) in height, but also can be quite large, up to 3 feet (1 m) tall (figure 105). They almost always are shown in full frontal view, rarely in profile. Arms are depicted up, sideways, down, or some combination. An anthropomorph located along a major trail in upper Pima Canyon has one arm down and the other arm raised, as though saluting or watching for something (figure 106). Arms held either up or down may be curved or rectilinear, often but not always matching the form of the legs, which may be straight or bent at the knees.

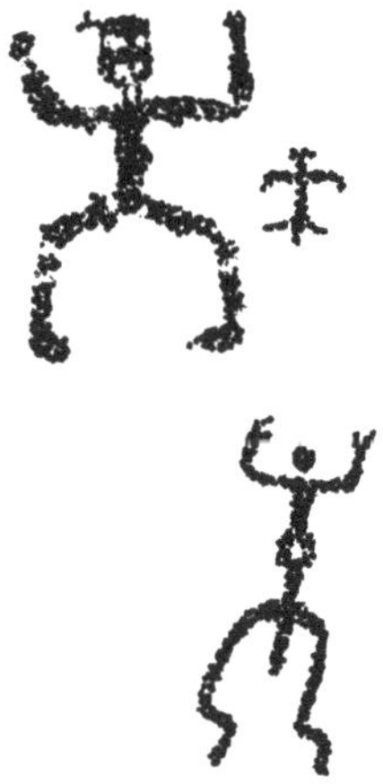

104. Three stick-figure anthropomorphs, Box Canyon. Large, upper anthropomorph is 31 cm in height.

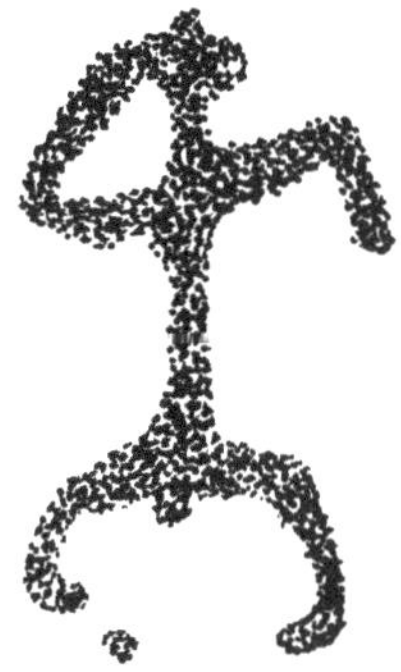

106. Anthropomorph saluting travelers on a major trail in Pima Canyon. Anthropomorph is 26 cm in height.

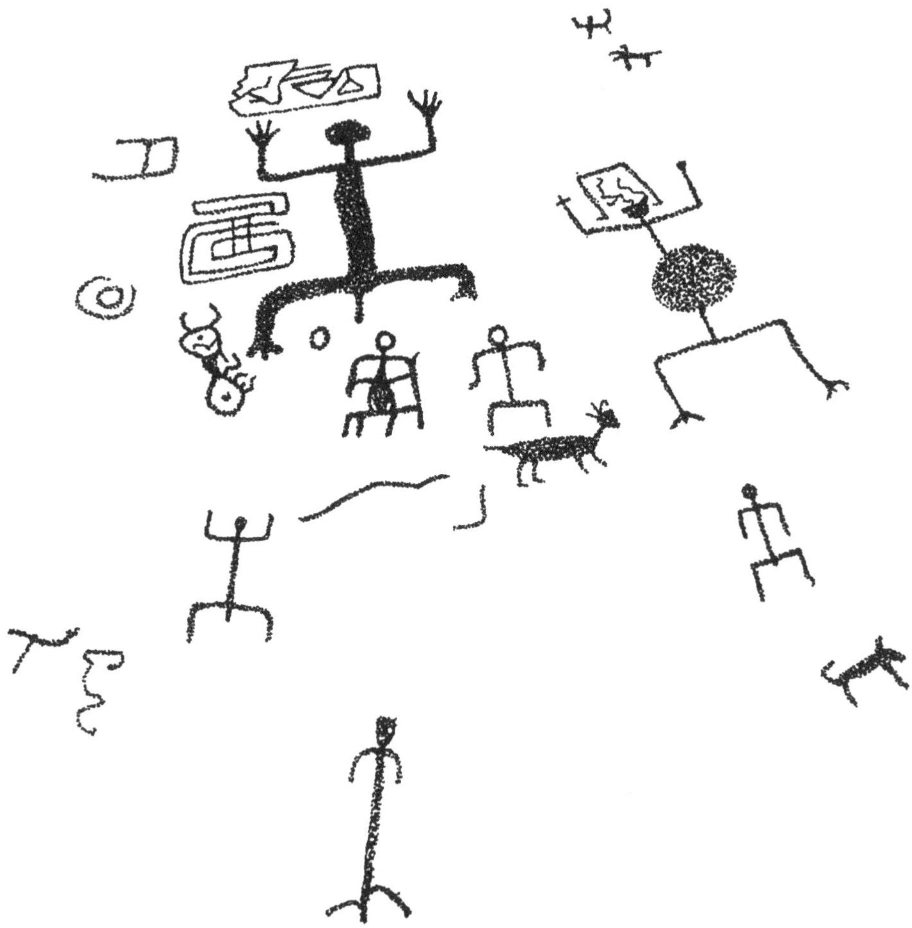

105. Large anthropomorphs, Beverly Canyon. Panel has been heavily vandalized. Both of the two large anthropomorphs are more than 1 m in height.

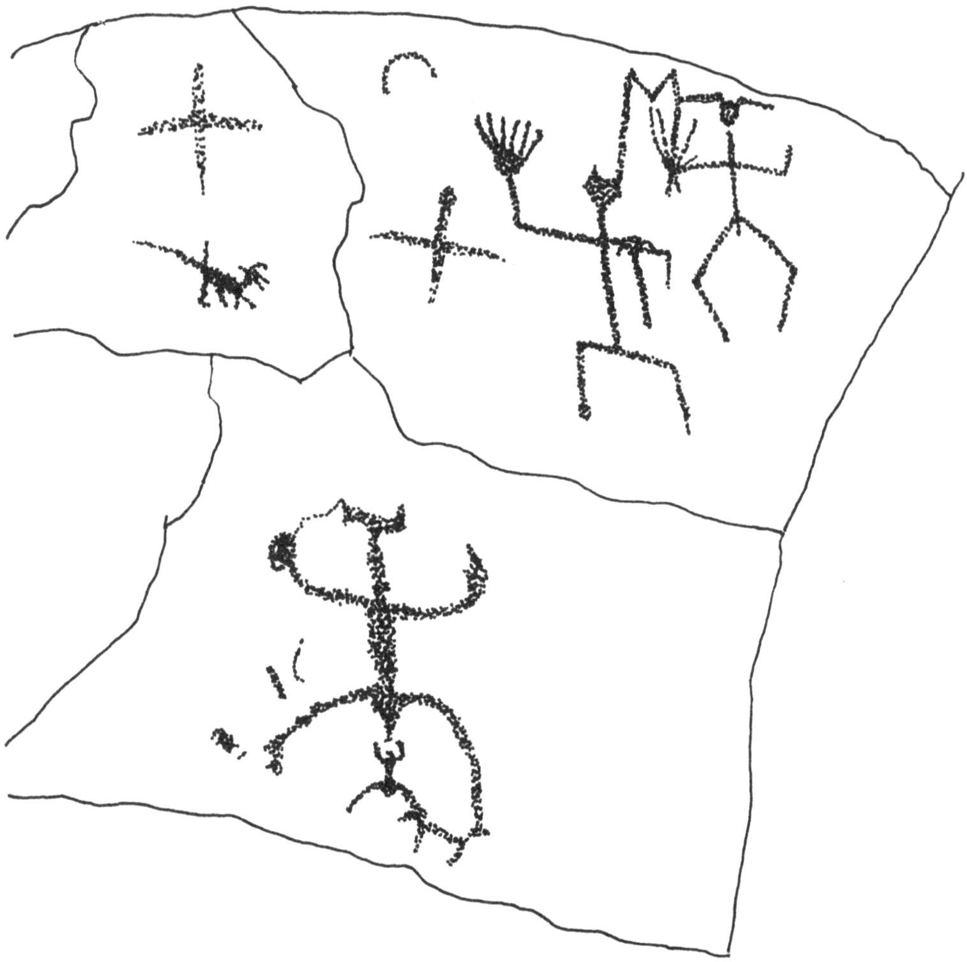

107. Anthropomorph with large six-fingered hand and other anthropomorphs, Hieroglyphic Canyon. Upper left anthropomorph with large hand is 33 cm in height.

The depiction of hands and feet is not common, but several interesting examples of exaggerated hands (or possibly wands) are present in Hieroglyphic Canyon and the 27th Street Locality (figure 107). Feet are typically straight lines at an angle to the leg, and a few examples have toes (figure 108). When depicted, fingers may be two to six in number. The three-digit form is similar to many of the lizard images. Sometimes it is difficult to distinguish between Hohokam lizard and human forms because anthropomorphs are often depicted with an exaggerated phallus and some lizards have short tails and humanlike heads (see discussion in chapter 5). This mixing of human and lizard traits most likely represents an important relationship between the two, perhaps in an otherworld mythic time or shamanic transformation.

Stick-figure anthropomorphs typically have straight lines for their torsos, although occasionally the bodies are curved, perhaps symbolizing motion—a trait common in other Southwestern rock art. Many of the anthropomorphs in the South Mountains have a large, solidly pecked circle in their midsection, as though representing a belly or central point in the abdomen (perhaps a symbolic portal or life-force connection). Archaeologists have labeled these "expanded mid-body" anthropomorphs. In a few instances in the South Mountains, anthropomorphs or lizardmen have concentric circle bodies. Again, these figures suggest a portal and are the central, most dramatic features in their respective panels.

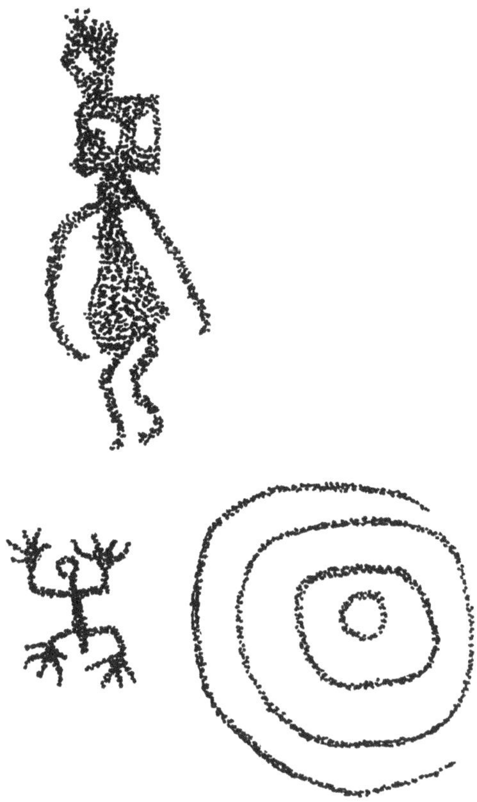

108. Anthropomorph with fingers and toes, 27th Street Locality. Anthropomorph is 17 cm in height. Another larger anthropomorph with an elaborate headdress is present above this petroglyph.

The shapes of heads and other details vary considerably among stick-figure anthropomorphs. Most often they are small, round, and solidly pecked, but sometimes they are circular and in outline form (negative or hollow). Small triangular heads also are not uncommon. Occasionally they are horizontally oriented in an oblong form. Some figures have no heads, only a short, straight up-and-down line. One of the surprising findings of our study is that a number of anthropomorphs have facial features. Circular and slanted eyes and mouths (even a few noses) were left unpecked in otherwise solidly pecked heads, giving the face a ghostlike appearance (see figure 108). Large, seemingly bulging eyes are not uncommon. In contrast, rarely do hollow heads have facial features.

Anthropomorphs with Headdresses

Headdresses, common on the South Mountain anthropomorphs, typically consist of a single, curved projection from the head, similar in form to a large feather (figures 109 and 110). However, some are more elaborate, with multiple projections. Some appear to represent horns, and a few look almost crownlike. A lizard/anthropomorph at the 36th Street Locality has what appears to be a halo, while the anthropomorph next to it has a long, flowing headdress (figure 111).

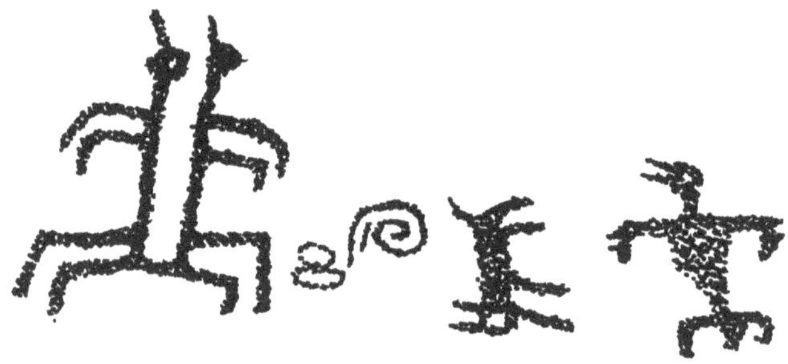

109. Two connected anthropomorphs with headdresses, 24th Street Locality. Anthropomorphs on left is 34 cm in height. These two attached figures may represent twins.

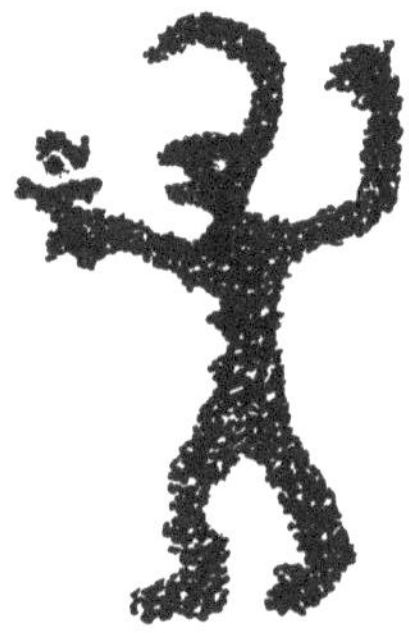

110. Anthropomorphs with typical bent, single-line headdress, western side of Box Canyon on top of Bird Hill. Anthropomorph is 29 cm in height and is holding something in one of its hands.

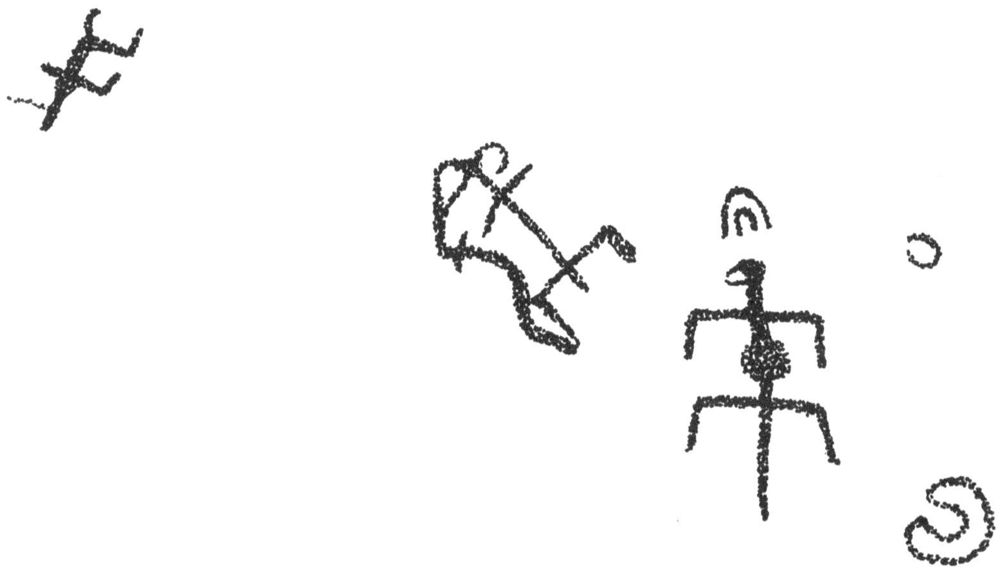

111. Anthropomorph with elaborate headdress, 36th Street Locality. Lizardman/anthropomorph to the right (with what appears to be a halo) is 32 cm in height.

Anthropomorphs with Flutes

Some stick-figure anthropomorphs are holding objects in their hands. These objects include canes and staffs, small and large unidentified circular objects, rake-like objects, bows and arrows, flutes, and strings or energy lines. Flute-players are rare, but we found five examples. Two bent-over flute-players are present on the eastern side of Bird Hill in Box Canyon (figures 103, 112). Both flute-players are in profile but face in opposite directions. Flute-players also are present in large panels at the 7th Street and 16th Street Localities and in Hieroglyphic Canyon (figure 113).

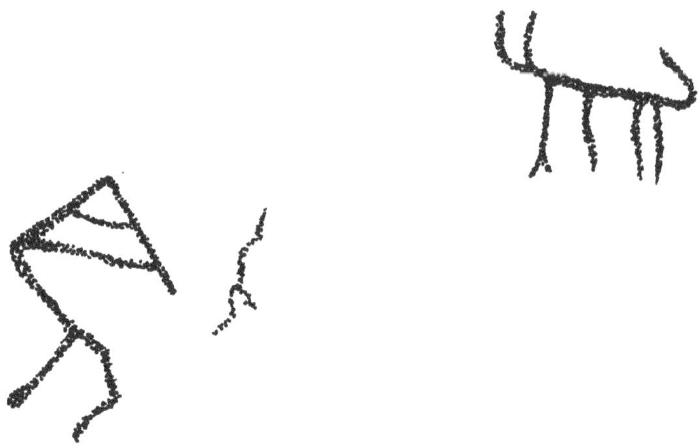

112. Bent-over flute-player and unidentified quadruped, Box Canyon. Flute-player is 24 cm in height.

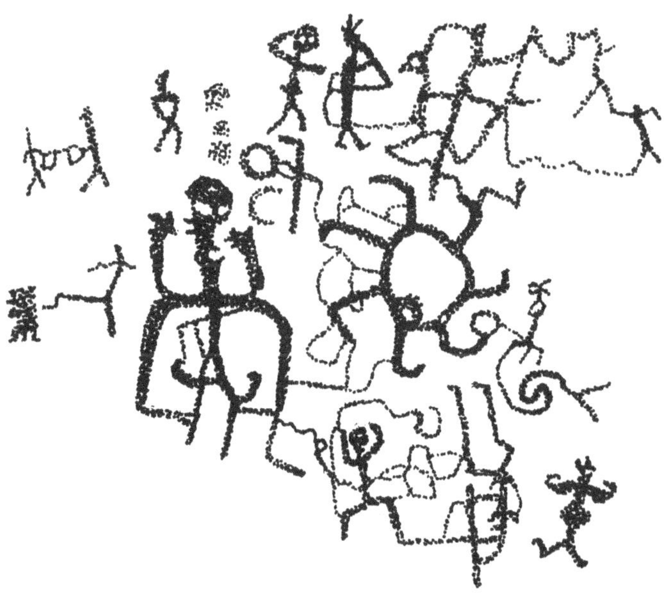

113. Flute-player (upper, central portion of panel), Hieroglyphic Canyon. Sun disk is 28 cm in diameter.

Frank Hamilton Cushing (1890), during his exploration of the Salt River Valley in the late 1880s, recorded meeting young Akimel O'odham men who played flutes made of river cane. These flutes were decorated with incised lines or burnt and painted designs, and plumes of downy eagle feathers were attached to the ends. Cushing reported that the music sounded sharp and flat, yet soft and sweet, like systematized bird songs.

Flute-player images depicted on Hohokam pottery are not entirely similar to those called "Kokopelli," which are found throughout the Anasazi region of Arizona, New Mexico, and Utah. The Hohokam flute-players are not humpbacked, although they are bent over; these figures are shown alone and are right-facing. Haury (1976:239) identified them as flute-players because they are "holding in both hands a straight object slanting downward from what would have been the face on the stylized head." Only twenty-eight ceramic fragments (sherds) from Snaketown, all of which dated to the Colonial period (ca. A.D. 750–950), had flute-player images. This low number of painted flute-players is consistent with the low number of rock art flute-players in the South Mountains.

The flute-player image occurs throughout the Southwest; it is found painted on ceramics, in kiva mural art, and as rock art. Flute-players are shown standing, sitting, kneeling, recumbent, dancing, hunting, or making love (Slifer 2000:101). The origin and evolution of this image is complex. Flute-players without humps first appeared around A.D. 800 or earlier in northeastern Arizona, occurred in large numbers by A.D. 1000, and then declined in popularity by the A.D. 1400s (Malotki 2001). Flute-player images are often associated with Kokopelli, but Ekkehart Malotki (2001) argues that this is a misnomer since the Hopi Katsina on which Kokopelli is modeled, "Kokopolmana," does not play a flute. Kokopelli-like figures have been interpreted variously as a trader from the south, a gambler, a hunter, a warrior, a priest, a clan symbol, or even an insect (Hill 1995). They are usually depicted as males, are said to have the power to bring rain and fertility, and can lure mountain sheep with their flute playing. Flutes also could have been used to produce sounds that opened portals into the supernatural world (Slifer 2000:102).

Anthropomorphs with Canes or Staffs

Anthropomorphs holding canes or staffs in their hands are scattered among nearly two dozen different locations in the South Mountains. Few locations have more than a single anthropomorph holding a cane or staff in the same panel.

In the 36th Street Locality, a panel inside a small rock shelter has two anthropomorphs with canes (figure 114). The lower human is deeply pecked and stands in bold pose, holding a long staff. The upper one is bent over and appears to be an older person. Perhaps these figures represent the same person during different stages of his

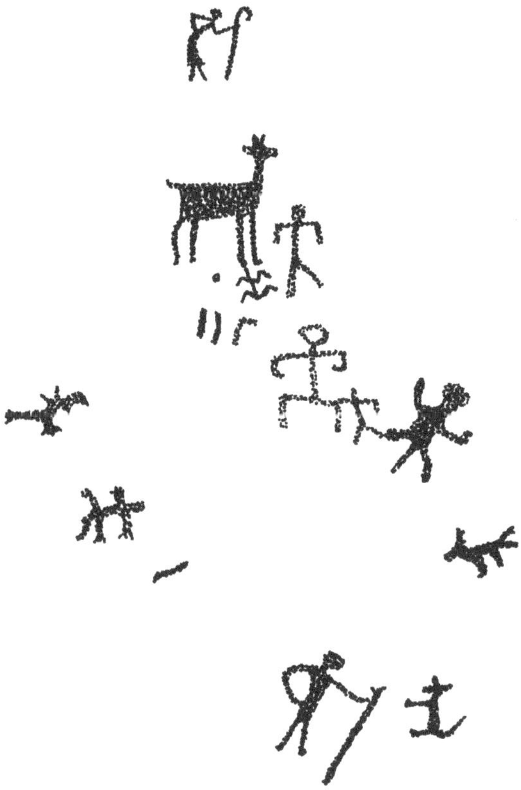

114. Two anthropomorphs with canes, 36th Street Locality. Lower anthropomorph with cane is 19 cm in height.

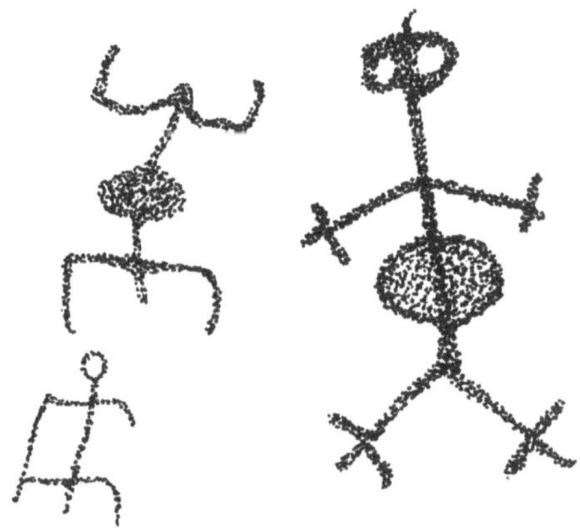

115. Anthropomorph holding a cane with two other anthropomorphs nearby, on a panel located above a natural water tank in Goodman Canyon. Large anthropomorph on right is 23 cm in height.

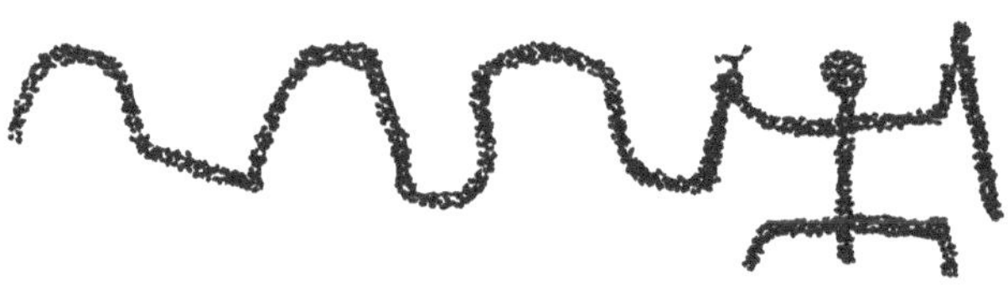

116. Anthropomorph holding a snake in one hand and a cane in the other, upper Pima Canyon. Anthropomorph is 13 cm in height.

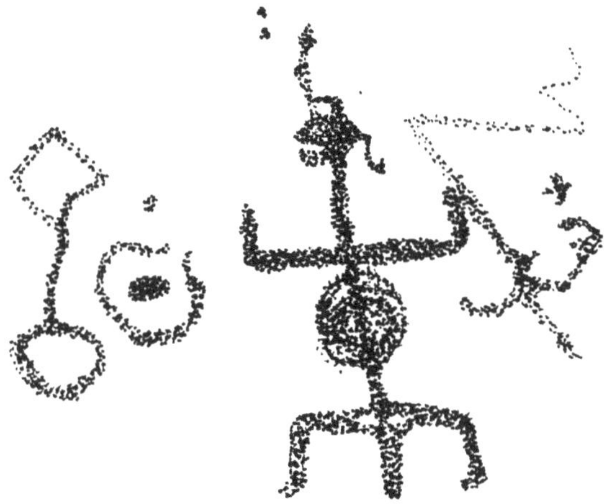

117. Anthropomorph with elaborate cane, near a spring along Mormon Loop Trail. Anthropomorph is 26 cm in height.

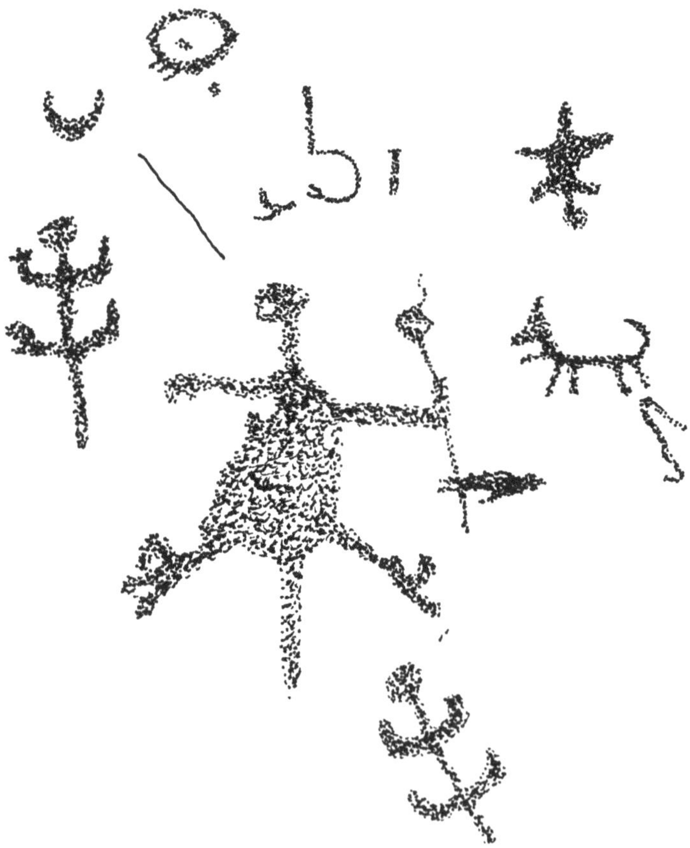

118. Anthropomorph/lizard with elaborate cane next to a natural water tank in Goodman Canyon. Anthropomorph/lizard is 49 cm in height.

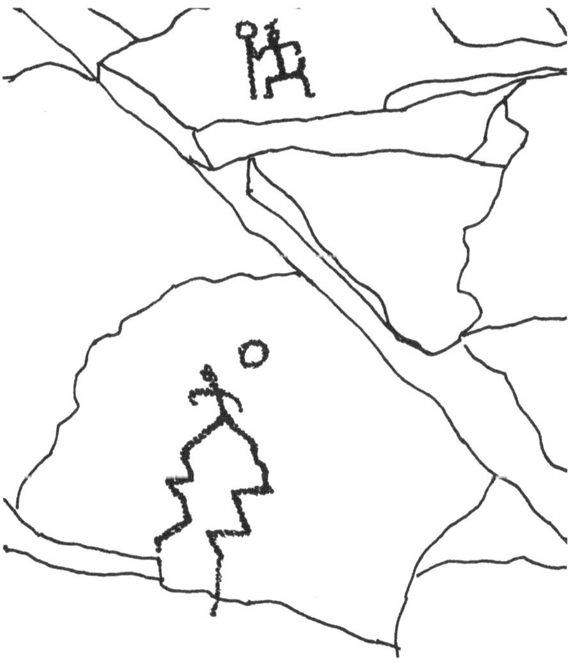

119. Anthropomorph holding cane and anthropomorph with lightning legs, upper Mormon Trail. Lower anthropomorph is 34 cm in height.

life. On a panel above a natural water tank in Goodman Canyon is an anthropomorph holding a cane below other elements that appear to be spirit beings (figure 115). An anthropomorph overlooking a wash in upper Pima Canyon holds a staff in one hand and a snake in the other, probably expressions of status and power (figure 116). An anthropomorph in Hieroglyphic Canyon holds a cane in one hand and a rakelike shape in the other. An anthropomorph or lizardman's staff is very elaborate in a panel along the Mormon Loop Trail (figure 117). There is a fancy top to a cane held by an anthropomorph in Goodman Canyon (figure 118). Adjacent to the Mormon Trail, high up on the northern side of the South Mountains, is a panel with an anthropomorph holding a staff that ends in a large ring (figure 119). Below this panel is an anthropomorph with lightning legs. Several panels in the South Mountains have multiple anthropomorphs that appear to be dancing. Often one of these individuals is holding a cane (figures 120 and 121). An elevated location in the upper portion of the 32nd Street Locality has an anthropomorph with a long crook; a small snake is located to the right of the anthropomorph. In Box Canyon, an anthropomorph holding a cane has another anthropomorph standing on top of him, surmounted by a spiral (figure 122). In the

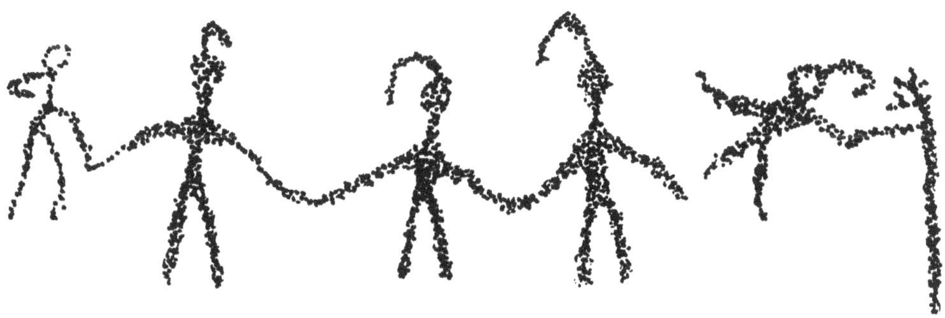

120. Anthropomorph holding cane and other anthropomorphs holding each other's hands as though dancing, 24th Street Locality. Cane is 23 cm in length.

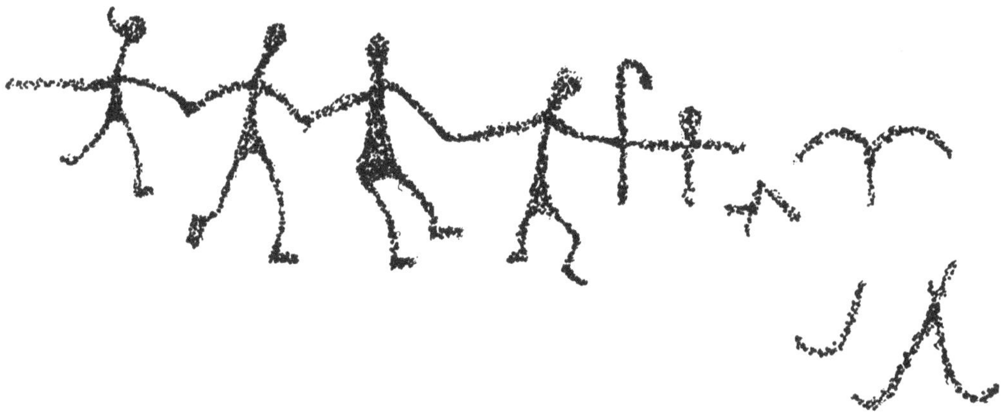

121. Anthropomorph holding cane, Kiwanis Trail. Largest anthropomorph is 18 cm in height.

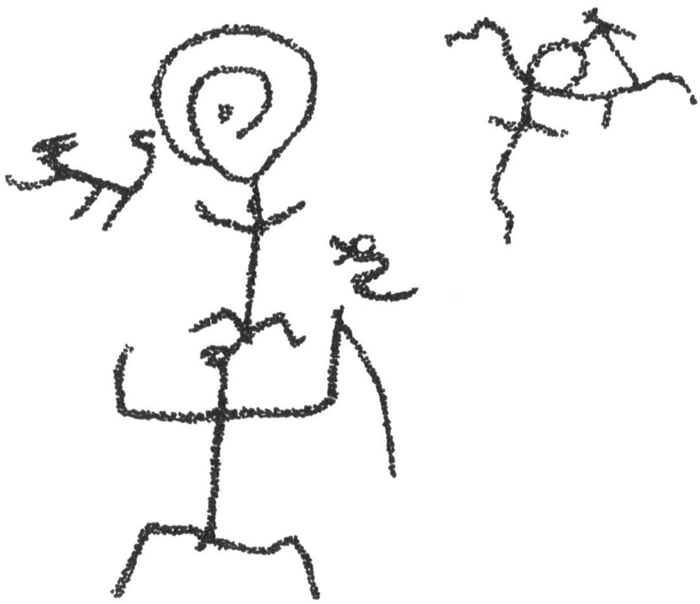

122. Anthropomorph holding cane and another anthropomorph above its head, Box Canyon. Anthropomorph with cane is 30 cm in height.

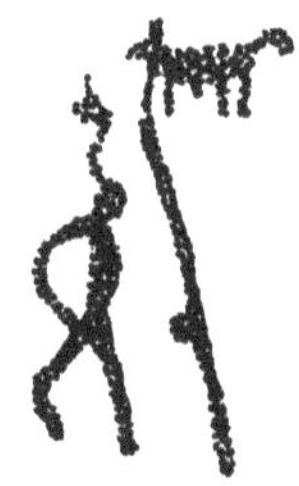

123. Anthropomorph standing beside staff with handle, 36th Street Locality. Anthropomorph is 30 cm in height.

western portion of the 36th Street Locality, an anthropomorph proudly stands next to a long staff with a handle in the middle (figure 123). In the eastern portion of this locality, an anthropomorph with a cane appears to be praying to a large anthropomorph with four arms and a headdress. Finally, an anthropomorph at the 51st Avenue site has a staff with a line connecting the staff to the anthropomorph's expanded midbody (figure 124).

Staffs, canes, and crooks are common symbols of authority and status in the American Southwest. O'odham singers carried long wooden wands, which were used in rain and curing ceremonies (Underhill 1946). Their oral traditions include

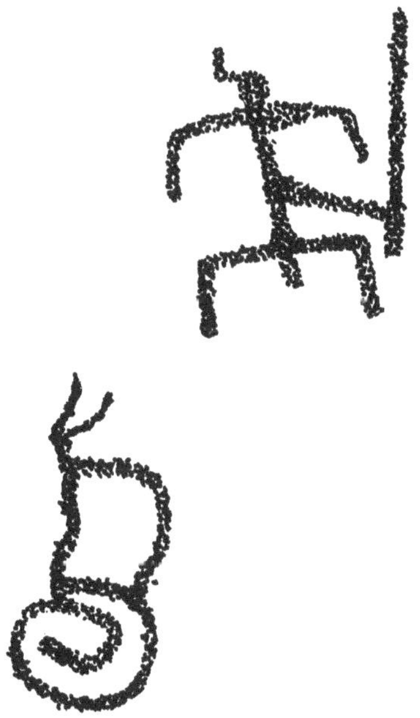

124. Anthropomorph with cane connected to midsection, 51st Avenue Locality. Anthropomorph is 18 cm in height.

accounts of shamans using canes for various magical feats. Shamans sent their canes underground to spy on their enemy's camps and also used canes to vault themselves across the heavens to escape a flood (Bahr et al. 1994). The Hopi chiefs carry a staff with a curved end, called a crook. The Hopi also place crooks at shrines and altars as prayer sticks. Pueblo Katsina dancers also carry crooks. Alexander Stephen (1936) stated that a Hopi crook represents the human body in old age: bent over looking at the earth from which we all came. The governor of Zuni Pueblo receives the official cane of authority after it has been blessed by the shamans, who breathe on the cane and handle it. Anthropologist Elsie Clews Parsons (1939:148) noted, "The canes have power; without them the officers would not be acknowledged, just as without his fetish bundle a chief was not a chief."

Humans with canes also occur on Hohokam red-on-buff pottery. Burden-basket carriers often hold canes with crooked ends. A few examples at Snaketown show individuals with a humpback, bent over, supporting themselves with a staff reminiscent of a shepherd's crook. These anthropomorph images, which appear to represent old age, have been dated only to the Colonial period (ca. A.D. 750–950) at Snaketown (Haury 1976).

Anthropomorphs and Snakes

A number of panels have anthropomorphs holding snakes in their hands (figures 125 and 126), standing next to snakes (figures 127–129), or having snakes as legs (figures 130 and 131). In Beverly Canyon, an image of a two-headed snake is next to an anthropomorph (figure 132). In the 36th Street Locality, an anthropomorph with four arms holds a snake.

Snakes may represent shaman spirit helpers. Alternatively, they could be actual snakes held by ceremonial participants. The Hopi still perform an annual snake-dance ceremony in which live rattlesnakes are handled by the dancers. Anthropomorphs holding snakes are found as rock art images throughout the Pueblo culture of the Colorado Plateau and Rio Grande regions (Schaafsma 1992; Slifer 2000).

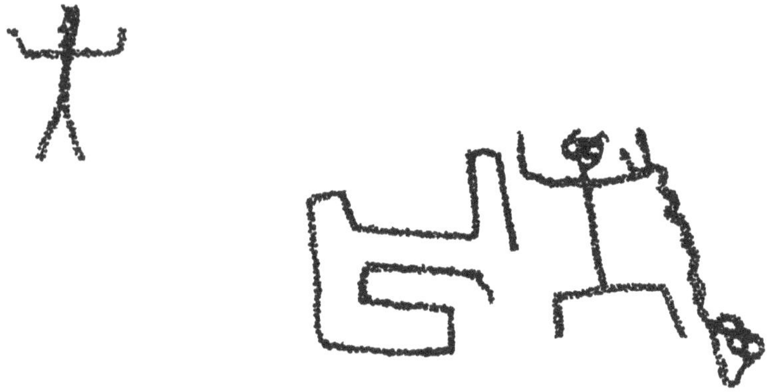

125. Anthropomorph holding snake, 36th Street. Anthropomorph is 27 cm in height.

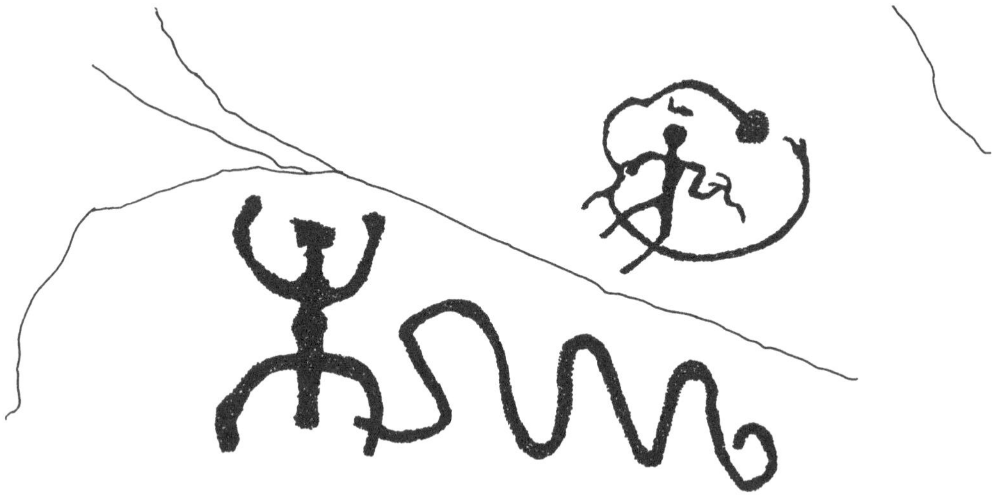

126. Anthropomorphs and snakes, Hieroglyphic Canyon. These figures suggest a snake dance similar to that of the Hopi. Lower anthropomorph is 15 cm in height.

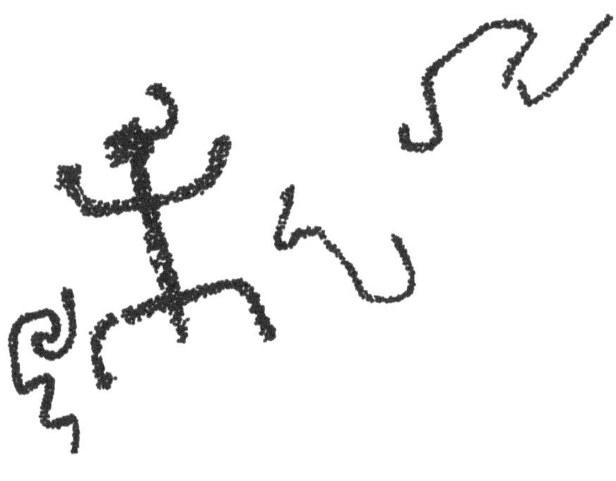

127. Anthropomorph flanked by snakes, 28th Place Locality. Anthropomorph is 17 cm in height.

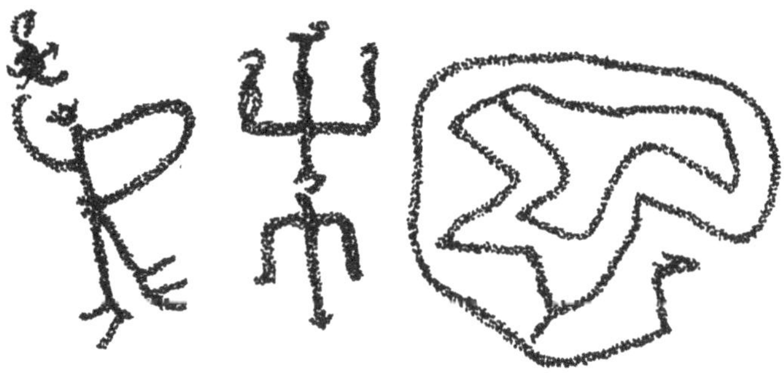

128. Unusual anthropomorphs holding objects beside coiled snake, Hieroglyphic Canyon. Anthropomorph on right is 28 cm in height.

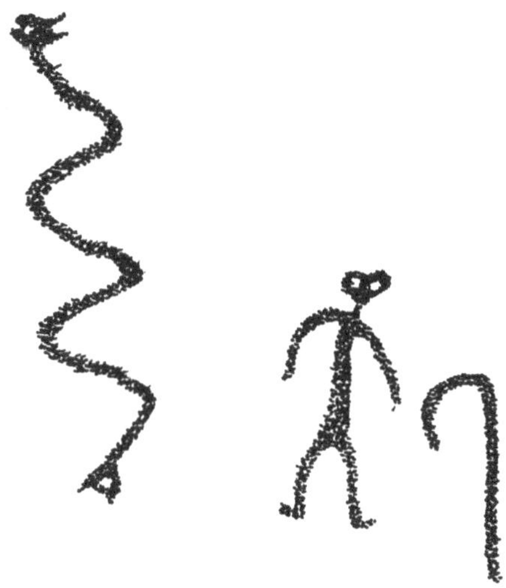

129. Anthropomorph, cane, and horned snake, Hieroglyphic Canyon. Anthropomorph is 17 cm in height.

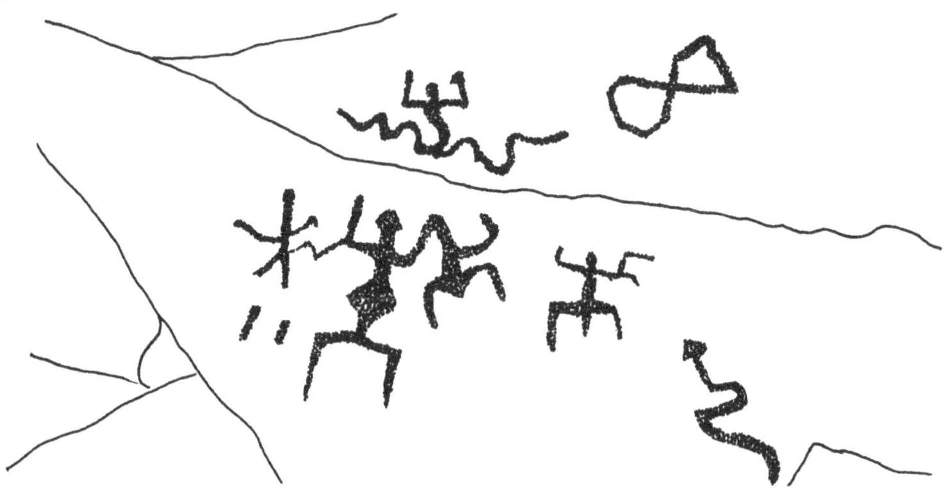

130. Anthropomorph with snake legs adjacent to a figure eight, Box Canyon. This anthropomorph is 19 cm in height. Four other anthropomorphs and a curved snake are present below the snake-legged anthropomorph.

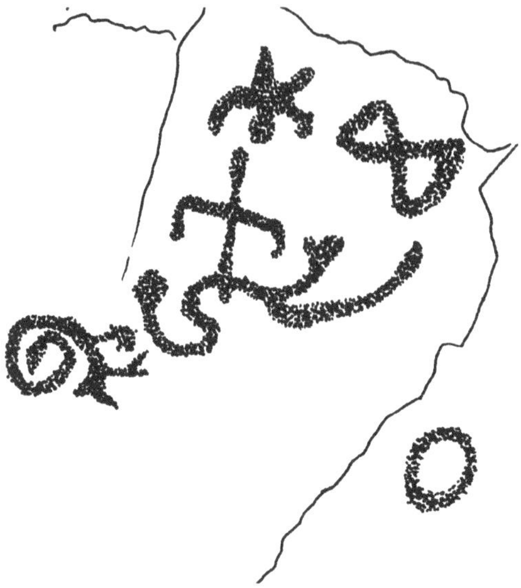

131. Anthropomorph with snake legs adjacent to a figure eight and other designs, Box Canyon. Figure eight is 11 x 7 cm.

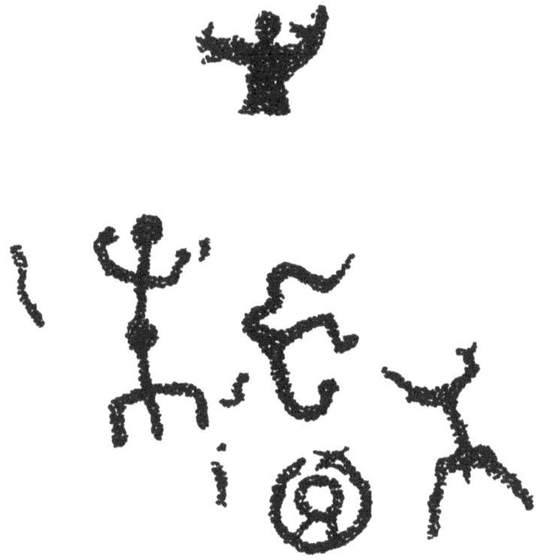

132. Anthropomorphs, thunderbird, and two-headed snake, Beverly Canyon. Anthropomorph on left is 26 cm in height.

Hunt Scenes

Anthropomorphs hunting four-legged mammals occur as rock art scenes in several locations. In all these hunt scenes, the humans are holding bows and arrows, pointing them at a large four-legged mammal. A hunter with a fancy headdress is present along the Mormon Loop Trail (figure 133). An unusual panel in the 32nd Street Locality has the hunter in profile, with his body a thick, single line as though depicting his legs close together (figure 134). In the Upper 12th Street Locality, a hunter occurs next to an anthropomorph playing a flute or possibly holding a blowgun (figure 135). At the 7th Street Locality, two different scenes on the same large panel show hunters with bows and arrows aimed at mountain sheep, and two anthropomorphs hold a "string" along which six or seven animals are walking (figure 136). A hunter in a panel in Hieroglyphic Canyon is pointing his bow and arrow at a faint mountain sheep but is looking in the opposite direction (figure 137). Panels in the 16th Street Locality have hunters pointing their bows upward at quadrupeds (figures 138 and 139). One of these panels also has an anthropomorph holding a crook. The panel in the 36th Street Locality shows four deer (and their tracks) being dispatched by a hunter using a bow and arrow (see figure 73).

The O'odham used a short self-bow made of mulberry wood to hunt large game such as deer and mountain sheep. Frank Hamilton Cushing (1890) observed that the O'odham were the best Indian archers he had seen during his travels in the American Southwest, especially at long distances.

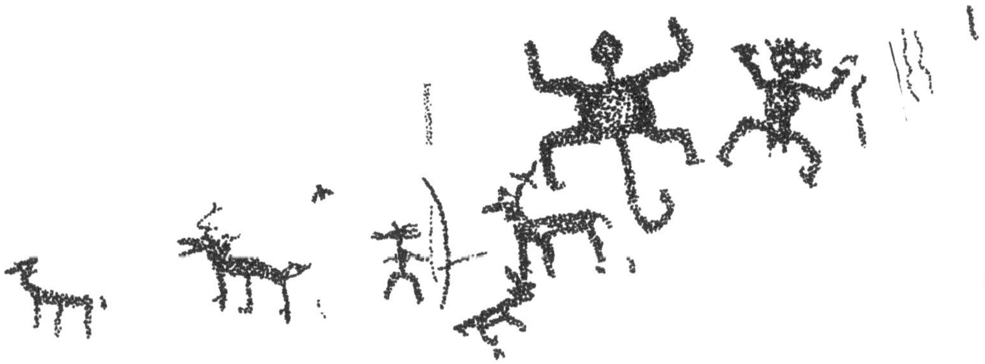

133. Hunter with bow and arrow among four quadrupeds, a lizard, and an unusual anthropomorph, Mormon Loop Trail. Anthropomorph holding bow is 8 cm in height.

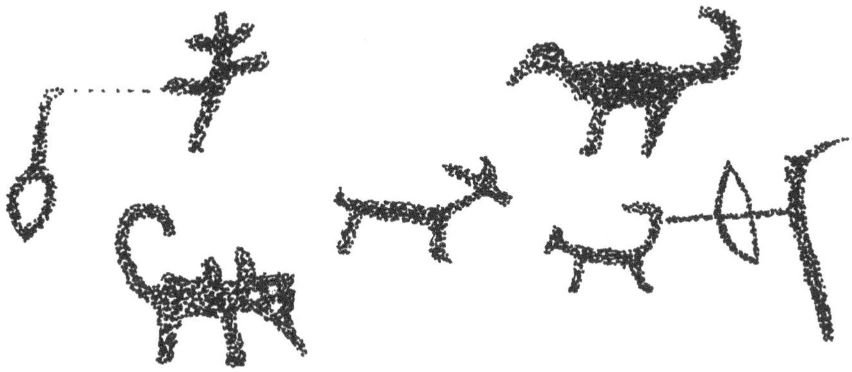

134. Hunter (legs together in a single line) with bow and arrow pointed at several quadrupeds, 32nd Street Locality. Anthropomorph is 16 cm in height.

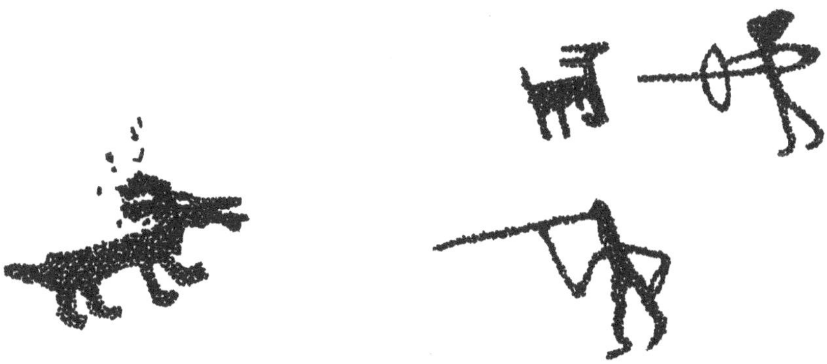

135. Hunter and anthropomorph holding a flute or blowgun, Upper 12th Street Locality.

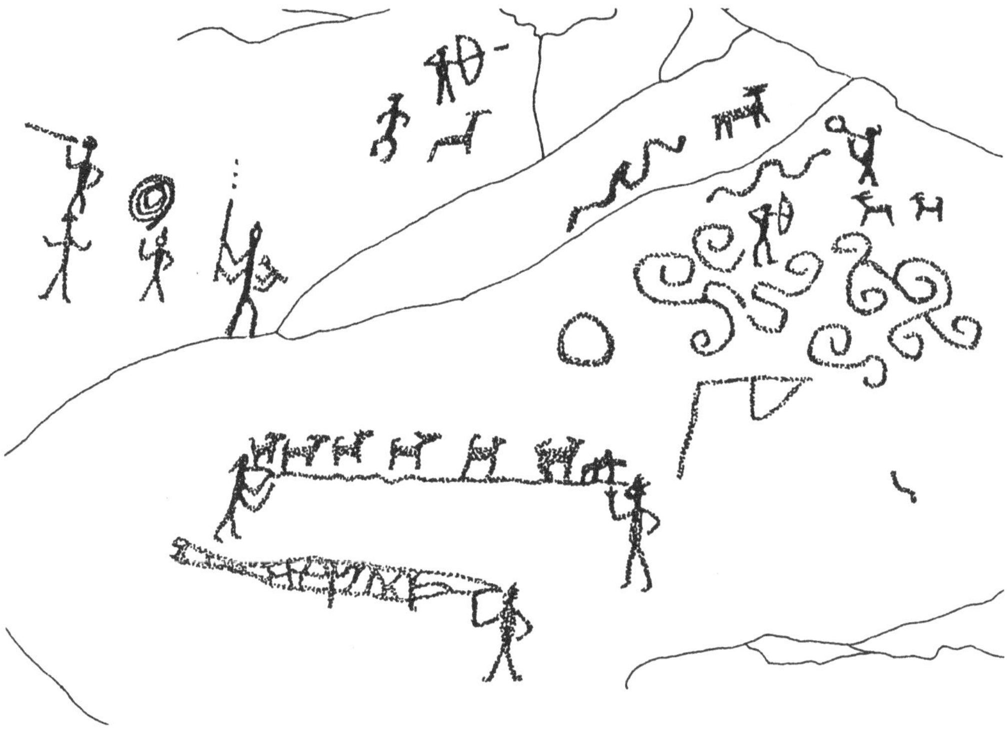

136. Hunters, acrobats, and flute-player, 7th Street Locality. Anthropomorph on right, holding a "string" on which animals are walking, is 20 cm in height. Four anthropomorphs in upper left are holding large objects and may be acrobats.

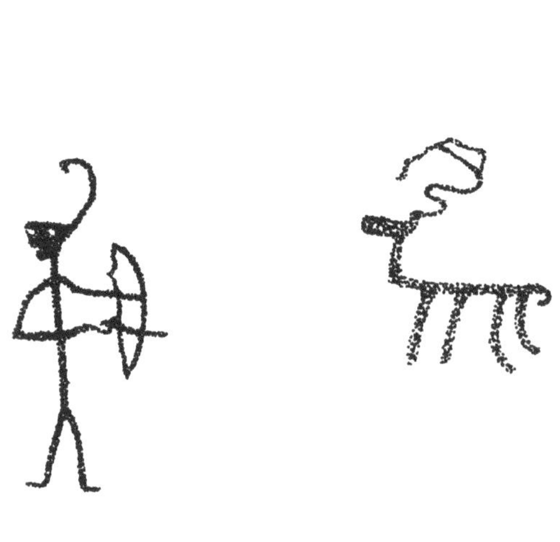

137. Hunter looking away from a quadruped, Hieroglyphic Canyon. Hunter is 28 cm in height.

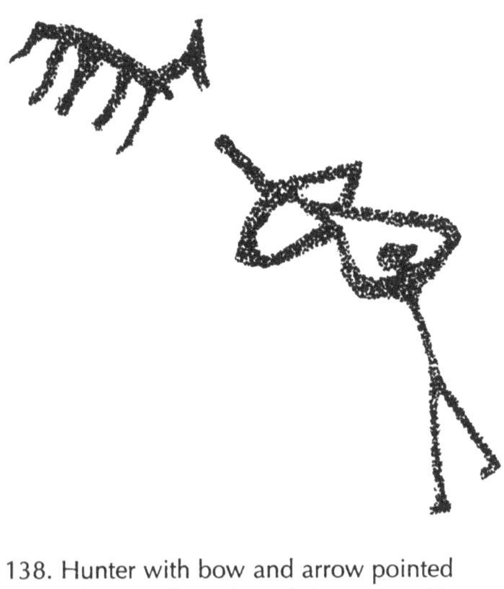

138. Hunter with bow and arrow pointed upward at quadruped, 16th Street Locality. Anthropomorph is 19 cm in height.

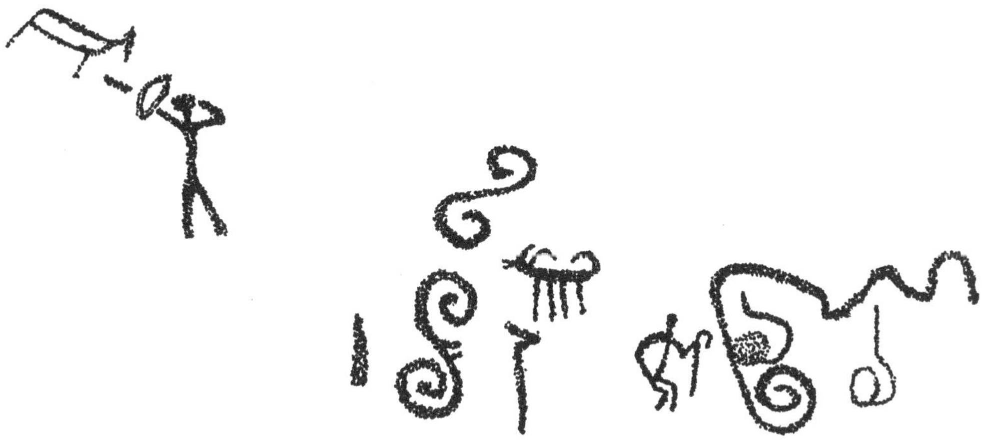

139. Hunter firing arrow upward at a quadruped, 16th Street Locality. Anthropomorph holding staff is 13 cm in height.

No hunt scenes have been found in the South Mountains that show hunters using an atlatl, a weapon associated with the Archaic people who hunted the area before the agricultural Hohokam. A few examples of the weapon itself, however, may be depicted (see chapter 3).

Archaeologist David Whitley (1994) has argued that most hunting scenes in North American rock art are shamanistic images. Rather than literal depictions of animal hunts, these images represent shamans seeking spirit helpers, specifically bighorn sheep, which are powerfully associated with rain and wind.

Dancing Anthropomorphs

A small number of panels have several anthropomorphs in a row, often holding each other's hands in apparent dance scenes. Usually, four or five individuals are present. Examples of these activity scenes occur at several localities. Sometimes one of the dancers in each group holds a cane or staff. The panel in Pima Canyon first illustrated by Cushing (1890:178) is an excellent example of a dance scene (figure 140). A portion of a complex panel in the 32nd Street Locality has several anthropomorphs in lively postures suggesting rhythmic movement (figure 141). Other panels with dancing individuals are found in Box Canyon, at the Twin Buttes Locality, and in Goodman Canyon (figure 142). An unusual panel on the eastern side of Box Canyon has four standing humans holding a line over their heads; another line is attached to the neck of a person who is sitting nearby (figure 143).

Dancing figures also occur on Hohokam painted pottery. These dancers are shown as stylized figures and lack details of gender or dress. They move in circles around the decorative field of the vessel or diagonally through it in bands, with arms connected. The most frequent manner of depiction on pottery is as a string

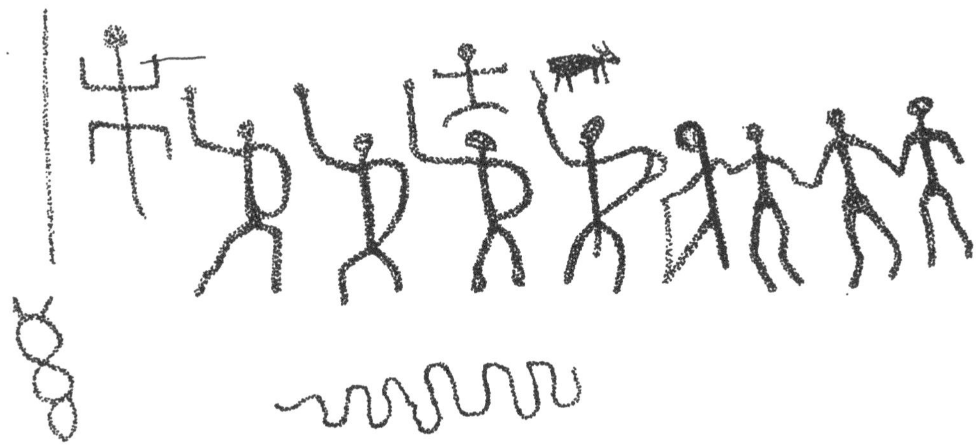

140. Dancers, upper Pima Canyon. This panel was sketched by Frank Hamilton Cushing in the late 1880s and photographed in the 1890s. Small, upper central anthropomorph is 10 cm in height.

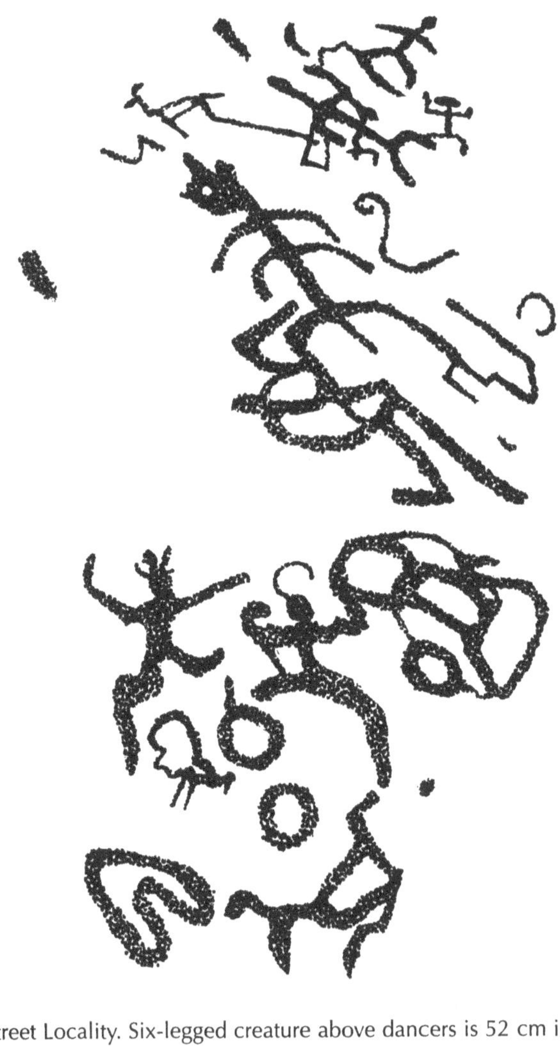

141. Dancers, 32nd Street Locality. Six-legged creature above dancers is 52 cm in length.

of dancers between painted fringes. According to Emil Haury (1976:237), "The emphasis placed on this art motif strongly reflects not only the Hohokam fondness for dancing but the nature of their dancing, a group or circle type. Russell's observations of Pima dancing appear to fit the aboriginal situation well . . . : 'The dancers stood in a circle with arms extended across the shoulders of those adjoining. This position did not permit much freedom, and movements were confined to stamping the feet and bending the body.'" Archie Russell, an Akimel O'odham, identified (to me) dancers in several rock art panels he observed in Box Canyon.

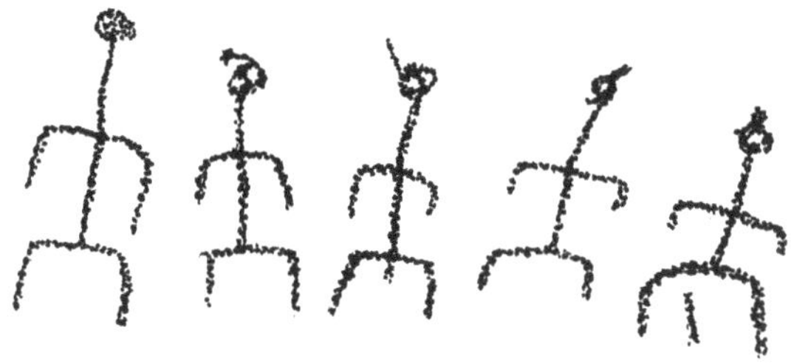

142. Dancers, Goodman Canyon. Anthropomorph on far right is 13 cm in height.

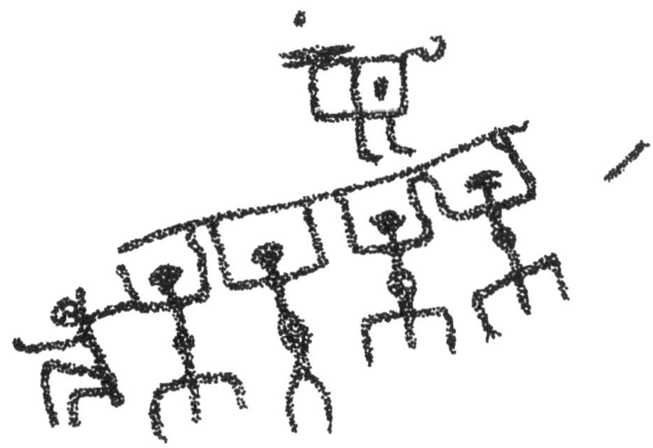

143. Dancers holding line over their heads, eastern side of Box Canyon. Center anthropomorph is 29 cm in height.

Acrobats

A SMALL NUMBER of rock art panels appear to be humans conducting acrobatic feats. In the 7th Street Locality, a large panel has several anthropomorphs that seem to be performing acts of skill (see figure 136). One anthropomorph is standing on the head of another and playing a flute. The bottom anthropomorph has outstretched arms as though to demonstrate his balancing skills. An anthropomorph just to the right of these two acrobats has a spiral perched on his head, and another anthropomorph farther to the right is holding a long staff and has a small animal on his back. A panel at the San Juan North Locality shows two individuals that are balancing one on top of the other, the lower anthropomorph holding the legs of the upper one, who has two horns and is holding a zigzag line in his right hand (figure 144). A deer is present to the left and above the two acrobats. In Hidden Valley, a panel has two large anthropomorphs that appear to be balancing one above the other, with their arms curved into circle forms.

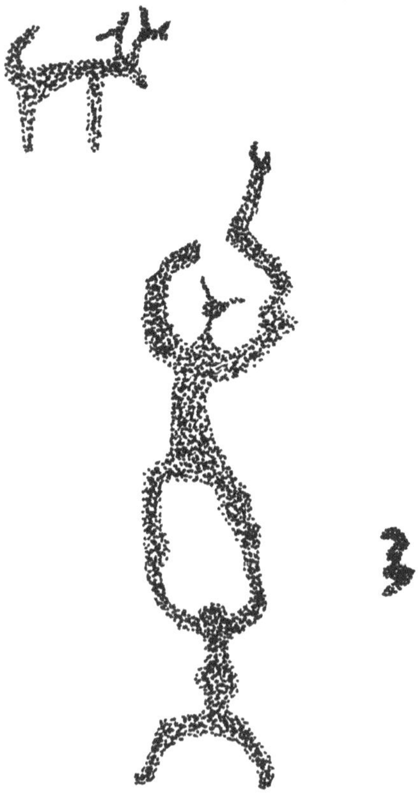

144. Acrobats and deer, San Juan North Locality. Lower anthropomorph is 21 cm in height.

Anthropomorphs and Geometric Designs

Numerous rock art panels have anthropomorphs in association with a variety of geometric elements, especially different types of circles. An anthropomorph in Hieroglyphic Canyon is attached to a spiral and a pregnant quadruped by a wavy line, perhaps representing a life force (figure 145). In Hidden Valley, a panel has an anthropomorph holding a shieldlike circle. Other panels have anthropomorphs in association with multiple concentric circles, almost as if the panel depicts humans watching a night sky or contemplating portals into the otherworld. Good examples of these are in the 27th Street Locality and the 28th Place Locality. In addition, a number of panels have anthropomorphs in association with circles, circles with dots, starlike crosses, and sun disks. These panels may have astronomical significance and are discussed in chapter 10.

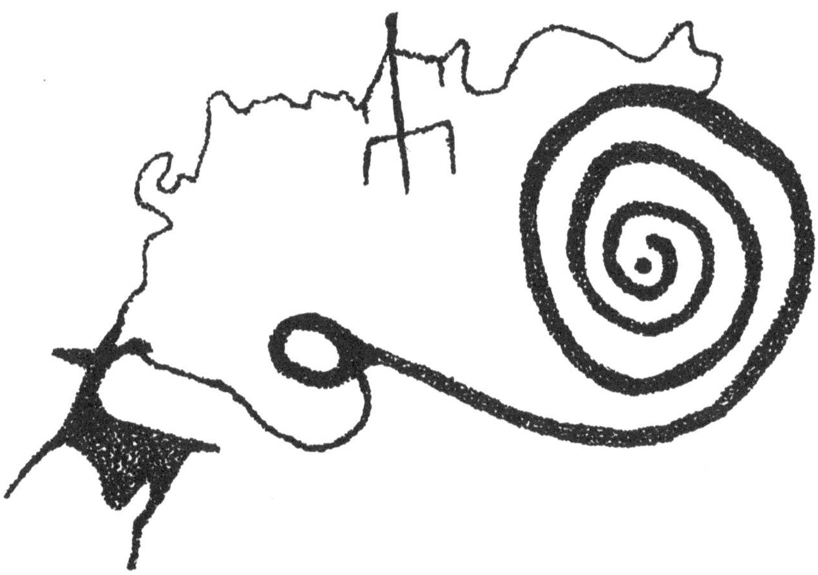

145. Anthropomorph attached by wavy lines, possibly energy or life-force connections, to pregnant quadruped and spiral, Hieroglyphic Canyon. Spiral is 13 cm in diameter (top to bottom).

Gender

North American Indian rock art is known to contain depictions of human sexuality and gender symbols (Hunger 1982; Slifer 2000; Wellmann 1974). This is also true for Hohokam rock art (Wallace and Holmlund 1986). Determining the gender of all anthropomorphs, however, is not possible.[1]

Although many anthropomorph images in the South Mountains have a penis, it cannot be assumed that all others are females. Female anthropomorphs are more difficult to identify, because anthropomorphs with female genitalia or breasts are rare in Hohokam art in general and in the rock art of the South Mountains in particular. Three anthropomorph petroglyphs, however, do appear to be females. One of these is in upper Pima Canyon at Johnson Camp (figure 146). This individual has what appears to be large breasts, although they also could represent a large stomach. The wavy lines may be life-force lines connecting her (it) to nearby anthropomorphs.

Another example is clearly a female. This large anthropomorph is located on a panel along a wash high up in Goodman Canyon (figure 147). The creator of this panel gave the anthropomorph a pair of small breasts and incorporated into the groin area a natural hole in the rock face that has a red water stain, perhaps representing menstrual flow.

A third example is a panel in lower Pima Canyon that shows two anthropomorphs holding hands. One of these figures has a straight line for a torso, which ends

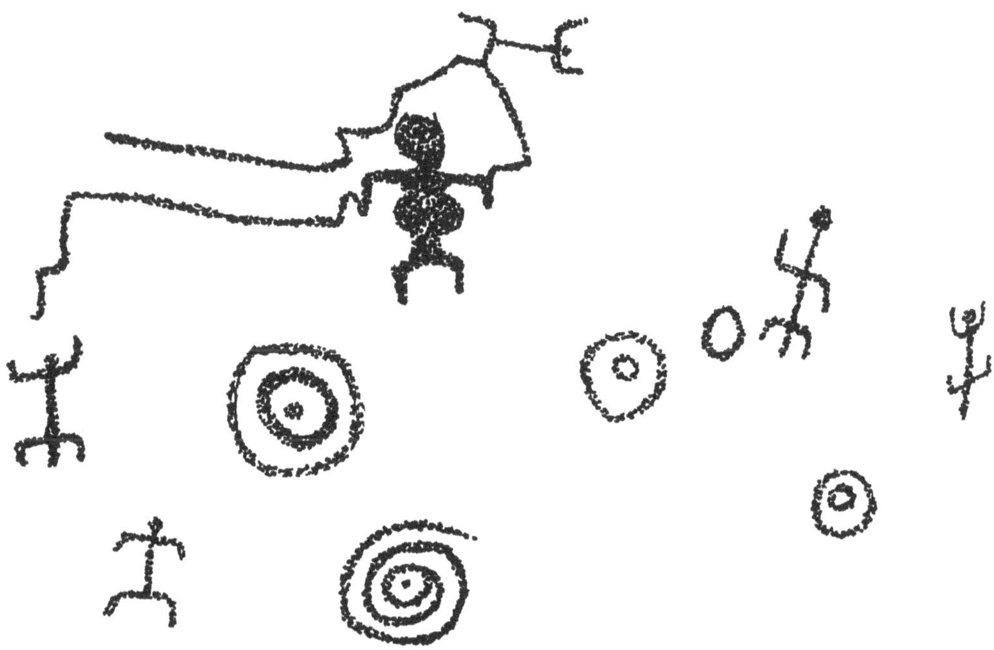

146. Possible female anthropomorph with what could be life-force lines, upper Pima Canyon. Female is 20 cm in height.

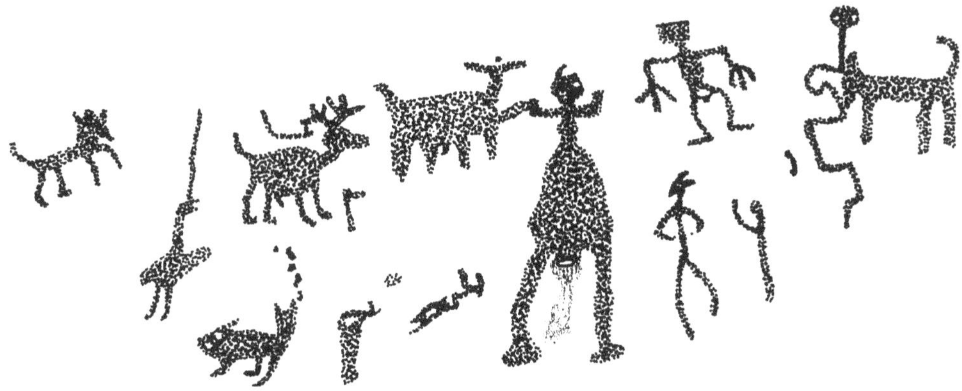

147. Female anthropomorph, upper Goodman Canyon. Natural, red-colored cavity in the rock face was incorporated into the female figure, giving the appearance of menstrual flow. Female anthropomorph is 36 cm in height.

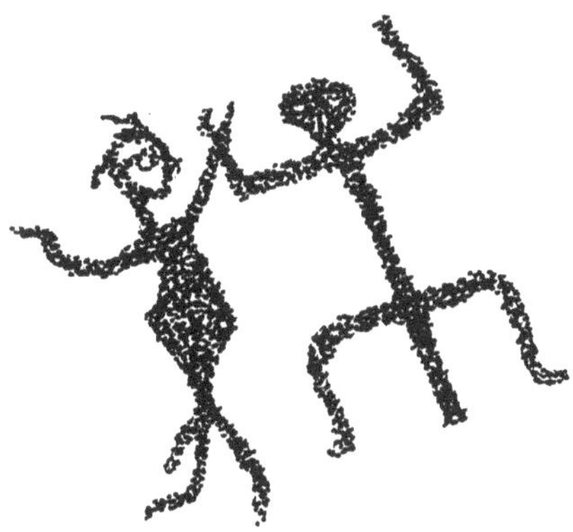

148. Possible male and female partners, Pima Canyon. Both anthropomorphs are 21 cm in height.

in a short penis, depicting a male. The other figure has a triangular torso with a possible sash behind the waist. The latter anthropomorph may be a female (figure 148).

Thus far, we have not found any vulva symbols in the South Mountains. These petroglyphs, characterized as bisected ovals and triangles, are present in the Zuni area and other parts of the Southwest (Slifer 2000), as well as throughout the Great Basin region (Woody and McLune 2000).

Sexual Scenes

Sexual scenes are uncommon in the rock art of the South Mountains, as they are for Hohokam rock art in general. Nonetheless, we found two examples. One panel in Hieroglyphic Canyon shows an anthropomorph seemingly holding a linear object in one hand as well as the back of another anthropomorph, who appears to have an erection and be wearing a bird mask (see figure 164). The other sexual scene is in the 16th Street Locality (figure 149). In this large, complex panel, a well-endowed and erect male is holding another individual from behind.

Spirit Beings

Some anthropomorph images in the South Mountains are not exactly human-like and probably represent spirit beings. While most anthropomorphs vary in size

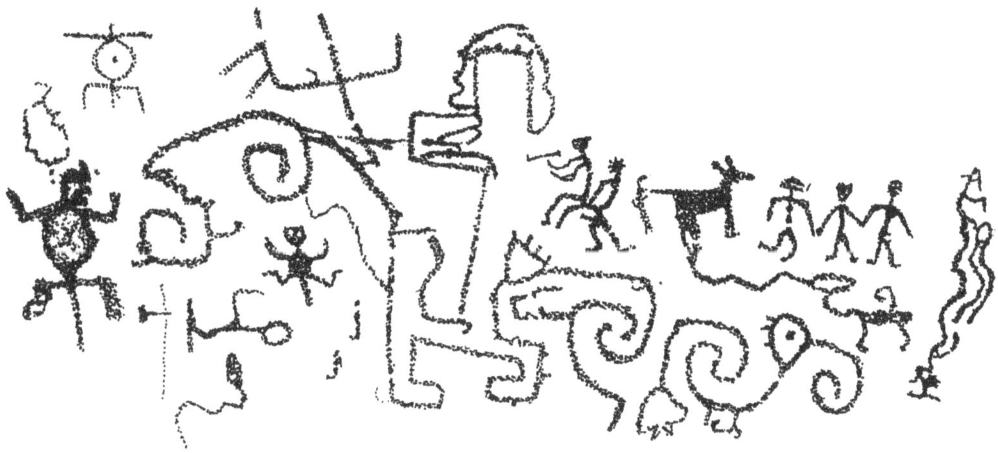

149. Sexual scene, 16th Street Locality; other portions of panel are not shown. Anthropomorph with flute is 13 cm in height.

from 9 cm to 24 cm in height, spirit beings are generally taller. In a few panels, incomplete anthropomorphs appear to be emerging from the stone, such as one on the southwestern side of Box Canyon (see figure 70). Some anthropomorphs have exaggerated characteristics: often these stick-figure anthropomorphs are large and have very long legs, giving them an ominous appearance. Good examples are present in Beverly Canyon, Goodman Canyon (figure 150), the lower and upper portions of the 32nd Street Locality (figure 151), Mormon Trail, Hieroglyphic Canyon (figure 152), the Southwest Side Locality, and Box Canyon. The large anthropomorph petroglyph in Beverly Canyon, at more than 3 feet (1 m) in height, is the tallest one in the South Mountains (see figure 105); unfortunately, this panel has been badly vandalized. Giants are mentioned in some O'odham oral traditions, and perhaps some of the long-legged anthropomorphs represent these giants.

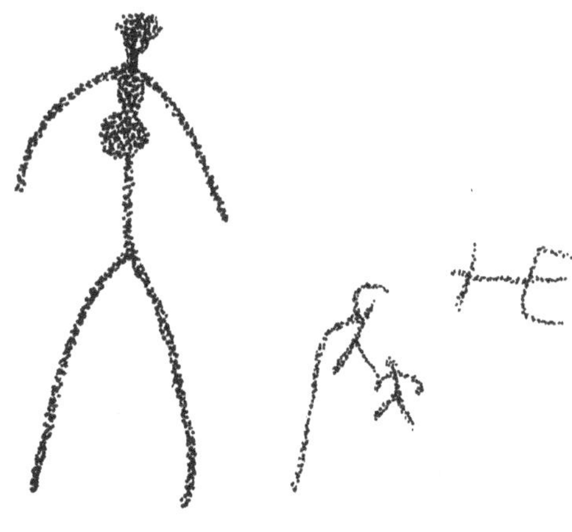

150. Large spirit being (left) and smaller anthropomorphs above spring in upper Goodman Canyon. Spirit being is 53 cm in height.

An interesting panel in the upper, southern end of Box Canyon has an anthropomorph with two large antennae (figure 153). This anthropomorph is holding a circle with a central dot, which is also being held by a smaller anthropomorph without antennae. The scene has the appearance of a shaman making a connection with his spirit helper through a portal, expressed by the circle, into the otherworld. Many other panels, including one with a pipette, are located at this natural water tank.

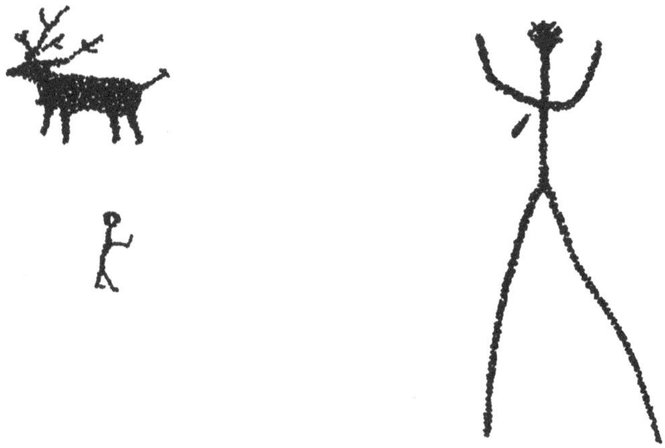

151. Large spirit being with smaller anthropomorph and deer, upper 32nd Street Locality. Spirit being is 60 cm in height.

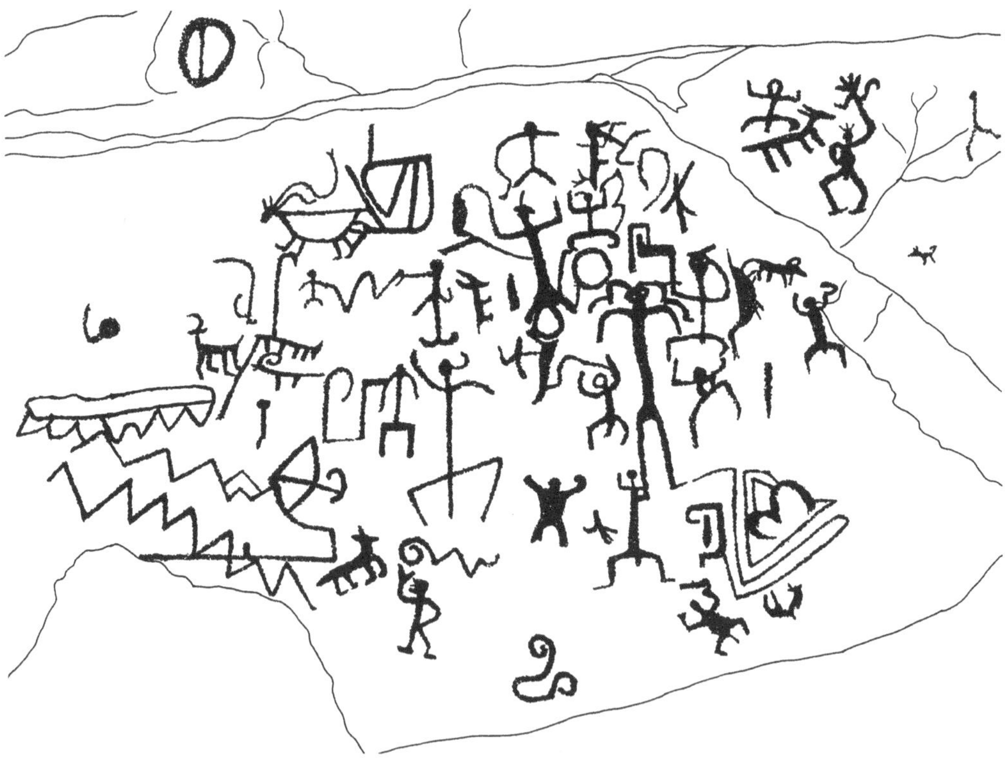

152. Large spirit being among numerous other anthropomorphs, quadrupeds, and geometric designs, Hieroglyphic Canyon. Large, central spirit being is 49 cm in height.

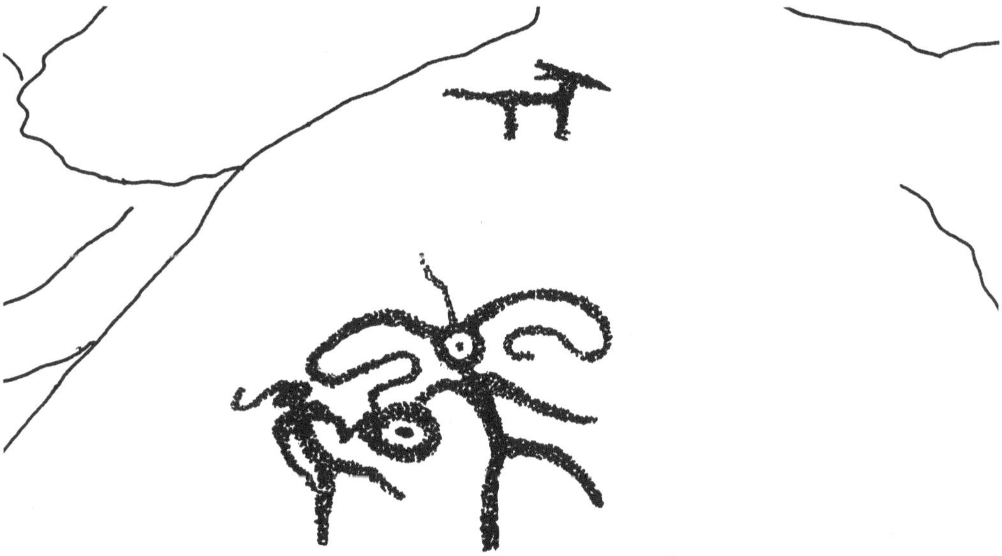

153. Spirit being with possible antennae and smaller anthropomorph next to a natural water tank at the southern end of Box Canyon. Spirit being is 45 cm in height.

A panel in an upper side canyon of Box Canyon has a small anthropomorph holding the leg of an anthropomorph twice its size (figure 154). Above the head of the larger anthropomorph is a large and elaborate rectilinear scroll.

Along the Mormon Loop Trail is a relatively large rock shelter in a cluster of boulders that contain abundant petroglyphs. One of the panels contains an interesting scene in which a square-bodied anthropomorph or spirit being is connected to a line that takes the form of a figure eight (figure 155). Other elements also are present. The panel is visible from the trail and may be a trail marker (Holden 1980).

In the upper reaches of the 32nd Street Locality, overlooking the Salt River Valley, we found a panel with a small anthropomorph connected to a large anthropomorph (figure 156). A thick, wavy line flows from the larger anthropomorph into and through the smaller one, as though it is transmitting power. Is the larger anthropomorph the Hohokam equivalent of I'itoi, the O'odham's cultural hero and powerful shaman, providing life force to a follower?

Hourglass Anthropomorphs

Ever since archaeologists found distinctive hourglass human designs on red-on-buff pottery sherds at the famous site of Snaketown in the 1930s, this particular design has been thought to be uniquely Hohokam. It is not, of course, but indeed the hourglass figure has become almost an icon for the Hohokam culture. Our study, however, revealed that this element is rare in the South Mountains

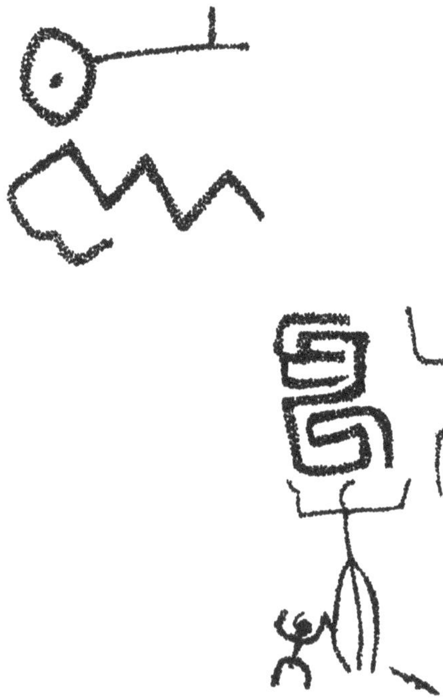

154. Spirit being with smaller anthropomorph holding its leg, along upper trail on the eastern side of Box Canyon. Central spirit being is 43 cm in height.

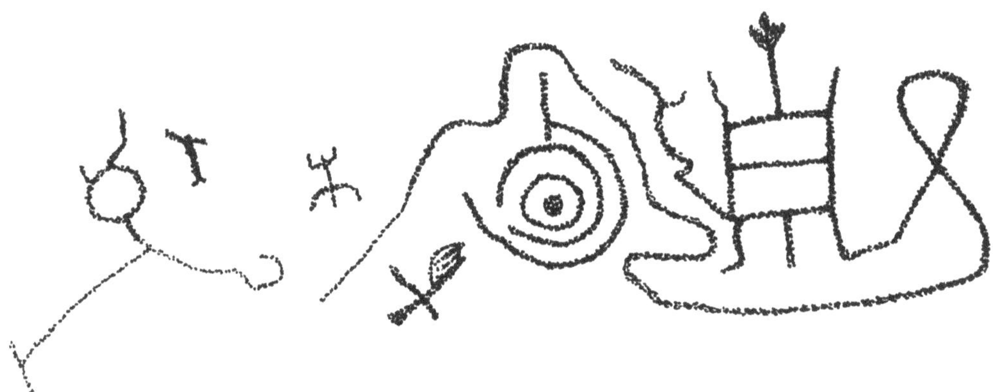

155. Spirit being with square body, Mormon Loop Trail. Panel is located next to a rock shelter along a trail and may be a trail marker. Spirit being is 30 cm in height.

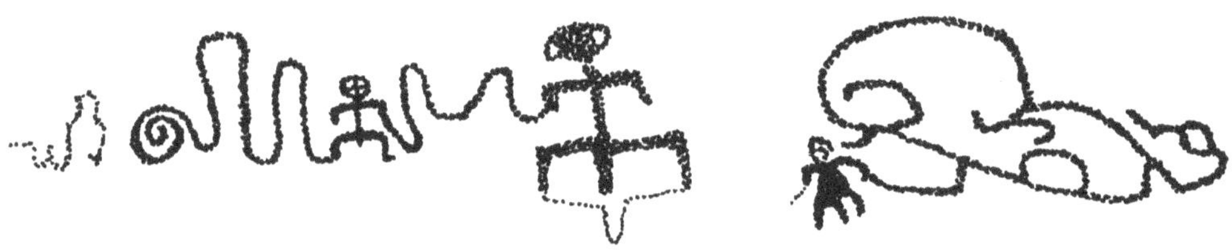

156. Spirit being transferring energy to a smaller masked anthropomorph, 32nd Street Locality. Large spirit being is 37 cm in height. Another small anthropomorph holds a meandering line on the right side of the panel.

petroglyphs: of more than two thousand anthropomorph petroglyphs, only fourteen have hourglass bodies (figure 157). Eleven of the fourteen petroglyphs are concentrated in Box Canyon; eight of these are on the western side of the canyon. The other three hourglass anthropomorphs are located in three different canyons east of Box Canyon.

Hourglass anthropomorphs occur alone and in panels with other elements. They vary in details, and no two are exactly alike; the most obvious difference is that some have hollow bodies and others are solid. One of the hourglass anthropomorphs in a panel on Bird Hill is holding a crook, and an hourglass anthropomorph in another panel has a rabbitlike face (figure 158). Another hourglass anthropomorph in this area has appendages attached to its elbows and unnatural legs.

Three prominent examples of hourglass anthropomorphs in Box Canyon include one on the eastern side that is surrounded by at least ten quadrupeds. Two or more of the quadrupeds are touching this figure, suggesting that the anthropomorph has spirit helpers or "pets." Another hourglass anthropomorph, located inside a split boulder, has upraised arms and has been placed next to two unusual bird images (figure 159). The third example has upraised arms and occurs with a bird image and other designs, including a dramatic sun symbol (now destroyed). This hourglass figure has fingers or rakelike objects in both hands, plus elbow appendages (see figure 157, *second row from top, second image from left*).

The other locations with hourglass anthropomorphs are all east of Box Canyon. An isolated panel about one-quarter mile (0.4 km) northeast of Box Canyon contains a single hourglass anthropomorph. This figure has the typical upraised arms and bent legs but has a bizarre head or headdress and a solidly pecked chest area (see figure 157, *bottom left*).

Approximately one mile (1.6 km) east of Box Canyon is a trail that follows a major wash up into the mountains. Midway up the canyon is an hourglass anthropomorph that has downward-pointing arms, straight legs, and an incomplete head shape (see figure 157, *bottom center*). The left hand is holding a bow with an arrow that follows a crack in the rock. The edge of the boulder above the figure's head has been chipped to form a shallow notch.

Farther east, about 3.75 miles (6 km) from Box Canyon, is the 32nd Street Locality. A panel there has an elaborate scene containing an hourglass anthropomorph, five quadrupeds, a rectilinear and a curvilinear spiral, a sun disk, a snake, and a double scroll (figure 160). The hourglass figure holds a line attached to the scroll. This panel faces the summer solstice sunrise.

Other Hourglass Designs

We also recorded seven hourglass designs that are not anthropomorphs. Four of these shapes are in Box Canyon, and single hourglass elements occur in three other areas.

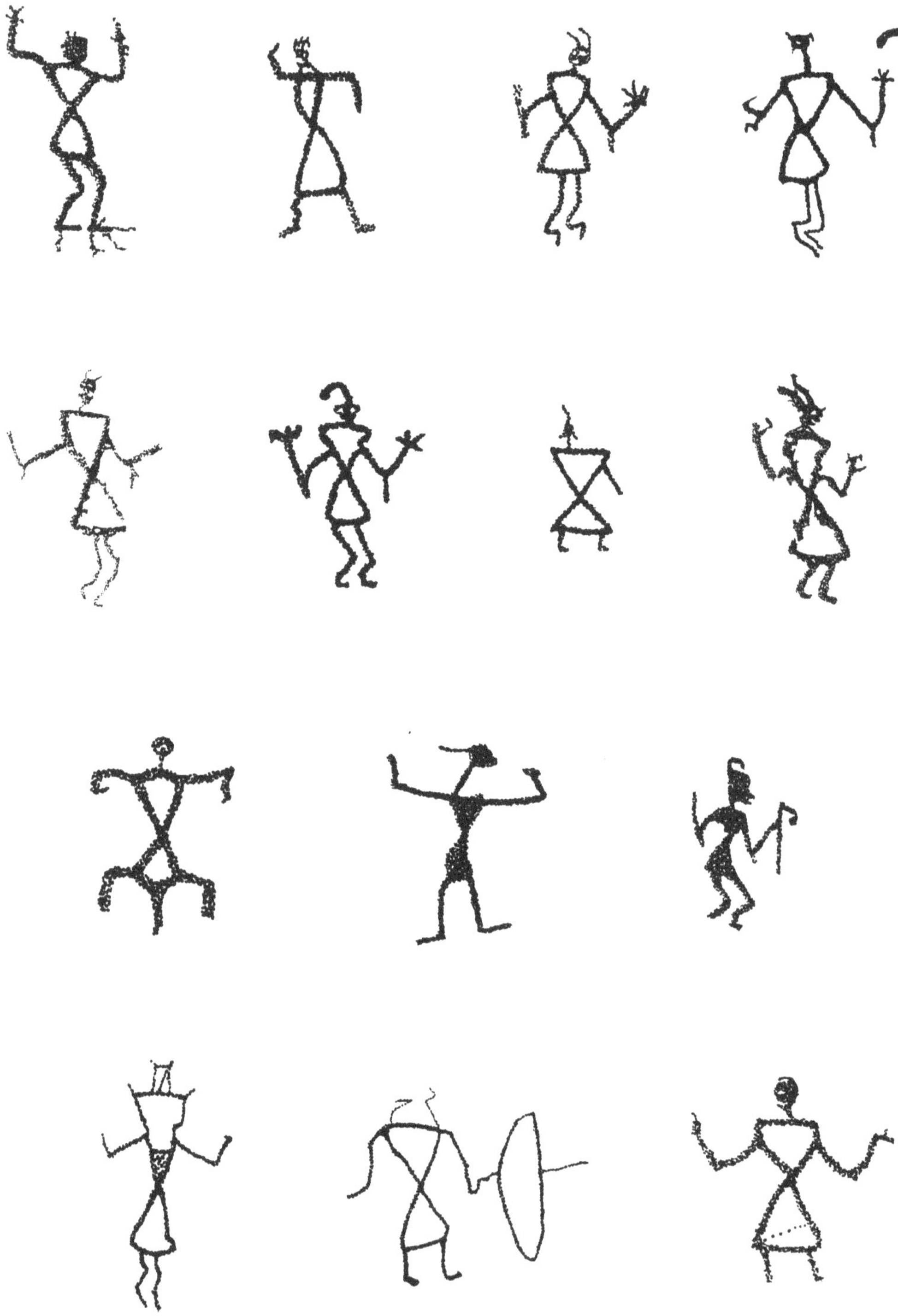

157. Hourglass anthropomorph petroglyphs in the South Mountains, various locations (from Bostwick 2000): **top three rows,** Box Canyon; **bottom left,** 12th Street Locality; **bottom center,** 16th Street Locality; **bottom right,** 32nd Street Locality. Petroglyphs vary from 23 to 47 cm in height.

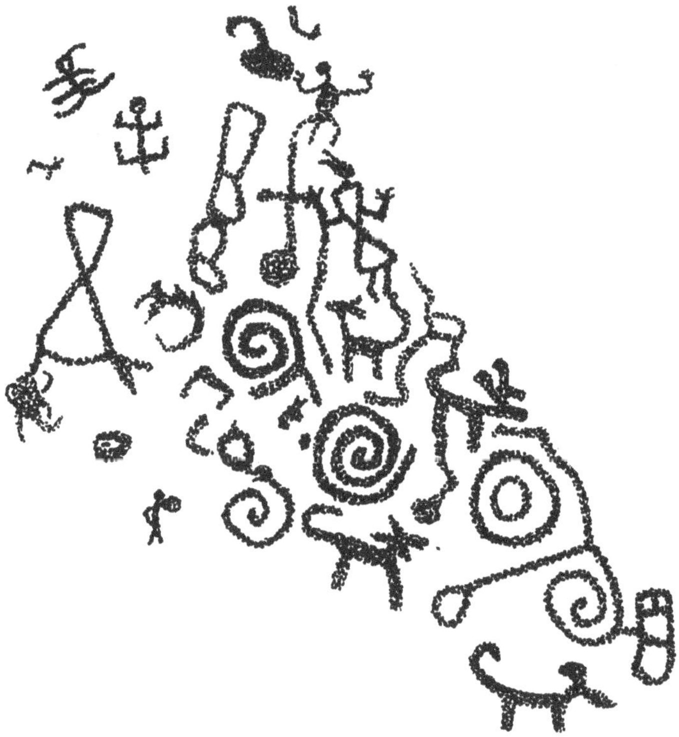

158. Hourglass anthropomorph with rabbitlike head in the middle of a complex panel, Box Canyon. Hourglass anthropomorph is 28 cm in height.

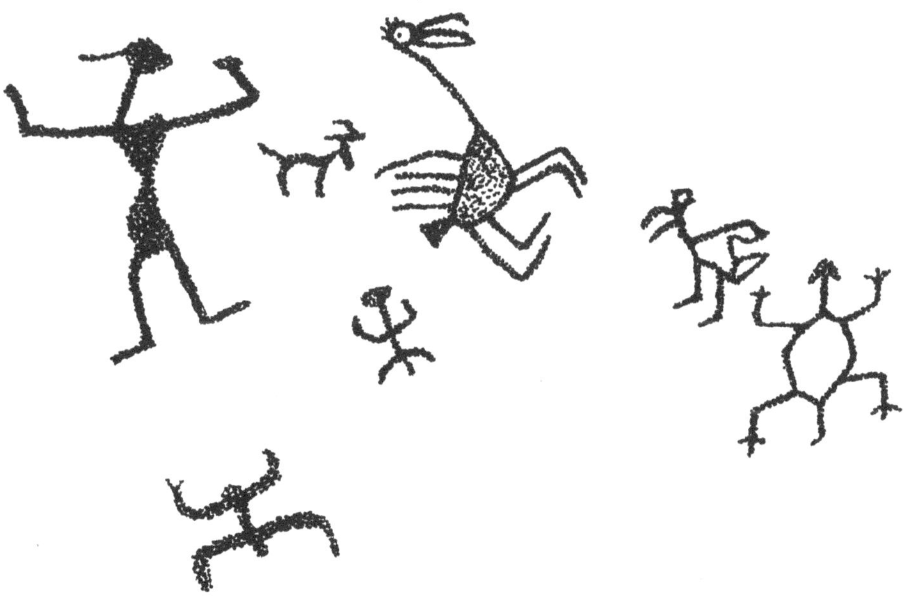

159. Hourglass anthropomorph with four-legged bird and other petroglyphs located inside a rock cleft on the eastern side of Box Canyon. Bird with four legs is 47 cm in length.

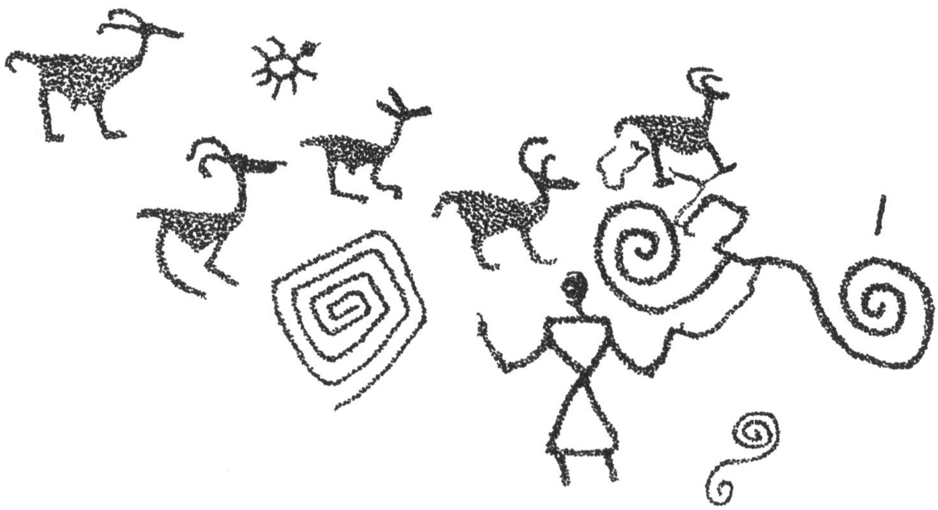

160. Hourglass anthropomorph attached to double spiral, 32nd Street Locality. Anthropomorph is 36 x 41 cm. Panel faces northeast.

An hourglass form in Box Canyon has a short appendage to the middle of its upper line and appears "twisted" in the middle (figure 161). A panel in upper Pima Canyon contains an hourglass element next to a stylized stick-figure quadruped and a human—all of which are reminiscent of Pueblo imagery (figure 162).

On the southern side of the mountains, at the top of a narrow ridge, is a southwest-facing panel (figure 163). In addition to an hourglass element that has numerous thin appendages attached to all sides, the panel also contains a sun, a zigzag, a stick-figure lizard and anthropomorph, two triangles, a partial triangle, and three arrow symbols. Almost all of these petroglyphs, except the arrow, are part of the roster of Hohokam images present in the Gila Style. However, the panel appears to have been pecked all at the same time and all the petroglyphs are partly repatinated, indicating that the panel is not recent. The arrows between the elements, each pointing to the next one in line, suggest a transformation. The series starts with the sun transforming into the hourglass (which appears electrified), which in turn transforms into the lizard, which then transforms into the humanlike figure. Perhaps this panel, located near the Gila River Indian Reservation, was made by an artist of the early Historic period using Hohokam rock art elements. The connection, as expressed by the arrows, between the different elements is intriguing; it suggests that the hourglass element represents the point at which supernatural power was received from the sun.

Hohokam Red-on-buff Pottery Hourglass Images

At the Hohokam village of Snaketown, hourglass anthropomorphs were painted on pottery in a variety of poses. Many of these are multiple figures that appear to be

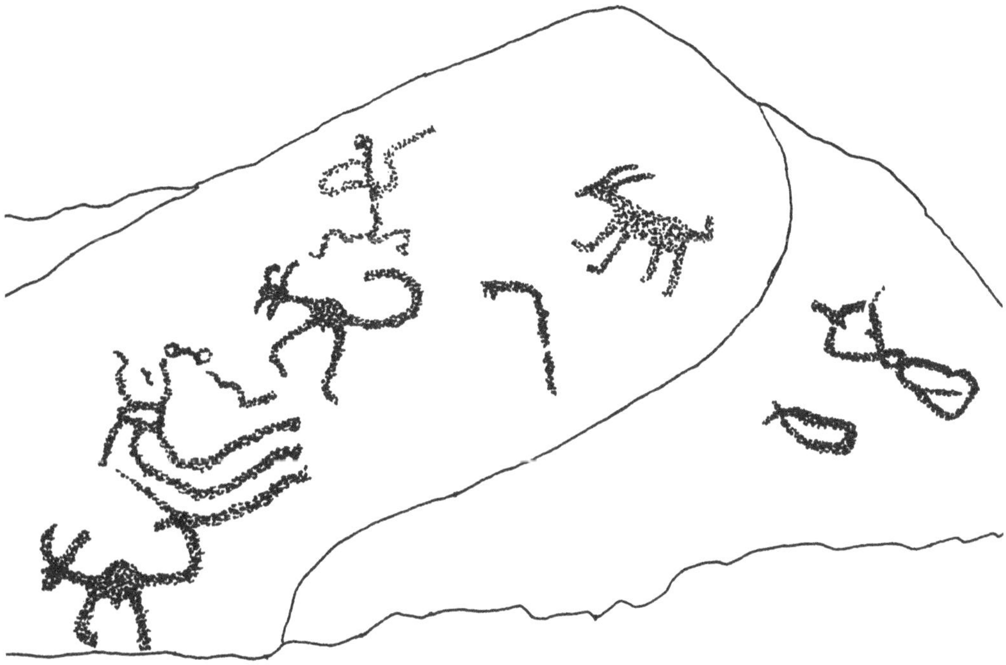

161. Twisted hourglass design, Box Canyon. Hourglass is 16 cm in length.

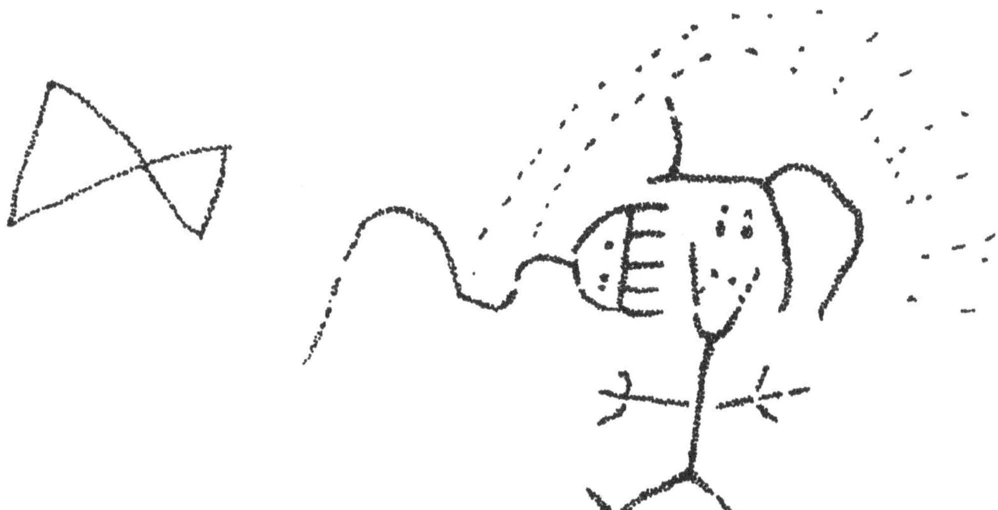

162. Unusual anthropomorph and hourglass petroglyphs, upper Pima Canyon. Anthropomorph is 52 cm in height.

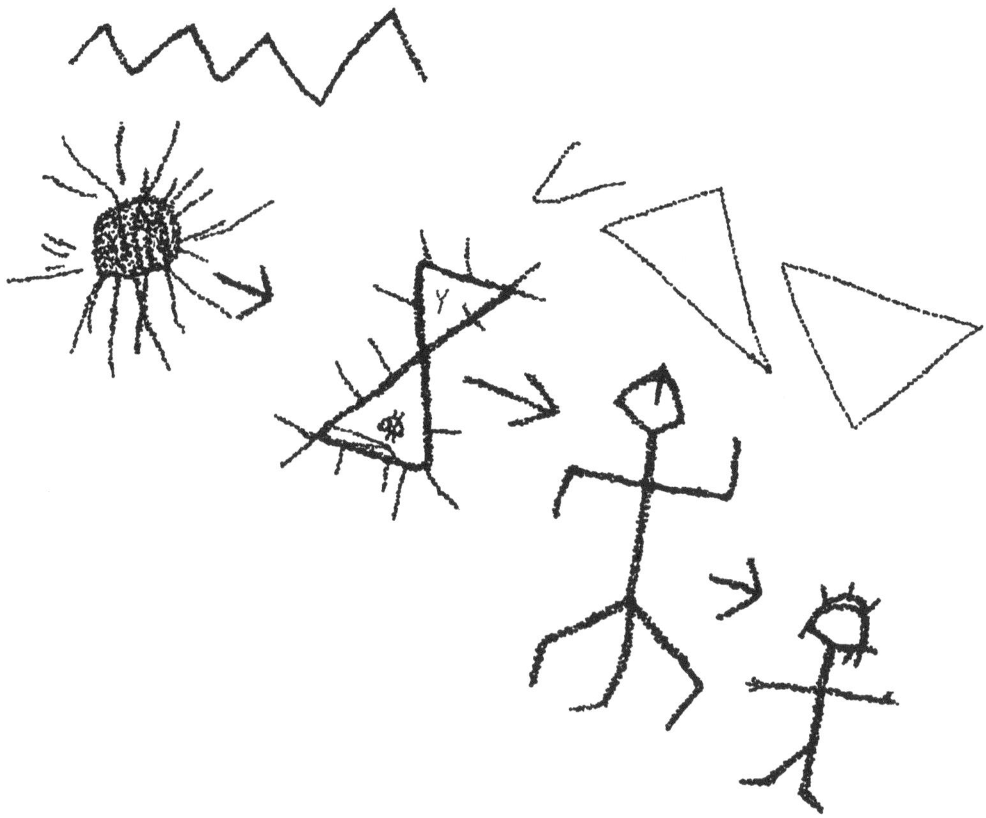

163. Hourglass design showing apparent transformation from sun to hourglass to lizard to human, in a panel located in the Desert Foothills Locality. Sun design in upper left is 22 cm in diameter. Lower right anthropomorph is 21 cm in height. Panel may postdate the Hohokam.

dancing; some are playing flutes; and others hold rattles, rakes, or other objects in their hands. These figures are generally similar to the South Mountains rock art images. The hourglass anthropomorph motif at Snaketown dates from the Colonial through Sedentary periods (ca. A.D. 750–1150). Emil Haury (1976:Fig. 12.86) charted only forty-five hourglass anthropomorph figures from among the tens of thousands of red-on-buff pottery sherds recovered from Snaketown, and they are even less frequent from other sites.

Other Southwestern Hourglass Anthropomorph Petroglyphs

Hourglass anthropomorph images are not common at other rock art sites in the Southwest. However, one at Tumamoc Hill in Tucson (Ferg 1979:Fig. 2) has a solidly pecked body, upraised arms, and a crook but no headdress or feet. Another hourglass anthropomorph is located in Saguaro National Park.

Hourglass anthropomorph figures also are rare for Anasazi and Sinagua rock art sites in northern Arizona. A Mogollon hourglass anthropomorph holding a bow and arrow similar to the one from the 16th Street Locality (see figure 157, *bottom center*) in the South Mountains is present as a petroglyph at the Three Rivers rock art site in western New Mexico. Hourglass shapes also occur on mask images at this site. In southeastern Arizona, 135 miles (216 km) southeast of the South Mountains, Wesley Jernigan (1992) documented a number of painted hourglass anthropomorph images at Mogollon rock art sites. Located in the Gila Mountains, these Mogollon Red Style figures vaguely resemble Hohokam figures. Because the Hohokam appear to have been present in the Safford area around A.D. 900, Jernigan suggests that Mogollon artists were influenced by the Hohokam. However, he notes that the Mogollon Red figures appear to be more static in their depictions and have less interaction with other figures compared to the Hohokam hourglass anthropomorphs. In addition, the Mogollon painted figures have birdlike feet, which do not occur on Hohokam hourglass anthropomorphs. Unlike the Hohokam figures, these hourglass anthropomorphs do not appear on Mogollon painted pottery.

Hourglass elements also occur on historic Hopi painted pottery. The hourglass, sometimes referred to as a bow-tie design, was recorded by Alexander Stephen on Payupki Polychrome, which dates from A.D. 1680 to 1780 (Patterson 1994). This design represents men's hair tied up in the form of a queue that rests at the nape of their neck.

Finally, the hourglass design is common in historic Apache and Diné (Navajo) rock art (Schaafsma 1980). One of the Diné warrior twins, Born-for-Water, is represented by small hourglass figures that are pecked, scratched in paint, or painted. These elements occur alone as well as in association with a Yeí anthropomorph. Born-for-Water is the twin brother of Monster Slayer; they are the children of the Sun and Changing Woman in the Diné origin story. Schaafsma (1980) argues that Diné borrowed the hourglass motif from Pueblo iconography, where it was associated with warriors and represented the scalp knot. Scalps in Pueblo society are closely tied to rain and fertility.

Interpreting Hourglass Anthropomorphs

Schaafsma did not identify this particular type of motif in her definition of the Hohokam Gila rock art style, although she did mention that sites near Phoenix have "men with geometric body shapes" (1980:91). Because none of the fourteen hourglass anthropomorphs in the South Mountains has genitalia, we cannot be certain that they are actually men.

We can only guess at the meaning of the hourglass anthropomorphs in the South Mountains. They may represent individuals with special status, including priests or shamans. One of them has a cane, often a sign of status in Southwestern groups, and another is shooting a bow and arrow. The hourglass body shape may depict a certain type of clothing, such as kilts or togalike apparel tied at the waist. Hohokam red-on-buff pottery hourglass anthropomorphs appear to depict ceremonial participants because they often occur as multiple individuals holding hands and are posed as though dancing (Haury 1976). Alternatively, the hourglass shape may represent something more abstract, and the hourglass form that looks electrified may indicate that the shape symbolizes a type of power or supernatural force (see figure 163). As a final possibility, the Hohokam hourglass anthropomorph may be a stylistic representation of a celestial body that the Hohokam charted in the sky. For example, the star group called Orion has a double triangle or hourglass configuration and is often called the Hunter or Mountain Sheep by the O'odham and Maricopa Indians (Miller 1997). Hohokam astronomy is discussed further in chapter 10.

Masks and Masked Faces

Any discussion of humans and spirit beings with humanlike bodies must include several unusual petroglyph panels that emphasize the face, masks (or faces), and individuals wearing masks. Inventories of Hohokam rock art elements typically do not list masks as one of the elements recorded. Masks also are absent from Hohokam ceramic designs. However, Henry Wallace and James Holmlund (1986) have suggested that some of the anthropomorphs in the Picacho Mountains may be wearing masks. In the South Mountains, a few rock art designs appear to be masks or figures wearing masks (Bostwick 2000). Some of these designs are executed in a style that looks different from Hohokam designs, raising the question, who made them?

In Hieroglyphic Canyon we found a complex panel that has a figure wearing a bird mask, bent over and apparently being attended by another anthropomorph (figure 164). The mask is in profile and has a long beak. The individual wearing it has a single-feather headdress that looks like a quail's topknot. In the upper right portion of this panel are two birds, one of which appears to be singing, as indicated by a series of scratched lines coming out of its mouth (see figure 99). The characteristics of the elements and their arrangement in this panel suggest a mythological or ceremonial narrative. Patination of the panel indicates that it predates the Historic period.

The other rock art panel with an anthropomorph wearing a bird mask is located along Kiwanis Trail, a major north-south route through the South Mountains via Telegraph Pass (figure 165). Situated in a wash on a large upright boulder, this scene is complex and consists of various geometric designs and a large anthropomorph wearing a bird mask in profile. This figure has a single, curved feather for a headdress and is facing to its right. It appears to be blowing smoke, or its breath, through the mask. The patination on this panel indicates that it too is prehistoric. A small rock shelter is present in front of this panel, and above the rock shelter is another panel consisting of four stick-figure human dancers (see figure 121).

Another panel that includes a mask design also is located along Kiwanis Trail (figure 166), about one-quarter mile (0.4 km) from the anthropomorph with the bird mask. This panel is very unusual compared to other rock art designs, although it is located near other petroglyph panels that appear more typically Hohokam. The mask panel has four major elements: (1) a round mask or face; (2) a large shield; (3) a life-sized handprint; and (4) a small circle design with a small appendage. The initials "M R" also are present below and to the left of the handprint.

The mask and shield are very large; most other circular rock art elements in the South Mountains are less than half the size. The mask has two eyes, a small mouth, and a long line for a nose. The top of the head has been extensively pecked to create what appears to be short-cropped hair or a helmet. The handprint is rare in Hohokam rock art and pottery design but is often associated with shield images in other areas of the Southwest (Schaafsma 2000).

The shield design is evenly divided into four sections with a central point, much like a wheel. Shield figures are not common in Hohokam rock art but are present in the Gila Bend area, where they are attributed to the Patayan people (Wallace 1989). A petroglyph panel in the upper 32nd Street Locality has a large shieldlike image next to a smaller anthropomorph (figure 167). Painted shield images next to cliff dwellings in northeastern Arizona have been interpreted as heraldic symbolism for

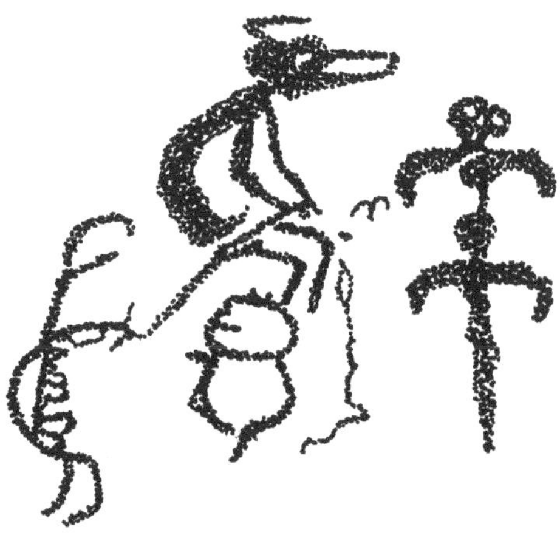

164. Anthropomorph wearing bird mask and single-feather headdress, Hieroglyphic Canyon. Anthropomorph with mask is 26 cm in height.

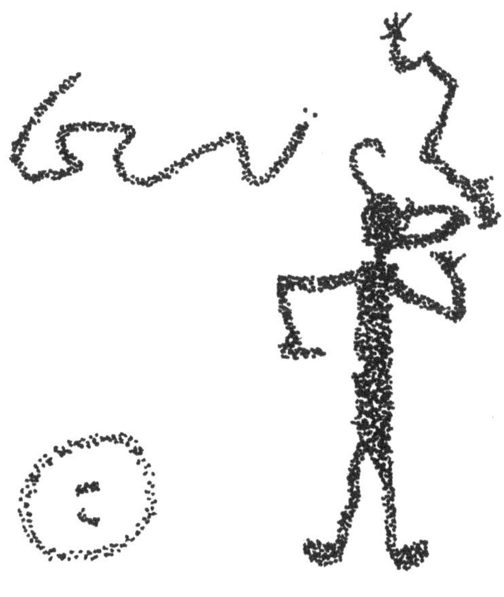

165. Anthropomorph wearing bird mask, Kiwanis Trail. Anthropomorph is 40 cm in height.

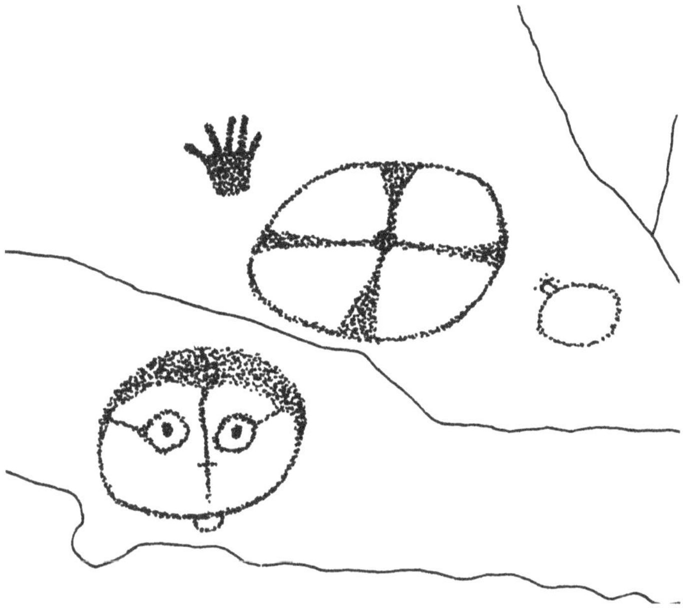

166. Face or mask, shield, and handprint petroglyphs located along Kiwanis Trail. Shield is 48 x 51 cm in diameter.

the groups that inhabited the cliff dwellings (Anderson 1971). Polly Schaafsma (2000:24–25) plotted the distribution of Pueblo shield designs; she suggests that shields were more than just social emblems: "Just as the shield and its design empowered and protected its wearer, it is likely that images of shields and the designs featured on them similarly would have transmitted their protective powers to the vicinity in which they were painted." Shield figures were most frequent on the Colorado Plateau and in the eastern Rio Grande regions from the mid thirteenth to late sixteenth centuries, reflecting increasing regional conflict at that time (Schaafsma 2000).

The O'odham used untanned leather shields to defend themselves in battle; they believed the shields had magical powers. Russell (1975:Figs. 45–47) shows examples of three O'odham shields: one is painted with a large swastika, a common rock art motif in the South Mountains; another is divided into four equal sections, each of which contains a circle.

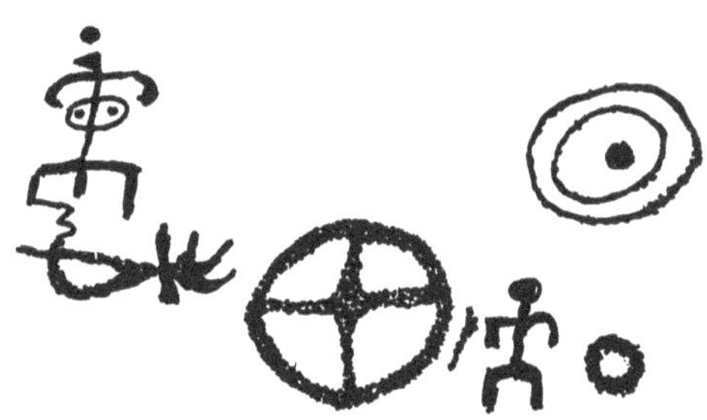

167. Shield design, 32nd Street Locality. Shield is 25 cm in diameter.

Another panel with a mask or face and shield is located on a boulder adjacent to a lower ridge trail in the southern portion of San Juan Canyon (figure 168). The head has simple facial features and a neck. The shield is divided into four sections, with the upper two

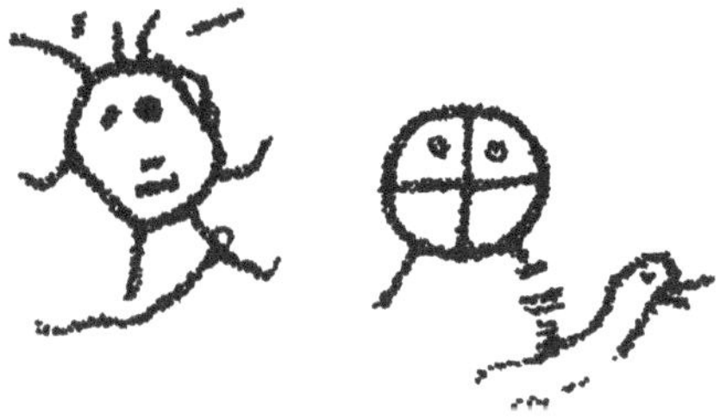

168. Face and shield located along a trail in the San Juan South Locality. Anthropomorph face is 13 x 10 cm.

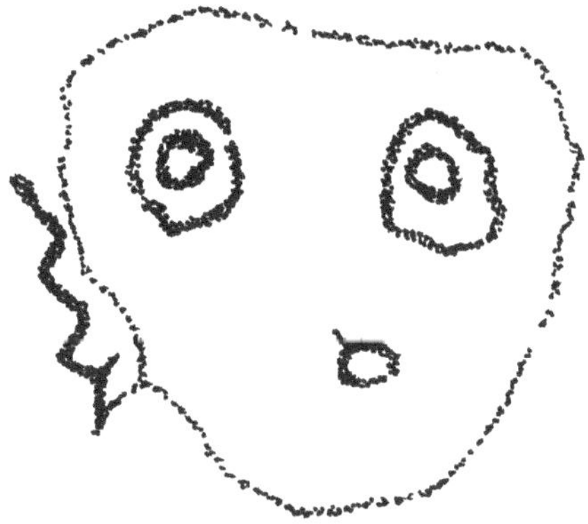

169. Face or mask petroglyph, 28th Place Locality. Mask is 44 x 50 cm. Scratches in neck area are not shown in this illustration.

sections containing circles. This shield has wavy appendages attached to its bottom, perhaps representing fringe or feathers. The panel has some repatination but, like the one along Kiwanis Trail, does not appear to be a Hohokam petroglyph style.

On the southern side of the mountains at the 28th Place Locality is a boulder with a large face that has concentric circles for eyes (figure 169). A small snake design was placed to the left side of the face, and a series of scratches occur on top of and adjacent to the face, especially in the neck area.

O'odham Mask Ceremonies

The O'odham people have an important ceremony that incorporates the use of masks. The "Vikita," or prayer-stick ceremony, considered the most sacred of all O'odham ceremonies, was performed to keep the world in order (Underhill 1946). It has four major components: (1) masked impersonators of the sun and the moon; (2) child actors; (3) masked clowns; and (4) prayer sticks and cornmeal. All of these components are also present in Puebloan Katsina ceremonies. Ruth Underhill (1946) believed that the Vikita (or Wi:gida) and Katsina ceremonies were related because of similarities in costumes, officiants, and rites. During the O'odham Vikita ceremony, sun and moon impersonators wear painted shieldlike masks. The Vikita ritual also includes masked clowns called Navitco (or Navitchu), who make shrill cries much like some Katsina dancers and are purported to have the power to bring rain (Russell 1975:168). Author and explorer Carl Lumholtz (1912) collected painted gourd masks worn by Vikita singers at the turn of the century; two of these masks were owned by Tohono O'odham shamans. The gourd masks were painted in three sections, with red zigzags representing clouds and lightning and dots symbolizing maize kernels.

Located 2 miles (3 km) northeast of the South Mountains is a rock shelter called Double Butte Cave. In this rock shelter, Frank Hamilton Cushing discovered several hundred cane cigarettes, seventy-five painted wooden prayer sticks, five effigy pahos, and Hohokam ceramics (Haury 1945). One of these pahos is made of cottonwood and looks similar to Hopi Katsina depictions, with its painted round head and single-feather headdress. Emil Haury (1945) suggested that the effigy dated before A.D. 1540 and represents a mask that was Puebloan in origin. He proposed that the effigy paho looks similar to the "Sio Humis" Katsina of the Zuni.

Katsina (or "Kachina") images of full-figured humans in ceremonial regalia, as well as elaborate masks, occur in a variety of mediums in the Southwest. These include rock art, ceramic designs, painted walls of kivas (ceremonial chambers), and artifacts such as wooden prayer sticks and altar images. Masks are especially widespread as rock art elements in Arizona, New Mexico, and Utah (McCreery and Malotki 1994; Schaafsma 1980, 1992). Estimates on when the Katsina cult was introduced into the American Southwest range from the eleventh century to the beginning of the fourteenth century; a Mesoamerican influence is generally acknowledged (Adams 1991; Schaafsma 1992, 1994; Sutherland 1996).

The small number of mask images in the South Mountains does not seem to indicate a strong Puebloan or Katsina presence. Nonetheless, the few examples are intriguing. Perhaps Puebloan traders visiting the area created them; one of the mask panels is located along a major north-south trail that crosses through the middle of the South Mountains. Another possible Katsina panel is located on Tempe Butte, near a major east-west trail along the Salt River (Bostwick 2000:Fig. 11; Loendorf and Loendorf 1995). Hopi yellow-ware ceramics have been found at several late Hohokam villages in the Salt River Valley (but none in the South Mountains), indicating that at least during the late fourteenth century the Hohokam interacted with these Puebloan people to the north. Sally Cole (1992) states that some of the Katsina iconography of the rock art found in the middle Little Colorado River area was probably made by visiting Hopi sometime after A.D. 1400. The presence of Pueblo-style wooden pahos with Hohokam sherds from Double Butte Cave suggests that the Hohokam may have known about and perhaps adopted certain Puebloan religious objects and images.

Conclusions

Images of humans and spirit beings with humanlike forms are scattered throughout the rocky canyons of the South Mountains, usually depicted with other desert life-forms and various geometric designs. Anthropomorphs take a variety of poses, but an angular posture with arms bent up is very common. These figures appear to be celebrating or perhaps providing a gesture of supplication to a higher power. In some panels, several small anthropomorphs are associated with a large one, often with slightly different details compared to the others.

A number of rock art panels show human figures in actions that are likely to be ceremonial or portraying scenes of cultural importance such as hunting, dancing, flute playing, or holding canes or staffs. Some human figures are oriented horizontally and appear to be floating in space; perhaps these represent the dead. Animals (of various types) are often noticeably larger than anthropomorphs in the same panel, possibly reflecting the animal's superior spiritual power compared to the anthropomorph.

We believe that some of the rock art panels in the South Mountains represent Hohokam shamans' records of journeys into the landscape of the spirits. It seems to us that various creatures from that sacred geography visited individuals on vision quests, perhaps teaching them magic songs. Some panels may be the products of rituals involving hunting magic to ensure successful hunts. The frequent occurrence of humanlike figures in the South Mountains rock art may well be the result of many years of ancient people initiating the young as well as seeking solitude and inspiration in this awe-inspiring landscape.

CHAPTER NINE

ABSTRACT MYSTERIES

Geometric Designs

The sunrise I'm going with.
The sunrise I'm following.
With zigzag lines I'm painted.
Following the sun,
With zigzag lines I'm painted.

—Elder Brother's song, Donald Bahr et al. (1994)

The petroglyph artists of the South Mountains included a wide range of geometric designs in their repertoire, with more than thirty different elements represented. Despite this range of abstract images, variations of the circle are most common; some geometric elements occur in relatively small quantities. Circles appear as simple rings, as rings within rings (concentric circles), with dots, in clusters, as chains, and in other configurations. The proliferation of circles makes them difficult to interpret because they occur in many different contexts and in combination with a variety of other elements. They were placed along trails as isolated elements and in association with other elements in complex panels. Anthropomorphs and animals are frequently associated with circles. In some panels, anthropomorphs are holding or standing on circles, suggesting an entryway. In others, the circles are placed above the anthropomorphs, perhaps representing an object or "hole" in the sky. Circles and crosses are discussed further in chapter 10 (on archaeoastronomy).

Table 2. Geometric Pottery Designs Similar to Rock Art Designs in the South Mountains

Geometric Element	Pioneer Period	Colonial Period	Sedentary Period
Asterisk	x	x	x
Circle	x	x	x
Circle with dot	x	x	x
Concentric circles	x	x	x
Crenulations			x
Diamond		x	x
Dots	x	x	x
Outlined cross		x	x
Scroll	x	x	x
Spiral	x	x	x
Square		x	x
Sun disk		x	x
Swastika			x
Whorl	x	x	x
"X"		x	x

Note: Pottery designs from Snaketown in dated contexts after Haury 1976

Some of the geometric elements in the South Mountains have their equivalents in Hohokam painted pottery designs (table 2). At Snaketown, Haury (1976) recorded 128 geometric element types on the painted pottery, although the most common element was the circle. He found that the use of certain elements evolved over time.

Clearly, Hohokam artists used certain geometric shapes both for painted designs on pottery and for petroglyphs. Red-on-buff painted pottery found in the South Mountains is dominated by geometric elements, primarily spirals and hatched lines. Henry Wallace (1983) has observed that Hohokam rock art shows much greater freedom in layout of design than do design patterns found on painted ceramics. This contrast in amount of variation may reflect different artistic conventions for the two mediums, or perhaps different genders or members of Hohokam society were responsible for each of the two.

The following describes a select group of geometric rock art images found in the South Mountains—pipettes, figure eights, spirals, swastikas and whorls, "X" designs, diamonds, zigzags, squares, textile patterns, and mazes. The meanings of these elements remain an enigma, and their depiction in a mountain landscape is intriguing. Some may represent the sacred, some appear to relate to water or weather phenomena, and others may symbolize objects in the sky. Geometric designs are often associated with anthropomorphs in the South Mountains. O'odham people once believed that anthropomorphic beings made the thunder and lightning and that some shamans had the power to control rain (Gifford 1940:61). Some geometric designs may symbolize group membership.

Pipettes

Twenty-three years ago, archaeologist Alan Ferg (1979) identified a unique geometric design at a Hohokam rock art site in the Tucson area of southern Arizona. He called it a "pipette," based on its similarity to a piece of laboratory equipment. Ernest Snyder had previously recognized this element in the South Mountains, but he did not name it. He later characterized it as "three connected rectangles, sometimes embellished with circles or stars" and "invariably vertically oriented" (Golio et al. 1995:95). In his Tucson study, Ferg (1979:109) defined the pipette design as having "bilateral symmetry with bulges of varying shapes at intervals." Ferg suggested that the pipette element dated to around A.D. 1150 to 1450. A few years after Ferg's study, Henry Wallace and James Holmlund (1986) recorded a number of pipette petroglyphs in the Picacho Mountains between Tucson and Phoenix. They also dated the pipette to the Classic period, based on its association with Classic period habitation sites.

J. J. Golio, Susie Bradshaw, Ernest Snyder, and Mike Golio (1995) undertook a study of pipette elements located throughout central and southern Arizona. They restricted their definition of the pipette to include only rectangular enclosures and collected data on fifty-nine pipettes from fourteen different locations, including twenty-one pipettes from the South Mountains.

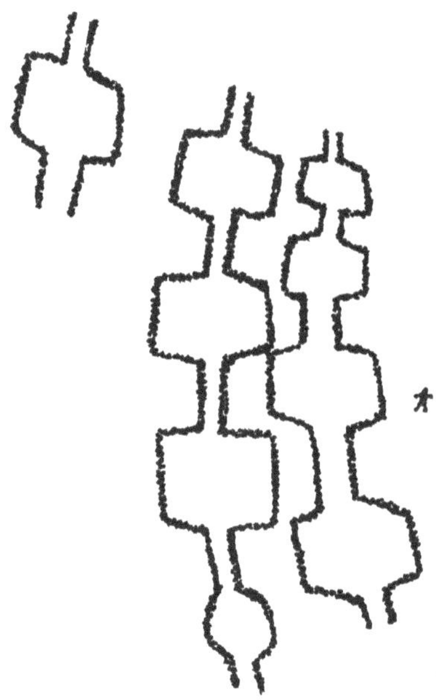

170. Three pipette petroglyphs in same panel, 20th Street Locality. Middle pipette is 93 cm in length.

In our study of the pipettes of the South Mountains, we retain the broader definition in which the boxes range from rectilinear to somewhat curvilinear. Within this broader characterization, we have identified thirty-five pipettes. We have found these unique designs at fourteen different localities, with Hieroglyphic Canyon containing seven of them (including the most elaborate and largest examples). East of Hieroglyphic Canyon in the 20th Street Locality is a boulder with three pipettes in the same panel, the most pipettes in a single panel (figure 170). Two panels have two pipettes each:

one in Hieroglyphic Canyon and one at the 28th Place Locality on the southern side of the South Mountains (figure 171).

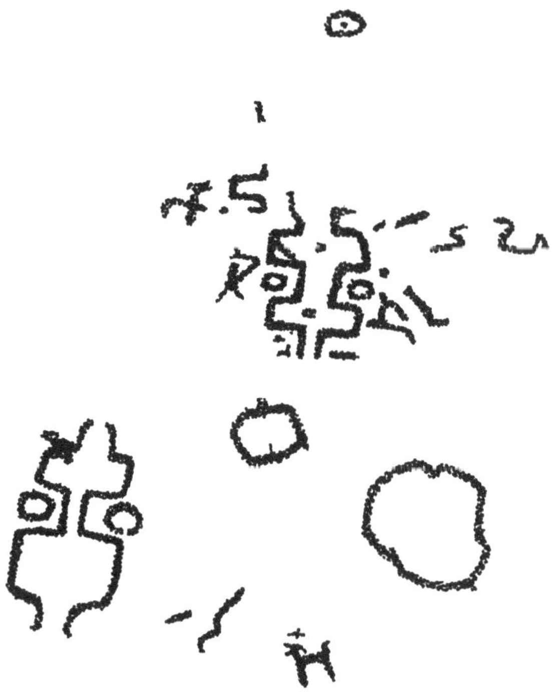

171. Two pipettes in same panel, 28th Place Locality. Lower pipette is 32 cm in length.

Pipettes face in all directions and also occur on horizontal surfaces. With only a few exceptions, such as a two-part horizontally oriented pipette in Hieroglyphic Canyon (figure 172), the long axes are oriented vertically. Most of the pipettes have two or three boxes in their design, with a long, slender one in Hieroglyphic Canyon having six boxes (figure 173). Four pipettes have only a single box and may not be considered pipettes in other studies (figures 174 and 175), but two of these examples in the South Mountains are in panels containing another fully executed pipette. At the southern end of Box Canyon, in a complex panel, we found a pipette that has double lines (figure 176). Slightly more than half of the pipettes have dual circles as part of the design, usually evenly spaced between two of the boxes, giving the pipettes the appearance of a stylized mask (figures 177 and 178). Most of the pipettes do not have other elements inside their boxes, but we identified several notable exceptions. A large pipette in Hieroglyphic Canyon appears to have a human figure inside the lower box (see figure 281). Next to this is another pipette with a circle in its center. A partial pipette in the lower reach

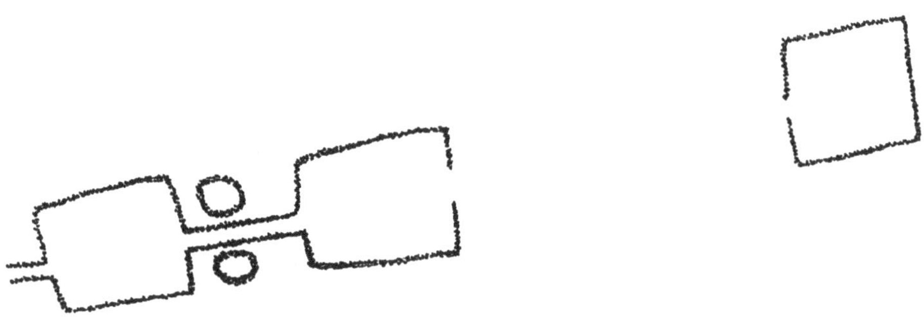

172. Horizontally oriented pipette with two separate parts, Hieroglyphic Canyon. Pipette section on left is 75 cm in length.

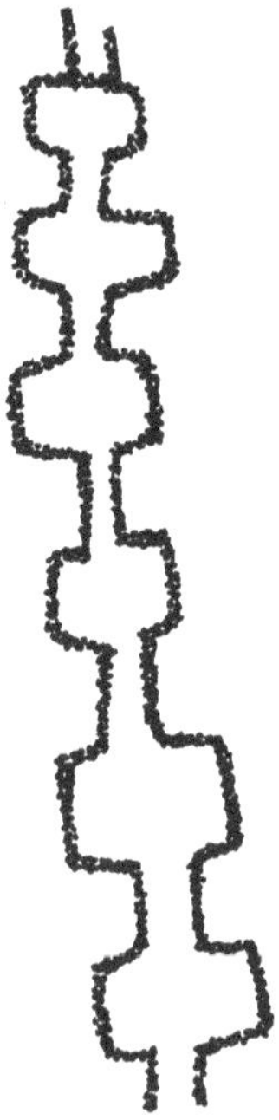

173. Pipette with 6 boxes, Hieroglyphic Canyon. Pipette is 69 cm in length.

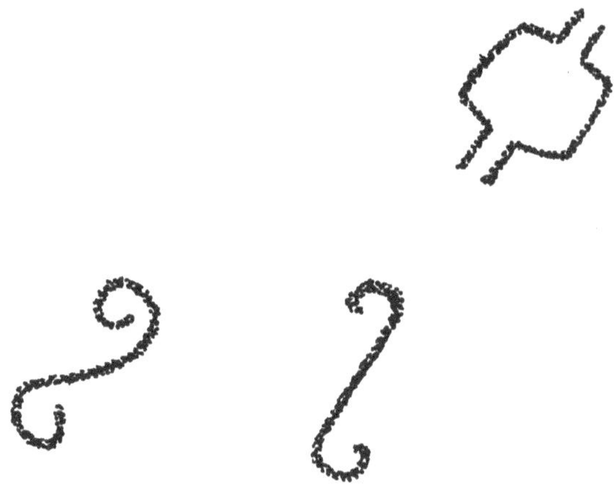

174. Single-box pipette near water tank, Valle Bonita Locality. Pipette is 24 cm in length.

of this same canyon also has a single circle in its center. At the 12th Street Locality, a lizardman is entering into a pipette (figure 179), and a panel in Box Canyon has a quadruped whose tail is inside the pipette (figure 180). In a large pipette on the southeastern side of the South Mountains, near the entrance to Pima Canyon, we noted a five-pointed star inside the upper box, a circle with a dot in the central box, and nested boxes inside the bottom box (figure 181). This panel is large and visible from afar. Ceramics collected from in front of this pipette panel have been identified as Santa Cruz/Sacaton Red-on-buff, which suggests that the panel dates to the late Colonial or Sedentary period (ca. A.D. 850–1150).

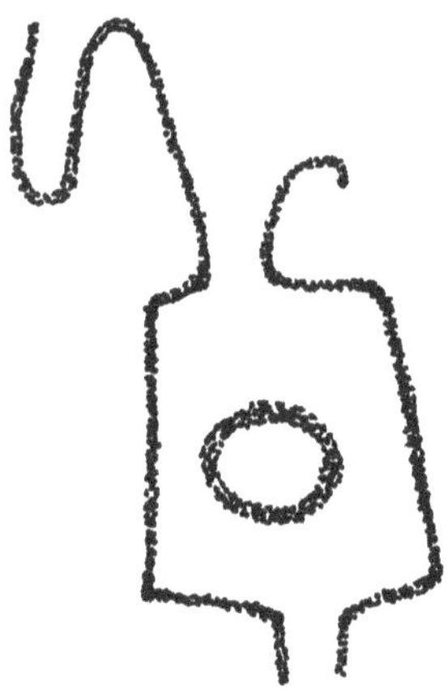

175. Single-box pipette, 20th Street Locality. Pipette is 36 cm in length.

The meaning of Hohokam pipettes remains a mystery. Because pipettes often have a pair of circles placed near the center boxes, causing those images to look like stylized faces or masks, Henry Wallace and James Holmlund (1986) suggested that such pipettes resemble the face of Tlaloc, a widespread Mesoamerican rain deity associated with serpents and mountain peaks. This suggestion is based on the discovery that rock art in the Jornada region of New Mexico after A.D. 1000 shows a

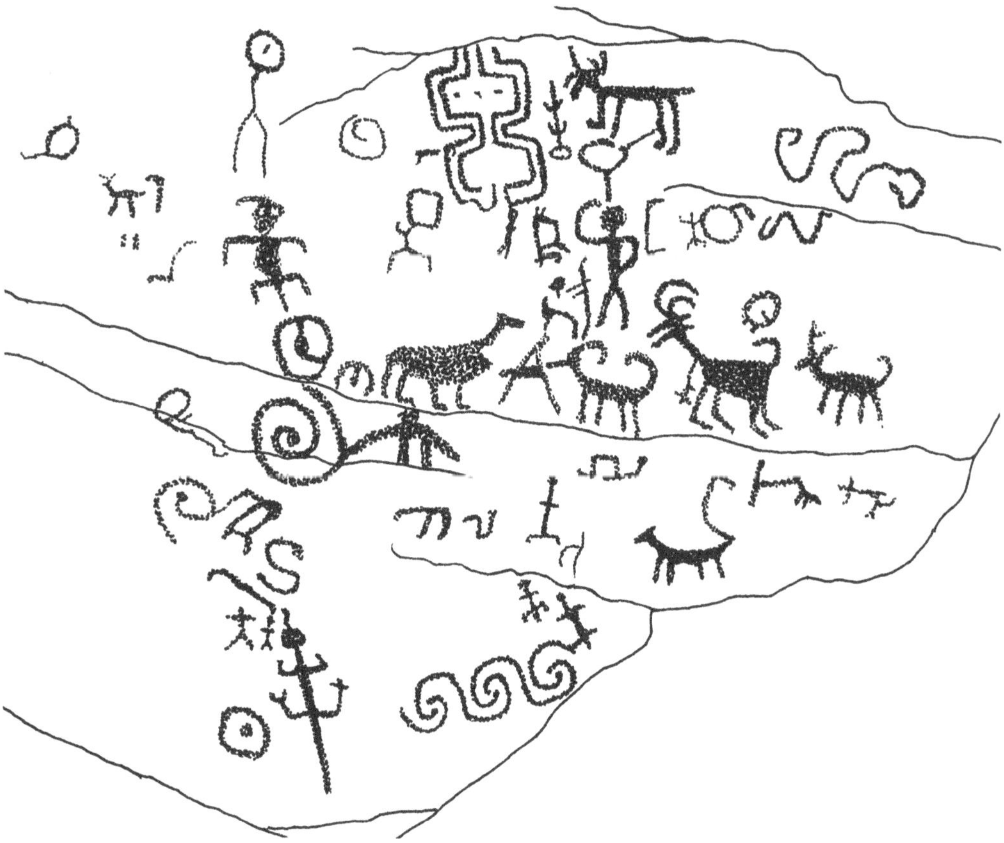

176. Double-line pipette and other petroglyphs, southern end of Box Canyon. Pipette is 30 cm in length. Panel is located above a natural water tank.

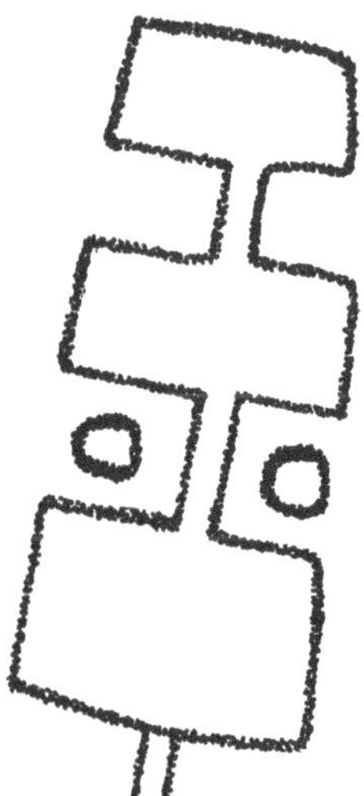

177. Pipette with double circles, Chandler Boulevard/32nd Street Locality. Pipette is 48 cm in length.

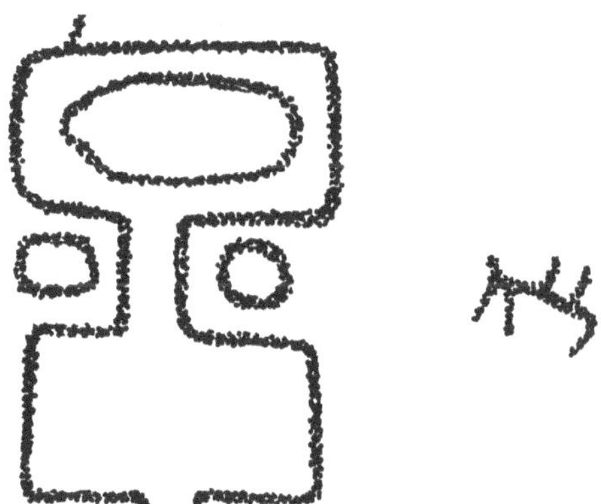

178. Pipette with double circles and upside-down quadruped, Pima Canyon. Pipette is 37 cm in length.

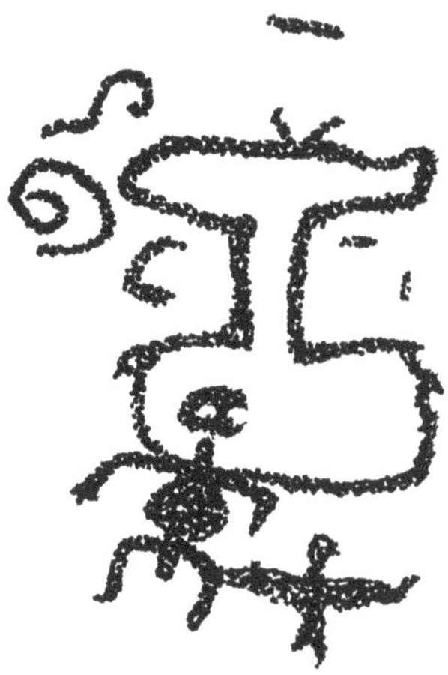

179. Anthropomorph/lizardman entering pipette, lower 12th Street Locality. A thunderbird is attached to the left knee of the anthropomorph. Anthropomorph is 17 cm in height.

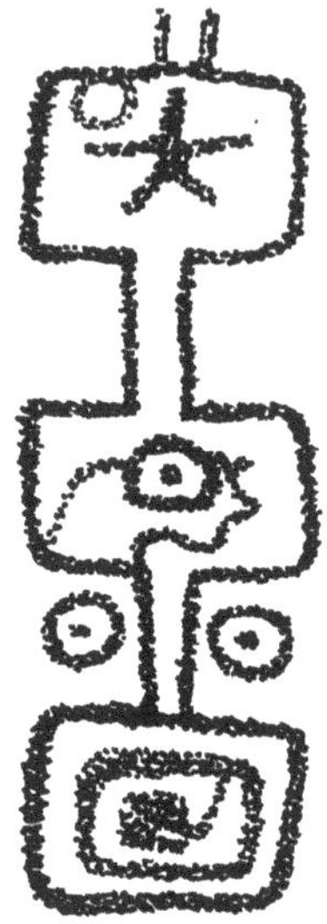

181. Pipette with other elements inside its boxes, southeastern side of the South Mountains, along trail near entrance to Pima Canyon. Pipette is 80 cm in length. Numerous other petroglyphs surround and underlie this pipette; some of these are very faint or have been rubbed over.

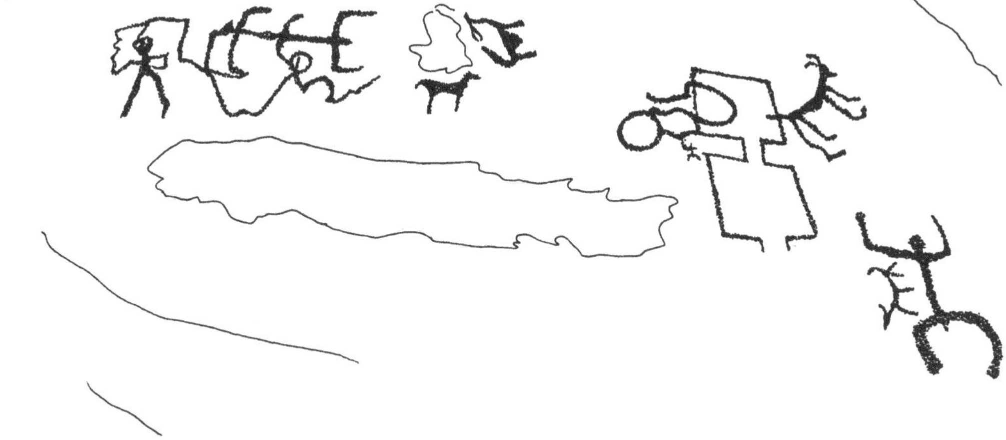

180. Pipette with quadrupeds and anthropomorphs, adjacent to a natural water tank in Box Canyon. Pipette is 56 cm in length.

dramatic influx of Mesoamerican religious images. One of the distinguishing characteristics of Jornada Style rock art is masks or faces with bulging eyes. However, Golio and others (1995) have shown that the depiction of pipettes exhibits considerable variation; indeed, two dozen of the pipettes they identified in central and southern Arizona do not include circles in the design. In the South Mountains, partial pipettes occur with complete pipettes in the same panel, as though representing pipettes not fully developed—or could they be like a single feather, which among Pueblo groups represents the whole bird and all its attributes?

Rock art researcher Ken Hedges (1994) has proposed, based on the neuropsychological model (discussed in chapters 2 and 11), that pipettes are portrayals of a visionary image received by a shaman in a trance state: in other words, a complex entoptic form. Hedges suggests that the pipette is a Hohokam version of the double crenelation, one of the basic phosphenes identified as an elemental form produced during a trance. Hedges also notes that double crenelations appear as designs on Hohokam red-on-buff pottery, as well as in Archaic period rock art throughout the western United States.

Frank Midvale suggested that Hohokam pipettes represent sacred shrines (Mitvalsky 1937). This theory is interesting, considering that some of the pipettes have smaller anthropomorphs in association with them. An example would be the large pipette in Hieroglyphic Canyon that has a human figure inside the lower box (see figure 281). Also, the panel with three pipettes at the 20th Street Locality has a tiny human pecked to its right (see figure 170). A boulder along a trail with a view of this three-pipette panel has a scene that includes an anthropomorph "saluting" a partial pipette. At the base of Hieroglyphic Canyon, an elaborate panel also has a small anthropomorph next to the larger pipette. A pipette in Pima Canyon has an upside-down quadruped next to it (see figure 178), and a pipette in Box Canyon is being touched by a large quadruped. At the 12th Street Locality, a human figure is partially inside the lower box, as though the pipette is a doorway (see figure 179). Perhaps this image symbolizes a shaman entering the world where spirits dwell.

Figure Eight

Figure-eight motifs are easily recognizable but occur in fewer than two dozen locations in the South Mountains, always with other geometric designs or life-forms (figure 182). Few panels contain more than one figure eight; we noted no concentrations of this image in any particular locality.

Figure eights are depicted in different orientations: up and down, sideways, and tilted (usually to the left). Rarely do they show elaboration, although a figure eight in the 36th Street Locality has a diamond shape inside the lower portion

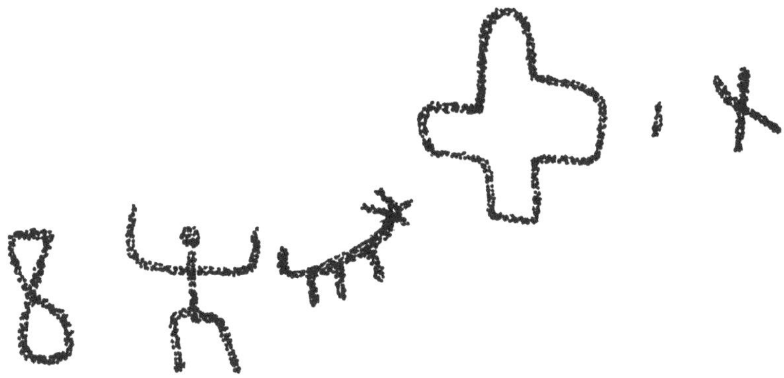

182. Figure eight, anthropomorph, quadruped, negative cross, and "X," 32nd Street Locality. Negative cross is 18 x 17 cm.

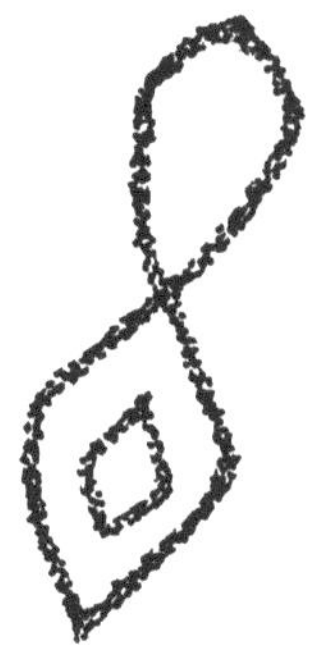

183. Figure eight with interior diamond shape, 36th Street Locality. Figure eight is 30 cm in length.

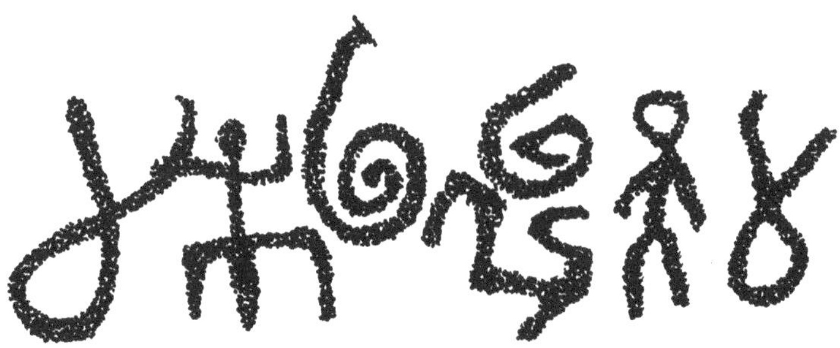

184. Partial figure-eight petroglyphs next to spirals and anthropomorphs, Upper 12th Street Locality. Anthropomorphs are 15 cm in height.

(figure 183). A few other figure-eight petroglyphs have short appendages: the two appendages of a figure eight at the 43rd Street Locality look like legs.

Partial figure eights take the form of an eight but are open at one end. A panel at the upper portion of a wash in the Upper 12th Street Locality has two partial figure eights, one on each side of the panel and being held by anthropomorphs (figure 184). Another partial figure eight appears next to a whorl petroglyph in the San Juan North Locality (figure 185).

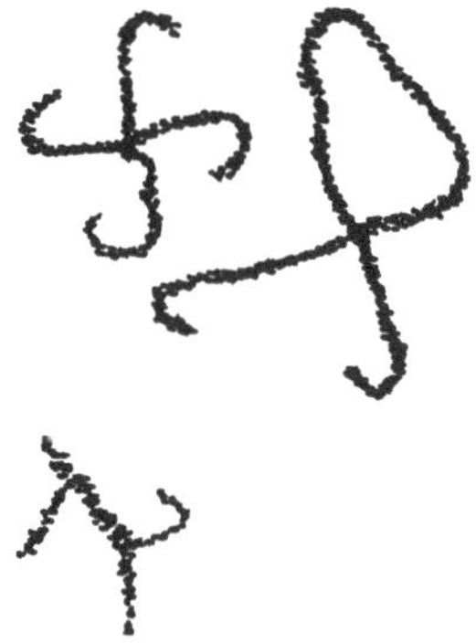

185. Partial figure-eight and whorl petroglyphs, San Juan North Locality. Whorl on left is 16 x 14 cm.

Spirals

Spirals are impressive designs, in part because of their difficulty to create. Maintaining a symmetrical swirl with a continuous, even weight line throughout requires considerable skill. Nearly 70 percent of the localities in the South Mountains contain at least one spiral, with a number of elaborate examples.

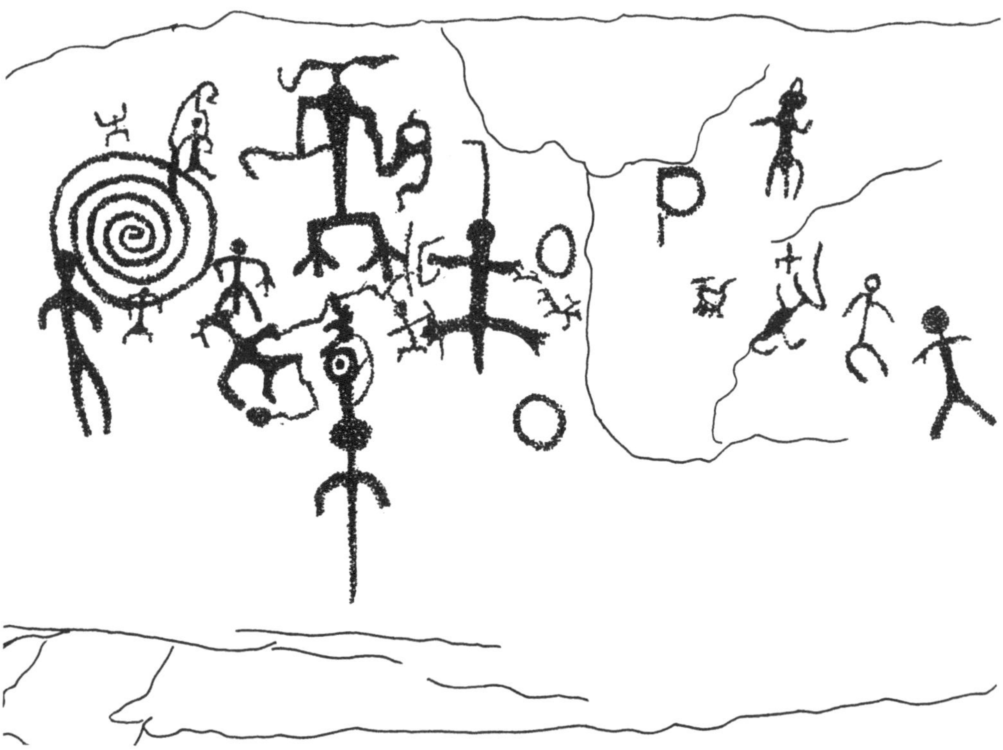

186. Large spiral and other petroglyphs, Hieroglyphic Canyon. Spiral is 25 cm in diameter.

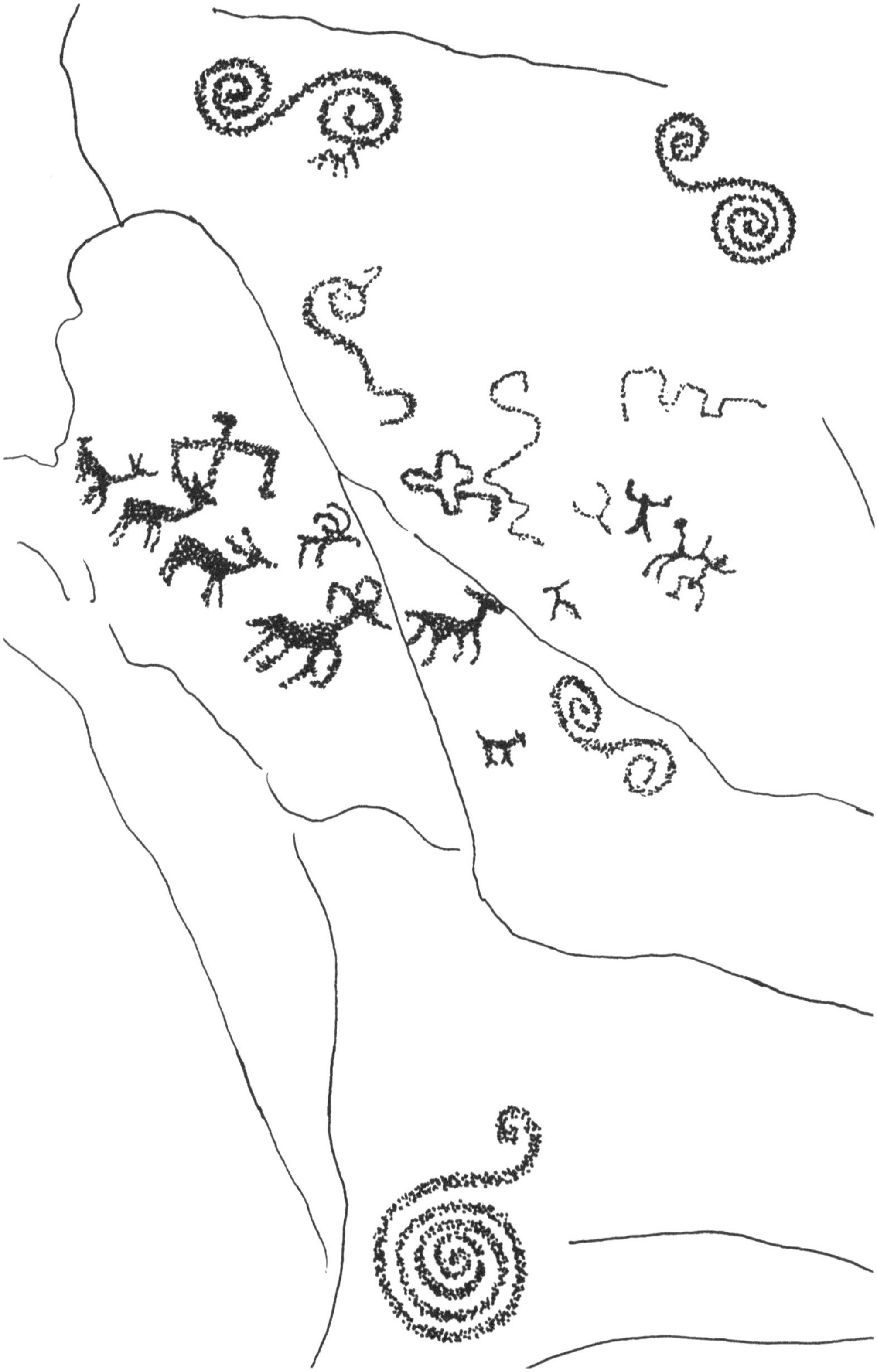

187. Spirals, 24th Street Locality. Lower spiral is 21 cm in diameter and faces northeast.

Spirals in the South Mountains occur in many variations. They may be alone or combined with other elements, both geometric designs and life-forms (figures 186 and 187). Several panels contain two spirals, each of which swirls in the opposite direction from the other, perhaps representing the concept of duality (figures 188 and 189). Some snakes have spirals at the ends of their tails, such as the snake with the headdress at the 32nd Street Locality (see figure 42). The spiral represents the

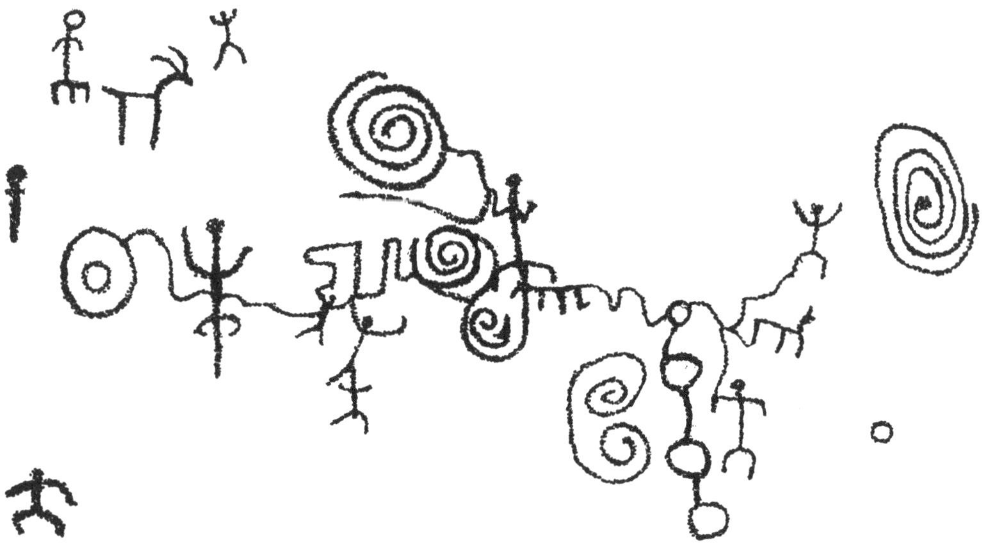

188. Two large spirals, quadrupeds, and anthropomorphs, 32nd Street Locality. Spiral on right is 35 x 41 cm in diameter. Panel faces northeast. Historic graffiti put on the panel later are not included in this illustration.

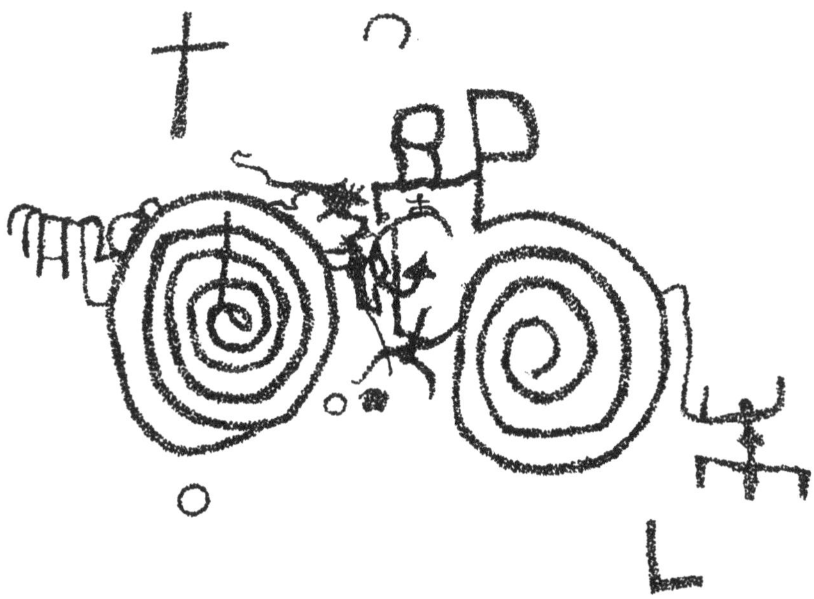

189. Two large spirals in a panel on Bird Hill in Box Canyon. Spiral on right is 50 cm in diameter. Panel faces west.

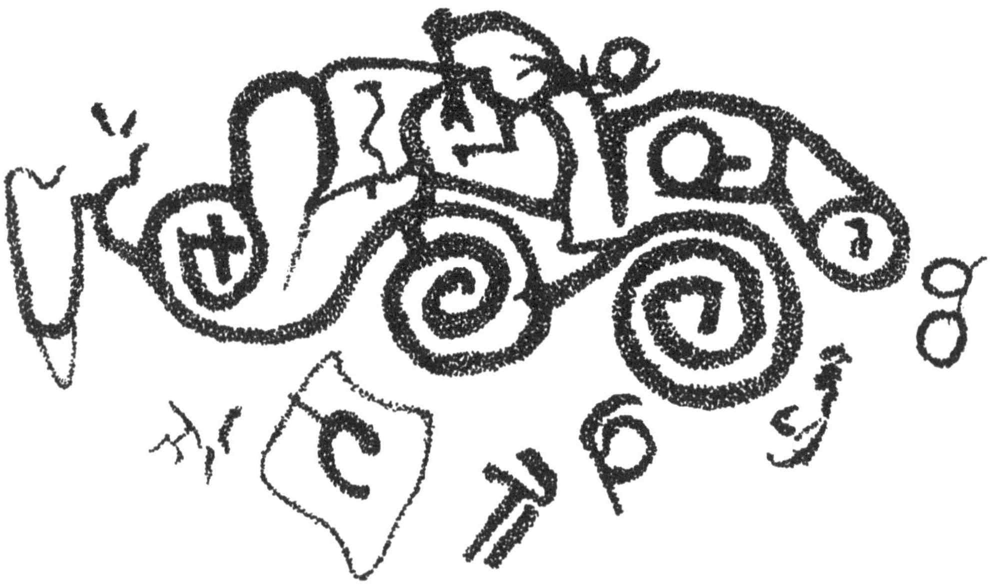

190. Multiple connected spirals, Box Canyon. Spiral on right is 16 cm in diameter. Panel faces southwest.

snake's body in a coiled form at the Chandler Boulevard/19th Way Locality (see figure 274, left). This panel is especially interesting because a double spiral is adjacent to the snake. A panel in the Southeast Side Locality has a snake body coiled into a curvilinear spiral that takes a cross form (see figure 48). A small lizard appears near this unusual snake element.

Spirals are especially common in Box Canyon. They are present at upper levels and down in the canyon. A well-patinated geometric design on Bird Hill in Box Canyon includes three connected spirals (figure 190). Another complex panel on Bird Hill has an anthropomorph standing on a spiral. A panel high on the eastern side of the canyon has two large spirals next to a large, solid cross and two anthropomorphs (see figure 189). This panel faces west. Another panel in the area has two large, double scrolls next to two smaller anthropomorphs and a solid cross. This panel also faces west.

A spiral panel in the 32nd Street Locality is the largest spiral found thus far; it contains nine rings (figure 191). An anthropomorph is holding the spiral in its left hand, and several very faint four-legged mammals surround the spiral. Among Hopi, the left hand is considered sacred and is used for removing masks or holding prayer sticks and feathers. Also at this locality is another panel with a large spiral, associated with several anthropomorphs and four-legged mammals, that has dramatic light and shadow solstice interaction (see figure 260). Another large spiral is present in the Southwest Side Locality near a major east-west trail associated with Hohokam ceramics (figure 192). This spiral has six rings and is placed above a large concentric circle with three rings. A quadruped is touching the outer line of the spiral. At the 36th Street Locality, a complex panel has two large spirals, one with five tri-

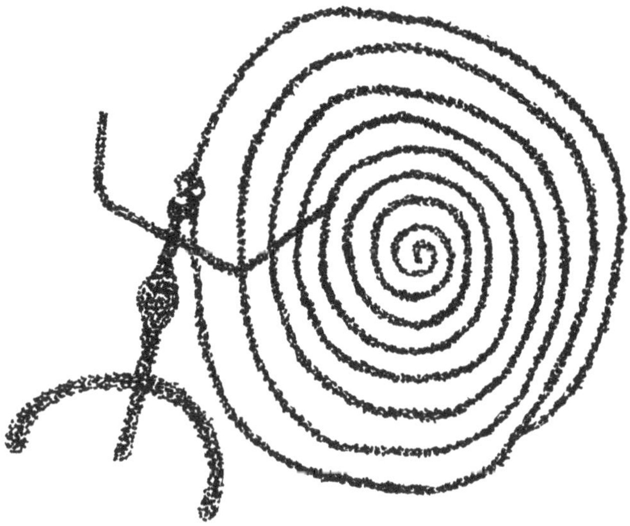

191. Anthropomorph holding large spiral, 32nd Street Locality. Spiral is 43 x 40 cm in diameter and anthropomorph is 30 cm in height. Other faint petroglyphs also are present but are not included in this illustration. Panel faces northeast.

angles attached to its tail; both spirals have six rings. A large spiral with a tail is part of an elaborate panel at the Four Pillars solstice site in the Twin Buttes Locality (see figure 254).

Utilizing the original but controversial work of LaVan Martineau (1973), rock art researcher Carol Patterson-Rudolph (1997) has argued that spirals are directional markers, with a clockwise spiral representing ascension and counterclockwise spirals indicating a descending direction. Among Puebloan cultures, spirals were said to represent the travel of the sun through the sky and underground during the course of a year, as well as symbolizing a people's journey in search of the center (Young 1988). Spirals also symbolize water, perhaps because water eddies sometimes look like they move in a spiral. For the Huichol Indians of northern Mexico, the spiral symbol was associated with rain and clouds, corn, serpents, the heart, and Grandfather Fire (Lumholtz 1912). In

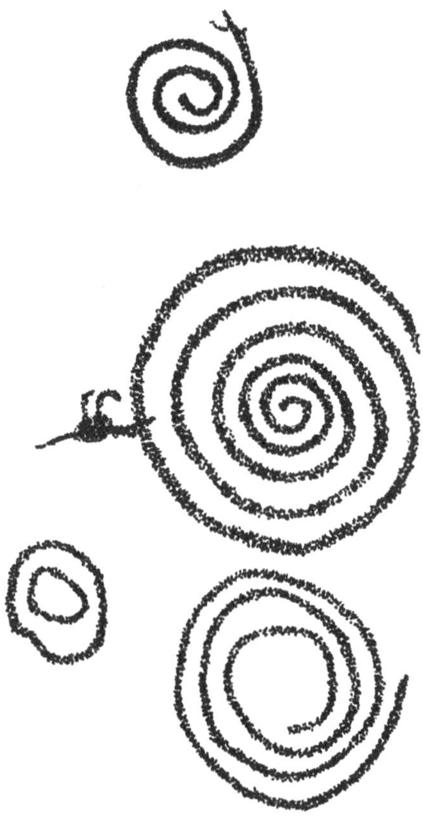

192. Spirals, Southwest Side Locality. Large, central spiral is 32 cm in diameter. Panel is located along an east-west trail and faces southeast.

Mexico, the spiral refers to Quetzalcoatl in his form as wind god (the wind that precedes a storm). He is also associated with water and agriculture. Some Pueblo people view spirals as whirlwinds. Commonly called dust devils, these whirlwinds are powerful spirals, and shamans are said to travel in them. Sometimes several of the great, twisting columns can be seen moving across the desert floor at the same time.

Swastikas and Whorls

An intriguing element found in the South Mountains is a geometric design called a swastika, which is formed by four intersecting lines that form a cross, the tip ends of which then bend at 90-degree angles. A whorl is similar but curvilinear. Whorl designs also are called pinwheels.

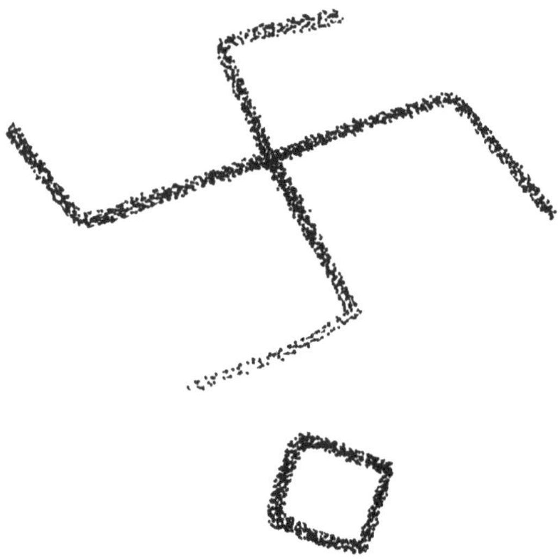

193. Swastika and square, Chandler Boulevard/32nd Street Locality. Swastika is 41 x 45 cm.

Swastikas and whorls appear by themselves and with other elements (figure 193). Some panels contain more than one. Most of the localities where swastikas and whorls are found contain no more than three of these elements. The largest quantity in one location is in Box Canyon, where we recorded ten. One of these panels, on the eastern side of Bird Hill, has two swastikas and a whorl in the same panel (figure 194). The two swastikas point in opposite directions and are separated by a large crack in the rock face. A swastika by itself on a rock outcrop on the eastern side of Box Canyon is at least twice as large as most other swastikas (figure 195). The winter solstice sun sets over another large swastika at the Chandler Boulevard/32nd Street Locality on the southern side of the South Mountains.

Swastikas or whorls may point in either a clockwise or a counterclockwise direction. Some have lines extending out of them (figures 196 and 197). An interesting panel on one of the higher ridges, south of the National Trail, has an elaborate whorl above an anthropomorph and next to a snake (figure 198). This panel faces to the southeast, where the winter solstice sun rises above the horizon.

Swastikas and whorls point either to the right or to the left, with one example pointing in both directions at the same time. A panel along the Kiwanis Trail has a whorl with a spiral for one of its arms. In the Holbert Trail Locality, a panel with two birds has a whorl with an added, curving appendage through its middle (figure 199).

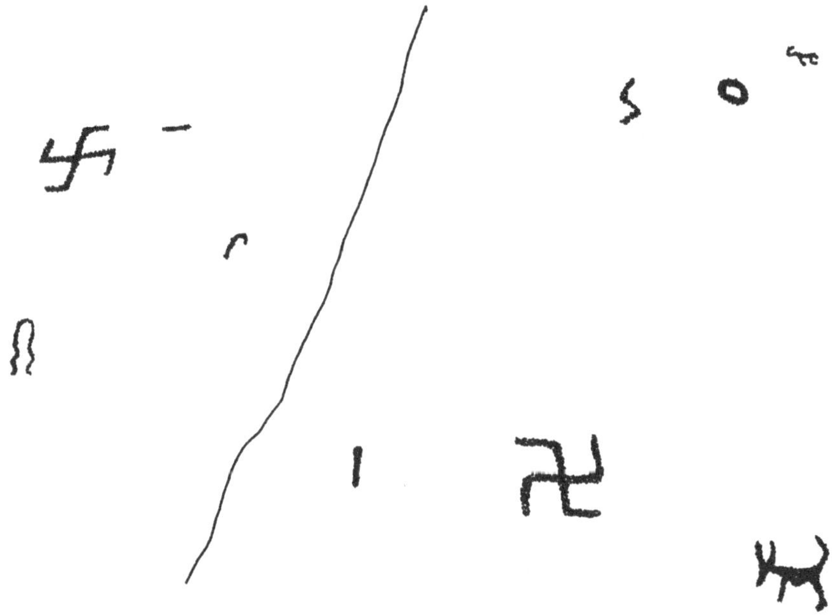

194. Panel with two swastikas oriented in opposite directions and separated by a natural crack in the rock face, located in Box Canyon on Bird Hill. Right swastika is 13 x 14 cm.

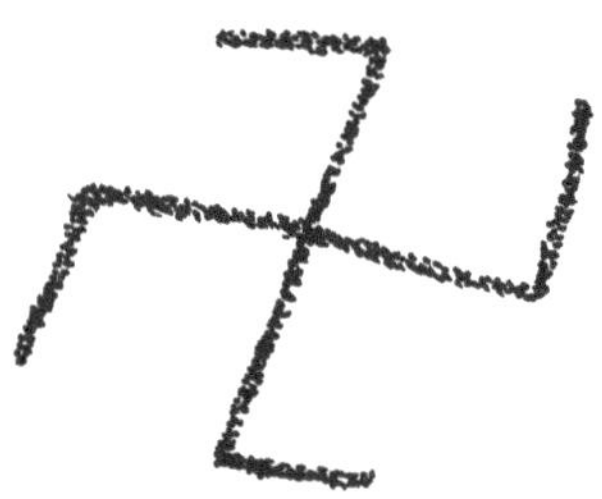

195. Swastika, eastern side of Box Canyon. Petroglyph is 36 x 37 cm.

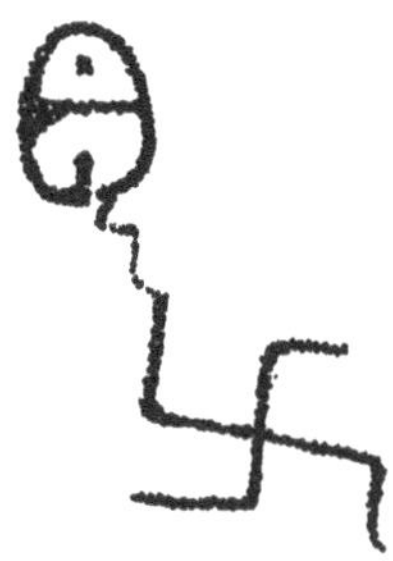

196. Swastika attached to circular design, 16th Street Locality. Swastika is 14 x 18 cm.

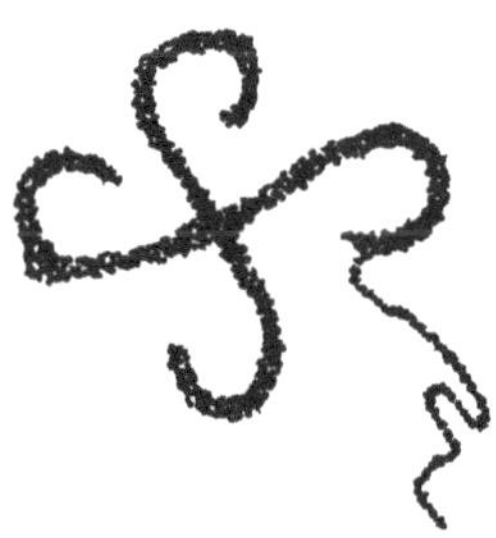

197. Whorl with attached wavy line, Box Canyon. Whorl is 29 x 33 cm.

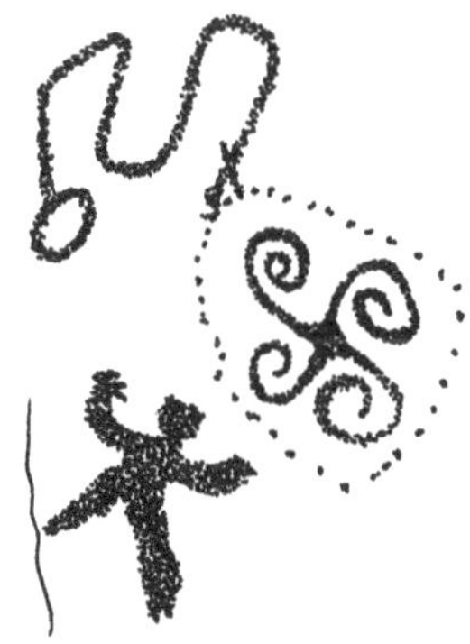

198. Elaborate whorl design with anthropomorph and snake, National Trail. Anthropomorph is 13 cm in height and has been repecked. Panel faces southeast, toward winter solstice sunrise.

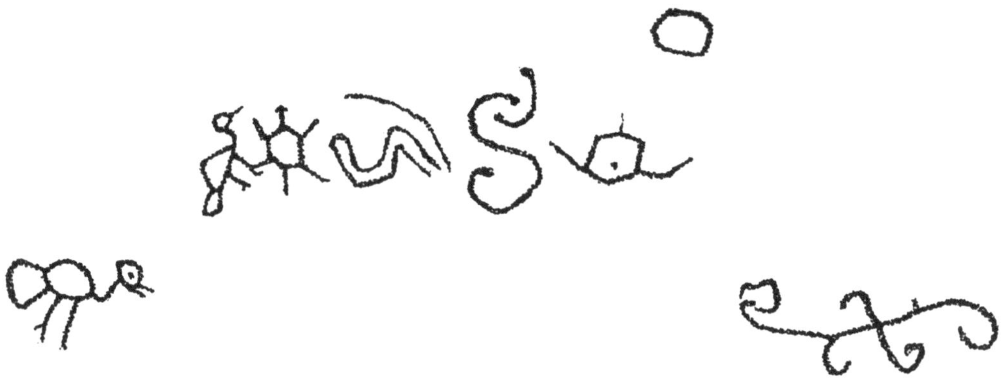

199. Elaborate whorl design, Holbert Trail. Bird on lower left is 30 cm in length.

Swastikas are an ancient and widespread symbol. In some places of the Old World, they represented the course of the sun through the heavens (Hall 1994). Clockwise swastikas could indicate masculinity and the sun, and counterclockwise swastikas symbolized femininity and the moon. As stated above, swastikas and whorls in the American Southwest have been interpreted as representations of whirlwinds, a common sight in the Sonoran Desert during hot summer months. In 1888, Frank Hamilton Cushing (1890) observed a Pima (Akimel O'odham) woman with a tattoo of a swastika on her shoulder. Cushing noticed that similar designs were present as rock art and on painted pottery. He surmised that the design represented the four winds to the Pima. Whorls were common geometric designs in O'odham basketry, some of which appear very similar to the rock art designs in the South Mountains. Anthropologist Alexander Stephen (1936) reported that whorl designs on Hopi pottery represented the breath of god. In his *Book of the Hopi,* Frank Waters (1963) stated that the swastika symbolizes the Hopi migration routes in the four cardinal directions, with the center in Hopi country in northern Arizona.

"X"

A DESIGN ELEMENT in the form of an "X" was clearly part of the Hohokam rock art inventory in the South Mountains. It occurs in many panels, often inconspicuously but sometimes in a dramatic fashion (figure 200). It also is present by itself occasionally. On the western side of the 36th Street Locality, a large "X" is in outline form next to an anthropomorph, a lizard, a figure eight, and other elements (figure 201). Another similar "X" is present on a prominent ridge along the eastern side of the same locality. An elaborate "X" design has curved ends and a line that splits the element in half in the San Juan North Locality (figure 202).

The most spectacular "X" panel in the South Mountains is located in the upper portion of the 24th Street Locality at the Yellow Rock Site (figure 203). This site is

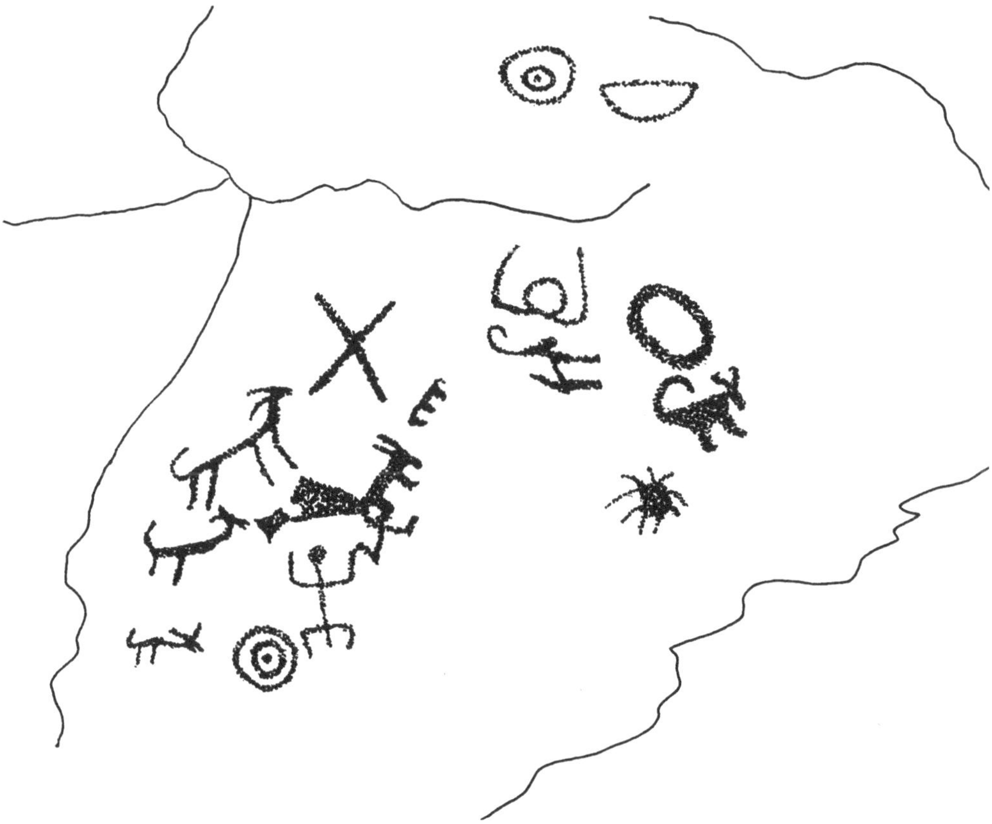

200. "X" design, 27th Street Locality. Central lizardman is 35 cm in length.

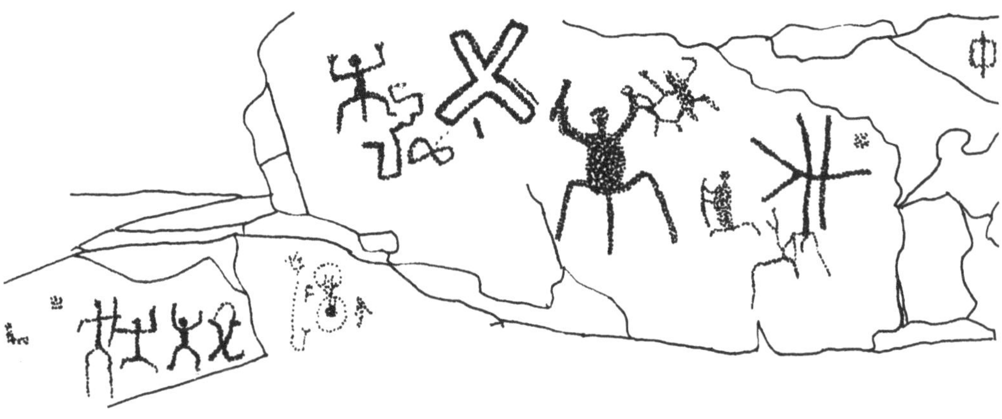

201. Negative "X" design and other petroglyphs, 36th Street Locality. Central lizardman is 35 cm in height.

situated next to a saddle on a long ridge and contains several panels and a cleared area with Hohokam pottery. An excellent view of the northern and eastern horizon of the Salt River Valley can be seen from the site. One of the panels has a natural "X"-shaped mineral vein in a yellow-colored rock outcrop. This natural "X" was outlined with pecking to form an outlined "X." Other elements are present on this panel, including a small anthropomorph, wavy lines, and a small, solid "X" directly above the large, outlined "X."

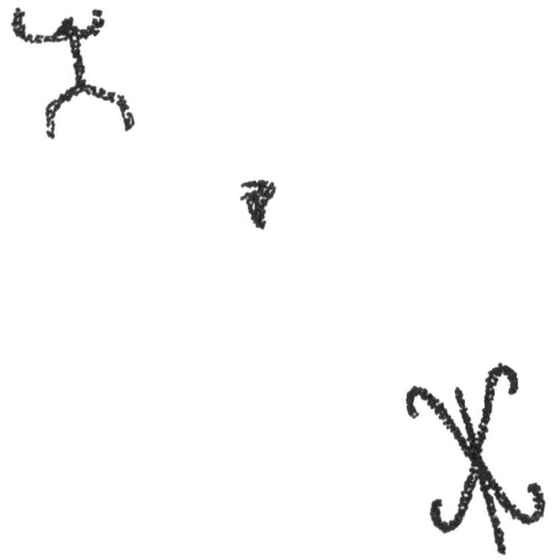

202. Elaborate "X" design and anthropomorph, San Juan North Locality. Anthropomorph is 21 cm in height.

"X" designs occur on shell tradeware artifacts from Casas Grandes, located in northern Chihuahua (DiPeso et al. 1974). They also are sometimes associated with Mogollon images of serpents and masks. Polly Schaafsma

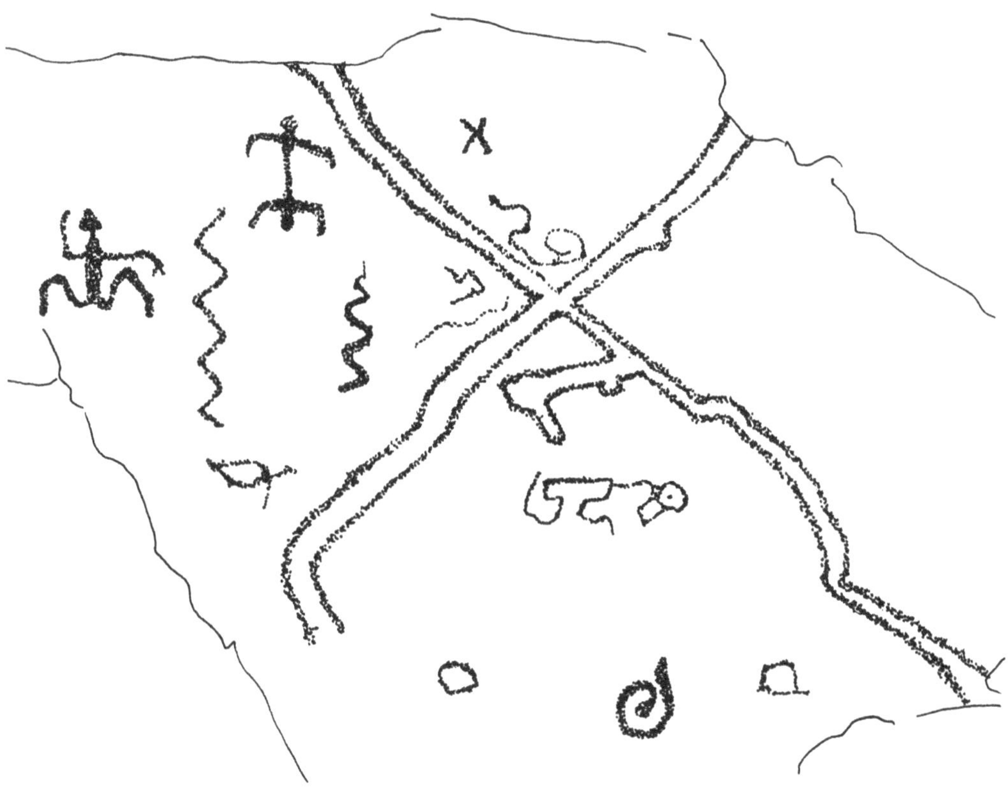

203. Large "X" petroglyph at the Yellow Rock Site, 24th Street Locality. Petroglyph outlines a natural vein in the rock outcrop. Outlined "X" is 2 x 1.4 m; upper anthropomorph is 22 cm in height.

(1989) has noted that the "X" design represents the track of the roadrunner among certain Pueblo groups. These tracks are powerful because they do not reveal which way the bird has gone.

Diamonds

Diamonds are not a frequent element in the South Mountains, but their various depictions are very interesting. A large diamond chain is present in a panel located along a wash in the Holbert Trail Locality (figure 204). We recorded several diamonds with one to six appendages at the following localities: San Juan North, 24th Street, 32nd Street, Beverly Canyon, Box Canyon, and Mormon Loop Trail (figure 205). Two of the diamonds have central dots. One complex diamond petroglyph near a spring along the Mormon Loop Trail has a face in its center (figure 206). A diamond with four appendages, or legs, in the 32nd Street Locality is situated on a high ridge that provides a view of the Four Peaks and the summer solstice sunrise. One of the legs points directly to Four Peaks (see figure 258).

Henry Wallace (1989) has suggested that in the Gila Bend area diamonds with appendages may be a design associated with the Patayan Culture. We have found nothing to suggest that the diamonds with appendages in the South Mountains are not Hohokam.

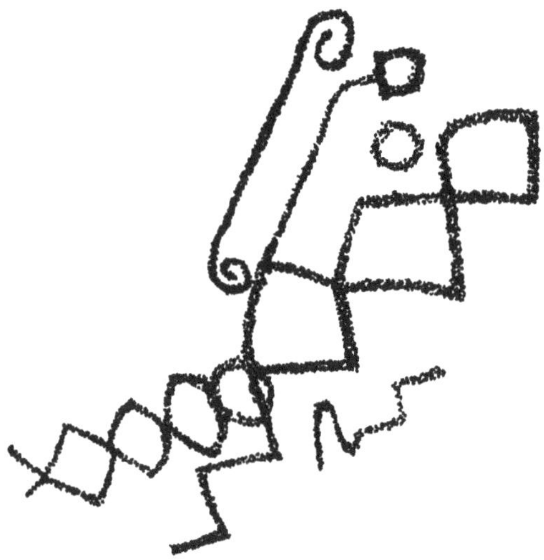

204. Two diamond chains touching each other, Holbert Trail. Combined diamond chains are 1 m in length. This is the left portion of a larger panel.

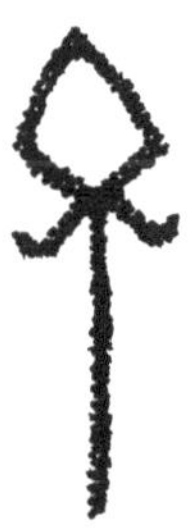

205. Diamond with legs and tail, 32nd Street Locality. Diamond is 26 cm in length.

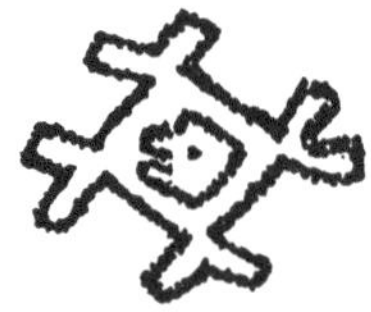

206. Elaborate diamond petroglyph with face inside, Mormon Loop Trail. Diamond petroglyph is 11 x 13 cm.

ZIGZAGS

ZIGZAGS OCCUR BY themselves and in panels with other designs. They are formed by a single zigzag line or by two to three parallel zigzag lines (figures 207 and 208). None was recorded with more than five parallel lines, but some of the zigzags have up to ten waves. Most often they are horizontal, but some are vertical and a few are oriented at a 45-degree angle. A curious panel in the Southeast Side Locality appears to be historic in age because of its lack of repatination and the nature of its design; it has a set of three zigzags among several other elements, including a fish and two bird images (see figure 12).

The South Mountains zigzag images appear to represent water or serpents in motion, or in some instances lightning. Several panels show anthropomorphs hold-

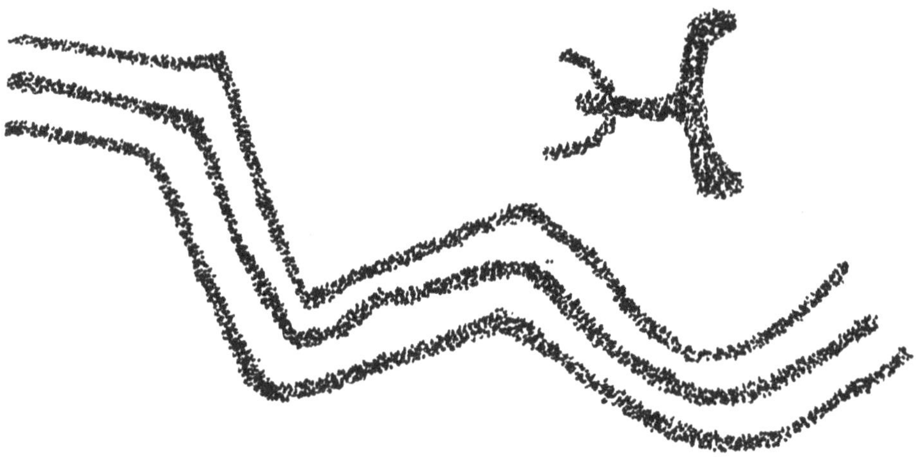

207. Zigzags and anthropomorph in alcove, Box Canyon. Zigzag is 83 cm in length.

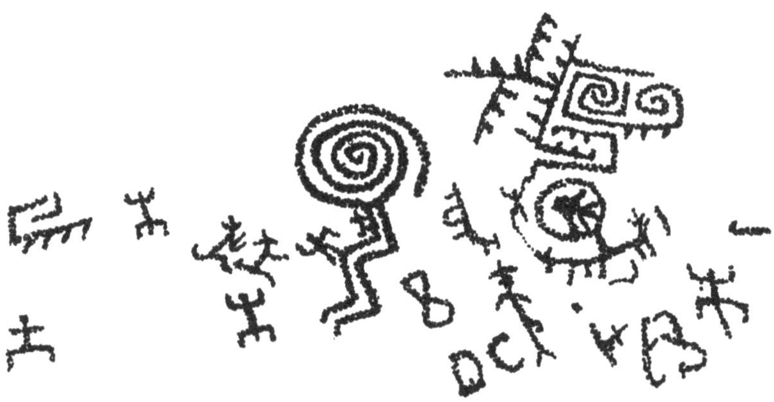

208. Zigzag attached to spiral, unusual mazelike design with hachured lines, and other petroglyphs, Hieroglyphic Canyon. Figure eight is 15 cm in length.

ing a zigzag line in one hand. A panel in Hieroglyphic Canyon has an anthropomorph holding a large waterbird and a lightning design (see figure 92). A rock art panel in Box Canyon has an anthropomorph above a large zigzag (see figure 207). In addition, anthropomorphs in Box Canyon and the upper part of the Mormon Trail (see figure 119) have zigzag legs, perhaps representing energy, motion, or the feeling a shaman attains when he goes into a trance.

Lightning is one of nature's most powerful forces and was especially so for native people of the American Southwest. Among the O'odham, shamans sought assistance from lightning for battle and other major purposes. An O'odham story describes a gambler who always lost until he convinced a shaman with the power of lightning to carve lightning symbols on his gambling sticks. One of the O'odham solstice deities is called Lightning Magician (Wupaki Makai); his house is located to the south, the direction from which summer thunderstorms approach the Salt River Valley (Russell 1975). Serpents are commonly understood to be both of the sky and of the ground: lightning in rain clouds and water springing from mother earth, spiritual and physical. The story of Quetzalcoatl is a Mesoamerican example of the spirit-serpent transformed to the physical. Frank Russell (1975:323) recorded an O'odham lightning song that describes lightning as "reddish snakes." For the Hopi, snakes also can represent lightning. Frank Hamilton Cushing (1979:195) stated that the Zuni often gave lightning the form of a serpent with a gliding, zigzag motion.

Squares

We recorded a small number of square elements in the South Mountains, usually as part of a complex geometric design (figure 209). In a few instances, they are an element in their own right. Some of the single square elements have central dots, similar to circles with dots, and some also have small openings (figure 210). In the lower level of the 32nd Street Locality, a panel has three squares, all with central dots (figure 211). Two of these squares are oriented in the same direction (north), with the central square oriented toward the northeast. The central square is oriented toward Four Peaks, where the summer solstice sun rises. In upper Pima Canyon, near the junction of Pima Wash and Mormon Loop Trail, we found a rock art panel with a square containing a central dot; an unusual crescentlike form is present below the square.

Another panel with a single square is located in the San Juan East Locality, near a wash and along a north-south trail. This panel has a series of tiny dots inside the square as well as "falling out" of the box in three lines, as though dropping water (figure 212). A tiny anthropomorph is located below the box, perhaps helping to release the water from it.

Several other box panels have multiple dots. A panel in Hieroglyphic Canyon has

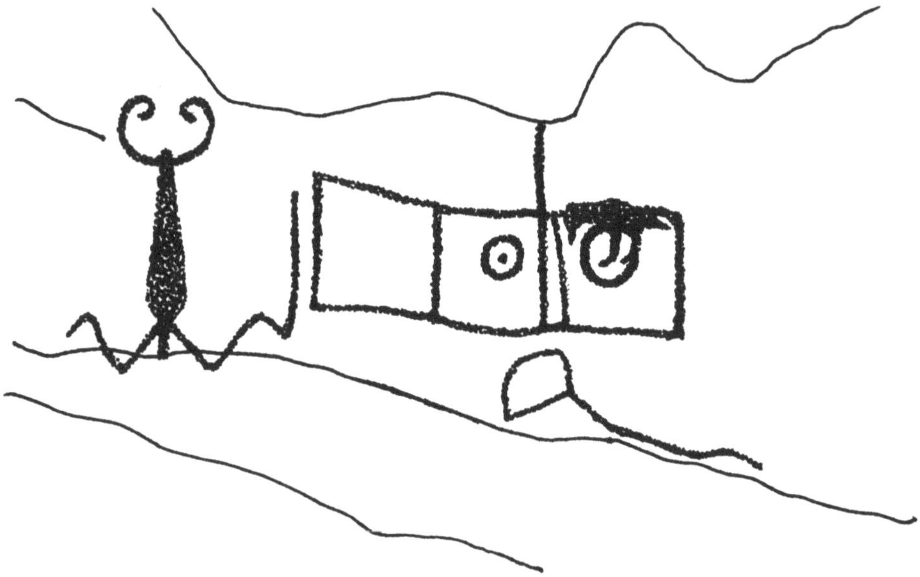

209. Squares with circles, 27th Street Locality.

210. Square with central dot, 32nd Street Locality. Square is 7 x 7 cm.

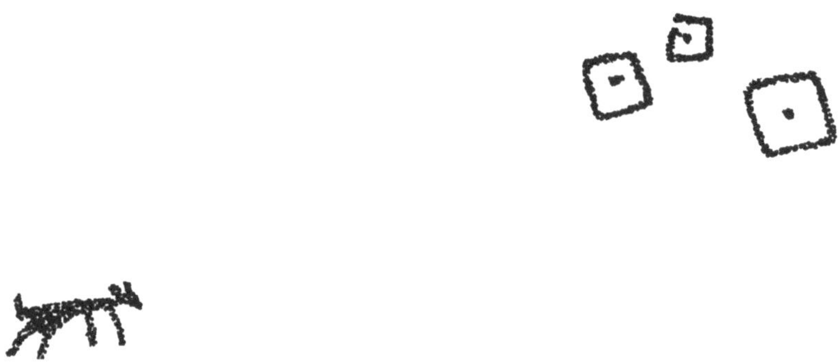

211. Three squares with central dots, 32nd Street Locality. Quadruped is 17 cm in length.

an anthropomorph with a big right hand standing beside a box containing twenty dots arranged in rows (figure 213). A square petroglyph at the bottom of Goodman Canyon has five dots spaced evenly within the box, as well as a straight line, which causes it to resemble a modern flag (figure 214). Another square with eight scattered dots occurs in the lower portion of the 32nd Street Locality. An "X" petroglyph is present to the left of this square (figure 215). A square design with an internal "X" is located on the north side of Twin Buttes, along a trail.

Several panels in the South Mountains have connected squares that form simple grids. Examples consist of a panel in Box Canyon with ten connected squares and a panel in the 32nd Street Locality that also has ten connected squares. In addition, a panel at the 28th Place Locality has a grid with four connected squares and appendages; a water-bird petroglyph is located next to this grid. An

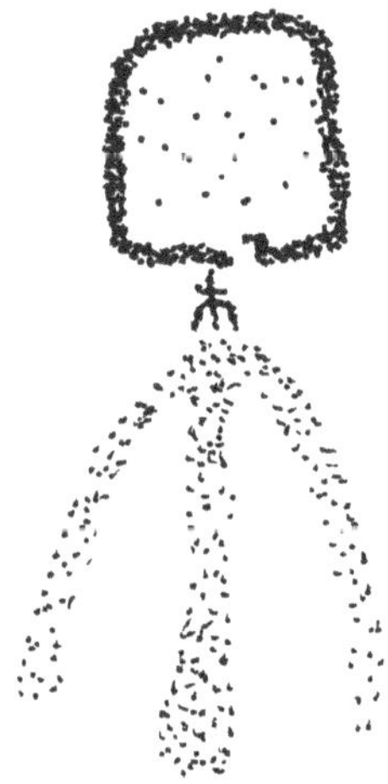

212. Box with small anthropomorph and pattern of dots as though water is falling, San Juan East Locality. Box is 9 x 10 cm.

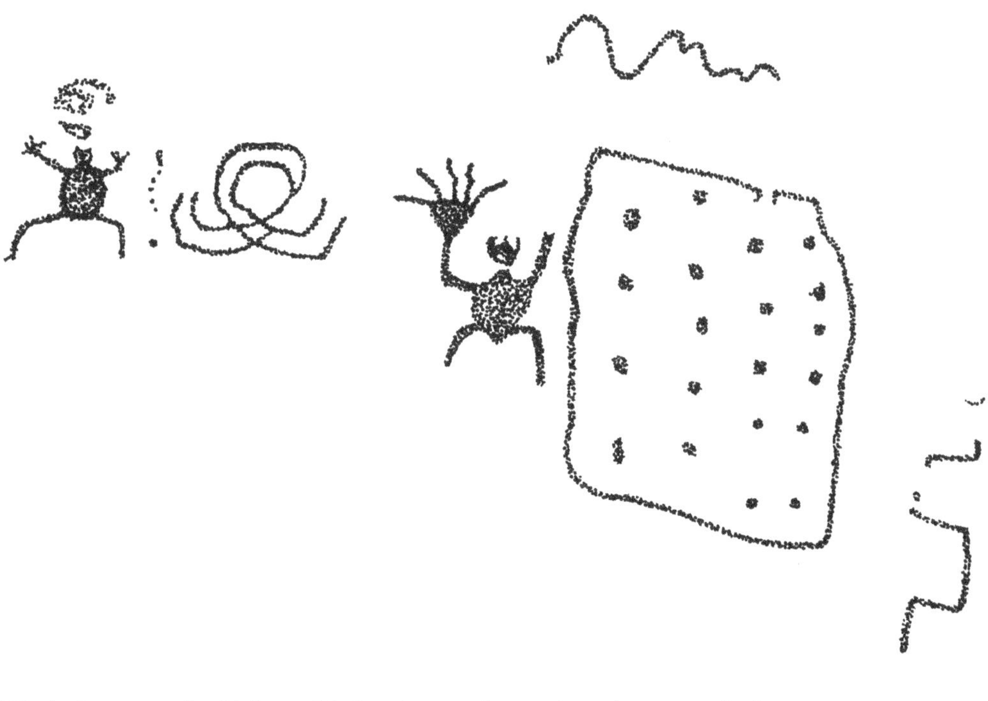

213. Anthropomorph with large right hand next to box with 20 dots, Hieroglyphic Canyon. Box is 47 x 38 cm.

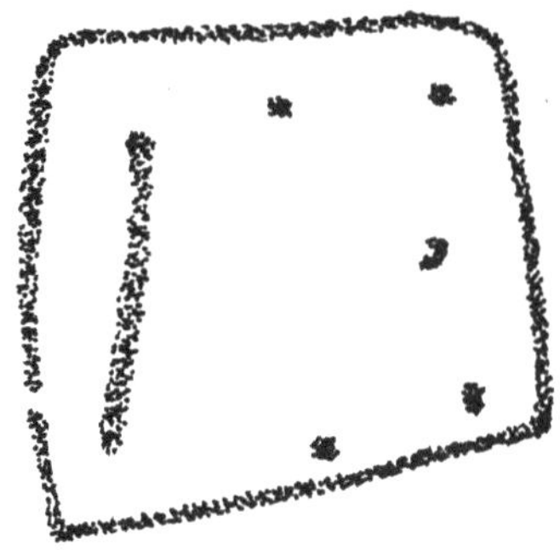

214. Box with 5 dots and line, Goodman Canyon. Box is 35 x 36 cm.

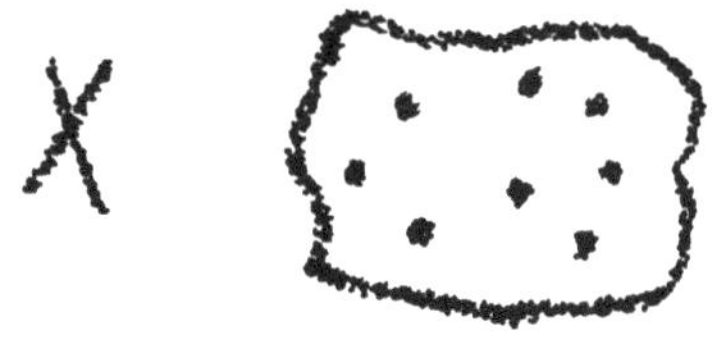

215. Box with 8 dots, 32nd Street Locality. Box is 14 x 17 cm.

unusual grid on a panel in the 32nd Street Locality has two squares connected to two circles; all four have central dots.

Squares with central dots occur as designs on painted red-on-buff pottery from Snaketown. For some Pueblo groups, square designs can symbolize a place or land (Fewkes 1903:161–162; Mallery 1893:746). Squares within squares sometimes represent shrines. The Hohokam squares also could symbolize farmers' fields.

Textile Patterns

A small number of rectangular gridlike designs have somewhat elaborate interior markings suggesting that they may represent textiles with decorations or pottery designs. We identified five of these patterned grid designs in four different localities: one each at 36th Street and 48th Street and two in Hieroglyphic Canyon on the northern side of the South Mountains, with another one at the Pecos Road Locality on the southern side of the mountains.

The textile design at the 36th Street Locality is by itself on a ridge outcrop (figure 216). A small masonry structure is located in a nearby saddle, and a trail connects the structure and the panel. Pecked human figures also are located nearby. This design is usually referred to as a cribbing design. The textile design at the 48th Street Locality is a double zigzag design and is situated near a wash with numerous other panels. A rock shelter is present nearby. Similar zigzag designs occur on Hohokam carved stone cylinders and bowls. The two textile designs in Hieroglyphic Canyon are the most elaborate of the five, being nested chevron patterns (figures 217 and 218). They were placed on two boulders near each other in a wash that contains a spring, and among a very dense concentration of other panels. Several rock shelters are present in this isolated canyon as well. Finally, the textile design at the Pecos Road Locality no longer exists or was moved to some unknown location during construction of the road in the mid 1990s. A photograph of this panel, taken in 1986, shows a complex grid design called a basket weave, or plaited pattern (figure 219). No habitation features were noted at that time, but the site was located along a major trail leading from the Gila River into the South Mountains.

Similar decorated boxes occur as rock art elements in the Jornada Style rock art of New Mexico and in the Paquimé region of northern Chihuahua. Polly Schaafsma (1998:36) called these elements "cuandros," or cartouches, and observed that a small number of them resemble masks.

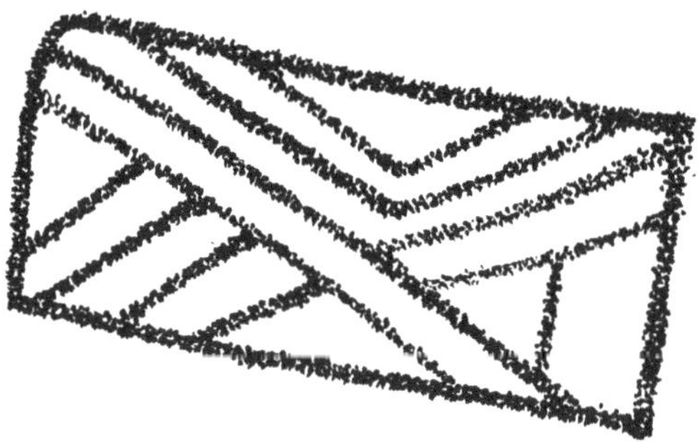

216. Textile pattern petroglyph, 36th Street Locality. Pattern is 40 x 20 cm.

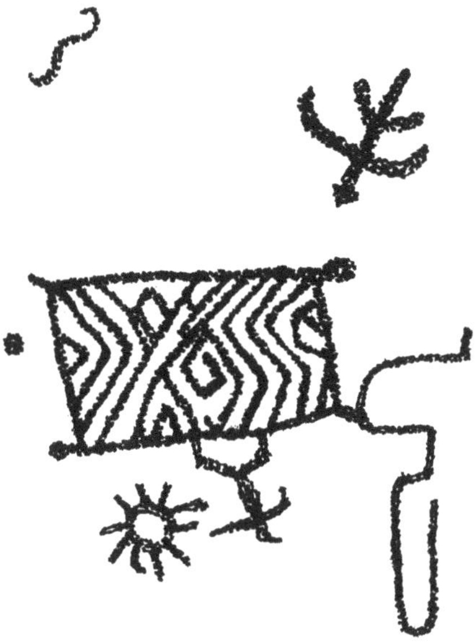

217. Textile pattern petroglyph, Hieroglyphic Canyon. An anthropomorph is standing on one of the edges of the textile pattern. This panel is located on a boulder that may have turned over; thus the panel would be turned around 180 degrees. Pattern is 20 x 38 cm.

Mazes

Several complex geometric panels in the South Mountains may represent mazes. Most do not present an unobstructed route into the middle of the geometric design, as in a traditional maze, but are merely meandering, interconnected lines taking complex curvilinear or rectilinear forms or combinations of the two. A rock art panel in upper Hieroglyphic Canyon has a small anthropomorph entering the geometric design (see figure 44). In the middle of the wash in Hieroglyphic Canyon, a large alcove occurs between several massive boulders. Inside this

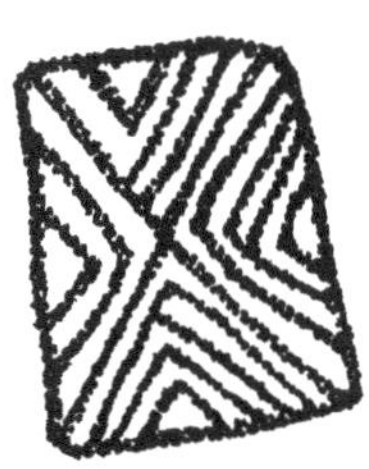

218. Textile pattern petroglyph, Hieroglyphic Canyon. Pattern is 26 x 23 cm.

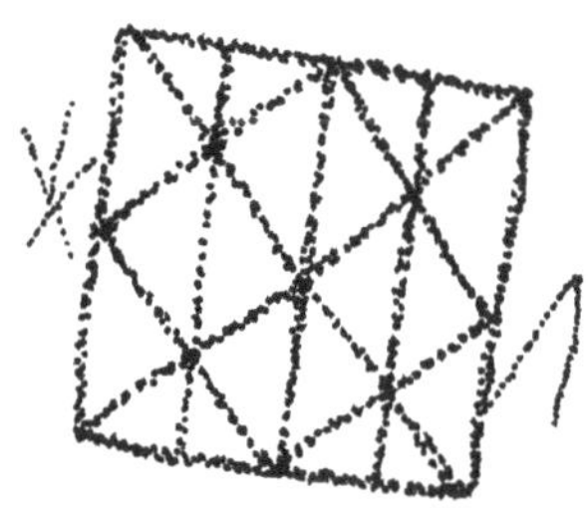

219. Textile pattern petroglyph, Pecos Road Locality. Panel has been destroyed or relocated from improvements to Pecos Road in the mid-1990s.

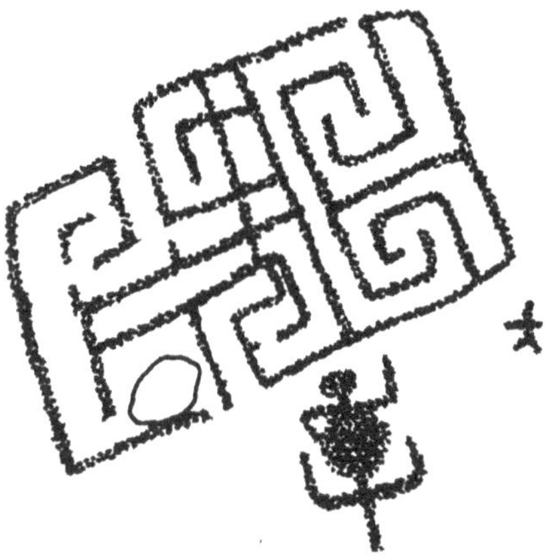

220. Mazelike design and lizard, Hieroglyphic Canyon. Lizard is 28 cm in length.

alcove is a panel of a maze with a well-executed lizard below it and a smaller stick-figure anthropomorph to the side (figure 220). The lizard has arms bent in opposite directions.

Two elaborate panels in the western portion of the 36th Street Locality have maze designs (figure 221). Both also have several anthropomorphs and other life-forms connected to the maze with wavy lines. Along the wash in Javelina Canyon is a beautifully pecked panel with a single geometric design that may represent a simple maze (figure 222). To the right of this panel are other panels that contain several anthropomorphs and negative crosses. A mazelike design, with both a rectilinear and a curvilinear form, is present in Goodman Canyon. Part of the design may represent a snake.

Frank Waters (1963) reported that, for the Hopi, the maze represents the universal plan of the Creator, which people must follow on the road of life. For the O'odham, the maze symbolizes life's journey, as well as the house of the gopher, who bored a spiral hole up to the surface of the earth from the underworld to allow people to emerge into this world. Anna Shaw (1968:15) tells a story about the origin of the Pima man-in-the-maze image: "After Se-Eh-ha [Se-ehe, or Elder Brother]

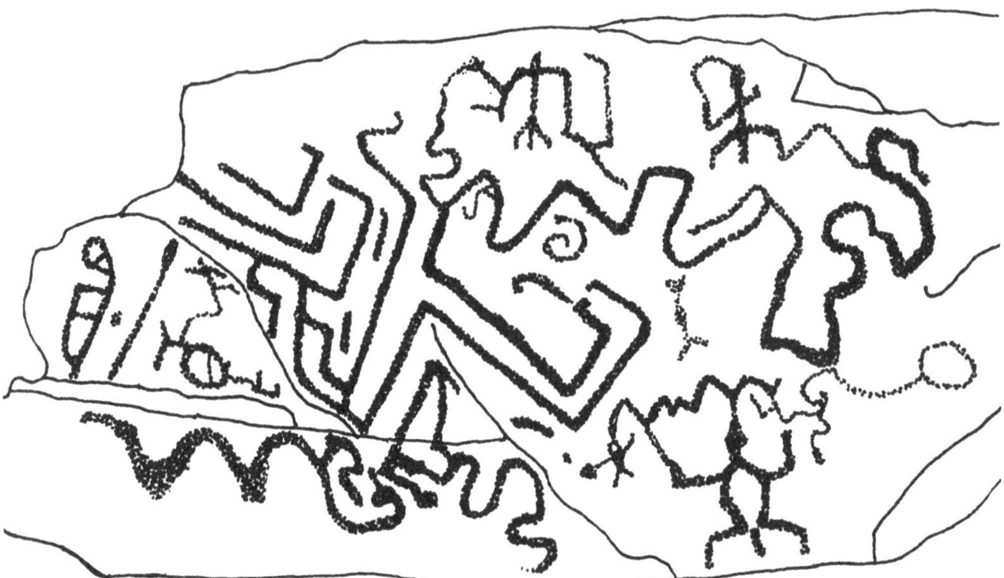

221. Mazelike design, 36th Street Locality. Lizard in lower right portion of panel is 20 cm in length.

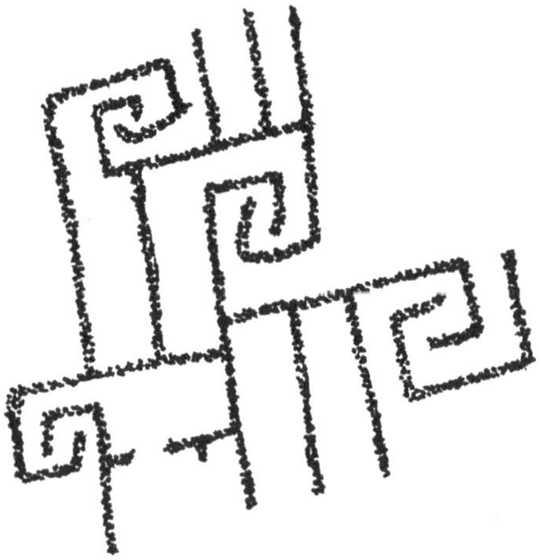

222. Mazelike design, Javelina Trail. Mazelike design is 52 x 57 cm. Panel has been vandalized with someone's initials.

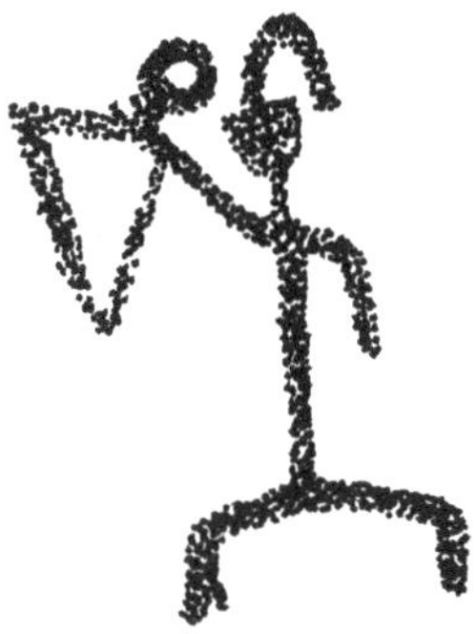

223. Anthropomorph holding triangle with small circle, Box Canyon. Triangle (which could be a surveyor's instrument) is 12 x 9 cm. Boulder containing this panel has been displaced from its original location, but it may originate from within Box Canyon.

returned to his home in the Greasy Mountains [South Mountains] he decided to build a new home, a dwelling that would be like a labyrinth with winding passages. His purpose was to bewilder the enemy should they come to destroy him. 'I'll be safe in my lodge in the center of my maze dwelling, he told himself.'"

Other Geometric Designs

The triangle is an infrequent but interesting geometric rock art element in the South Mountains. At two localities, Mormon Trail and Box Canyon, anthropomorphs hold large triangles (figure 223). Perhaps these individuals are surveyors and the triangles are their instruments.

A variety of other geometric designs occur in small numbers. These include grids, frets, and scrolls, which also were painted on Hohokam red-on-buff pottery (figure 224). The stepped fret is a common design on Pima baskets.

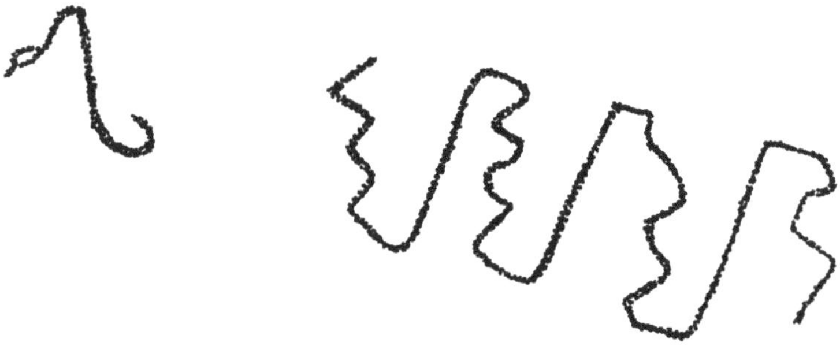

224. Fretlike design with snake, 32nd Street Locality. Snake is 16 cm in length.

Conclusions

A WIDE RANGE of geometric elements appear in the South Mountains, although variations of the circle dominate the inventory. Interpreting these rock art designs is difficult. Curiously, some of them—such as the cross, swastika, spiral, and figure eight—are easily recognizable symbols still in use today by cultures around the world. Rock art researchers have expressed two views concerning geometric designs: one interprets them as symbolic of something, often some religious concept, while the other portrays them as simply decorative designs. We prefer the former view. We believe that some of the circular elements and crosses in the South Mountains may have had astronomical meanings to the Hohokam (discussed in chapter 10). In addition, small clusters of circles or other simple geometric designs are located along trails as though they were trail markers. Other circular elements may represent portals into other worlds. Much remains to be learned about these enigmatic rock art elements.

CHAPTER TEN

SALUTING THE SUN

A Hohokam Calendar

For many people, the blue of the overarching sky means infinity, mystery, power. The sky is peopled with gods: sky gods, sun gods, wind gods, rain gods. Gods threw thunderbolts, carried the sun from east to west, protected it from hungry demons. The first astronomers of the planet attended to the needs of these deities.

—J. McKim Malville and Claudia Putnam (1989)

All cultures try to understand the universe in which they live, to determine their place within that universe. Archaeologists are increasingly aware that astronomy was one of the principal tools used by ancient cultures to study their universe and chart its patterns. Observations of those patterns, such as seasonal changes, were incorporated into larger worldviews and used to guide everyday living. Many past cultures observed the movements of objects in the sky, recording or marking the changing patterns of daily and nightly appearances. This information allowed them to create efficient calendar systems to better measure the cycles of nature and to put human activities in balance with those cycles. We believe the Hohokam were dedicated sky watchers and thoroughly familiar with the annual movements of certain celestial bodies.

Inventing Calendars

Native Americans have long had strong connections to the rhythms of the universe through observation of the sun, moon, and stars (Cope 1919; Williamson 1984). These rhythms create a sense of time, establishing the days, months, seasons, and years. When these time periods are tracked, they can be used to record important events and schedule future human activities. When activities are thus arranged, the result is a calendar. Today people are only vaguely familiar with the night sky and how it can be used to establish a calendar. Astronomer Ray Williamson (1984:5) comments on this prehistoric/modern contrast: "It is difficult for modern urbanites to imagine that men and women less technologically advanced paid such close attention to the effects of the stars and purposely observed sunrise every day. Yet there is abundant evidence that they did and that their modern descendants still do watch the sky for such things as planting, religious ritual and guidance in their daily affairs."

The fundamental unit of time measurement for nearly all calendars in the world is the "day"—the period of one rotation of the earth about its axis, or from a human perspective, the time taken by the sun to complete its daily journey and return to the morning sky (Richards 1998). Thus, calendars are schemes for grouping days into longer units, such as months and years. Months were originally based on the cycle of the moon, which waxes and wanes with regularity. A year represents the time taken by the earth to revolve around the sun in its orbit, or from ancient people's viewpoint, the time it takes the sun to move in a full circle against the backdrop of the stars.

According to paleobotanist Vorsila Bohrer (1994), ancient and historic agricultural people of the American Southwest defined their universe by the path of the sun. The apparent pattern of the sun's path provided the quadrilateral model of the cosmos prevalent among Mesoamerican cultures of ancient Mexico. The "corners of the earth," in this model, are marked by four sacred locations: the summer solstice sunrise on the northeastern horizon; the summer solstice sunset on the northwestern horizon; the winter solstice sunrise on the southeastern horizon; and the winter solstice sunset on the southwestern horizon (figure 225). Two pairs of "solstice houses" sit where the path of the sun intersects the earth at opposite horizons, with the equinox located halfway between the two solstice points. This solstitial model also sanctioned the counterclockwise motion followed by many Southwestern peoples, including the O'odham (Pima and Papago), during ceremonial dance circuits. M. Jane Young (1988:96) has commented the Zuni regard the winter and summer solstice points "as the most critical times of the year, for it was then that the sun appears to stand still for four days during its journey along the horizon." Elaborate rituals were developed and are still being performed to get the sun moving again—particularly to ensure that it turns around and continues its journey back along the horizon.

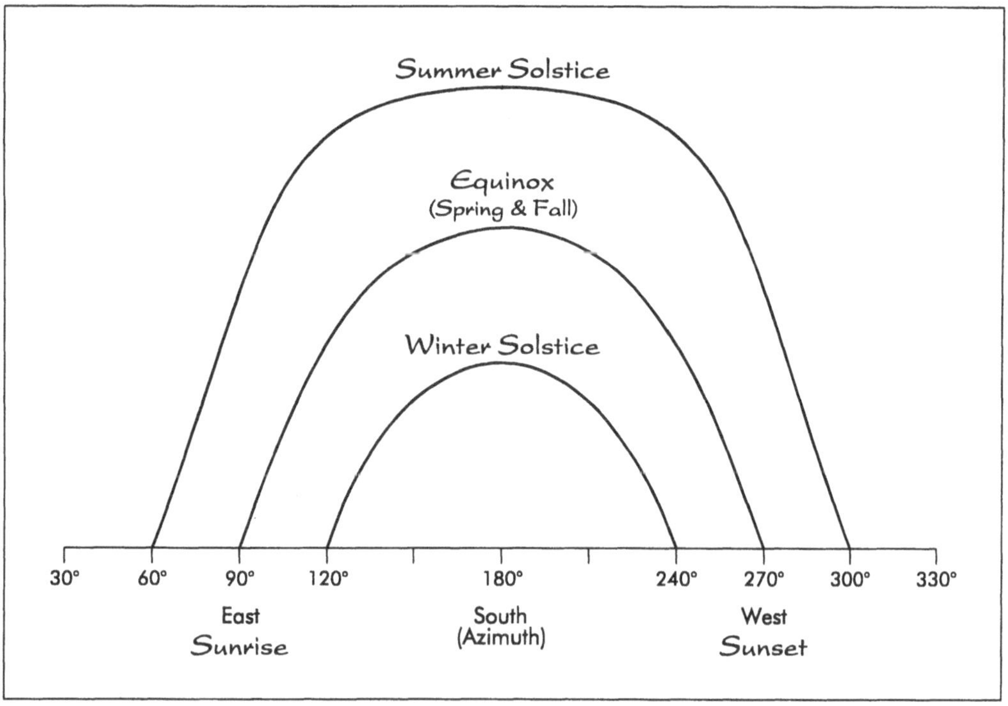

225. Annual movement of the sun's daily path through the sky in the Salt River Valley.

Archaeologists and archaeoastronomers have thoroughly documented that Mesoamerican cultures coordinated time and space by orienting rock art, buildings, and settlements with the movements of certain celestial bodies (Aveni 1980; Broda 1993; Cohodas 1975; Edmonson 1988; Malmstrom 1997). Ancient Puebloan buildings in Chaco Canyon, New Mexico, also are aligned with the rising and setting sun and moon (Sofaer 1997). Those orientations provided a constant reminder of the importance of conducting human affairs according to nature's cycles. The ability to make correct astronomical observations (and the control of that knowledge) was often used as a means to reinforce the status of an individual or group within a society.

The Hohokam certainly must have interacted with Mesoamerican cultures, because trade items from Mexico—including copper bells, ceramics, exotic birds, pyrite-encrusted mirrors, and other items—are found at Hohokam sites (Haury 1976). Hohokam ceremonial and ritual systems were likely influenced by Mesoamerican religions. David Carrasco (1990) has identified three of the main religious and ideological principles common to all Mesoamerican cultures: (1) world making, (2) world centering, and (3) world renewing. World making, recorded in mythologies about how the universe was made, expressed the organization of society by and around ceremonial centers modeled after the structure of the universe. World centering related concepts of the universe to the human body and was expressed through the performance of ritual specialists. World renewing was a ceremonial rejuvenation of time, human life, agriculture, and the gods—all organized according to astronomical and calendrical events. All three of these principles can be identified in Hohokam material culture and site structure.

According to O'odham oral traditions (e.g., Russell 1975), the sky is seen as a vault, with Earth Doctor spitting water into the sky to create stars and throwing a block of ice to make the sun. He then commanded Gray Spider to spin a web connecting the edges of the sky with the earth. Ethnobotanists Edward Castetter and Willis Bell (1942) reported that the sun, moon, and certain planets and constellations served as signposts for the O'odham calendar for scheduling festivals and other important activities. The O'odham believe in the omnipotence of the sun and tracked where it rose and set on the horizons. In addition, the O'odham used the dawn location of the constellation Pleiades, called "The Travelers," as a seasonal marker. A delegated individual observed celestial movements and provided information about when to plant to the headman, who then called the men of a village together, six days prior to planting, to inform them of the planting schedule. This anticipatory planting calendar resembles the Puebloan calendar system.

The historic O'odham had a twelve- or thirteen-month lunar calendar that started two nights before the appearance of a new moon in July, called saguaro harvest moon. (The twelve-month calendar may be a result of historic acculturation.) The thirteen monthly calendar divisions, listed below, were named after different moons or from observations about the condition of the environment (Lumholtz 1912:76).

Hot Moon
Rainy Moon
Short Planting Moon
Dry Grass Moon
Touches Mildly Moon (the cold touches lightly)
Low Cold Moon
Inner Bone Moon (the middle of the winter)
Heat Moon (the animals are in heat)
When the Animals Have Lost Their Fat
When the Trees Are Without Leaves
Green Moon
Yellow Moon (flowers on trees, bushes, and plants)
Flowers Disappear Moon (plants begin to make fruit)

The solstices were important seasonal events, with the creation myth formally celebrated during the sacred four-day winter solstice period. Two of the O'odham

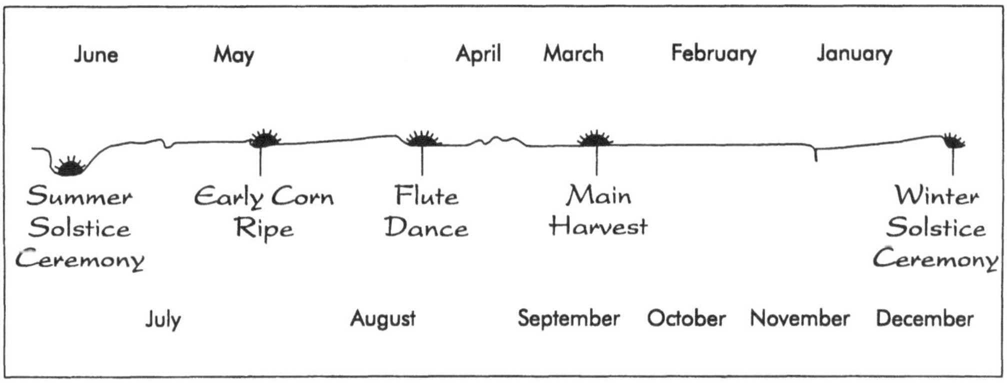

226. Ritual horizon calendar at the Hopi village of Shimopovi (after Forde 1931:Fig. 68, and Zeilik 1989:Fig. 10.4).

deities were believed to live at the solstitial points on the horizon: Tcopiny Makai (Sinking Magician) in his "house" at the northeast and northwest solstitial points and Vakolif Makai (South Magician) at the southeast and southwest houses.

The Hopi of northern Arizona also have a thirteen-month calendar, associating a specific ceremony with every moon (Ellis 1975). In addition, the Hopi conduct ceremonies for summer solstice sunrise and for winter solstice sunset (figure 226). Prayer sticks with roadrunner feathers are used during the winter solstice ceremonies when the sun needs strength and swiftness to get through this dangerous period (Fewkes 1920).

Astronomer Michael Zeilik (1987, 1989) studied the calendar systems of the Pueblo cultures and defined three different types of calendars: (1) horizon calendars, (2) light and shadow markers, (3) and lunar phase counts. Among the Zuni, the priest of the sun, or Pekwin, is responsible for keeping the village calendar. Anthropologist Ruth Bunzel (1992:512) described the role of the Pekwin: "As Priest of the Sun he is the keeper of the calendar. He sets the dates for the solstices, from which all other ceremonies are dated. His calculations are based on observations of the sunrise in the winter and the sunset in summer. These observations are made at shrines outside the villages. When the sun rises (or sets) behind certain landmarks, the date for the solstice is at hand. . . . It is at the solstices that the sun is celebrated with great public ceremonies. For some period of time before, the Pekwin observes fasts and continence and makes frequent offerings of prayer sticks to the sun and moon and the ancients." The Pekwin officiates at all ceremonies at which priests are present and is responsible for setting up the altars for all ceremonies that require altars. The Pekwin also blesses the road for the Katsina spirits when they visit the Zuni.

Archaeological evidence from several Hohokam sites in the Phoenix region suggests that the Hohokam utilized all three of the calendar systems used by the

Puebloans. The multistoried adobe Big House at Casa Grande has several astronomical features in two of its stories. A circular hole in a west wall provides a portal to view the horizon at summer solstice sunset, and a hole in an east wall allows a ray of light to pass through onto another interior wall during equinox sunrise (Evans and Hillman 1981; Molloy 1969). Archaeologists have proposed that the upper stories of this unique adobe building may have permitted lunar observations as well.

Other Hohokam sites also show astronomical functions. Rooms marking solstice sunrise on the eastern horizon have been recorded at Pueblo Grande platform mound (Mixon 1989) and Mesa Grande platform mound (Howard 1995). The Papago Buttes Hole-in-the-Rock formation in Phoenix creates a light interaction with manmade depressions, or cupules, that mark summer solstice and the equinoxes (Mixon and White 1991). A southwest-facing spiral pecked on Tempe Butte, which is next to the Salt River, is marked by a distinct triangle of light during the summer solstice solar zenith (approximate noon). An oval compound made of boulders, located on a hilltop in the Phoenix Mountains, 10 miles (16 km) north of the South Mountains, has masonry rooms and petroglyphs that align with or mark the equinoxes and the summer and winter sunrise and sunset (Bostwick and Plum 1997). A circle with a central dot is the predominant petroglyph element at this site, including an upright boulder with thirteen circle/dots that perhaps represent the moon—a clan sign for the extinct Puebloan Moon clan included the circle/dot (Michaelis 1981).

Petroglyph Celestial Designs

Ancient astronomy throughout the American Southwest combined observation of the movements of celestial bodies with features of the terrestrial landscape. For some Pueblo groups, sky symbolism was prominently depicted in warrior societies. High places, where storm clouds gather and lightning strikes, are often viewed as the "home" or domain of the gods; respectful visitors to these places carry offerings to invoke the resident spirits (Schaafsma 2000). The South Mountains provide numerous locations with outstanding views of distant horizons. Several rock art designs with what appear to be symbolic shapes may represent celestial objects. These include crosses, circles, concentric circles, circles with dots, crescents, and sun disks.

Three different types of crosses occur in the rock art of the South Mountains. One is the simple stick-figure cross, like a mathematical addition sign (+). Another form is the outlined cross, which has a stick-figure cross outlined entirely with another line. The third cross form is just the outline, without the interior cross but sometimes having other small geometric designs in its interior. This latter cross form is called a negative or hollow cross.

Stick-figure crosses are scattered throughout the South Mountains, alone and with other petroglyphs (figure 227). Determining if the stick-figure cross is historic

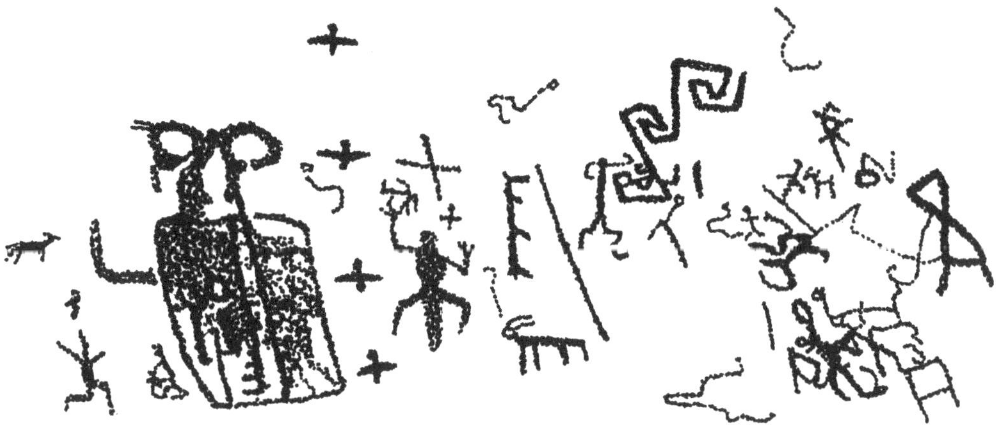

227. Four crosses next to large anthropomorph, Hieroglyphic Canyon. Large anthropomorph on left is 53 cm in height. Panel faces northeast.

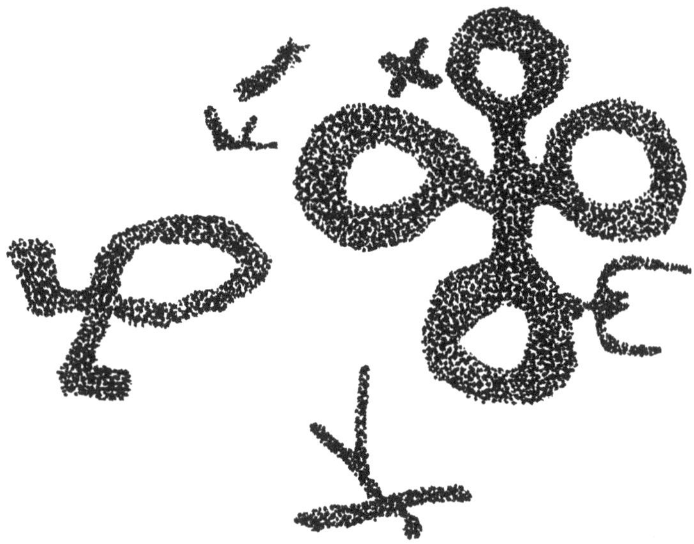

228. Cross with a circle at the end of each arm, 34th Street Locality. Cross with circles is 35 x 34 cm. Panel is on a low, sloping boulder and faces south.

or Hohokam in origin requires observing the degree of repatination, the quality of workmanship, and the nature of the surrounding petroglyphs. An elaborate stick-figure cross in the 34th Street Locality has a circle at the end of each arm (figure 228). Several stick-figure crosses occur on three high knolls along the southern ridge of Pima Canyon, overlooking the middle Gila River Valley. Another prominent stick-figure cross is located in a saddle on the eastern side of Goodman Canyon, overlooking a concentrated area of rock art panels within this narrow canyon. Several panels in the South Mountains have anthropomorphs holding stick-figure crosses; we noted interesting examples at the 27th Street and 36th Street Localities (figure

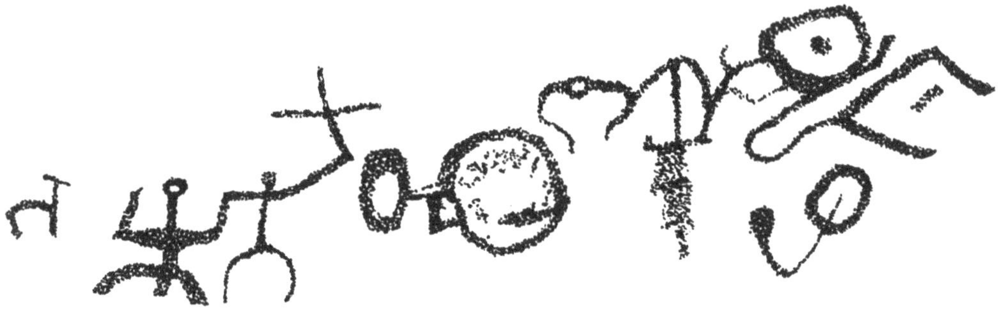

229. Anthropomorph holding cross, 27th Street Locality. Anthropomorph on far left is 13 cm in height. Panel faces southwest.

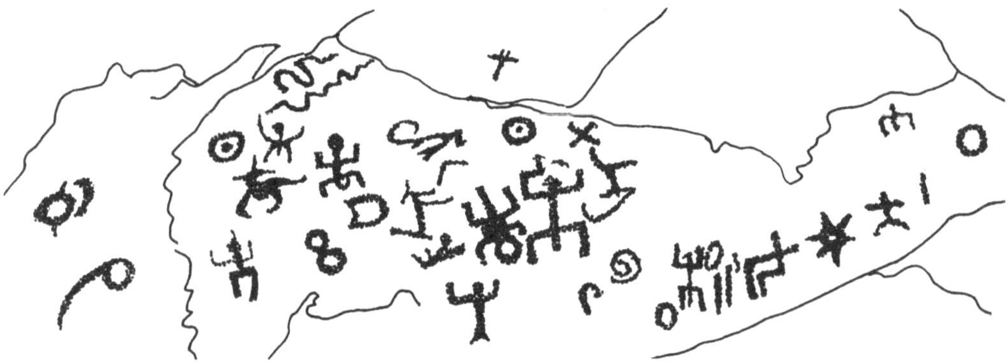

230. Panel with sun disk (lower right), cross with attached lines, circles, anthropomorphs, and other designs, 28th Place Locality. Sun disk is 8 cm in diameter. Panel faces southeast.

229). A few stick figure crosses have two lines extending from the cross, as though representing motion (figure 230).

Outlined crosses occur in about a dozen locations, with no more than two in any one locality (figure 231). Both rectilinear and curvilinear outlines are depicted, but outlined crosses are primarily curvilinear (figures 232 and 233). A fine example is located at a spring in the lower portion of the 24th Street Locality. This outlined cross is next to a small swastika and an elaborate rectilinear scroll (figure 234). A large outlined cross (48 x 38 cm) is present in Goodman Canyon (see below). On a high ridge within the upper portion of the 32nd Street Locality is an outlined cross with an attached line that loops back to the cross, perhaps suggesting motion (figure 235). Along the Javelina Trail, a rock art panel contains an outlined cross that is held by an anthropomorph. This panel faces southwest. A panel in the 36th Street Locality also has an anthropomorph holding an outlined cross (see figure 287).

Negative or hollow crosses are slightly more common than outlined crosses (figures 236 and 237). These cross types may be either rectilinear or curvilinear. With one exception, no more than three negative crosses occur in the same locality. That

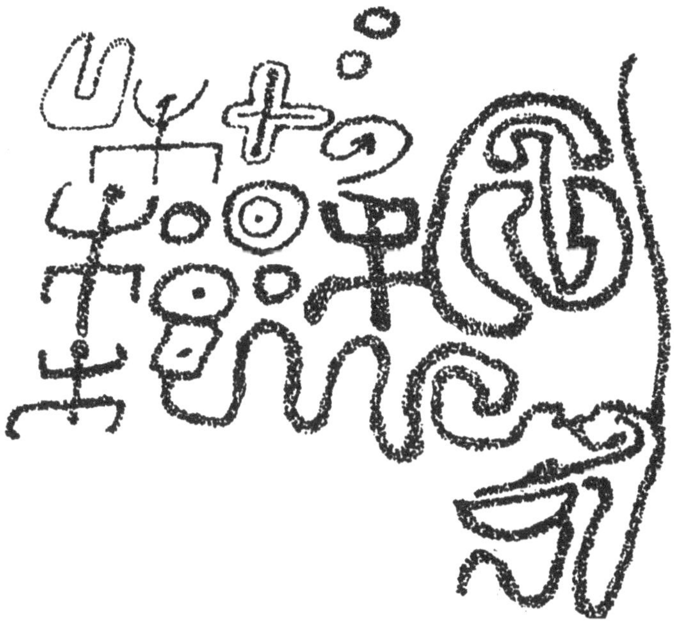

231. Outlined cross, 32nd Street Locality. Outlined cross is 19 x 19 cm. Panel is located near a rock shelter and faces northeast.

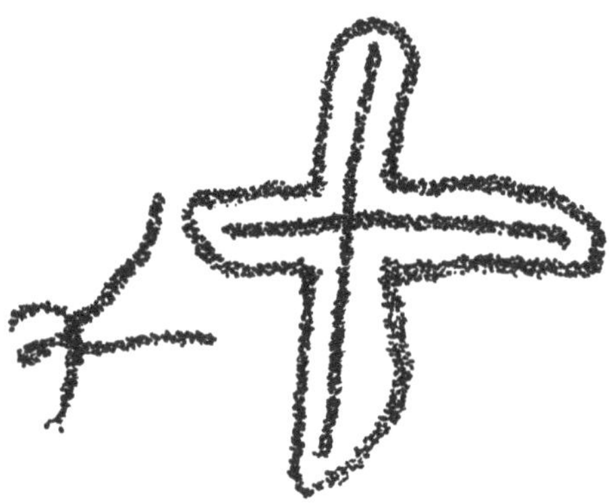

232. Outlined cross, Goodman Canyon. Outlined cross is 48 x 38 cm. Summer solstice sun sets over the outlined cross. Panel faces southeast.

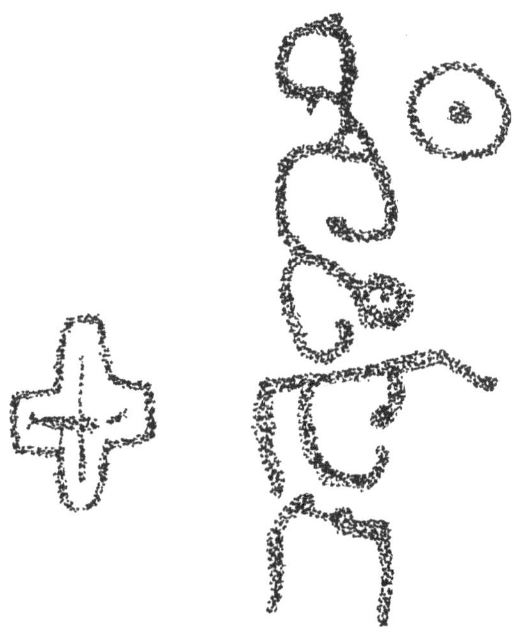

233. Outlined cross and geometric designs, San Juan North Locality. Outlined cross is 16 x 20 cm. Panel faces southwest.

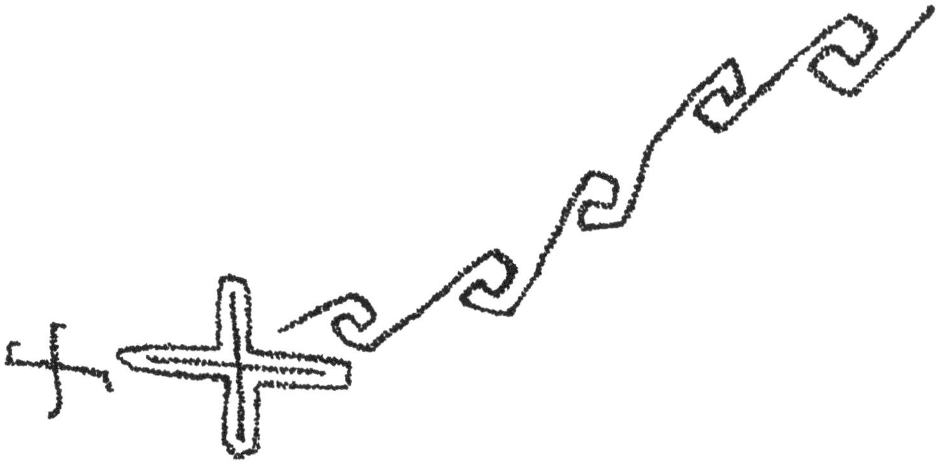

234. Outlined cross, swastika, and rectilinear scroll, 24th Street Locality. Outlined cross is 37 x 37 cm. Panel faces northeast.

exception is a spectacular panel located along the Mormon Loop Trail that contains seven negative crosses among numerous other geometric and representational elements (see chapter 11). One of the crosses in this panel has a circle in its center, another has a V shape inside it, and a third has a single line in its interior (see figure 288).

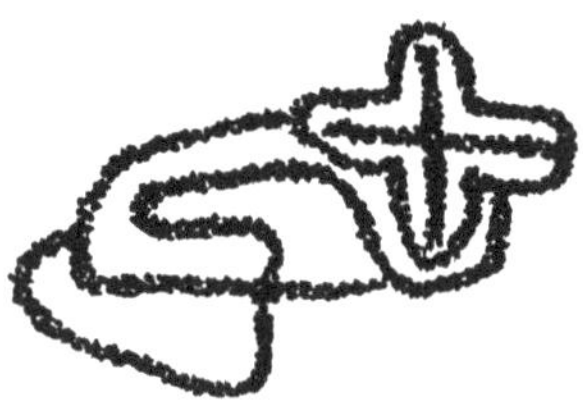

235. Outlined cross with attached lines, 32nd Street Locality. Outlined cross is 15 x 16 cm. Panel faces northeast.

Outlined crosses are very common in southern and western Arizona and southern California. A number of archaeologists have argued that the outlined cross symbolizes the planet Venus as the morning star, or evening star, based on its symbolism in Mesoamerica, where it is equated with the Mesoamerican god Quetzalcoatl (Johnson 1995). Because the morning star appears in the eastern sky before sunrise, it represents Quetzalcoatl as "he who precedes the sun" out of the underground. As the evening star it represents death, which is actually "birth" into the spirit world. And in eight days, Venus is "reborn" in the predawn sky. According to geographer Vincent Malmstrom (1997), the 584-day synodical cycle of Venus was recognized by the Maya in the seventh century, and they correlated their solar calendar with this cycle by observing that five revolutions of Venus around the sun were equivalent to eight earth cycles. In other words, Venus will appear in the sky in the exact same place every eight years. The Maya used the Venus cycle to predict eclipses of the sun by the moon.

The Venus cycle undergoes four phases in its movement through the sky. For part of the cycle it disappears completely below the horizon. The shape of Venus's

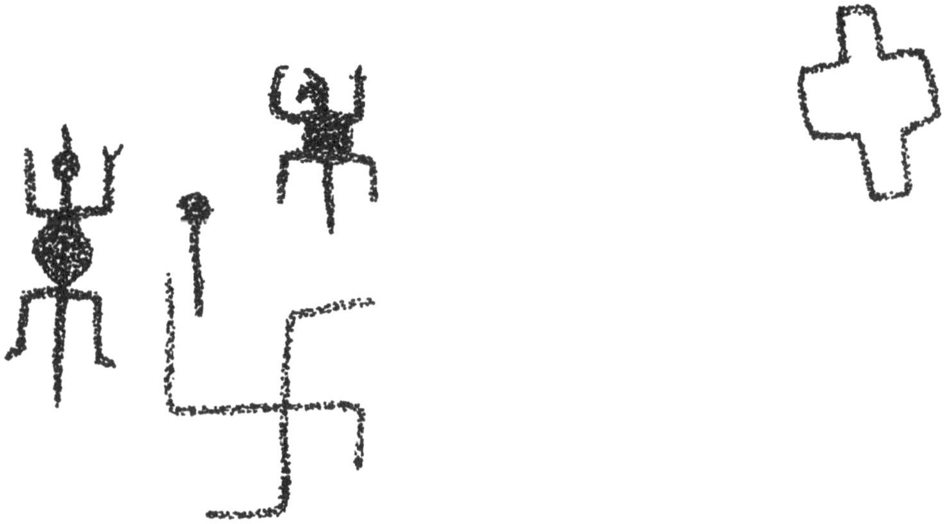

236. Negative cross with lizards and swastika, Central Avenue Locality. Negative cross is 25 x 17 cm. An outlined cross petroglyph is located nearby.

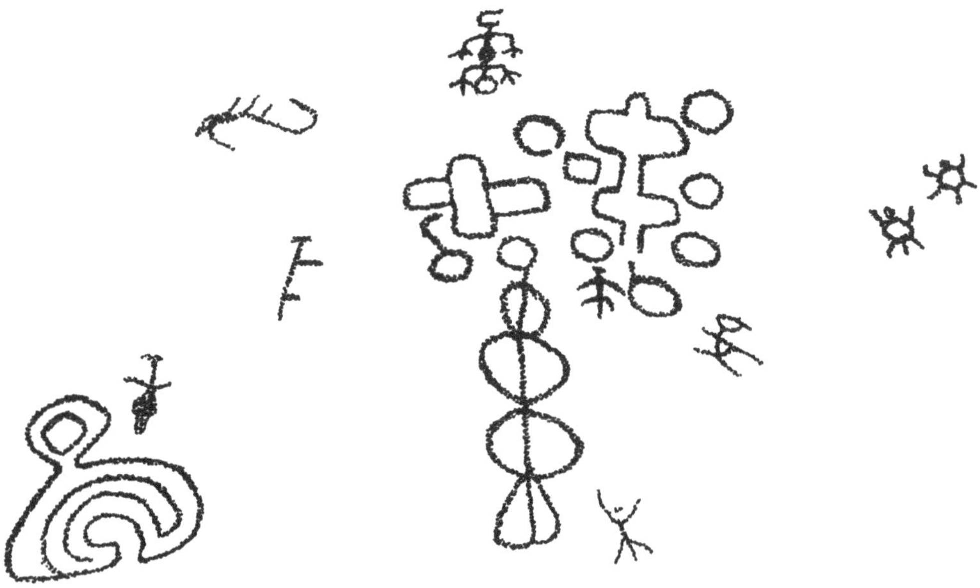

237. Negative cross, pipette, and other petroglyphs at lower entrance into Hieroglyphic Canyon. Pipette is 48 cm in length.

movement across the sky and below the horizon takes the form of an incomplete figure eight. It may not be a coincidence that several partial figure-eight designs occur in the South Mountains petroglyphs.

The moon may be represented in the rock art of the South Mountains as circles, partial circles, circles with central dots, and crescent shapes (figures 238–241). These may symbolize different phases of the moon. A panel at the 28th Place Locality has a four-legged mammal jumping over a circle with a central dot and a short appendage; an anthropomorph with upraised arms and a snake are located nearby. At a spring near the Mormon Loop Trail we found a panel with an anthropomorph holding an elaborate staff in one hand and a circle/dot next to it (see figure 117). A panel high up on the northern side of the mountains has three concentric circles with central dots; one of these has seven rings (see figure 244).

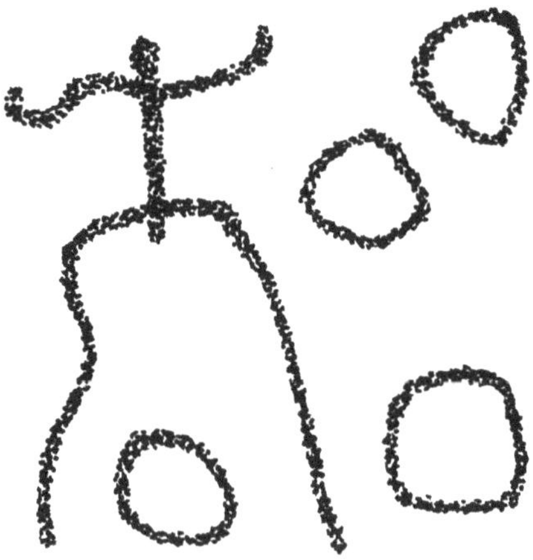

238. Anthropomorph with circles, 43rd Street Locality. Anthropomorph is 44 cm in height.

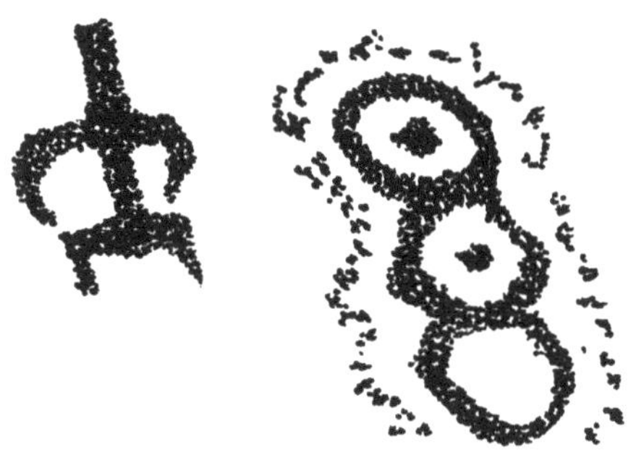

239. Lightly outlined circle chain and anthropomorph, 16th Street Locality. Circle chain is 24 cm in length.

• In the South Mountains rock art study we have not yet been able to test potential lunar alignments at sites containing possible moon petroglyphs, partly because the lunar maximum cycle is 18.6 years. In other words, a person must wait more than eighteen years to observe the moon rising and setting in the same place in the sky. It is worth noting that crescent-shaped designs occur above anthropomorphs and four-legged mammals in several panels in the South Mountains. An anthropomorph having a big left hand and associated with crescent forms and crosses is present in Hieroglyphic Canyon (see figure 107). An anthropomorph along a ridge trail in the 34th Street Locality has a crescent moon–shaped head. Finally, a panel at the 32nd Street Locality has thirteen circular dent patterns in a long arch across the face of a low boulder; these could represent thirteen moons (figure 242).

Concentric circles also could have represented celestial objects, although some

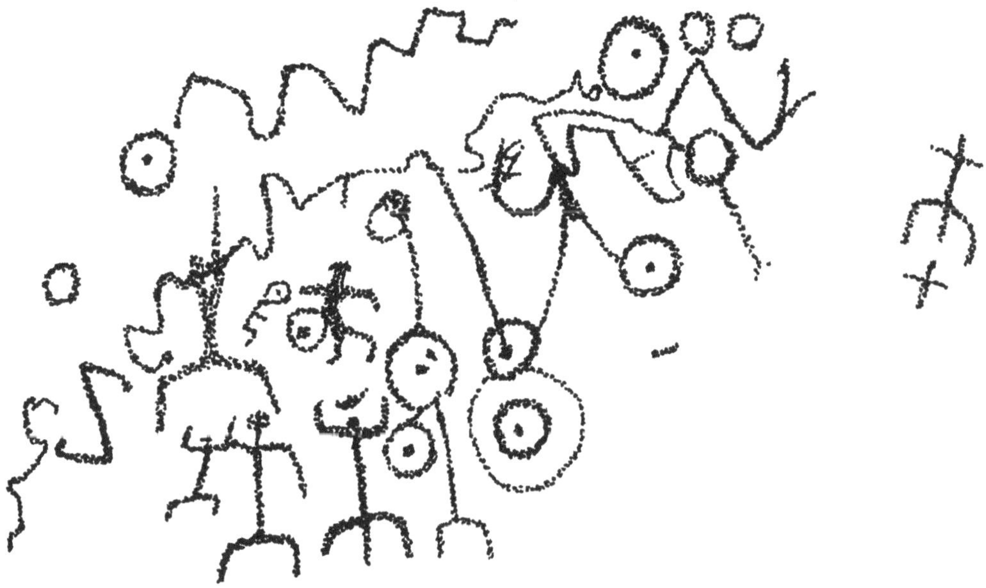

240. Circles with dots and anthropomorphs, Javelina Trail. Large anthropomorph on right is 36 cm in height.

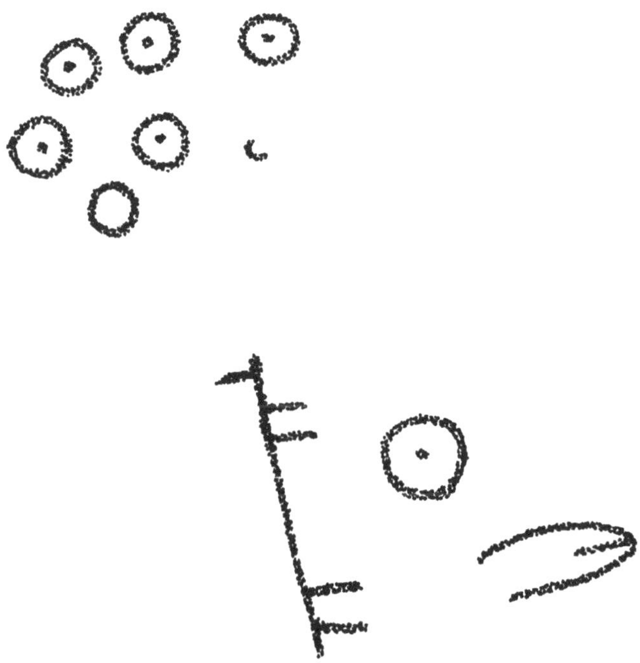

241. Circle variations, crescent, and vertical stick-figure quadruped, Goodman Canyon. Quadruped is 62 cm in length.

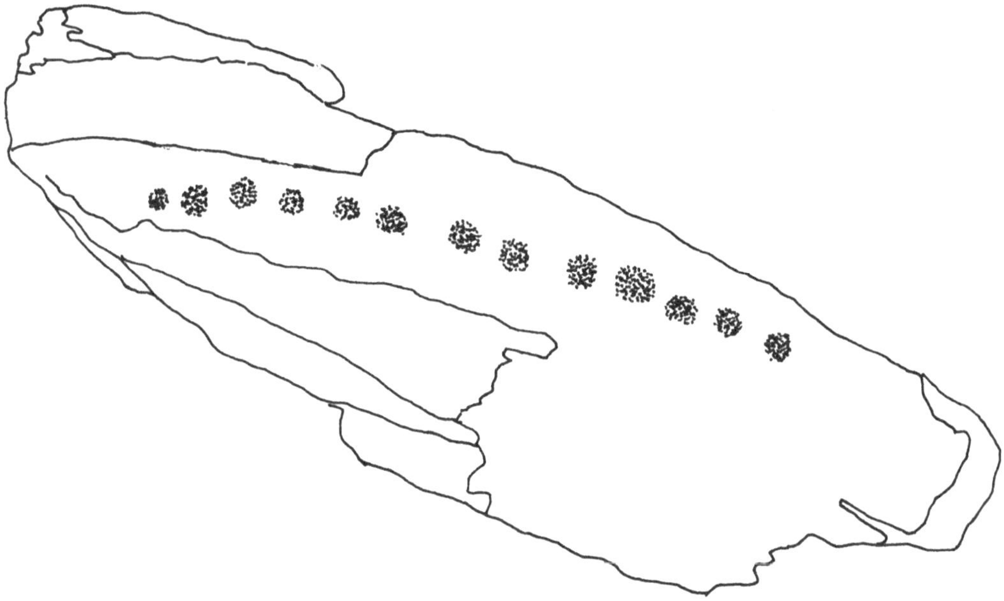

242. Thirteen dots in a row, possibly representing full moon cycles, 32nd Street Locality. Dots are 5 to 9 cm in diameter. Panel faces northeast.

have the appearance of tunnels or collapsing portals (figures 243–245). Anthropologist Florence Ellis (1975) reported that concentric circles with central dots symbolize the sun to some Pueblo groups. A Hopi informant told Polly Schaafsma (1980:11–12) that the concentric circle with central dot represents the earth. Peter Faris (1993) has suggested that the concentric circle symbolizes the sun with a halo, as seen in a moist atmosphere during the monsoonal summer rains.

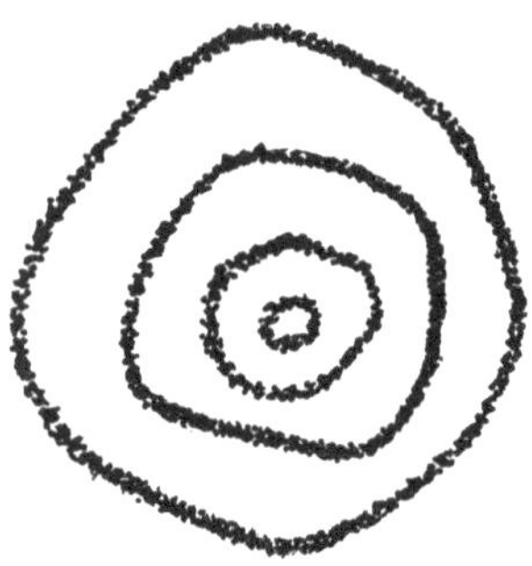

243. Concentric circles, Box Canyon. Petroglyph is 47 cm in diameter.

Concentric circles occur in large numbers in the South Mountains and are present at more than three-quarters of the localities. Occasionally they occur alone, but usually they are associated with other elements in the same panel. A panel in the 27th Street Locality has six concentric circle designs next to several anthropomorphs (figure 246). Sometimes concentric circles form part of the body of an anthropomorph or lizard (as in the Desert Foothills, 28th Place, and Mormon Trail Localities). A concentric circle design in Hieroglyphic Canyon has eight rings.

Circles with ticks (short appendages along their edges) have the appearance of radiating suns (figure 247). Harold Colton (1946:7) identified similar petroglyphs in

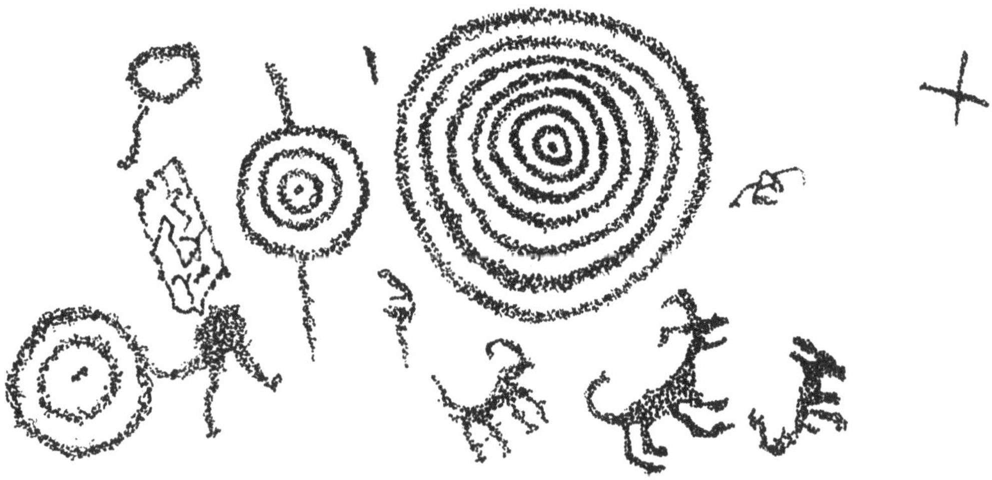

244. Concentric circles, upper 24th Street Locality. Large concentric circle is 44 cm in diameter.

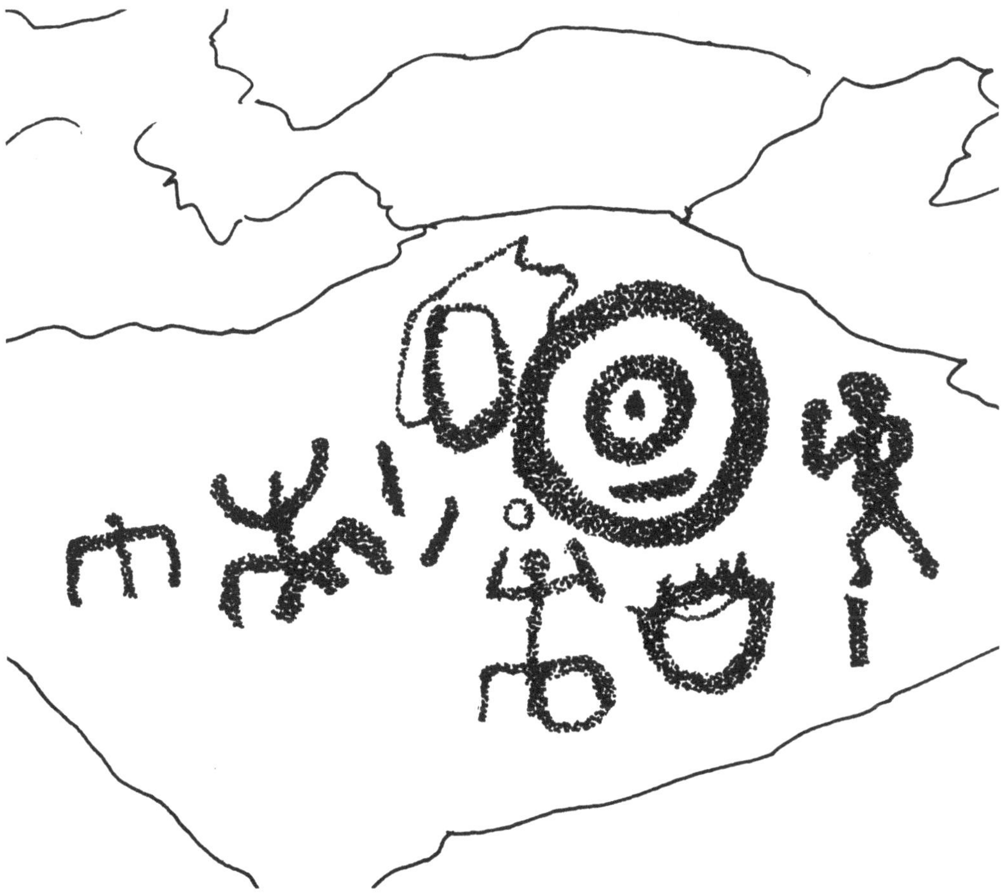

245. Concentric circles, 28th Place Locality. Right concentric circle is 14 cm in diameter. Panel faces northeast.

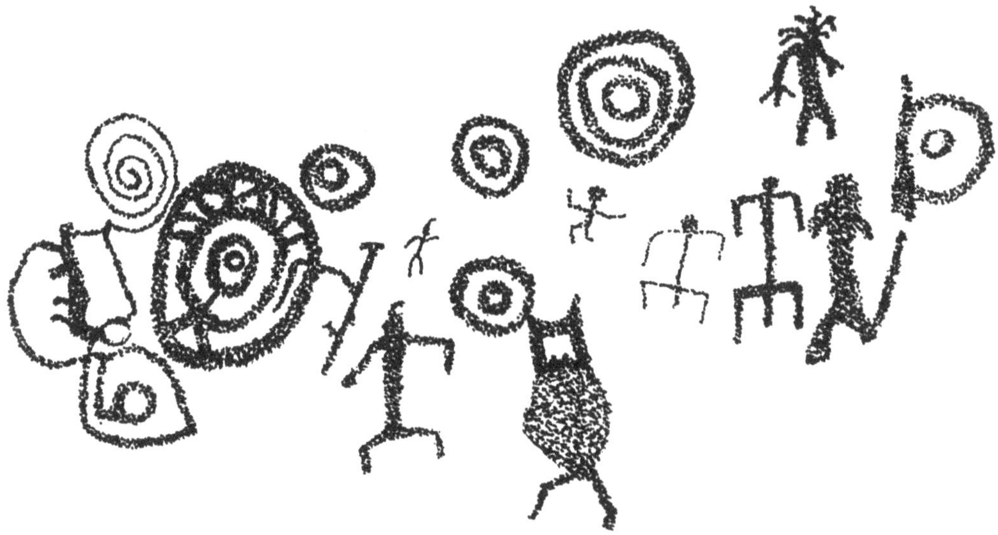

246. Concentric circles, 27th Street Locality. Large concentric circle is 22 cm in diameter. Panel faces southwest.

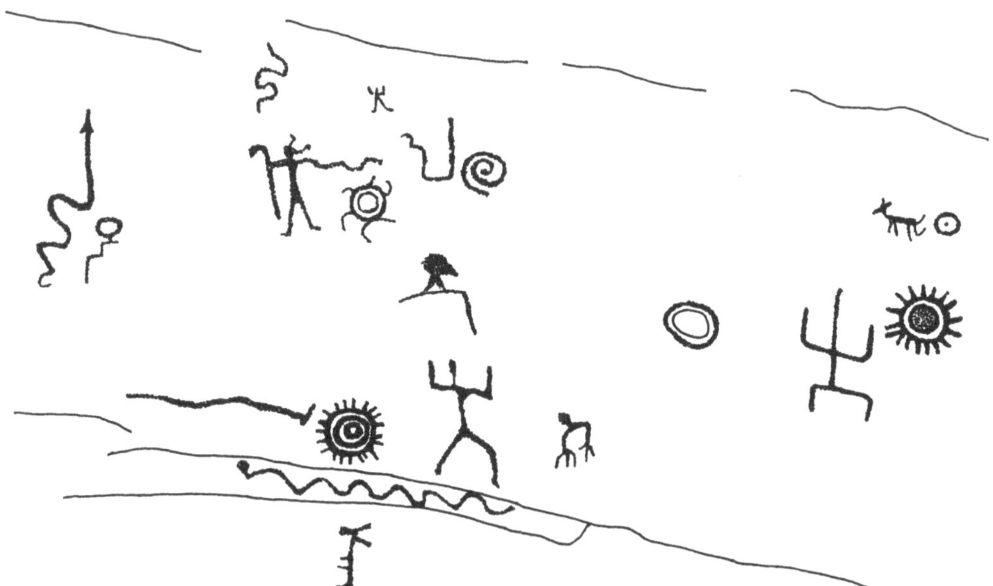

247. Sun disks, Hieroglyphic Canyon. Sun disk on right is 32 x 36 cm. Panel faces northeast.

northern Arizona as Puebloan sun symbols. Henry Wallace and James Holmlund (1986) recorded numerous sun disk petroglyphs at Hohokam and Archaic period sites in the Picacho Mountains. Astronomer Ed Krupp (1989) has noted that these symbols, which he calls sunbursts, are common throughout the world.

We recorded more than fifty of these sun disk petroglyphs at nearly two dozen locations in the South Mountains (figures 248 and 249). They show considerable

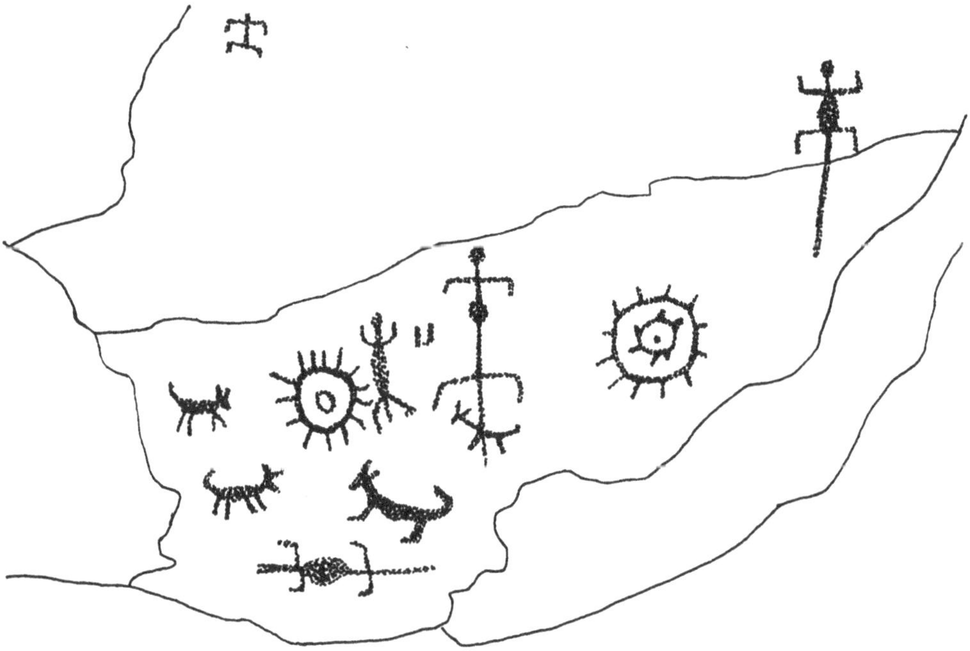

248. Sun disks, Pima Canyon. Sun disk on right is 24 cm in diameter. Panel faces southwest.

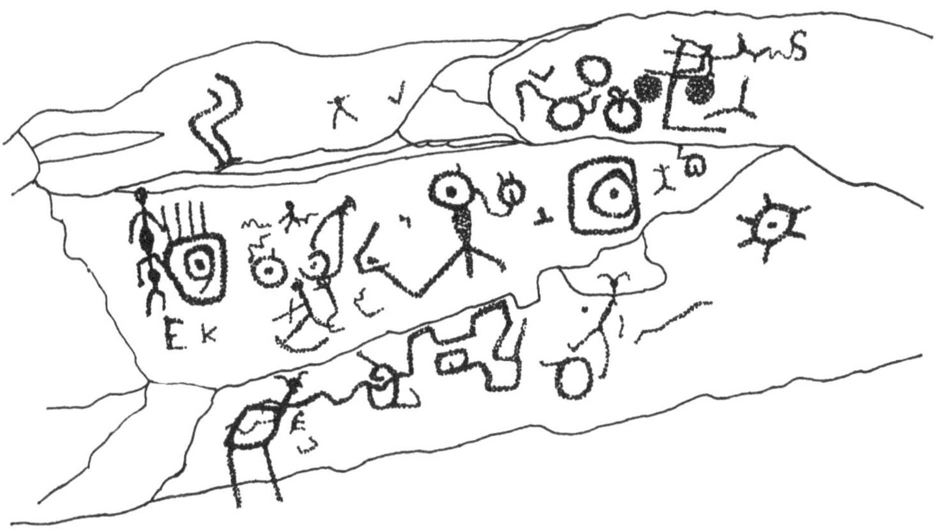

249. Sun disk (far right) and other geometric petroglyphs, Upper Pima Canyon Locality. Sun is 15 cm in diameter. Panel faces northwest.

variation in form and occur in the same panels with anthropomorphs, four-legged mammals, snakes, turtles/tortoises, pipettes, and other geometric designs. In several of these panels, the sun disk is placed above an anthropomorph as though suggesting a sun in the sky (figure 250). The sun disks have between four and seventeen rays, with almost every number in-between (figure 251). Rays can be short or long, straight, curved, or rectilinear (figure 252). Some of the suns are concentric circles;

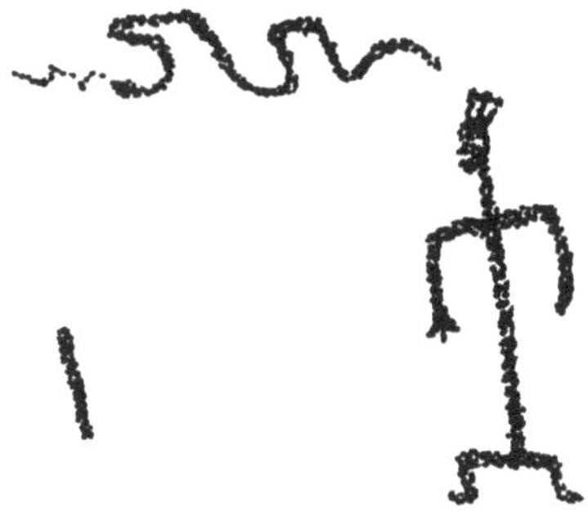

250. Sun disk, anthropomorph, and snake petroglyphs, Box Canyon. Sun disk is 20 cm in diameter. Panel faces southwest.

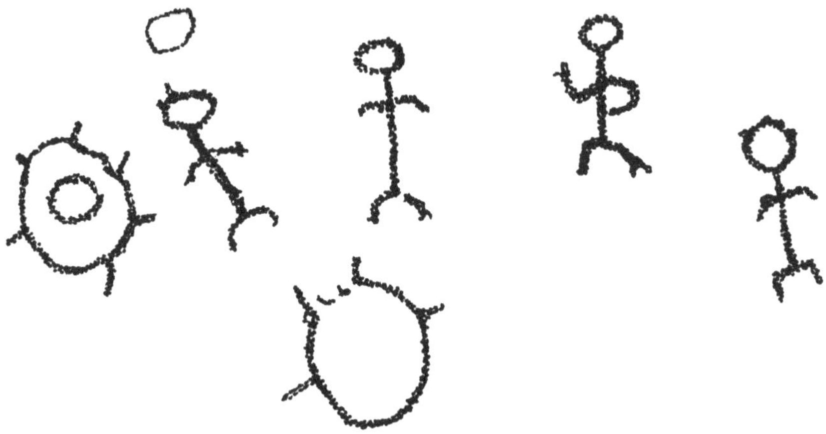

251. Sun disks and anthropomorphs, Goodman Canyon. Anthropomorph with bent arms is 29 cm in height. Panel faces southwest.

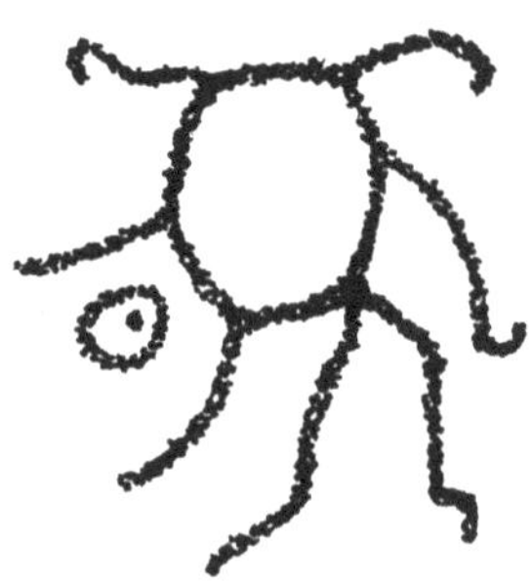

252. Stylized sun disk, Hieroglyphic Canyon. Sun disk is 19 x 18 cm and heavily repatinated, suggesting considerable age. Panel faces northwest.

others have central dots. A sun disk located along the Mormon Trail is made from a large spiral. The sun disk at the Four Pillars solstice site in the Twin Buttes Locality has a long tail (see figure 253, *top left*).

Observing the Sun in the South Mountains

If the Hohokam had a calendar, how did they create it? Our rock art study in the South Mountains shows that some of the Hohokam who visited the South Mountains marked important locations where the sun rises and sets on the eastern and western horizons.[1] The Hopi and Zuni observed the sunrise on the eastern horizon to establish ceremonial and agricultural calendars (McCluskey 1977; Young 1988). Solar locations marked in the South Mountains include the summer solstice, the winter solstice, and the spring and fall equinoxes, the midpoint between the two solstices (see figure 225). During the summer solstice the sun rises at its northernmost location on the horizon (approximately 60 degrees azimuth from the South Mountains). For four days around the summer solstice, the sun will rise in that same location and set in a corresponding location on the western horizon. The sun will then begin traveling south, rising and setting farther south each day until equinox (in September), when it rises due east (90 degrees azimuth). The sun continues to rise farther south for the next few months, until it reaches its southern "house," wherein it rises in the same location for four days during the winter solstice. It then proceeds to "turn around" and rise north of that point every day until it passes the spring equinox (horizon midpoint) in March and eventually completes its annual cycle at the summer solstice in June. A year or two of observations from a set location with good views of the eastern and western horizons will provide enough information to allow a calendar to be developed, enabling the prediction of future sunrise and sunset locations. For cultures that appear to have revered the sun, such as the Hohokam, individuals or groups could use this information to maintain status within their society. Indeed, to be a Hohokam "sky watcher" most likely was a position of high responsibility.

The union of sky and earth in Hohokam times can be replicated today both through observations and with computer simulations. Anyone willing to commit to two or more years of horizon observations can test various theories about Hohokam astronomy. An important part of observing is to demonstrate relationships between celestial bodies and points on the landscape with archaeological features such as rock art. These celestial body/landscape relationships must repeat themselves at regular intervals to be meaningful and, consequently, marked by ancient observers.

Ancient Mesoamerican cultures, such as the Maya and Aztec, had precise calendars that were central to the operation of their empires (Aveni 1980). Prehistoric groups in the American Southwest may not have had, nor would they have needed, such detailed calendars to help track ritual cycles and establish agricultural schedules. But equally important, observing and marking significant celestial body/landscape relationships took on sacred values. Astronomer Michael Zeilik (1989:190) has used the term *hierophany* to describe the act of honoring and celebrating an established celestial body/landscape relationship during times of interaction. To pray and make offerings to an event representing a supreme spiritual relationship helps maintain balance in the world, called by many native people "centering the world" (Lamphere 1983).

The sun has long been the most important celestial body and spiritual being to Native Americans. In O'odham oral traditions, when Elder Brother was assassinated he followed the path of the sun, rising in the east and descending in the west to the underworld (Bahr 1971). During this journey, Elder Brother came to four notches (possibly Four Peaks) that the sun uses when rising; he then slid down four times to Makai's house, at the winter solstice (Lloyd 1911).

Robert and Ann Preston (1987) have identified two techniques by which prehistoric people of the American Southwest monitored the sun's position: (1) imaging, in which sunlit rays and shadows directly interact with petroglyphs; and (2) sighting, which is the direct viewing of the sun's position from a particular petroglyph. During our multiyear rock art study we made observations of the sunrise and sunset on the horizons as seen from several rock art sites in the South Mountains.

We noticed that the location of some rock art panels aligned with certain points on the eastern and western horizons (table 3). Most seem to be tied to the summer and winter solstices, though several other points in the sun's journey (such as the equinoxes) also appear to have had importance. The Hohokam could have used these petroglyph markers to construct a basic solar calendar. The rock art sites associated with cleared spaces also may have been used for ceremonial purposes to salute the sun during the solstices, thus becoming an act of celebration and reverence, as well as a source of spiritual power.

Four Pillars Site

Located next to a cleared area in a high-elevation saddle with a spectacular view of the eastern horizon is a cluster of boulders containing rock art. This site in the Twin Buttes Locality contains four areas, or loci, of rock art (map 4). The northern locus (Locus 1) consists of an elaborate panel with multiple elements, and other individual petroglyphs, on a large boulder directly adjacent to the eastern edge of the cleared area (figure 253, *top row*). It includes a complex scene on the west side of the boulder, a large sun disk with a swirling tail on the north side, and an anthropomorph on the south side. A zigzag is present on another side, and a snake design occurs on top of the boulder. In addition, a whorl design has been placed by itself

Table 3. Astronomy-Related Rock Art Sites in the South Mountains

Locality	Interactions	Designs
Central Avenue		
* Lookout Site	summer solstice sunset	outlined cross
Chandler Boulevard/19th Way		
* Chuckwalla Site	summer solstice sunrise	large lizard
Chandler Boulevard/32nd Street		
* Arrow Site	summer and winter solstice sunset	sun disk, swastika
Desert Vista		
* Lizard Monolith Site	winter solstice sunset	lizard
Goodman Canyon		
* Saddle Site	winter solstice sunset	outlined cross
Hieroglyphic Canyon		
* Sunstone Site	winter solstice sunset	sun disk
* Hieroglyphic spring	summer solstice sunrise	geometric
Mormon Trail		
* Lizard Site	summer solstice sunrise	lizard
* Trail anthropomorph	summer solstice sunrise	anthropomorph
* Split Dome Site	summer solstice sunrise	geometric
Pima Canyon		
* Lizard Site	summer solstice sunrise	large lizard
Summit Trail		
* Whirling Whorl Site	winter solstice sunrise	anthropomorph, whorl
Twin Buttes		
* Four Pillars Site	summer and winter solstice sunrise	long line, sun disk
* Sungod Site	summer and winter solstice sunrise	bird
24th Street		
* Morning Star Site	summer solstice sunrise	snake with diamond tail
32nd Street		
* Moon panel	moon's annual cycle?	13 dots
* Diamond Site	summer soltice sunrise	diamond with appendages
* Sun Disk Site	summer solstice sunrise	spiral and quadruped
* Rake panel	summer solstice zenith	rake and other designs
* Anthropomorph panel	summer solstice sunrise	anthropomorph
36th Street		
* Lizardman Site	equinox	lizard with headdress
* Hourglass anthropomorph panel	summer solstice sunrise	hourglass human
* Waterbird Site	winter solstice sunset	waterbird

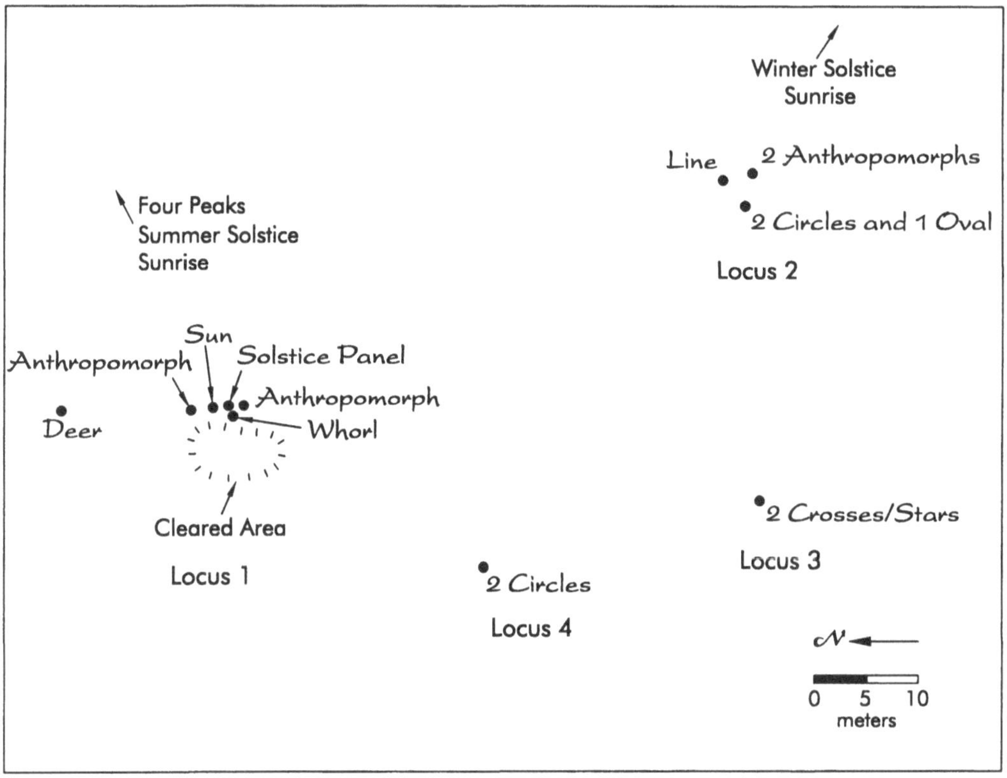

4. Four Pillars solstice site plan map

on an upright stone in front of the main panel. A lone human figure is present a short distance to the north, with a deer a little beyond that.

Another locus is present about 100 feet (35 m) to the southeast of Locus 1. Locus 2 is a small petroglyph cluster containing a single line, three crude circles, and two dancing anthropomorphs (figure 253, *middle row*). To the southwest of Locus 1 is Locus 3, where a low-lying panel shows two small crosses or stars that face east (figure 253, *bottom row, left*). Locus 4, between Loci 1 and 3, consists of a large boulder with two small circles that face northwest (figure 253, *bottom row, right*).

The main panel on the west side of the boulder in Locus 1 contains an interesting combination of elements (figure 254). It also exhibits a dramatic relationship to the sun and the surrounding landscape. The panel consists of a quadrilateral geometric pattern with four circles divided by two long, perpendicular lines. A spiral, a solid star (oriented to the north), an anthropomorph, two four-legged mammals, and other elements are also depicted. The anthropomorph is connected by a line to one of the four-legged mammals and seems to preside over the rest of the panel. One of the long lines in the panel extends out of the main area toward the edge of the boulder in a northeastern direction. Early one morning we learned that this long line has astronomical significance when viewed from a small boulder at the western edge of the cleared area in front of the panel—it points to a location on the horizon where

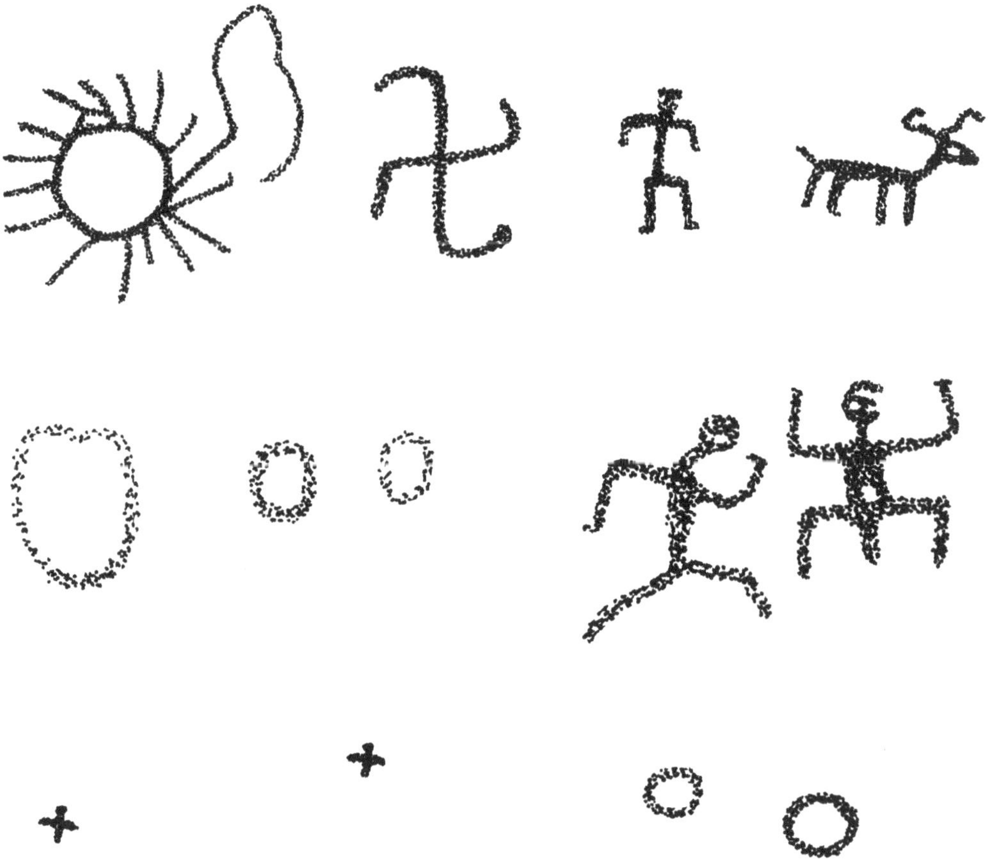

253. Petroglyph elements at Four Pillars Site, Twin Buttes Locality. Locus 1, **top row, left to right:** sun disk with tail on panel facing northwest is 27 cm in diameter; whorl is 18 x 22 cm; anthropomorph is 14 cm in height; deer is 13 cm in length. Locus 2, **middle row, left to right:** small circle in set of three is 7 cm in diameter; anthropomorph with upraised arms is 17 cm in height. Locus 3, **bottom row, left:** cross/star on left is 9 x 10 cm; panel faces east. Locus 4, **bottom row, right:** circle on left is 7 cm in diameter; panel faces northwest.

the sun rises during the summer solstice, June 21. This sunrise location happens to occur between two of the peaks of Four Peaks, 40 miles (60 km) east, creating an awesome view of the sun. This finding was of critical importance to our astronomy study because it determined that Four Peaks (which the O'odham considered sacred) was a significant landmark on the eastern horizon for the Hohokam as well. We also realized that other sites in the South Mountains could be similarly aligned, and thus we sought out other panel clusters that provided a view toward Four Peaks.

We made other important discoveries at the Four Pillars Site, too. Because the sun moves along the horizon throughout the year, we watched it rise during the winter solstice, December 21. Much to our delight, when observed from the northern edge of the cleared area, the sun rose over the sun disk petroglyph with the swirling tail. Consequently, this cluster of petroglyphs marks both solstice sunrise locations on the horizons, when the longest and shortest days of the year occur.

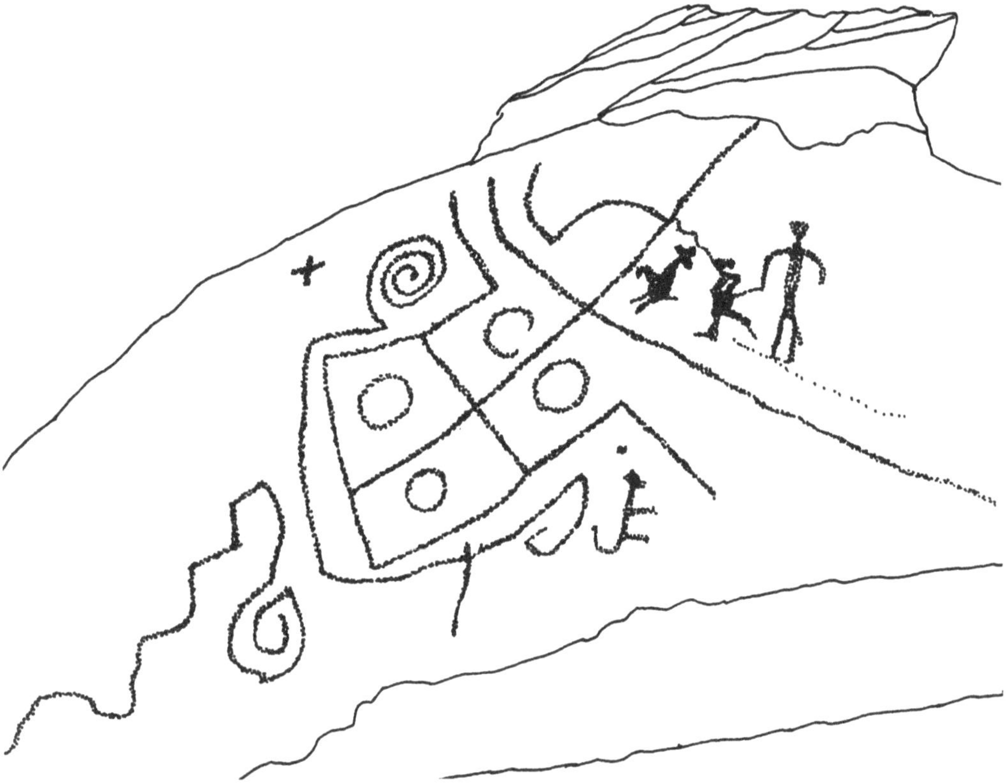

254. Solstice panel, Locus 1, Four Pillars Site, Twin Buttes Locality. Anthropomorph is 29 cm in height. Panel faces southwest.

Other rock art clusters at this site mark solstice sunsets. Located about 100 feet (35 m) to the southeast of the Four Pillars panel is a small knoll comprising several large boulders. On the southwestern side of this boulder pile is an alcove in which a single line, 6 inches (15 cm) long, has been pecked. The top of the line aligns with the rising of the winter solstice sun on the southeastern horizon. In addition, the winter solstice sun sets over two petroglyph crosses when viewed from a cleared area in front of them. Finally, the summer solstice sun sets over two circles on a large boulder when viewed from the alcove in which the winter solstice sunrise petroglyph line is located (see figure 253).

We collected Hohokam red-on-buff ceramics dating to the late Colonial/early Sedentary period (ca. A.D. 850–1050) at the Four Pillars Site. The presence of this pottery suggests that the Hohokam had an interest in astronomy relatively early in their occupation of the Salt River Valley. According to Vorsila Bohrer's (1994) agricultural model of the quadrilateral universe, the main panel at this site may depict the four corners of the universe, with the four circles representing the four solstice sunrises and sunsets: thus, the name Four Pillars Site.

Sungod Site

A few hundred meters to the northeast and below the Four Pillars Site, near the top of the Mormon Trail, is another high-elevation solar panel. We called it the Sungod Site (map 5). Situated in a flat saddle, it offers a great view of the northern and eastern horizons. During Hohokam times, the area had been cleared of boulders, creating a large depression or "room" where numerous petroglyphs have been pecked on bedrock and on small boulders. A formal entrance into the room, marked by upright stones, is located to the south. We recovered unidentified Hohokam red-on-buff ceramics, probably dating from the Colonial or Sedentary period (ca. A.D. 750–1150), from inside the entrance to the room.

One of these panels has two anthropomorphs holding hands (figure 255). One has a head that looks like a sun with rays and is holding an unidentified object

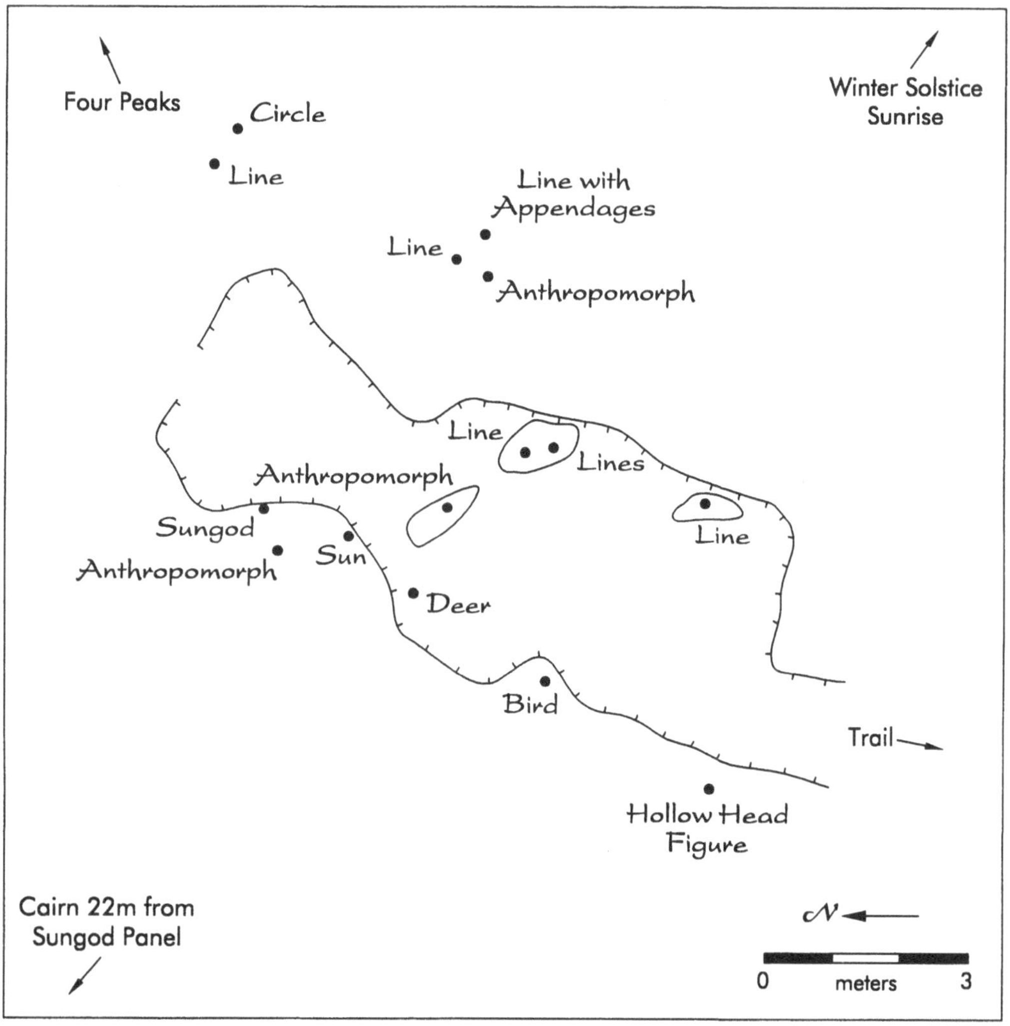

5. Sungod Site plan map

(which may be the moon); the other figure has a headdress. Both figures face east. A large partial figure eight (possibly representing the path of Venus) and two circles connected with a line are present on a flat surface above these two figures. Another panel, on the thin edge of a flat boulder, has a sun disk associated with an upside-down anthropomorph, a small and a large "X," and other elements (figure 256).

During the winter solstice at the Sungod Site, the sun rises over a distant ridge, the precise location of which is marked by a stylized thunderbird design placed on top of a flat boulder at that point on the horizon (figure 257). An upright stone inside the room marks the spot where the summer solstice sun rises. A stone cairn is located to the northwest of the room, near where the summer solstice sun sets.

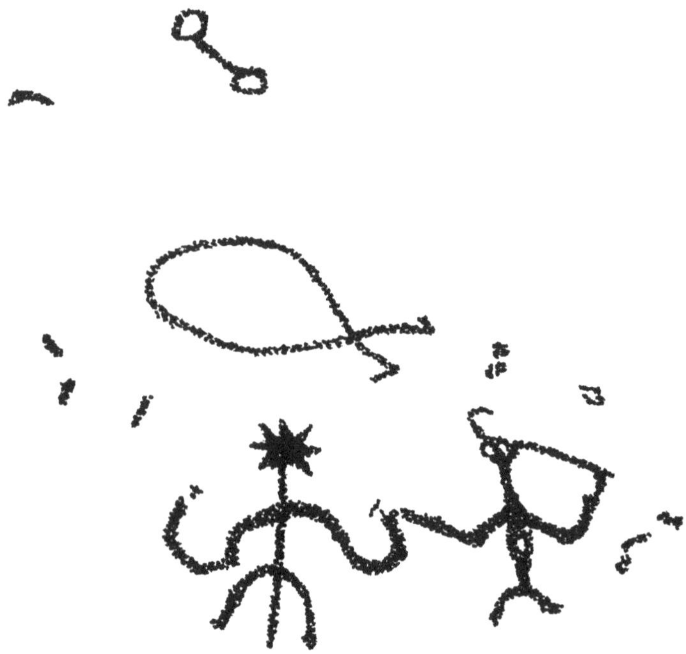

255. Anthropomorph with sunlike head and holding an unknown object, Sungod Site, Twin Buttes Locality. Anthropomorph with sunlike head is 23 cm in height. Panel faces northeast.

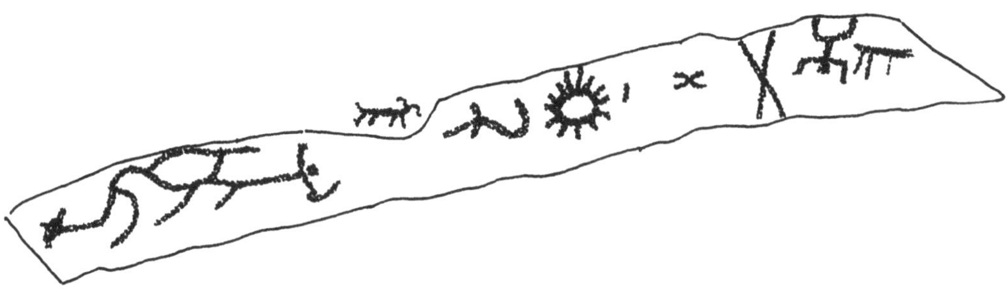

256. Sun disk and other petroglyphs inside cleared area at the Sungod Site, Twin Buttes Locality. Sun disk is 9 cm in diameter.

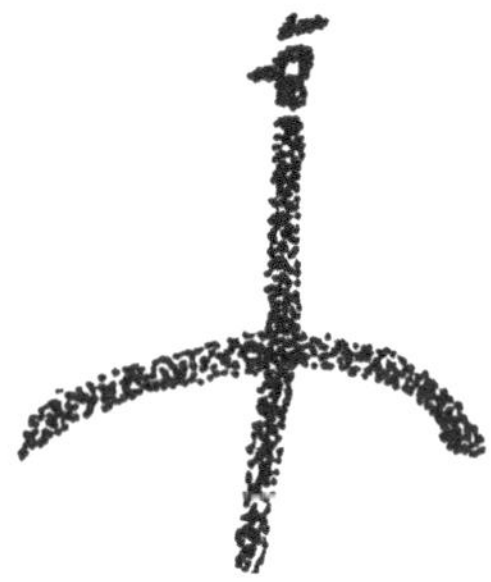

257. Bird petroglyph over which the winter solstice sun rises at the Sungod Site, Twin Buttes Locality.

32nd Street Locality

Armed with the information obtained from the Twin Buttes Locality, we selected other sites at which to observe the rising and setting sun. We had noted a relationship between Four Peaks and the summer solstice, so we looked for sites with an unobstructed view of Four Peaks. The 32nd Street Locality provided such views. Four Peaks can be viewed over the petroglyphs, where the southeastern appendage, or leg, of the diamond aligns with the summer solstice sunrise over Four Peaks (figure 258). West of this rock art is a site with an unusual sun disk image and two anthropomorphs (figure 259). A cleared area is present in front of the panel. One of the anthropomorphs is much taller than the other. The sun disk has been partitioned in half and has one of its rays curved like a scorpion's tail. An individual standing with his or her back to this panel can view the summer solstice sunrise over Four Peaks.

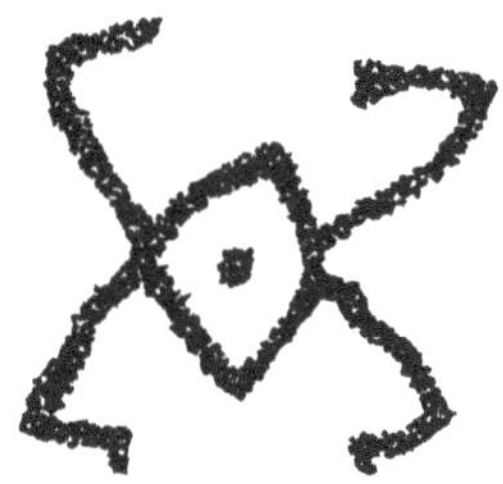

258. Geometric design that has one of its legs align with the summer solstice sunrise, 32nd Street Locality. Petroglyph is 19 x 17 cm.

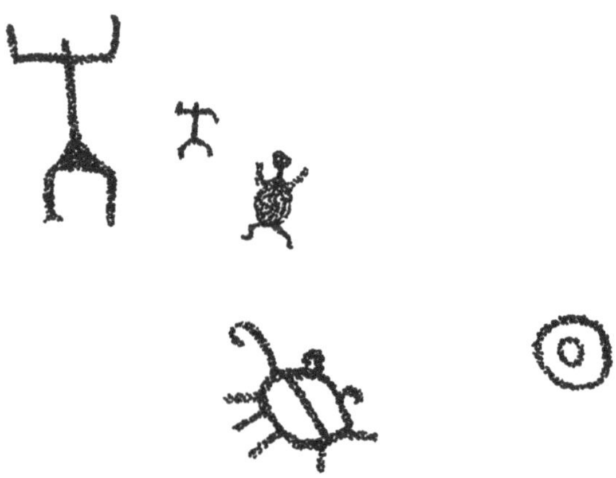

259. Panel with unusual sun disk petroglyph that faces the summer solstice sunrise at the 32nd Street Locality. Large anthropomorph on left is 28 cm in height.

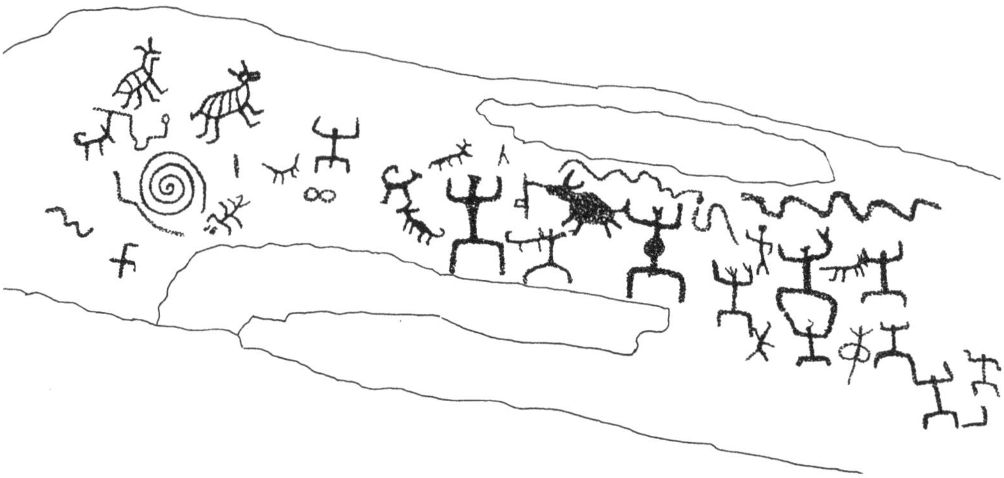

260. Panel with light and shadow interactions during the summer solstice zenith (solar noon) in which a ray of light appears to come out of the mouth of a quadruped on the left side of the panel before moving down through the spiral and off the bottom of the rock, 32nd Street Locality. Snake on right is 64 cm in length.

In the same locality, another panel faces the summer solstice sunrise and may contain the image of a powerful Hohokam "astronomer" or a deity (see figure 160). An hourglass anthropomorph holds in its left hand a large, connected double spiral. Five mountain sheep surround the human figure, and a sun disk petroglyph is present in the upper left portion of the panel. Two other spirals, including a rectilinear type, are present next to the human figure. Double spirals may symbolize the annual or daily movement of the sun (Bohrer 1994).

In the upper reaches of this locality, to our surprise, we discovered a solar zenith marker utilizing light and shadow effects. On a ridge overlooking Phoenix is a panel with several anthropomorphs and quadrupeds, a large spiral, and other elements (figure 260). At midday during the summer solstice, a triangular ray illuminates the panel. The point of this ray appears to come out of the mouth of a quadruped; over the next twenty minutes it moves down the panel through the center of the spiral until it disappears off the bottom of the rock (see color plate section).

Other Localities

The quickest route up the northern side of the South Mountains is the Mormon Trail. At the bottom of the trail, where the mountains meet the upper bajada, is the southwest-facing Lizard Site. A cleared area in front of this boulder is perfect for viewing the interaction between rock art and the summer solstice sunrise over Four Peaks. The sun rises over a crack in the rock that separates an anthropomorph and two lizards, including one with a concentric circle body. A small circle is present above the large lizard.

A panel in the 36th Street Locality contains two lizards that interact with a moving light pattern a little before noon during the equinox. Another panel at this locality consists of a large arrow design and a small anthropomorph holding a crook (figure 261). This panel looks younger than the nearby lizard panel. During the equinox, a ray of light forms under the anthropomorph's feet and the bottom of the crook.

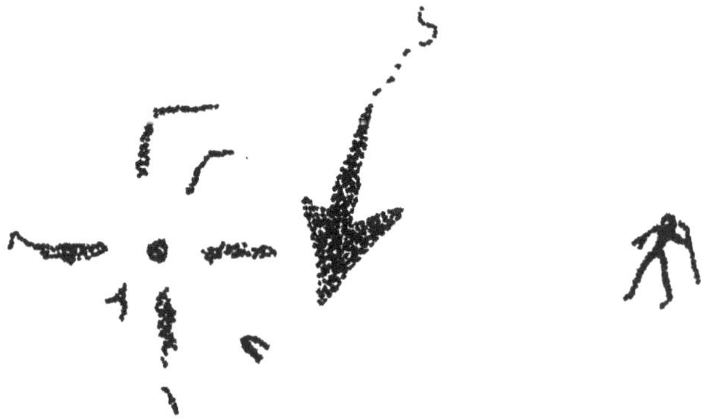

261. Panel with light and shadow interactions during the equinox zenith in which a ray of light forms under the anthropomorph's feet, 36th Street Locality. Anthropomorph is 5 cm in height. Because it shows relatively little repatination, this panel may postdate the Hohokam.

Located near the bottom of Hieroglyphic Canyon is the Sunstone Site, a massive boulder with three geometric designs in a row (figure 262). One looks like a squarish sun with rays, another like an asymmetrical asterisk, and the third is a line with a slight hook at the end. During the winter solstice the sun sets on the western horizon over the squarish sun symbol. The other two elements may or may not mark a celestial event.

Goodman Canyon is bordered on both sides by steep ridges. In a saddle midway

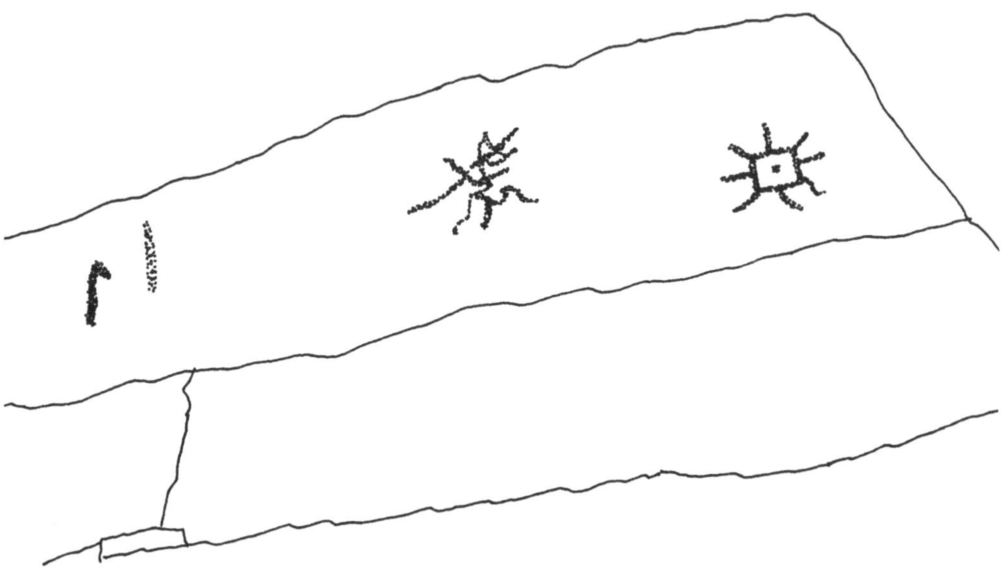

262. Panel over which the sun sets during winter solstice, Hieroglyphic Canyon. Sun symbol is 30 cm in diameter.

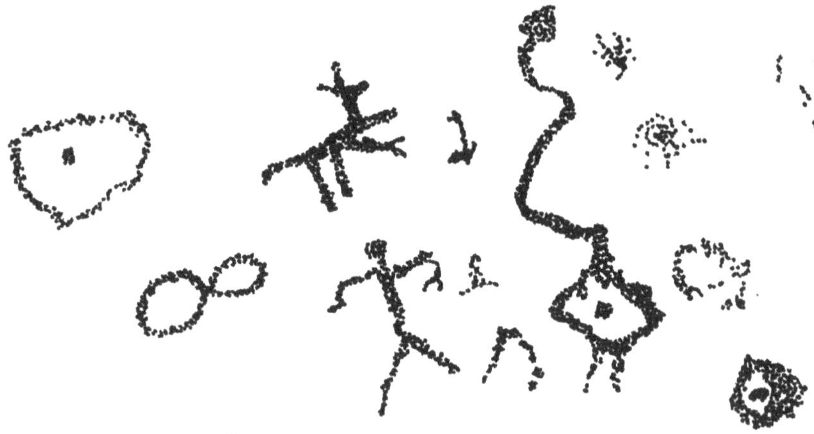

263. Panel over which the summer solstice sun rises in alignment with a nearby upright slab and Four Peaks, 24th Street Locality. Anthropomorph is 30 cm in height.

up the eastern ridge is a dense concentration of rock art panels associated with an artifact scatter that we named the Saddle Site. We collected Hohokam ceramics dating to the late Colonial and Sedentary periods (ca. A.D. 850–1150) here. One large boulder has numerous circle designs and anthropomorphs; on top is a large outlined cross that faces to the southeast. During the winter solstice, the sun sets over this cross.

The 24th Street Locality incorporates several steep canyons and ridges west of the Mormon Trail. High up on a ridge is a rock art panel on a large, rectangular boulder with a cleared area in front. We call this the Morning Star Site. The large panel contains several elements, including an anthropomorph, a four-legged mammal, two figure eights, circles, and a large snake with a diamond and central dot for a tail (figure 263). The panel faces southwest, but an individual standing in front of the panel has a view to the eastern horizon and Four Peaks. An upright slab with a natural V-shaped groove has been set upright about 1.5 feet (0.4 m) in front of the panel. On

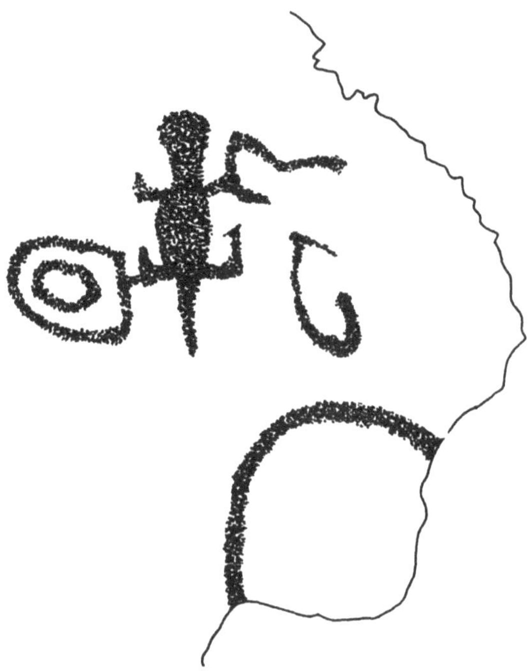

264. Panel over which the summer solstice sun rises, Chandler Boulevard/19th Way Locality. Lizard is 32 cm in length.

the summer solstice, the sun rises over Four Peaks in alignment with the snake petroglyph and the upright slab.

Astronomy-related sites are also present on the southern side of the South Mountains. A small site located at the Chandler Boulevard/19th Way Locality has a panel with a fat, chuckwalla-like lizard petroglyph (figure 264). The summer solstice sun rises over this panel on the northeastern horizon.

Another of these southern locations is the Chandler Boulevard/32nd Street Locality, where a cluster of petroglyphs includes two panels with sun disk elements—a large one and a small one. The winter solstice sun sets over the large sun symbol. In addition, the winter solstice sun rises over a swastika located near the large sun symbol but facing in the opposite direction.

Conclusions

Our research on Hohokam astronomy in the South Mountains is incomplete. Nonetheless, four years of sunrise and sunset observations have revealed that several rock art sites exhibit deliberate solar interactions during the winter and summer solstices, the "turning points" in the annual movement of the sun. The Hohokam also appear to have marked the spring and fall equinoxes. Furthermore, certain rock art designs and limited observations suggest that the Hohokam may also have charted the movements of other celestial bodies, such as the moon and Venus. We are only beginning to understand what knowledge the Hohokam may have had of the heavens, but what little we have learned shows that the serious study of ancient astronomy has great potential.

CHAPTER ELEVEN

DREAMS, MEMORIES, AND SIGNS

A Summary of South Mountains Rock Art

The traditions of the Pimas are kept by those who show special aptitude in remembering them and who gradually become recognized as the tribal historians. To them the boys are regularly sent that they may listen for four nights to the narrative of how the world was made and peopled; whence the Pimas came and how they struggled with demons, monsters, and savage enemies.

—Frank Russell (1975)

This book shares our many years of exploration of rock art throughout the rugged desert landscape called the South Mountains. In the process of studying these ancient petroglyphs and their associated features and artifacts, we have been able to produce at least preliminary answers to several questions and in so doing provide insights that may lead to better understanding of how rock art fit into the Hohokam world.

Who Made the Rock Art and How Old Is It?

The majority of the rock art in the South Mountains was created by the prehistoric Hohokam, an artistic people who farmed the Phoenix region with extensive irrigation systems for more than a millennium. Hohokam ceramic types recovered from fourteen different localities in the South Mountains and thus proximally associated with rock art date primarily from the eighth through eleventh centuries, with a small quantity of sherds dating from the eleventh through fourteenth centuries (see chapter 3). Hohokam pottery was found near springs, along trails, in open areas, and in front of rock art panels.

A few of the rock art panels in the South Mountains may have been made by hunter-gatherer people from the Archaic period, which predates the Hohokam occupation of the region. These early petroglyph elements, associated with the Archaic tradition at other rock art sites in the Salt River Valley and elsewhere, include atlatls, meanders, rakelike designs, and circle clusters. The latter two motifs are infrequent in but not absent from the Hohokam rock art inventory. All of the rock art panels that may be Archaic in the South Mountains are situated among other rock art panels that appear to be Hohokam. Dating this rock art is problematic because archaeologists have identified no other Archaic sites within the South Mountains.

A few panels also appear to date later than the Hohokam but are not modern graffiti. These petroglyphs may have been produced in the Protohistoric or early Historic period (ca. A.D. 1500–1900), perhaps by the native O'odham people who have lived in villages along the Gila River for many centuries. The style and manner of execution is a little different for these panels compared to the Hohokam rock art (see figures 12–16). Some elements from these panels, such as cattle brands and human profiles, do not appear in the roster of Hohokam elements, although designs similar to those of the Hohokam are present in the Protohistoric or early Historic period petroglyphs.

How Was the Rock Art Made?

Petroglyph artists used various techniques to create their designs in the South Mountains. The simplest method is the pecking of a design by directly hammering the rock face with a pointed stone. River cobbles with battered edges occur throughout the South Mountains, often near rock art panels. These implements are sometimes flaked to create a sharpened edge and are called "hammerstones" by archaeologists. Hammerstones we found ranged from about the size of a golf ball to slightly larger than a man's clenched fist.[1] We also found a broken stone axe, the dulled blade of which had been used as a hammerstone.

Some petroglyphs, by contrast, are well pecked and have fine marks indicating that they were made with a stone chisel hit with a hammerstone. This technique is called indirect percussion. Experiments have shown that small, oblong river cobbles serve very well as rock art chisels when pounded lightly with a hammerstone. Archaeologists have found several of these tools in association with Hohokam rock art sites in the Picacho Mountains, but none in the South Mountains.

A third technique used to create rock art is scratching the rock face with a sharp stone. A few petroglyph designs were made entirely by scratching, typically as geometric designs such as grids and parallel lines. Close inspection of petroglyph designs, however, reveals that sometimes a portion of a pecked element also was scratched. These examples more often than not appear as though the petroglyph artist combined these techniques simply for expediency—scratching a design is generally quicker than pecking it, because scratching requires less concentration and hand-eye coordination.

The intensity of pecking varies considerably in the rock art of the South Mountains. Occasionally different designs in the same panel are only lightly pecked. In some cases, however, light pecking may have been done intentionally to create a near-invisible effect, perhaps symbolizing a state of transition. Changing light con-

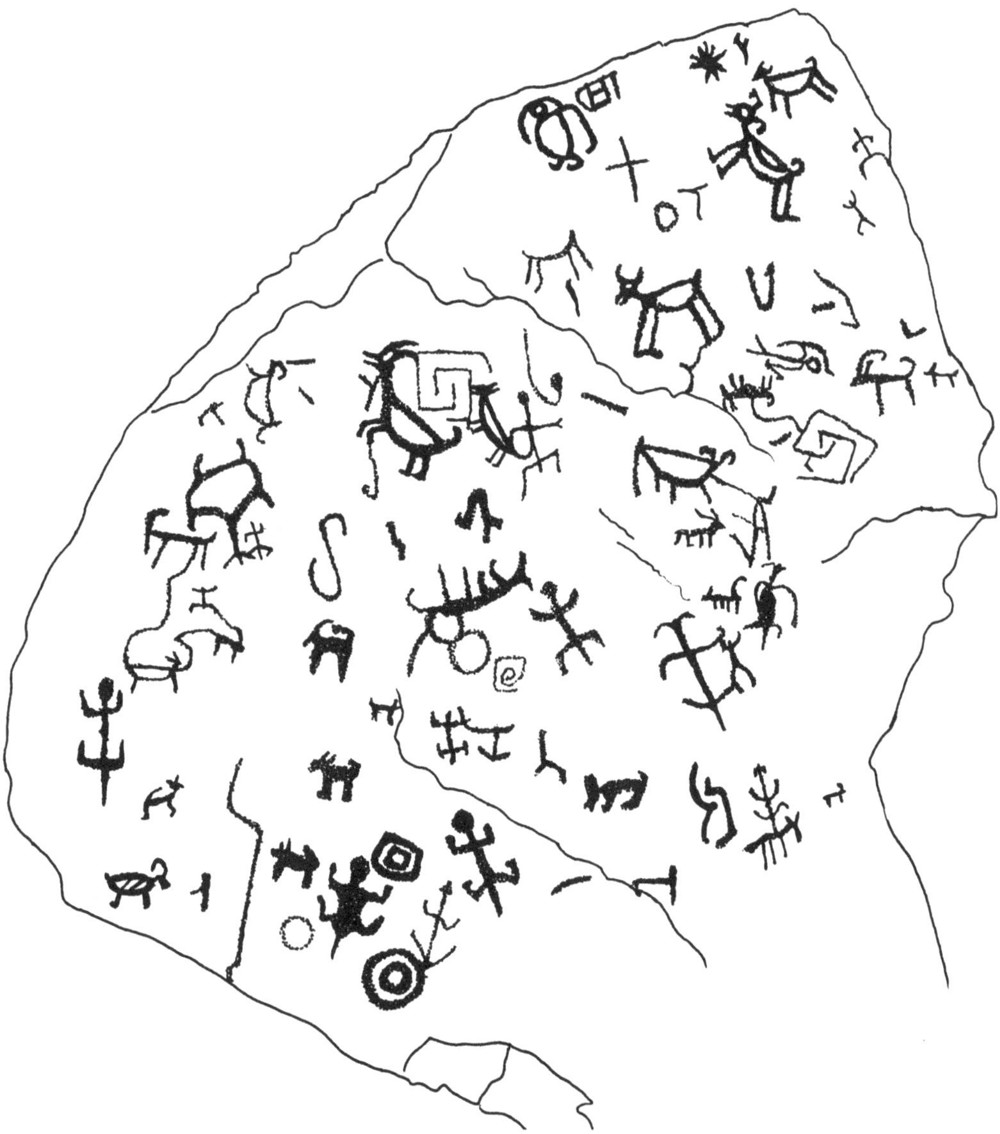

265. Panel with multiple pecking episodes, upper 16th Street Locality. Asterisk or sun disk at top of panel is 10 cm in diameter.

ditions can make these kinds of petroglyphs disappear and reappear at different times of the day. Some elements appears to have been repecked after they were originally made, although this trait does not seem to be especially common.

Some petroglyph panels clearly had been made over a long period of time. Fainter elements are located next to more visible elements and are sometimes under more recent petroglyphs (figure 265). In some panels, anthropomorphs were pecked into an existing scene, suggesting that the panels were visited over time and remained important well after they were originally made. Perhaps individuals returned to certain panels during the course of their lifetime, adding elements in the panel. Some panels may have been revisited over many generations, perhaps by initiates or apprentice shamans, to experience the "power of place" and assimilate deeper mythical meaning. A complex panel in the 36th Street Locality is a fine example of this phenomenon (figure 266). It appears to have been added to over time, with some figures deeply pecked, some lightly pecked, and some partially pecked and partially scratched. Anthropomorphs on the left side of the panel appear to have been made first, followed by the pipette in the middle. Designs on the right side appear to have been added later. In addition, the pipette has been repecked, especially its lower portion. The "barbell" design to the right of the pipette was probably added at the same time the pipette was repecked.

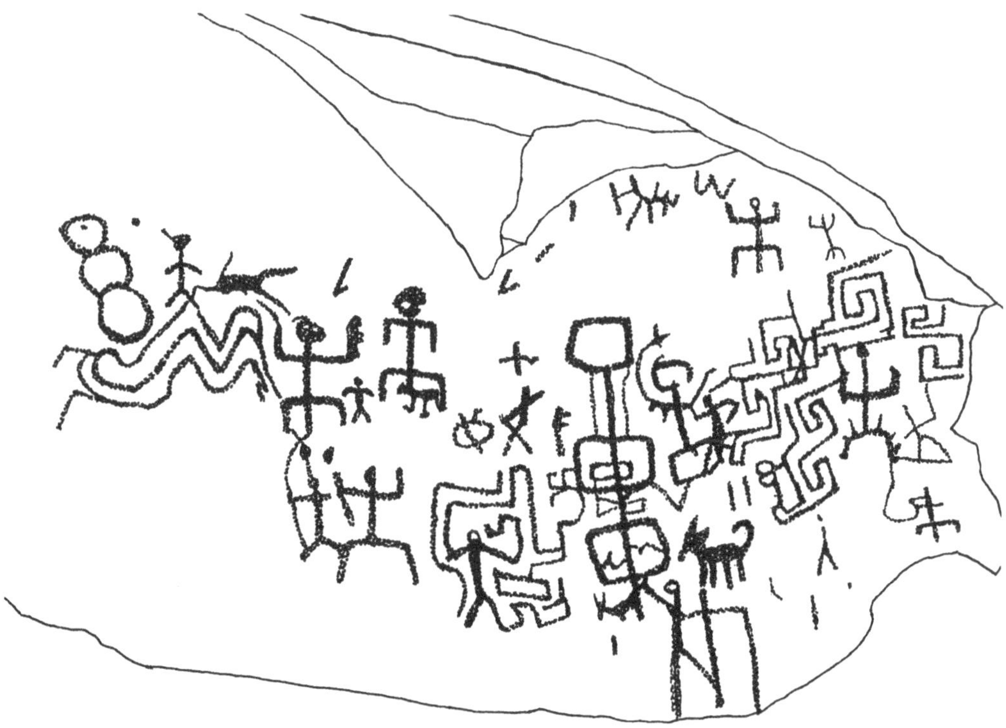

266. Panel with multiple pecking episodes suggesting that anthropomorphs were added into existing scenes and connected to earlier design elements by lines, 36th Street Locality. Pipette is 52 cm in length.

The rock faces in which petroglyphs were pecked or scratched do not appear to have been prepared before the element was pecked, that is, the rock faces were not smoothed or ground before a petroglyph was added. In some instances, however, existing panels or elements appear to have been rubbed over during prehistoric times, resulting in the distortion or obliteration of certain elements. An example would be the area of a large panel in upper Hieroglyphic Canyon that has been extensively rubbed over, leaving only faint traces of the previous designs. In contrast, elements nearby were not touched and remain quite visible.

On only a few occasions did the Hohokam incorporate natural holes into the South Mountains rock art. In most of these instances, holes served as anthropomorph heads. In the upper portion of Goodman Canyon, a natural hole in a rock face with a red stain was incorporated as the groin of a female petroglyph, suggesting menstrual flow (see figure 147). A panel in the upper portion of the 32nd Street Locality incorporates a large, natural hole as part of the scene but not as part of a design element. In this panel, several anthropomorphs and other life-forms surround the hole. An anthropomorph with upraised arms is located just below the hole, perhaps contemplating entering the hole as a portal into the stone.

We are not aware of any rock art in the South Mountains that was painted, called "pictographs." But the harsh desert sun slowly destroys painted rock art in the Sonoran Desert, and Hohokam painted rock art is not common anywhere. A few petroglyphs in the South Mountains have slight coloration inside their pecked elements, suggesting that they once may have been painted or stained as well. However, water stains and traces of graffiti stain occur on some of the rock art panels, and chalking of rock art designs by photographers was once common.

We did not find any evidence that rock art panels were created from preliminary sketches or outlines made on the rock faces with light pecking, such as the Anasazi rock art panels that Peter Pilles (1975) recorded in the Little Colorado River region of northern Arizona. The Hohokam rock artist may have sketched a scene with charcoal from a burnt stick before pecking it with a chisel and hammerstone. If so, traces of that charcoal have not survived the centuries of desert weather.

Where Are the Rock Art Sites Located within the South Mountains?

Rock art panels are scattered throughout the South Mountains from the lowest elevations in the foothills, around 1,200 feet (366 m), to the top of some of the higher peaks, at more than 2,400 feet (732 m). Rock art is found at the base of the mountains, at the mouths of canyons, inside canyons, along ridges, on top of knolls, on top of peaks, on isolated boulder piles, and at springs, seeps, and water tanks. In other words, rock art should be looked for nearly anywhere suitable rock faces occur in the mountains, even up the sides of steep talus slopes.

Nearly all of the different rock types in the South Mountains, including granodiorite, chloritic granodiorite, alaskite, granite, and gneiss, were used for rock art. More than fifty geographic localities contain concentrations of Hohokam rock art. Clusters of rock art are visible on all sides of the mountains, but the vast majority are located in the eastern half. The western half is composed of rock types that provide fewer suitable boulders and exposed bedrock. The eastern side also contains springs, locations with solar alignment potential, and isolated canyons and grottos that may have been selected for their cultural rather than physical characteristics. Some locations, such as Box Canyon, have special acoustic qualities (Waller et al. 1999).

Ernest Snyder (1966) argued that the northeastern concentration of rock art sites should be attributed to the presence of several large Hohokam villages to the northeast of the mountains. However, other villages were present to the northwest, west, and south as well. Other possible reasons for the eastern focus of the rock art sites include the following: (1) the northeastern face of the mountain has the most dissected terrain, with numerous canyons, isolated areas, and springs; (2) these locations are ideal places for vision quests or ceremonies relating to the heavens; (3) many burials at Hohokam villages have the head oriented to the east (among the O'odham, east is a sacred direction and the original home of their culture hero, Elder Brother); and (4) certain areas in the South Mountains have views of Four Peaks, the most prominent landmark on the eastern horizon of the Salt River Valley—at those locations, rock art indicates a solstice sunrise alignment with Four Peaks.

Our study confirmed one of Snyder's observations: a dense concentration of rock art all along the northeastern face of the mountains at around 1,500 feet (457 m) in elevation. We found many flat and cleared areas, as well as artifacts, associated with these sites. Most have outstanding views of the Salt River Valley and the distant horizons, and these views may have been an important characteristic. Rock art sites decrease in density and occurrence above this elevation, but small panels also occur along ridge tops in the higher reaches of the mountains.

In general, different rock art designs or elements are widely distributed throughout the fifty-two localities we have inventoried. All but one locality contains at least one anthropomorph, although the hourglass-shaped anthropomorph form is concentrated in Box Canyon. Four-legged mammals—mountain sheep, deer, coyotes/dogs, and unidentified quadrupeds—occur at more than 80 percent of the localities. Most localities also contain geometric designs, with circles nearly as ubiquitous as anthropomorphs, occurring at more than 90 percent of the localities. The 28th Place Locality, in particular, contains a large number of circles (at least sixty). Two design elements that are notably difficult to make—concentric circles and spirals—also are scattered throughout the South Mountains; both are present at more than 70 percent of the localities. The 48th Street and Southeast Side Localities have a relatively large number of concentric circles, and Box Canyon contains the most spirals.

Other Archaeological Features Found in the South Mountains

Rock art panels make up by far the most numerous site type. Dry-farming agricultural sites consisting of bordered fields, check dams, and terraces are present at the mouths of some canyons, such as the 12th Street Locality, and on sloping pediment such as that north of Beverly Canyon. Associated with these fields, as well as in areas of natural resources, are numerous stone tools archaeologists call "primary flake tools." These large cutting and chopping implements made from hard river cobbles were likely used in the processing of plant products, including agave and cactus.

Trails occur throughout the mountains, leading up and down most of the canyons and along the ridges. The presence of rock art panels and artifacts adjacent to these trails indicate that they are ancient in origin. Numerous Hohokam ceramics are present at the Telegraph Pass Locality, where a major north-south trail crosses the South Mountains. Petroglyphs are located all along the Mormon Trail, a steep trail that connects the base of the northern side of the South Mountains with the upper canyons (in particular, Hidden Valley and the Twin Buttes area).

Single masonry rooms and possible pithouses, previously unknown before our study, are present at some rock art sites, suggesting temporary habitation. These rooms have been identified at the base of the mountains at around 1,200 to 1,300 feet in elevation (366–396 m), as well as at ridge-top sites located along the escarpment at approximately 1,500 feet (457 m) in elevation. For example, we discovered masonry rooms in the upper portions of the 32nd Street and 36th Street Localities, and a site in the upper portion of the Mormon Trail has seven depressions associated with two rock art panels. Farther up this ridge is the High Terrace site, a flat area with numerous Hohokam ceramics and scattered rock features. In addition, dense clusters of artifacts in Box Canyon suggest that pithouses may have once been present there, along with the numerous rock art panels and trails.

Rock shelters occur throughout the mountains. They are present at many of the rock art sites in the upper elevations, where massive boulder piles provide grottolike openings with sheltered space. Although petroglyphs are often located near rock shelters, in only a few instances is the rock art placed near the entrance of or inside the rock shelter, such as in Box Canyon and in Goodman Canyon (see figures 103 and 65).

Other archaeological features associated with rock art consist of metate slicks, water basins, mortar holes, and mineral extraction areas. A well-worn metate slick is present on top of a large boulder covered with rock art in the Southeast Side Locality, not far from the entrance to Pima Canyon. Another metate slick is present in a boulder at the 34th Street Locality. In the 32nd Street Locality, a shallow basin has been cut into the top of a large outcrop knoll. Water collects in this basin during rainstorms. A lizardman petroglyph has been pecked next to the basin. In the Upper

Pima Canyon Locality, at Johnson Camp, four deep mortar holes are associated with a natural water tank and a major concentration of rock art panels.

In the eastern portion of the 48th Street Locality, a large granodiorite rock outcrop has several small rock art panels. In scattered spots on this outcrop are parallel scratches where a sharp object has been used to remove patches of dark manganese minerals that are deposited on the surface of the rock outcrop. These scratches may not be contemporaneous with the Hohokam rock art on the same outcrop: the manganese could have been used for pigment to make paint.

What Kinds of Images Were Made as Petroglyphs?

We recorded a variety of life-forms and geometric images as petroglyphs in the South Mountains:

- scorpion
- centipede
- beetle
- dragonfly
- cocoon or larva
- tadpole
- frog
- tortoise/turtle
- Gila monster
- lizard
- snake
- fish
- mountain sheep
- deer
- coyote/dog
- mountain lion
- javelina
- heron or egret
- hummingbird
- roadrunner
- thunderbird
- bluebird
- bat
- stick-figure anthropomorph
- hourglass anthropomorph
- spirit being
- atlatl
- bow and arrow
- crook/staff
- rattle
- composite animals
- mask
- pipette
- circle
- concentric circles
- circle with dot
- shield
- circle chain
- circle cluster
- figure eight
- spiral
- swastika
- whorl
- scroll
- fret
- solid cross
- negative cross
- outlined cross
- diamond
- zigzag
- square
- square with dot
- triangle
- "X"

"H"
"I" (barbell)
"A"
grid
textile pattern
maze
map
sun disk
moon
meander
line
scratches

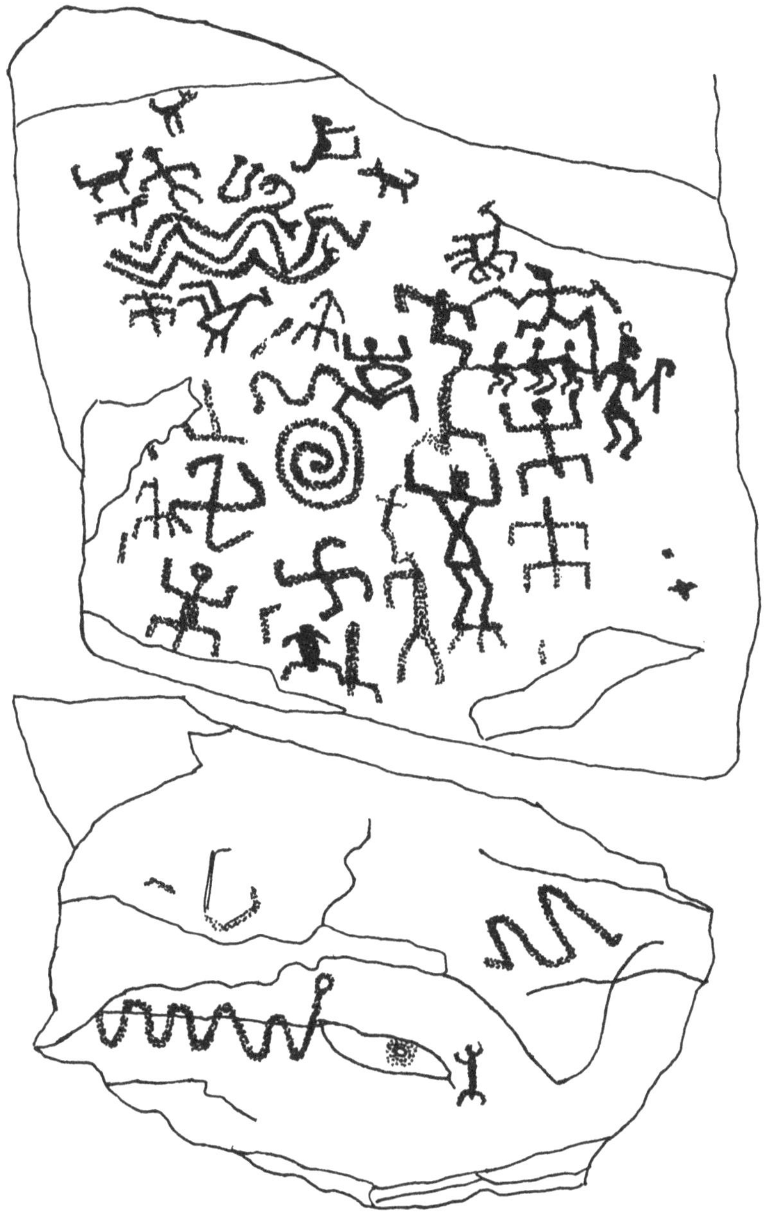

267. Hourglass anthropomorph in complex panel, Box Canyon. Hourglass anthropomorph is 34 cm in height; whorl is 17 x 16 cm. In the lower panel, a hole appears to have been drilled into the rock and is framed by petroglyphs.

Three basic elements—anthropomorphs, quadrupeds, and circles—occur most frequently. Anthropomorphs represent more than one-quarter of the total inventory of more than seven thousand recorded elements. The frequent depiction of humans or spirit beings in this rock art suggests that many of the panels are telling stories about someone's experiences or thoughts (figures 267 and 268). A variety of other life-forms, especially four-legged animals, participate in these stories. Most of the animals appear similar to creatures that live in the desert mountains, although some animal petroglyphs are composite creatures or are unidentifiable (figures 269 and 270). Geometric designs occur in all localities as simple forms and complex patterns. Amorphous lines also are common.

One unusual design found in the South Mountains but not identified at other Hohokam sites is a bat image (figure 271). Two panels (at Goodman Canyon and the 27th Street Locality) contain upright creatures that have small heads and wide

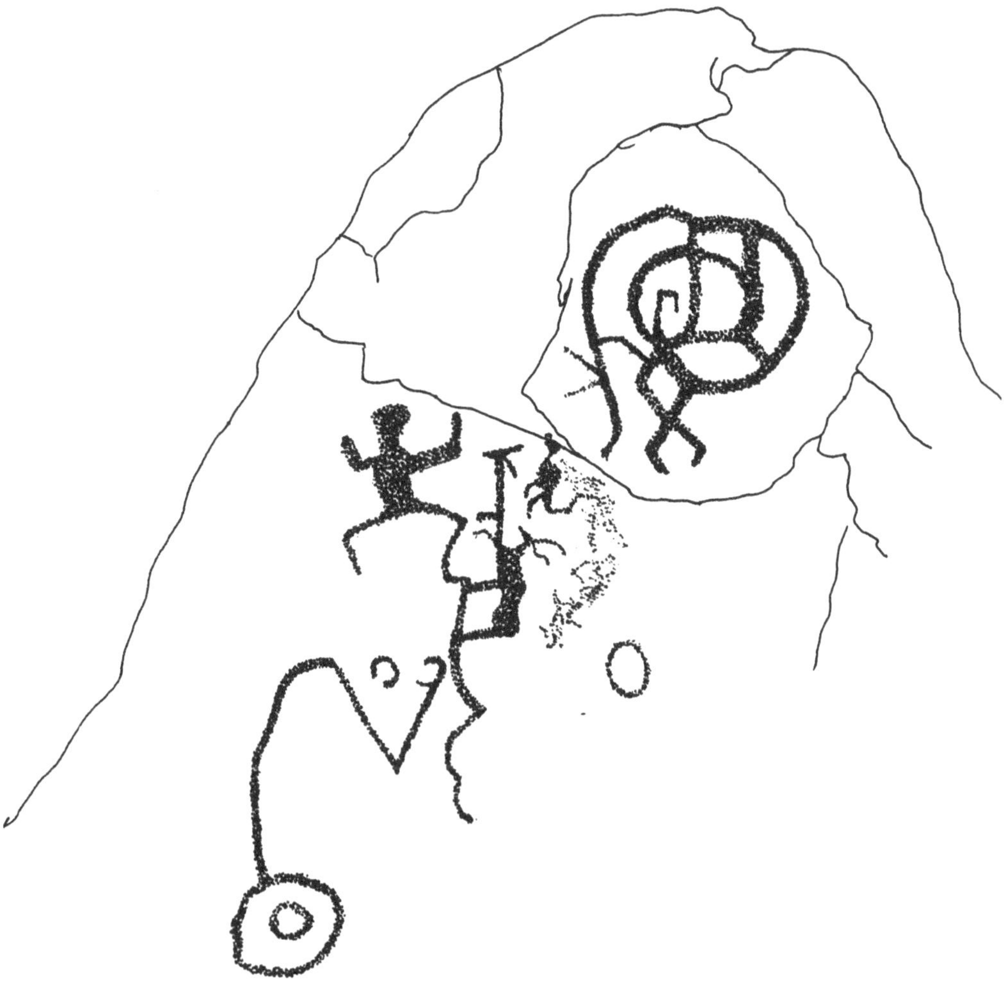

268. Anthropomorph, quadrupeds, and geometric designs, Box Canyon. Anthropomorph is 26 cm in height.

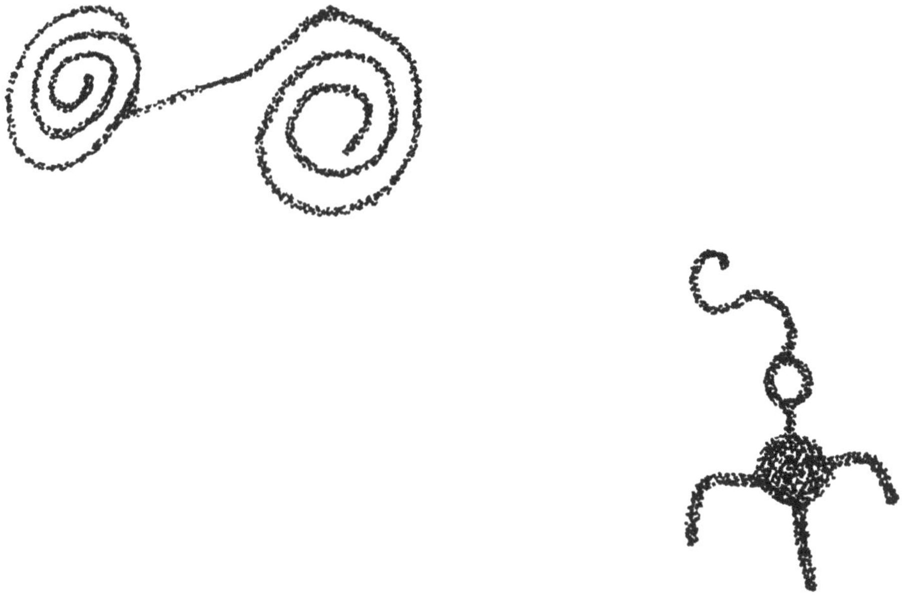

269. Double spiral and unusual life-form (possibly a spirit being), Box Canyon. Spirit being is 37 cm in length.

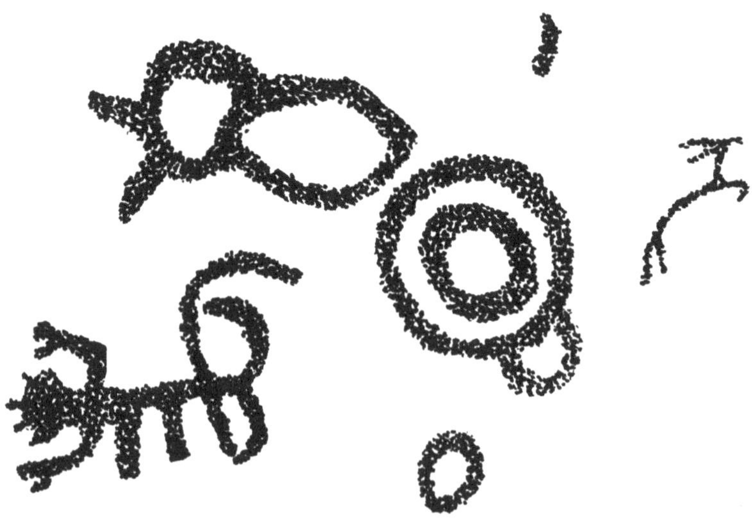

270. Multilegged creature with two tails next to circle designs, 28th Place Locality. Creature is 17 cm in length.

bodies, as though representing wings that are semi-spread. An O'odham circle song describes a reddish bat that rejoices in the songs being sung by the O'odham.

It is worth noting what is absent as rock art in the South Mountains. A scarcity of plant images seems unusual, because plants used as food and other products were extremely important to the Hohokam. Only a single petroglyph, a panel at the 32nd Street Locality, may represent a plant, and it appears to have a head with a headdress (figure 272). Both human and animal tracks are rare in the South Mountains, as is typical for other Hohokam rock art sites. An exception is a panel with four deer and their tracks at the 36th Street Locality (see figure 73). Although a relatively large quantity of bird petroglyphs are present, none appear to be quail images, which are common on Hohokam painted pottery. We did not find a few of the life-forms that Ernest Snyder (1966) identified but did not illustrate or describe in his mid 1960s South Mountains rock art inventory: these include skunk, rabbit, and squirrel (which are rare Hohokam rock art motifs). Birds that Snyder identified as turkeys we called waterbirds because of their long legs and long, arched necks. Finally, the pit-and-groove rock art style found at Archaic period (pre-Hohokam) sites in the American Southwest and Great Basin regions is absent from the South Mountains. The scarcity of this very old rock art style is consistent with the small number of Archaic rock art elements.

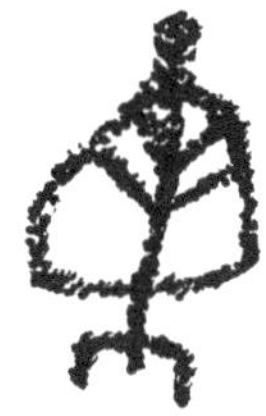

271. "Possible bat, Goodman Canyon. Petroglyph is 27 cm in height and 18 cm in width. It is located in a large panel with anthropomorphs, quadrupeds, and geometric designs.

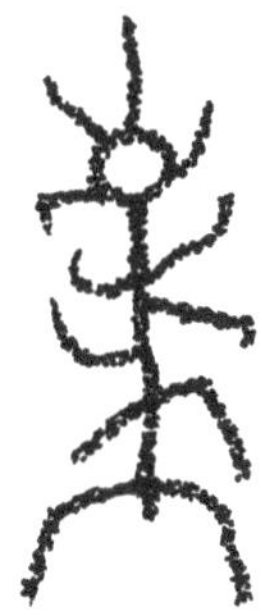

272. "Corn man," 32nd Street Locality. Petroglyph is 35 cm in height and located by itself in a cluster of boulders at the base of the mountains.

Why Was Rock Art Created?

Many rock art elements are combined in panels that appear to record dreams or memories, including experiences in the supernatural world. Some of the rock art images likely represent signs or symbols concerning people's relationship to the landscape and to the sky. Anthropomorph images are present in large quantities in the South Mountains and probably represent both humans and spirit beings. These figures are depicted carrying canes and crooks, playing flutes, holding snakes, hunting four-legged mammals with bow and arrow, dancing with other anthropomorphs, wrestling with animals, performing acrobatic feats, engaging in sexual acts, and wearing bird masks and headdresses that may indicate transformation. An interpretive sign posted at the Gila River Heritage Park at the Gila River Cultural Center, located south of the South Mountains, described the O'odham people's view of Hohokam rock art: "Images of animals, of cosmic signs, of maze-like designs, of human and reptilian forms have been pecked out of volcanic stone by rock or bone tools. Clusters of these figures are incised in the rock face east or south, catching the full rays of the morning sun. These galleries served ritual purposes. They may have been retreats for Hohokam prayers before the hunt. They may have been places to symbolically celebrate the spiritual forces affecting community life."

For archaeologists, a currently popular theory concerning the meaning of Hohokam rock art involves shamanism (Whitley 1994) and the neuropsychological model (Lewis-Williams and Dowson 1988), both of which are applicable to the South Mountains rock art (discussed in chapter 2). The entoptic geometric signs (see figure 3) associated with this model are typically seen by shamans, or religious spe-

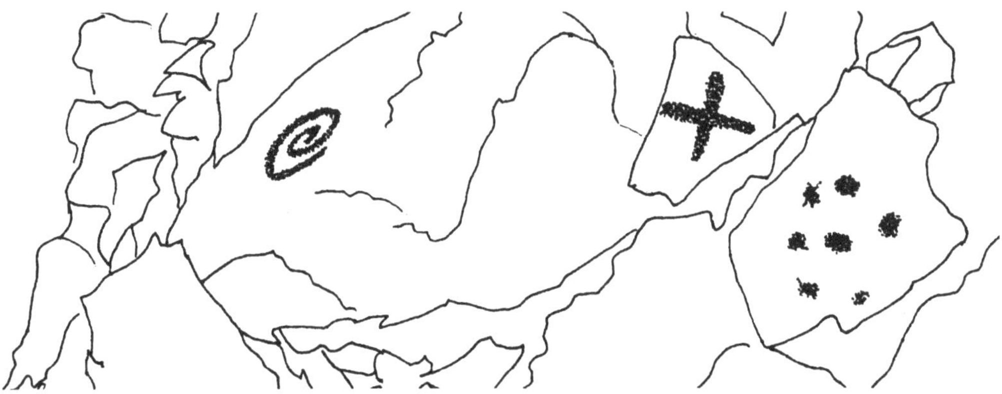

273. Possibly trance-induced geometric elements, River View Locality. Cross or "X" is 19 x 17 cm.

cialists, who undergo a spiritual transformation during their trances. Entoptic images can become embedded within a culture's art traditions, taking on iconographic meanings. Some of the South Mountains geometric petroglyphs—such as zigzags, circle clusters, spirals, dots, and others—may have originated as trance-induced images (figure 273). Anthropomorphs and other life-form images often occur with these geometric images, suggesting an important relationship between humans and entoptic forms in Hohokam rock art (figure 274).

The O'odham people of the Sonoran Desert have medicine people, called shamans, who communicated with animal spirits to receive power songs that are used in curing ceremonies, as well as for prophecies, controlling the weather, and assisting with warfare. The animal spirits contact the O'odham through dreams and during vision quests. Anthropologist Donald Bahr (1994:232) describes a "landscape of the spirits" where shamans visit to communicate with their animal spirit

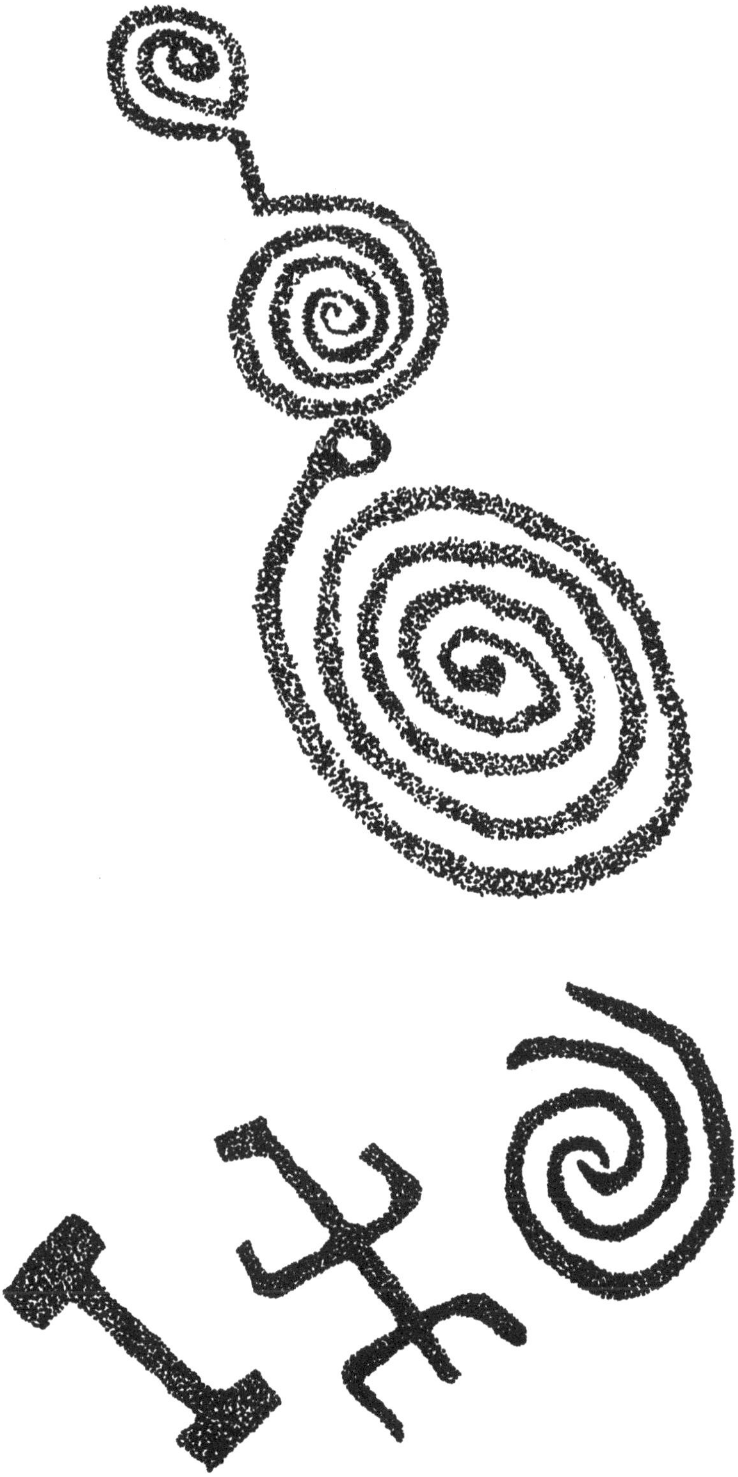

274. Two adjacent panels with interesting geometric designs and an anthropomorph, Chandler Boulevard/19th Way Locality. Large spiral is 30 cm in diameter; anthropomorph is 23 cm in height.

helpers. The South Mountains (Greasy Mountain to the O'odham) appear to be one of those places.

Akimel O'odham (Pima) ethnographer Frank Russell (1975) could find no evidence that the historic Pima made rock art, although they treated Hohokam rock art sites with reverence. Therefore, we have no ethnographic information concerning O'odham shamans and rock art. Nonetheless, several studies have shown that shamans around the world created rock art, often as records of their dreams or trance experiences. Shamanistic art typically depicts visual images associated with the shaman's travels into the landscape of the spirits (Halifax 1982):

Maps—depicting the sacred geography traveled by the shaman
Paths to the underworld—a sacred tree or a hole or portal often represented by spirals or concentric circles
Spirit beings—animals, birds, and other life-forms
Representations of death and dismemberment—stick figures, individuals without part of their bodies, skeletal figures, upside-down or sideways figures
Animal transformations—humans assuming animal forms, or creatures that are combinations (called "therianthropics")
Life energy—represented by lines or sinuous movement
Flight—symbolized by birds and flying humans
Solarization—sun symbols, halos around humans

Interpretive analyses of rock art sites can search for the presence or absence of the preceding universal shamanistic art motifs to determine whether some of the rock art is shamanistic in origin.

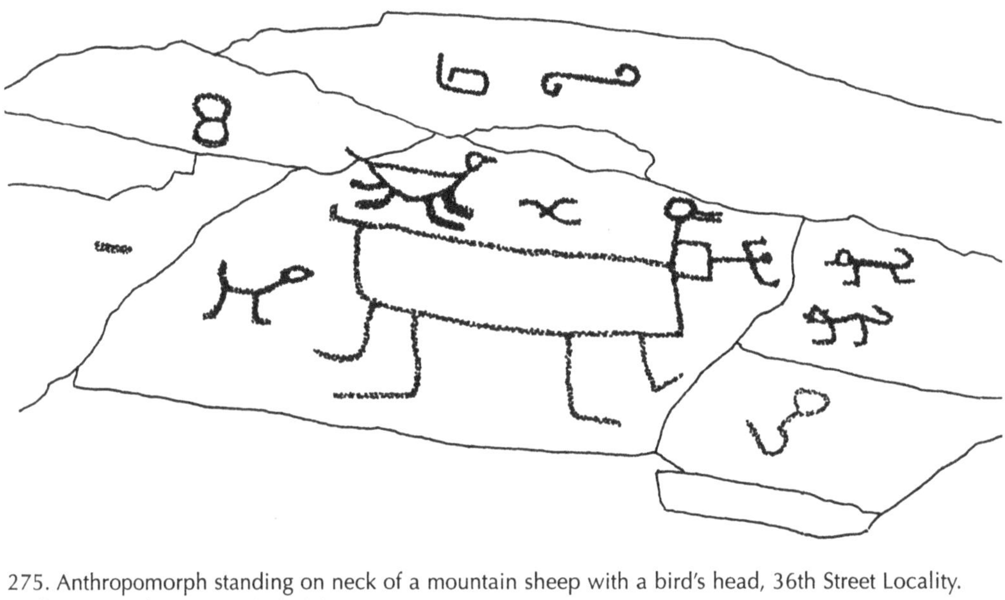

275. Anthropomorph standing on neck of a mountain sheep with a bird's head, 36th Street Locality. Anthropomorph is 20 cm in height.

The rock art of the South Mountains expresses all of the shamanistic art motifs listed above, being filled with large mammals, birds, venomous insects, serpents, composite creatures, spirit beings, and ghostlike figures—much of which involves creation mythology—and all in association with human figures that are typically smaller in size. Humans often are standing on or are attached with a wavy line to the various other creatures (figure 275). Animal designs often have exaggerated, unrealistic, or anatomically incorrect body forms. For example, many mountain sheep and deer are depicted with unnatural horn shapes and long tails. Some apparently human petroglyphs are depicted upside-down or have wavy bodies, suggesting death or transformation. Other humans are part animal or are wearing animal or bird masks. A few anthropomorphs have horns, and others have sun rays coming out of their heads. Feather headdresses are common.

Several individual burials have been identified as shamans at four different Hohokam villages in the Salt River Valley: Pueblo Grande, Las Colinas, Casa Buena, and Grand Canal Ruin (Bostwick and Downum 1994; Mitchell 1994). Archaeologists consider these individuals shamans because of the unusual and exotic materials found with them in their graves, including quartz crystals, minerals, stone concretions, clay effigies, and carved bone tools. O'odham shamans considered quartz crystals very powerful and used them for healing, locating deer, assisting in warfare, and bringing rain (Underhill 1946). In support of the premise that some of the South Mountains petroglyphs may have been shamanistic, we found a quartz crystal next to a rock art panel in Goodman Canyon, where a natural water tank is located.

The South Mountains would have been an ideal location for shamans or initiates to seek out visions and communicate with animal spirit helpers. Frank Hamilton Cushing (1979:209) noted that a Zuni who undergoes a vision quest has a profound experience: "His perceptions will become startlingly manifest in the various visions and signs he sees. These will seem to him, I can again personally assure you, far more real than the most absolutely actual things he had ever beheld or experienced."

Numerous examples presented in the preceding chapters may be shaman scenes. We found a dramatic example of a shaman scene in Goodman Canyon, where a panel in a hidden alcove contains a lizard, a bird, and a deer perched above a human holding a cane, possibly serving as his spirit helpers (figure 276). In the 32nd Street Locality, an anthropomorph appears to be transforming into two deer (figure 277). A panel at the 36th Street Locality has several anthropomorphs connected with lines to each other and to other elements including a two-headed serpent and a four-legged mammal that is a reversed mirror image of itself (figure 278). One of the anthropomorphs is holding a star. A maze also is present in this panel, which has all the characteristics of shamanistic art.

Geometric designs often appear in apparently meaningful association with humans, animals, and birds (figure 279). In some panels, human figures are holding,

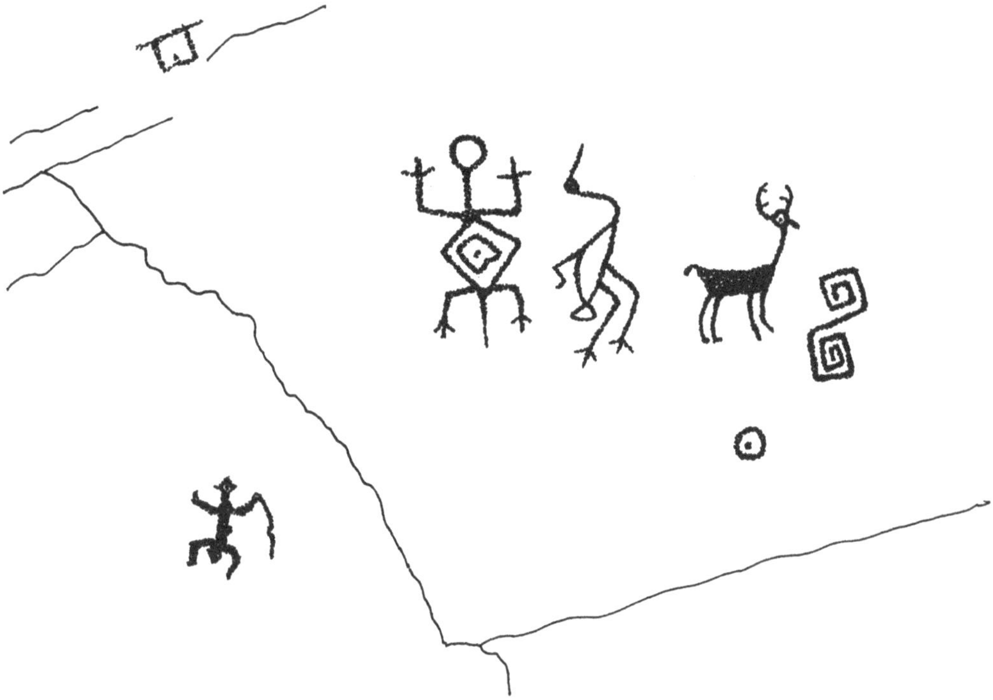

276. Anthropomorph and his spirit helpers, Goodman Canyon. Anthropomorph is 21 cm in height. Panel is located within a hidden alcove next to a natural tunnel.

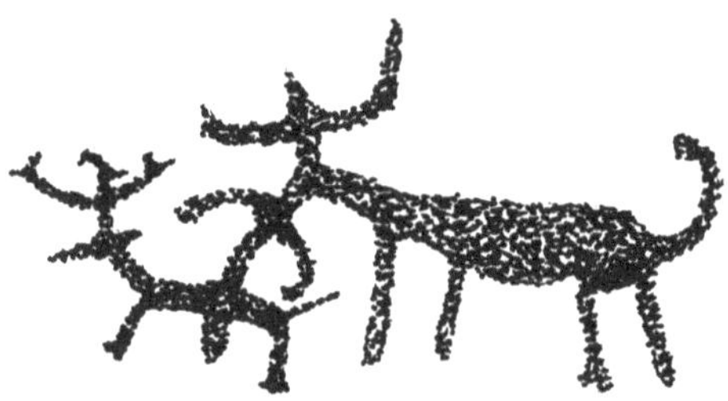

277. Anthropomorph transforming into two deer, 32nd Street Locality. Petroglyph is 44 cm in total length.

standing next to, or entering circles (figure 280). These panels may represent portals into the spirit world, where humans in trance states travel to interact with spirit beings.

One important role of the O'odham shaman is to influence the weather to ensure adequate rain to fill the rivers, recharge the mountain springs, and give life to desert plants. When the rivers ran, vast fields of corn and other crops could be irrigated. When food was plentiful, people lived well and had time to create beautiful arts and crafts. When the rains did not come, however, life on the desert was diffi-

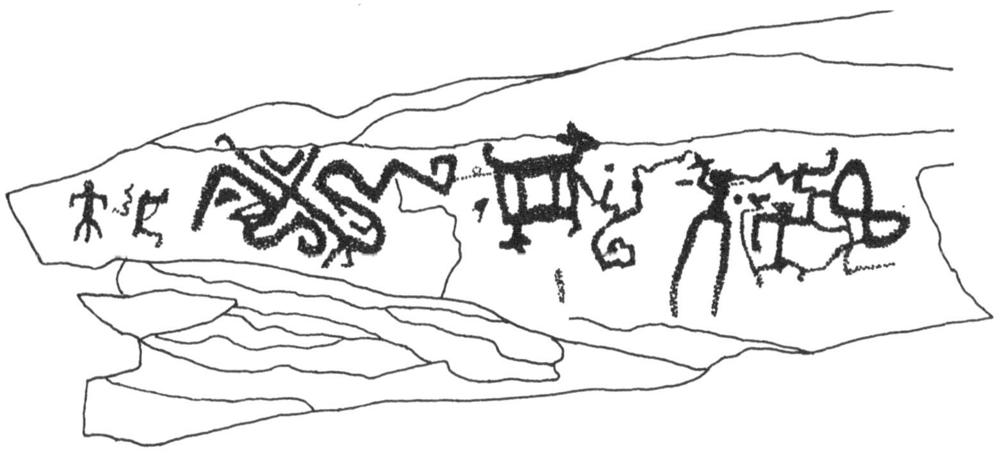

278. Possible shaman scene with reverse mirror-image quadruped, 36th Street Locality. Figure eight on right is 15 cm in length.

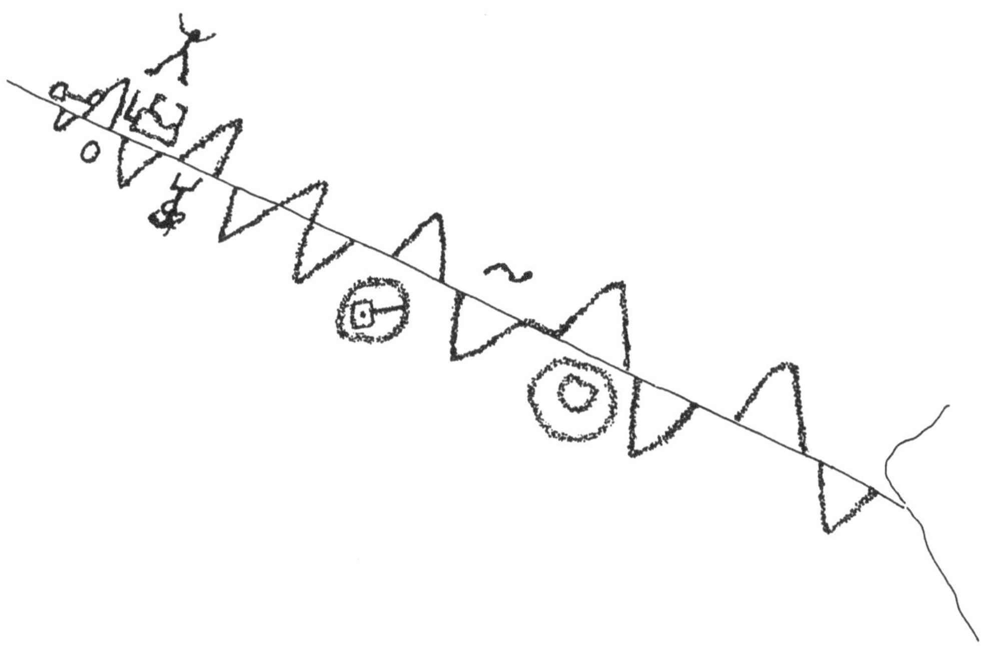

279. Anthropomorph with elaborate geometric design, 48th Street Locality. A large crack in the rock was incorporated into the composition. Panel is 2 m in width and faces east.

cult. It is no surprise that rituals praying for rain were interwoven throughout the O'odham's religious and ceremonial lifeways.

The Hohokam would have been no less concerned about adequate rain and most likely had rituals that encouraged it to fall. Hohokam painted ceramic designs and petroglyphs are full of water symbols. These include water-related life-forms and geometric designs. Water animals consist of dragonflies, tadpoles, frogs, salamanders,

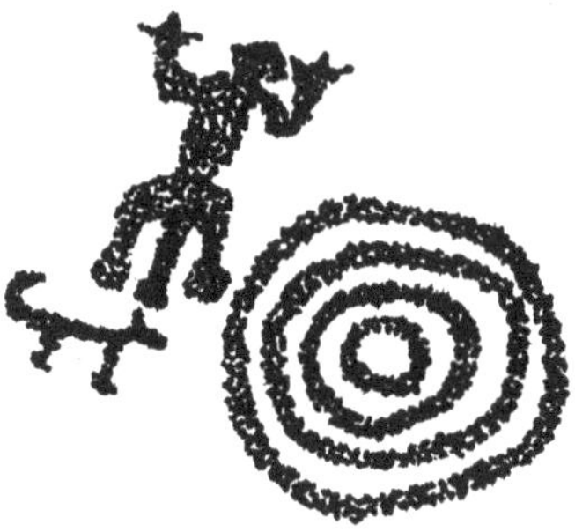

280. Lizardman and concentric circles, Box Canyon. Lizardman is 27 cm in height.

snakes, turtles, waterbirds, and thunderbirds. The O'odham associate the mountain sheep with the wind and rain; if the Hohokam had the same belief, that would be reason enough for the comparatively large numbers of mountain sheep petroglyphs in the South Mountains rock art. In addition, two panels with flute-player images in the South Mountains have mountain sheep petroglyphs in the same panel; it may be no coincidence that Zuni rain priests were flute-players. Geometric designs in the rock art of the South Mountains that may be water symbols include spirals, scrolls, wavy lines, and zigzags (lightning). An O'odham rain song describes the behavior of lightning as "moving very zigzag, roaring beautifully" (Saxton and Saxton 1973:335).

A large number of pipettes, nearly three dozen, are present in the rock art of the South Mountains. Some of these unusual designs look like faces with bulging eyes; Henry Wallace and James Holmlund (1986) have equated them with the Mesoamerican rain god Tlaloc (figure 281). This custodian of the clouds is a storm god who wears a mask and is associated with mountains and lightning. He often carries a serpent in one hand and is said to scatter the rain like seeds. A Tlaloc Cult was present at Casas Grandes in northern Chihuahua, a Mesoamerican trade center undoubtedly visited by Hohokam traders (DiPeso et al. 1974). However, not all pipettes have a facelike appearance, and some may have represented portals or had some other significance (figure 282).

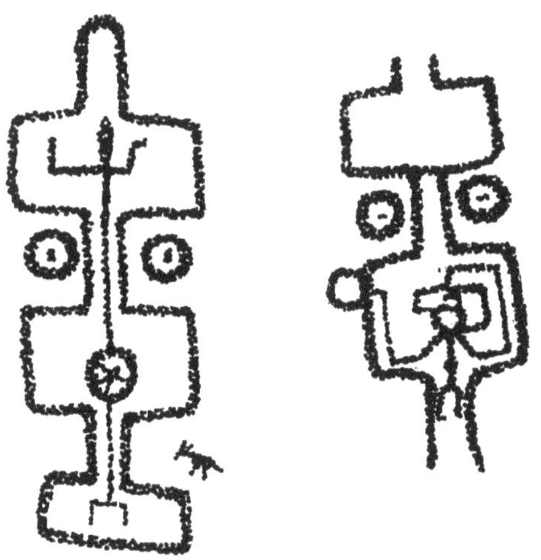

281. Two large pipettes, Hieroglyphic Canyon. Pipette on left is 1.23 m in length. Other faint petroglyphs, including stick-figure anthropomorphs, are present under and adjacent to this pipette.

Not all rock art in the South Mountains is shaman related. Some geometric elements located along trails, such as spirals and groups of circles, appear to be trail markers or directional indicators (figures 283 and 284). Other petroglyphs may be territorial markers. Two panels on the southern side of the mountains may be maps of the local area or larger region. A flat-

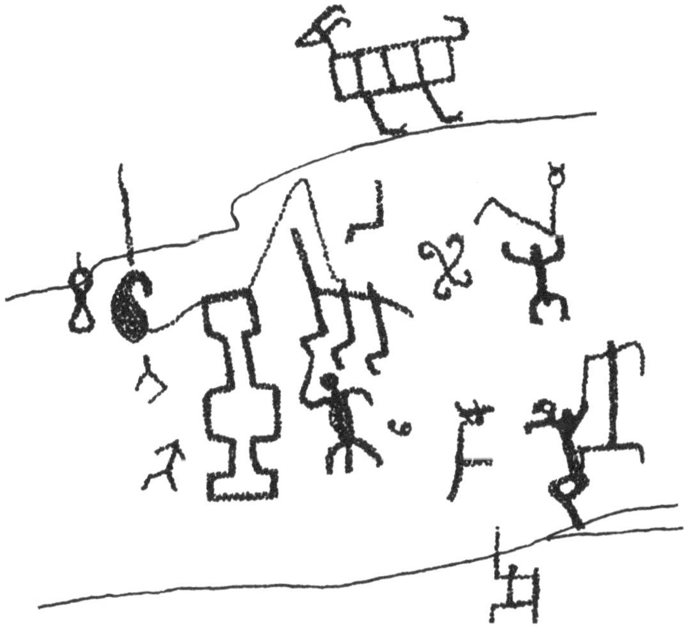

282. Pipette attached by lines to lightning and to a tadpole, Box Canyon. Pipette is 46 cm in length.

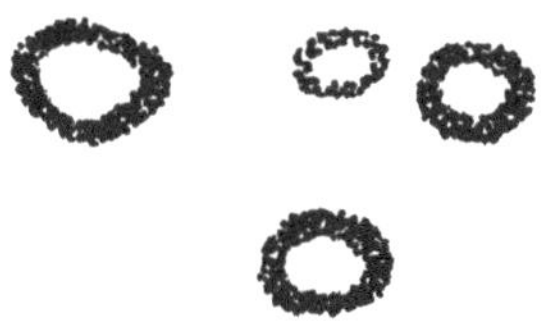

283. Circle petroglyphs, possibly trail markers, located along an east-west trail, Pecos Road Locality.

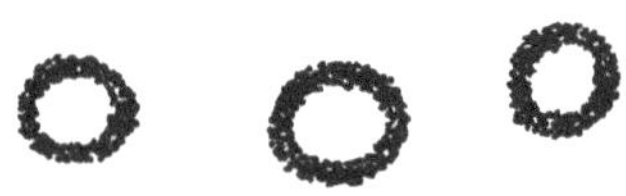

284. Circle petroglyphs, possibly trail markers, located along an east-west trail, upper 32nd Street Locality.

lying panel on the southeastern side of the South Mountains has three thick lines that merge and several smaller associated elements (figure 285). The three lines look like the Salt River and Gila River flowing to their junction west of the South Mountains, eventually joining with a south-flowing Colorado River that debouches into the Gulf of California. Design elements located along the lines could represent villages or sacred locations. An interesting four-legged mammal with a large, curved tail is present in the panel. Is this a Hohokam map of the region, a map of the O'odham sacred salt pilgrimage to the Gulf of California, or neither?

Another possible map panel is pecked into a small, well-patinated boulder along the upper reaches of the Telegraph Pass Trail on the southern side of the South Mountains. This panel also has thick lines that curve across the face and sides of

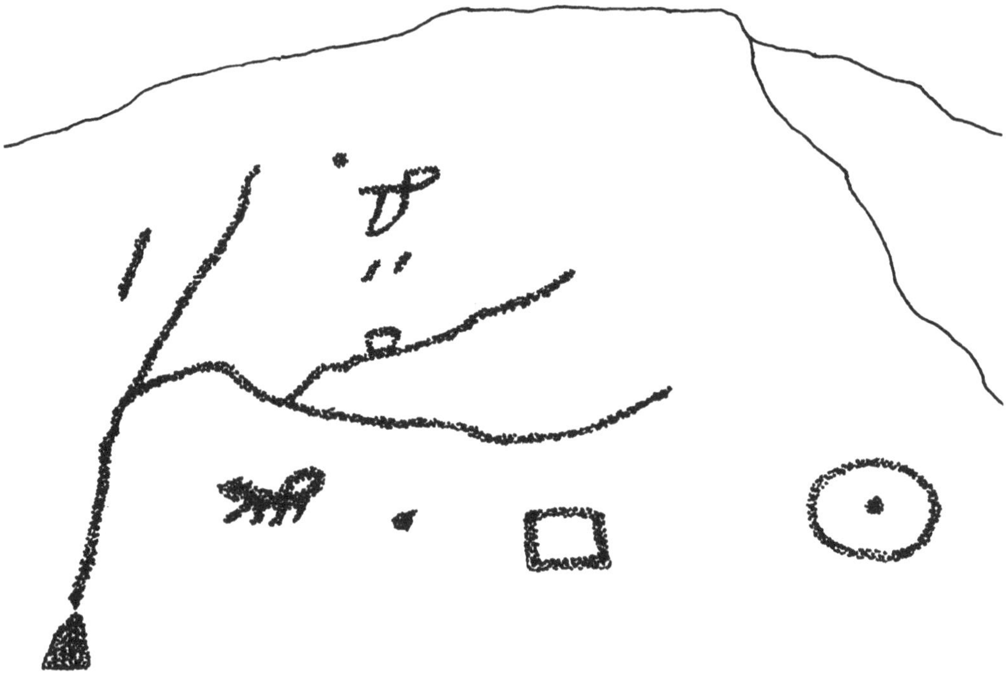

285. Possible map, Southeast Side Locality. Square is 7 x 7 cm. This panel may depict the Colorado, Salt, and Gila Rivers.

the boulder, as well as several smaller elements (figure 286). This panel could be a map of the trails that join in Telegraph Pass, an important travel route through the mountains.

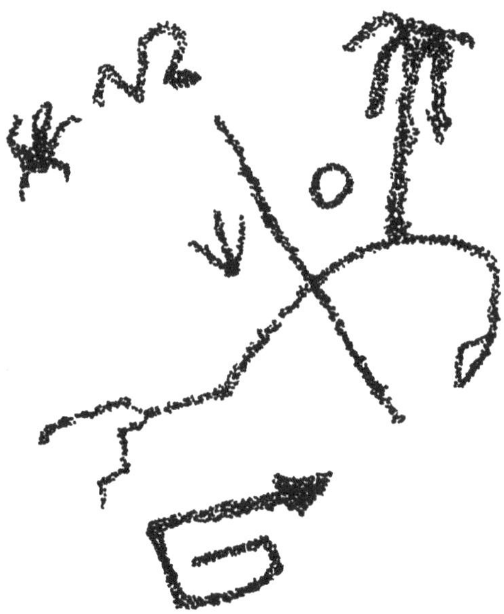

286. Possible map, Telegraph Pass. Rectilinear scroll is 10 x 6 cm.

Some of the panels in the South Mountains containing circles and other geometric elements (for example, crosses) may represent celestial bodies including the sun, moon, and Venus (discussed in chapter 10). Sun disk motifs occur throughout the South Mountains and are often placed above human figures in the same panel. A variety of cross designs, possibly symbolizing stars and Venus, also occasionally occur in these same panels, as though representing a heavenly scene (figure 287).

A large and elaborate panel along the Mormon Loop Trail may represent a celestial scene, with several stars at the top of the panel and a series of dramatic zigzags spread across the middle, possibly symbolizing the Milky Way (figure 288). Alternatively, the zigzags may symbolize lightning during powerful storms that cause floods. A variety of different types of anthropomorphs are scattered throughout this panel, some of them entering circles. Perhaps they are observing or participating in the events or concepts represented in the panel. In an interesting parallel, the O'odham shaman's ladder to the sky is known as the zigzag ladder.

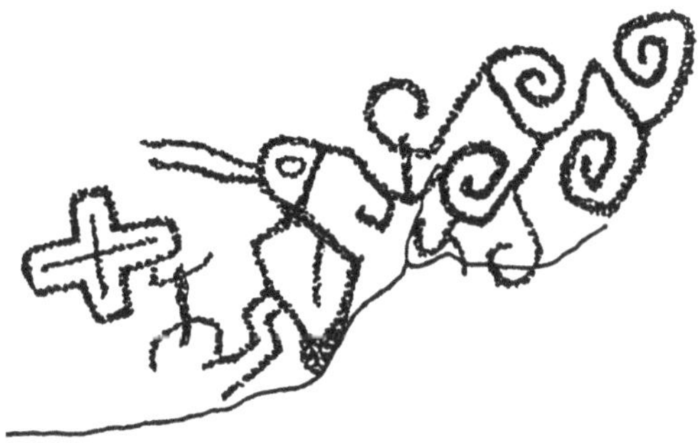

287. Anthropomorph holding an outlined cross and standing on the foot of a large waterbird, 36th Street Locality. Outlined cross is 16 cm in width. Panel faces southwest.

There may be a connection between the sun and shamanism. Anthropologist Donald Bahr (1983) has noted that O'odham shamans use the power of the sun to influence light and wind. Ethnographer Frank Russell (1975) stated that the sun gives the O'odham shaman his trance vision and magic power. Perhaps an example of this solar power is depicted in a rock art panel located on the southern side of the South Mountains—although this panel may postdate the Hohokam (see figure 163). This panel possibly implies the transformation of sun power to the human through the hourglass and lizard elements.

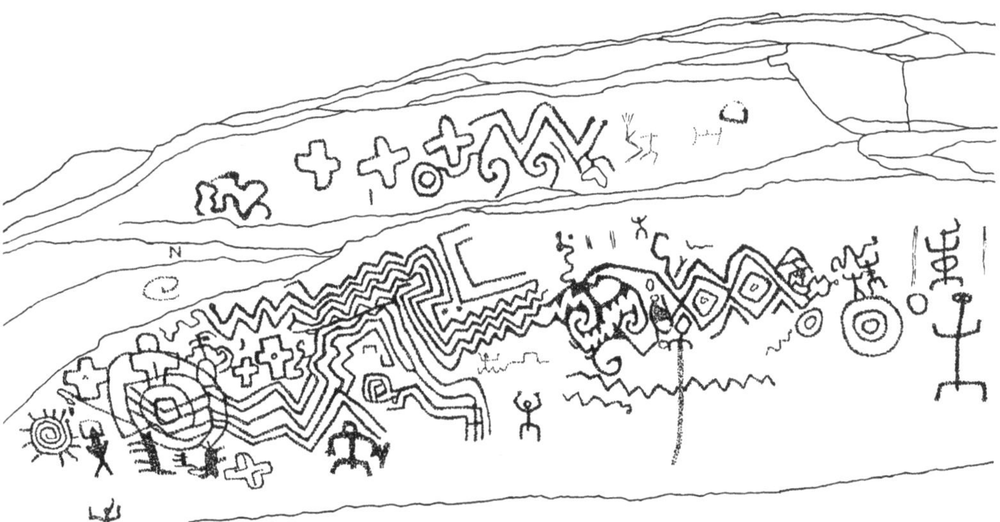

288. Large, complex panel located along the Mormon Loop Trail. Negative crosses in upper portion of panel are 20 x 20 cm. Panel faces southeast.

Mesoamerican archaeologist Burr Brundage (1982) has proposed that a sky religion developed in Mesoamerica around the eighth century. This sky religion charted the annual movement of the sun and other celestial bodies and was directed by a priestly class who had separated themselves from the older shamanistic religion. They worshiped Quetzalcoatl, a deity with shaman powers closely tied to the planet Venus and associated with images of a plumed or horned serpent. The Mesoamerican sky religion incorporated a sacred ball game, which was practiced wherever ball courts were built; the sun and moon were important symbols associated with the game. Mayan stories say that the ball represented the daily movement of the sun from the sky into the underworld. The Hohokam also began constructing and using ball courts in the latter part of the eighth century, the same time that a suite of new art motifs first appear in Hohokam art. In addition to the new art motifs, which include various life-forms found in the rock art of the South Mountains, several ritual items such as incised palettes, ceramic and carved stone censers, and carved shell were introduced. Brundage suggests that this dramatic change in Hohokam culture can be attributed to their participation in the widespread Mesoamerican sky religion.

Plumed and horned serpents occur in a number of rock art panels in the South Mountains, but their presence does not necessarily indicate that the Hohokam had a sky religion similar to what Brundage suggests occurred in Mesoamerica. Nonetheless, it appears that the Hohokam were keen astronomical observers, with a knowledge of the sun's annual cycle. Much more study is needed to more fully understand the extent and importance of their knowledge.

Is the Rock Art in the South Mountains a Writing System?

Only the Olmec, Maya, and Zapotec cultures of Mesoamerica developed true forms of writing in the New World (Robinson 1995). These prehistoric peoples used ideographic glyphs, a system similar to ancient Egyptian and Chinese writing systems. The Maya also had a remarkable numbering system that used dots and bars for numbers, and they were the first people in the world to use zero. Sometime in the early fourteenth century, the Aztecs developed a writing system that was less abstract than the Mayan. It has been called a pictographic form of writing that is little more than an elaborate mnemonic device, the subject matter of which includes religious subjects, historical annals, records of events, diaries, year counts, tribute paid, lines of descent of important kin groups, landownership records, and other things. These are similar to subjects Garrick Mallery (1893) reported for American Indian art in the late nineteenth century.

Although not a writing system, Hohokam rock art does appear to be a form of communication. Hohokam petroglyph artists used a similar, limited set of elements or motifs, often in combination, over a broad region. Many of these rock art panels are in highly visible locations along trails and in cleared areas, suggesting that the concepts, stories, or messages that they contain would have been seen and understood by persons other than the artist. We have suggested this rock art represents dreams, memories, and signs. Much of the Hohokam rock art element inventory in the South Mountains also was painted on Hohokam red-on-buff pottery. On the basis of an analysis of the ceramic designs from the Hohokam village of Snaketown, Emil Haury (1976) suggested that Hohokam art was in the beginning stages of storytelling. Perhaps Hohokam rock art can be called a form of protowriting, which had certain conventions or rules that we have not yet discovered.

How Does the Rock Art of the South Mountains Fit into the Gila Style?

Polly Schaafsma defined Gila Style rock art in 1980, based in part on rock art recorded in the South Mountains by Ernest Snyder in the mid 1960s. However, this style remains too broadly defined, and its regional variability is largely unknown. Close examination of the large quantity of rock art in the South Mountains indicates that several different styles or substyles may be present. Formally identifying these different styles is difficult because archaeologists have not yet systematically developed the required criteria. Further study of these variations in execution and forms may show that some have chronological significance.

One of the findings of our study is that the Hohokam who made rock art in the South Mountains were not overly concerned with exact representation of life-forms, including humans and animals. Correct anatomical details appear not to have been required or desired. Stick-figure humans are typical, and full-figure humans with genitalia and other detailed body parts are rare. Even mountain sheep and deer are not depicted as Hohokam hunters would have seen them. Indeed, many large four-legged mammal petroglyphs are anatomically incorrect, exhibiting such peculiarities as mountain sheep horns pointing forward or overly long tails—curious discrepancies because the Hohokam certainly were capable of pecking accurate designs. In contrast, certain geometric designs such as spirals and concentric circles are well executed and consistently symmetrical in their depiction, as though the artist intended to make them as accurate as possible.

For both humans and animals, the intent seems to have been more important than accuracy. Donald Bahr (1997) has noted that when Pimas recall the dreams in which they were visited by animal spirits, they are hesitant to report or describe the spirits in detail. Merely remembering the presence of the animal spirits and any songs they gave to the dreamer was enough. Much of the South Mountains rock art has this dreamlike appearance with its stick-figure humans, simple compositions, and infrequent elaborations.

NOTES

Chapter 1. Learning the Landscape

1. At the time of my survey I knew about Ernest Snyder's (1966) rock art survey, but his published map was too small to be useful for revisiting his sites. Some time later I learned that Margerie Green and Richard Effland had conducted an archaeological survey in 1984 of the Pecos Ranch on the southeastern side of the South Mountains. They recorded nine rock art sites, several of which no longer exist. One of the panels, located along an east-west trail, consisted of three circles, similar to possible trail-marking panels found along other trails in the South Mountains.

2. When recording the petroglyphs in the South Mountains we quickly learned how difficult it is to record all the details and nuances of a rock art panel. The rock surfaces of boulders and outcrops are generally rough and often pebbly in texture. These uneven surfaces reflect light, obscuring some petroglyphs during certain times of the day. Between this trick of the light and the Hohokam artist's penchant for only lightly pecking some designs, photographs of the rock art sometimes do not fully capture all of the more difficult-to-identify petroglyphs that may be present. Even field sketches can be incomplete if accomplished during a single visit or at the wrong time of the day (generally late morning to early evening).

3. The establishment of South Mountain Park can be attributed largely to the efforts of James Dobbins, Dwight Heard, William Hartranft, Senator Carl Hayden, and Senator Ralph Cameron. The official transfer of the property occurred with several purchases by the City of Phoenix beginning in 1927. Charles M. Holbert was appointed as park custodian in 1929. Much of the initial development of the park—including trails, roads, ramadas, and office buildings—was undertaken from 1933 to 1940 by the Civilian Conservation Corps as part of President Franklin Roosevelt's New Deal employment program.

4. Park development and management is currently guided by the 1989 South Mountain Park Master Plan. This master plan encourages the preservation of natural and cultural resources within the park and promotes the educational values of those resources. In 1999, the South Mountain Environmental Education Center was built, a decade after it was recommended by the 1989 master plan.

Chapter 2. Investigating Ancient Art in the Sonoran Desert

1. The first five decades (1880s to 1930s) of archaeological investigations in the Salt River Valley were largely undertaken by archaeologists associated with museums located in the eastern

United States. One of the main objectives of these expeditions was to obtain museum specimens, with rock art mostly a curiosity. Local archaeologists took over in the 1930s, but interest in rock art remained limited. Not until the 1960s was Hohokam rock art studied seriously, and only beginning in the 1980s did archaeologists undertake its systematic recording.

2. I have experienced entoptic phenomena after strenuous hikes at a rapid pace into the South Mountains. In particular, at the end of the hike I have seen a flickering light in front of my eyes that took the form of a spinning whorl (commonly called a "pinwheel"). This geometric design disappeared after a brief rest.

Chapter 3. Dating Rock Art in the South Mountains

1. Among the petroglyphs at the 28th Place Locality are several pecked and scratched dates, including "1900" and "Feb 7, 1905". Pecked initials also are present, in addition to Hohokam designs (pipettes, spirals, concentric circles, anthropomorphs, and snakes).

2. In the early 1920s, naturalist Charles Sheldon recorded personal signatures expressed as geometric symbols by Seri Indians in Sonora, Mexico (Carmony and Brown 1979:185). Two examples were tattooed on the individual's arm. Some of these signatures are similar to the South Mountains petroglyphs and the O'odham cattle brands. Anthropologist Jesse Walter Fewkes (1892) also recorded Puebloan signatures that were clan symbols.

Chapter 4. Small Critters

1. A large petroglyph next to a natural tunnel in the Hidden Canyon area has been identified as a "bug" in the popular literature. However, this four-legged creature has a segmented, boat-shaped body similar to other petroglyphs in the South Mountains that are mountain sheep; these figures often have faint horns. Close examination of a well-known historic photograph with Frank Midvale and Orland Higgins in front of the so-called bug panel indicates that the petroglyph was retraced with white chalk for the photograph; a set of faint mountain sheep horns may not have been chalked for the photograph. This panel has been heavily vandalized and is now hardly recognizable.

Chapter 7. Friends of the Upper World

1. Elsewhere (Bostwick 1998b) I initially identified the roadrunner and hummingbird petroglyphs as waterbirds because of the stylistic similarity of their body forms with other waterbird designs.

Chapter 8. Humans and Spirit Beings

1. Dennis Slifer (2000:46–48) has noted that Puebloan rock art anthropomorphs identified as females are less abundant and less obvious than males. Females may be characterized by facial markings, hairstyles, clothing, body positions (squatting), head shape, breasts, widened hips, genitals, and the use of natural holes as vulvas.

Chapter 10. Saluting the Sun

1. There is always the possibility that the alignment of petroglyphs and the position of the sun on the horizon is merely coincidental. However, the frequent occurrence of these alignments in the South Mountains and the apparent selection of specific locations where other rock faces equally suitable in their physical characteristics were not chosen suggests that many of the alignments were intentionally marked by the Hohokam. Furthermore, these sites often have cleared

areas from which to view the alignments. (For discussions of archaeoastronomy methodology, see Hardman and Hardman 1992, C. Johnson 1992, and Young 1986).

Chapter 11. Dreams, Memories, and Signs

1. We collected seven cobble hammerstones from five rock art localities in the South Mountains. Localities and dimensions are listed below, with multiple hammerstones from a single location indicated in parentheses.

Mormon Trail	5 x 5 x 4 cm
20th Street	6 x 5 x 3 cm
Southeast Side	12 x 10 x 10 cm
34th Street (2)	10 x 8 x 6 cm
	9 x 8 x5 cm
36th Street (2)	8 x 5 x 4 cm
	8 x 8 x 5 cm

The broken axe used as a hammerstone was found in the upper 32nd Street Locality; it measures 10 x 7 x 4 cm.

REFERENCES CITED

Abbott, David R.

1993 The Pueblo Viejo Ceramics. In *Pueblo Viejo: Archaeological Investigations at a Classic Cemetery in El Reposo Park, Phoenix, Arizona,* ed. Mark Zyniecki, pp. 60–198. SWCA Archaeological Report No. 92-75. Flagstaff, Ariz.

1997 Ceramics. In *Archaeological and Archival Investigations of Las Canopas: The Esteban Park Project,* ed. Mark R. Hackbarth, pp. 87–104. Pueblo Grande Museum Anthropological Papers No. 6. Phoenix.

2000 *Ceramics and Community Organization among the Hohokam.* University of Arizona Press, Tucson.

Adams, E. Charles

1991 *The Origin and Development of the Pueblo Katsina Cult.* University of Arizona Press, Tucson.

Alcock, John

1985 *Sonoran Desert Spring.* University of Chicago Press, Chicago.

Amsden, Charles A.

1936 *An Analysis of Hohokam Pottery Designs.* Medallion Papers 23. Gila Pueblo, Globe, Ariz.

Anderson, Keith

1971 Excavations at Betatakin and Keet Seel. *Kiva* 37:1–29.

Aveni, Anthony

1980 *Skywatchers of Ancient Mexico.* University of Texas Press, Austin.

Bahr, Donald M.

1971 Who Were the Hohokam? The Evidence from Pima-Papago Myths. *Ethnohistory* 18(2): 245–66.

1983 Pima and Papago Medicine and Philosophy. In *Handbook of North American Indians,* vol. 10: *Southwest,* ed. Alfonso Ortiz, pp. 193–200. Smithsonian Institution Press, Washington, D.C.

1997 *Ants and Orioles: Showing the Art of Pima Poetry.* University of Utah Press, Salt Lake City.

Bahr, Donald M., Juan Gregorio, David I. Lopez, and Albert Alvarez

1974 *Piman Shamanism and Staying Sickness.* University of Arizona Press, Tucson.

Bahr, Donald, Juan Smith, William Smith Allison, and Julian Hayden
1994 *The Short Swift Time of Gods on Earth: The Hohokam Chronicles.* University of California Press, Berkeley.

Bartlett, Katharine, and Harold S. Colton
1940 A Note on the Marcos de Niza Inscription near Phoenix, Arizona. *Plateau* 12(4):53–59.

Beck, W., D. J. Donahue, A. J. T. Jull, G. Burr, W. S. Broecker, G. Bonani, I. Hajdas, and E. Malotki
1998 Ambiguities in Direct Dating of Rock Surfaces Using Radiocarbon Measurements. *Science* 280:2132–39.

Benson, Elizabeth P.
1997 *Birds and Beasts of Ancient Latin America.* University of Florida, Gainesville.

Bohrer, Vorsila L.
1994 Maize in Middle American and Southwestern United States Agricultural Traditions. In *Corn and Culture in the Prehistoric New World,* ed. Sissel Johannessen and Christine A. Hastorf, pp. 469–512. Westview Press, Boulder, Colo.

Bostwick, Todd W.
1998a Managing Rock Art in an Urban Setting: The Challenges of South Mountain Park. In *American Indian Rock Art,* vol. 22, ed. Steven M. Freers, pp. 119–128. American Rock Art Research Association, Tucson.
1998b Songs of the Waterbird: Hohokam Petroglyph Bird Designs in the South Mountains, Phoenix, Arizona. In *Rock Art Papers,* vol. 13, ed. Ken Hedges, pp. 7–30. San Diego Museum Papers No. 35. San Diego.
1999 Hourglass Anthropomorph Petroglyphs in the South Mountains, Arizona. *American Indian Rock Art,* vol. 23, ed. Steve Freers, pp. 121–32. American Rock Art Research Association, Tucson.
2000 Rock Art Mask Designs in the South Mountains, Arizona. *American Indian Rock Art,* vol. 24, ed. Frank G. Bock, pp. 103–12. American Rock Art Research Association, Tucson.
2001a Gold-Gold-Gold: The Rise and Fall of Mining in Phoenix's South Mountain Park. *Journal of Arizona History* 42(1):59–80.
2001b North American Indian Agriculturalists. In *Handbook of Rock Art Research,* ed. David S. Whitley, pp. 414–58. AltaMira Press, Walnut Creek, Calif.

Bostwick, Todd W., and J. Claire Dean
2000 An Experiment in Removing Spray Paint Graffiti from a Hohokam Rock Art Panel with Graffiti-B-Gone. In *American Indian Rock Art,* vol. 24, ed. Frank G. Bock, pp. 103–10. American Rock Art Research Association, Tucson.

Bostwick, Todd W., and Christian E. Downum
1994 Site Structure and Ceremony at Pueblo Grande. In *Archaeology of the Pueblo Grande Platform Mound and Surrounding Features,* vol. 2: *Features in the Central Precinct of the Pueblo Grande Community,* ed. Todd W. Bostwick and Christian E. Downum, pp. 297–386. Pueblo Grande Museum Anthropological Papers No. 1. Phoenix.

Bostwick, Todd W., and Jerry B. Howard
1992 *An Archaeological Survey of the South Mountain National Trail, and a History of South Mountain Park, Phoenix, Arizona.* Pueblo Grande Museum, Phoenix.

Bostwick, Todd W., and Stan Plum
1997 Under Ancient Skies: A Prehistoric Hohokam Observatory. *The Practical Observer* 82:116–19.

Bostwick, Todd W., and Glen E. Rice

1986 *A Cultural Resource Inventory for the Southwest Loop Freeway Project.* Arizona State University OCRM Report No. 66. Tempe.

Bourke, John G.

1884 *Snake-Dance of the Moquis of Arizona.* Scribner, New York. 1984 reprint, University of Arizona Press, Tucson.

Broda, Johanna

1993 Astronomical Knowledge, Calendrics, and Sacred Geography in Ancient Mesoamerica. In *Astronomies and Cultures,* ed. Clive L. N. Ruggles and Nicholas J. Saunders, pp. 251–95. University Press of Colorado, Niwot.

Brown, David E., and Neil B. Carmony

1991 *Gila Monster: Facts and Folklore of America's Aztec Lizard.* High-Lonesome Books, Silver City, N.Mex.

Bruder, J. Simon

1983 *Archaeological Investigations at the Hedgpeth Hills Petroglyph Site.* Museum of Northern Arizona Research Paper No. 28. Flagstaff.

Brundage, Burr C.

1982 *The Phoenix of the Western World: Quetzalcoatl and the Sky Religion.* University of Oklahoma Press, Norman.

Brunson[-Hadley], Judy

1989 The Social Organization of the Los Muertos Hohokam: A Reanalysis of Cushing's Hemenway Expedition Data. Ph.D. diss., Department of Anthropology, Arizona State University, Tempe.

Bunzel, Ruth L.

1992 Zuni Ceremonialism. In *Three Studies by Ruth Bunzel.* University of New Mexico Press, Albuquerque.

Carmony, Neil B., and David E. Brown, eds.

1979 *The Wilderness and the Southwest: Charles Sheldon's Quest for Desert Bighorn Sheep and Adventures with the Havasupai and Seri Indians.* University of Utah Press, Salt Lake City.

Carrasco, David

1990 *Religions of Ancient Mesoamerica: Cosmovision and Ceremonial Centers.* Harper and Row, San Francisco.

Castetter, Edward F., and Willis H. Bell

1942 *Pima and Papago Agriculture.* University of New Mexico Press, Albuquerque.

Cockrum, E. Lendell, and Yar Petryszyn

1992 *Mammals of the Southwestern United States and Northwestern Mexico.* Treasure Chest Publications, Tucson.

Cohodas, Clemency

1975 The Symbolism and Ritual Function of the Middle Classic Ballgame in Mesoamerica. *American Indian Quarterly* 2(2):99–130.

Cole, Sally J.

1990 *Legacy on Stone: Rock Art of the Colorado Plateau and Four Corners Region.* Johnson Books, Boulder, Colo.

1992 *Katsina Iconography in Homol'ovi Rock Art, Central Little Colorado Valley, Arizona.* Arizona Archaeologist 25. Arizona Archaeological Society, Phoenix.

Colton, Harold S.

1946 Fools Names Like Fools Faces. *Plateau* 19:1–8.

Conway, Thor

1993 *Painted Dreams: Native American Rock Art.* Northword Press, Minocqua, Wis.

Cope, Leona

1919 Calendars of the Indians North of Mexico. *University of California Publications in American Archaeology and Ethnology* 16(4):119–76.

Cornet, Jim

1975 *Wildlife of the Southwest Deserts.* Nature Trails Press, Desert Hot Springs, Calif.

Cummings, Byron

1953 *First Inhabitants of Arizona and the Southwest.* Cummings Publication Council, Tucson.

Curtin, L. S. M.

1949 *By the Prophet of the Earth: Ethnobotany of the Pima.* 1984 reprint, University of Arizona Press, Tucson.

Cushing, Frank Hamilton

1890 Preliminary Notes on the Origin, Working Hypothesis, and Primary Researches of the Hemenway Southwestern Archaeological Expedition. *Congres Internacional des Americanistes, Compte-Rendu de la Septieme Session,* pp. 151–94. W. H. Kuhl, Berlin.

1979 *Zuni: Selected Writings of Frank Hamilton Cushing,* ed. Jesse Green. University of Nebraska Press, Lincoln.

Daniels, Thomas F., and Mary L. Butterwick

1992 Flora of the South Mountains of South-Central Arizona. *Desert Plants* 10(3):99–119.

Deloria, Vine, Jr.

1991 Reflection and Revelation: Knowing Land, Places, and Ourselves. In *The Power of Place,* ed. James A. Swan, pp. 28–40. Quest Books, Wheaton, Ill.

DiPeso, Charles C., John B. Rinaldo, and Gloria J. Fenner

1974 *Casas Grandes: A Fallen Trading Center of the Gran Chichimeca.* Amerind Foundation, Dragoon, Ariz., and Northland Press, Flagstaff, Ariz.

Doelle, William H., David A. Gregory, and Henry D. Wallace

1995 Classic Period Platform Mound Systems in Southern Arizona. In *The Roosevelt Community Development Study: New Perspectives on Tonto Basin Prehistory,* ed. Mark D. Elson, Miriam T. Stark, and David A. Gregory, pp. 385–440. Center for Desert Archaeology Anthropological Papers No. 15. Tucson.

Doyel, David E.

1991 Hohokam Cultural Evolution in the Phoenix Basin. In *Exploring the Hohokam: Prehistoric Desert Peoples of the American Southwest,* ed. George J. Gumerman, pp. 231–78. Amerind Foundation, Dragoon, Ariz., and University of New Mexico Press, Albuquerque.

Drucker, Philip

1941 *Culture Element Distributions,* vol. 17: *Yuman-Piman.* University of California Anthropological Record 6(3). Berkeley.

Dudley, Tom

2000 Aquatic Insects of the Sonoran Desert. In *A Natural History of the Sonoran Desert,* ed. Steven J. Phillips and Patricia Wentworth Comus, pp. 357–64. Arizona-Sonora Desert Museum Press, Tucson, and University of California Press, Berkeley.

Edmonson, Munro S.

1988 *The Book of the Year: Middle American Calendrical Systems.* University of Utah Press, Salt Lake City.

Eliade, Mircea

1964 *Shamanism: Archaic Techniques of Ecstasy.* Bollingen Series 76. Princeton University Press, Princeton.

Ellis, Florence H.

1975 A Thousand Years of the Sun-Moon-Star Calendar. In *Archaeoastronomy in Pre-Columbian America,* ed. Anthony F. Aveni, pp. 59–88. University of Texas Press, Austin.

Evans, John, and Harry F. Hillman

1981 Casa Grande, an Ancient Astronomical Observatory. *Arizona Highways* 57(10):32.

Faris, Peter

1993 A Meteorological Model for the Concentric Circle Sun Symbol of the American Southwest. *Southwestern Lore* 59(2):23–27. [Colorado Archaeological Society, Denver.]

Farrell, Mary M., and Jeffrey F. Burton

1992 Dating Tom Ketchum Cave: The Role of Chronometric Dating in Rock Art Analysis. *North American Archaeologist* 13(3):219–47.

Ferg, Alan

1979 The Petroglyphs of Tumamoc Hill. *Kiva* 45(1–2):95–118.

Fewkes, Jesse Walter

1886 *Hopi Snake Ceremonies.* Bureau of American Ethnology, Washington. 1986 reprint, Avanyu Publishing, Albuquerque.

1892 A Few Tusayan Pictographs. *American Anthropologist* 5:9–26.

1903 Hopi Katchinas Drawn by Native Artists. *Twenty-first Annual Report of the Bureau of American Ethnology,* pp. 3–126. Washington, D.C.

1912 Casa Grande, Arizona. *Twenty-eighth Annual Report of the Bureau of American Ethnology,* pp. 25–180. Washington, D.C.

1919 Designs on Prehistoric Hopi Pottery. *Thirty-third Annual Report of the Bureau of American Ethnology.* Washington, D.C. 1973 reprint, Dover Publications, New York.

1920 Sun Worship of the Hopi Indians. *Smithsonian Institution Annual Report, 1918,* pp. 493–526. Smithsonian Institution, Washington, D.C.

Fischer, R.

1975 The Cartography of Inner Space. In *Hallucinations: Behaviour, Experience, and Theory,* ed. R. K. Siegel and L. J. West, pp. 197–239. Wiley, New York.

Foster, Michael S., ed.

1994 *The Pueblo Grande Project,* vol. 4: *Material Culture.* Soil Systems Publications in Archaeology No. 20. Phoenix.

Furst, Peter

1976 Shamanistic Survivals in Mesoamerican Religion. In *Actas del XLI Congresso International de Americanistas,* vol. 3, pp. 149–57.

Gifford, E. W.
1940 *Culture Element Distributions,* vol. 12: *Apache-Pueblo.* Anthropological Records 4(1). University of California, Berkeley.

Golio, J. J., and Ernest Snyder
1993 Petroglyph Surveys of South Mountain, 1991/1964. In *Rock Art Papers,* vol. 10, ed. Ken Hedges, pp. 1–6. San Diego Museum Papers No. 20. San Diego.

Golio, J. J., Susie Bradshaw, Ernest Snyder, and Mike Golio
1995 An Analysis of the Pipette Element in Hohokam Rock Art. In *Rock Art Papers,* vol. 12, ed. Ken Hedges, pp. 95–106. San Diego Museum Papers No. 33. San Diego.

Grant, Campbell
1978 *Canyon de Chelly: Its People and Rock Art.* University of Arizona Press, Tucson.

Green, Margerie, and Richard Effland, Jr.
1984 *Archaeological Investigations at the Pecos Ranch Development Property, Maricopa County.* Archaeological Consulting Services Cultural Resource Report No. 22. Tempe.

Griffith, James S.
1992 *Beliefs and Holy Places: A Spiritual Geography of the Pimeria Alta.* University of Arizona Press, Tucson.

Halifax, Joan
1982 *Shaman: The Wounded Healer.* Crossroad, New York.

Hall, James
1994 *Illustrated Dictionary of Symbols in Eastern and Western Art.* Westview Press, Boulder, Colo.

Hamann, Diane L.
1995 Hohokam Rock Art of Southern Arizona: A Regional Overview. In *Rock Art Studies in the Americas,* ed. Jack Steinbring, pp. 77–82. Oxford Monograph No. 45. Oxford, U.K.

Hanson, Jonathan, and Roseann B. Hanson
1997 *50 Common Reptiles and Amphibians of the Southwest.* Southwest Parks and Monuments Association, Tucson.

Hardman, Clark, Jr., and Marjorie H. Hardman
1992 Linear Solar Observatory Theory: The Development of Concepts of Time and Calendar. *North American Archaeologist* 13(2):149–72.

Hartmann, Gayle Harrison
1985 The Black Sheep Pictograph Site: Interpretation and Relationships. *Kiva* 50(2–3):95–109.

Haury, Emil W.
1945 *The Excavation of Los Muertos and Neighboring Ruins in the Salt River Valley, Southern Arizona.* Papers of the Peabody Museum of American Archaeology and Ethnology 24(1). Cambridge, Mass.
1976 *The Hohokam: Desert Farmers and Craftsman.* University of Arizona Press, Tucson.

Hayden, Julian
1985 Food Animal Cremations of the Sierra Pinacate, Sonora, Mexico. *Kiva* 50:237–49.

Hedges, Ken
1985 Rock Art Portrayals of Shamanistic Transformation and Magical Flight. In *Rock Art Papers,* vol. 2, ed. Ken Hedges. San Diego Museum Papers No. 18. San Diego.
1994 Pipette Dreams and the Primordial Snake-Canoe: Analysis of a Hallucinatory Form

Constant. In *Shamanism and Rock Art in North America,* ed. Solveig A. Turpin, pp. 103–24. Rock Art Foundation Special Publication No. 1. San Antonio, Tex.

Hedges, Ken, and Anita McDaniel
1986 A Sampler of Hohokam Rock Art. In *Rock Art Papers,* vol. 3, ed. Ken Hedges, pp. 117–28. San Diego Museum Papers No. 20. San Diego.

Heizer, Robert F., and Martin A. Baumhoff
1962 *Prehistoric Rock Art of Nevada and Eastern California.* University of California Press, Berkeley.

Hill, Erica
2000 The Ceremonial Analysis of Animal Interments and Ritual Practice in Southwestern North America. *Kiva* 65(4):361–98.

Hill, S.
1995 *Kokopelli Ceremonies.* Kiva Publishing, Santa Fe.

Hodge, Frederick W.
1896 Pueblo Snake Ceremonials. *American Anthropologist* 9:133–36.

Holden, Wes
1980 Rock Writings of South Mountain, Phoenix, Arizona. *Artifact* 18(1):43–51. [El Paso Archaeological Society.]

Horowitz, Mardi J.
1964 The Imagery of Visual Hallucinations. *Journal of Nervous and Mental Disease* 138:513–23.

Howard, Jerry B.
1995 *Preserving Temples of Clay: A Stabilization Plan for the Mesa Grande.* Mesa Southwest Museum, Mesa, Ariz.

Huffman, T. N.
1983 Trance Hypothesis and the Rock Art of Zimbabwe. *South African Archaeological Society, Goodwin Series* 4:49–53.

Hunchak, J. F.
1980 Hypnotic Induction by Entoptic Phenomena. *American Journal of Clinical Hypnosis* 22:223–24.

Hunger, Heinz
1982 Ritual Coition as Sacred Marriage in the Rock Art of North America. *American Indian Rock Art,* vol. 9, ed. Frank G. Bock, pp. 1–9. American Rock Art Research Association, San Miguel, Calif.

Hyman, Marion, and Marvin E. Rowe
1997 Plasma-Chemical Extraction and AMS Radiocarbon Dating of Rock Painting. In *American Indian Rock Art,* vol. 23, ed. Steve Freers, pp. 1–10. American Rock Art Research Association, Tucson.

Jaeger, Edmund C.
1961 *Desert Wildlife.* Stanford University Press, Stanford, Calif.

James, Steven R.
1994 Hohokam Hunting and Fishing Patterns at Pueblo Grande: Results of the Archaeofaunal Analysis. In *The Pueblo Grande Project,* vol. 5: *Environment and Subsistence,* ed. Scott Kwiatkowski, pp. 240–318. Soil Systems Publications in Archaeology No. 20. Phoenix.

Jernigan, Wesley

1992 *Hour-Glass Rock Art Figures of Southeastern Arizona.* Eastern Arizona College Museum of Anthropology Publication No. 4. Thatcher.

Johnson, Boma

1995 A Unique Expression of the Venus Star Symbol among the Petroglyphs of the Lower Colorado River. In *Utah Rock Art Papers,* vol. 14, ed. Carol Patterson-Rudolph, pp. 59–74. Utah Rock Art Research Association, Salt Lake City.

Johnson, Clay

1992 Establishing a Uniform Terminology for Descriptions of Solar Interactions with Rock Art Panels. In *Utah Rock Art,* vol. 10, ed. Nina Bowen, pp. 33–57. Utah Rock Art Research Association, Salt Lake City.

Johnson, Marsha

1992 The Genus Bursera (Burseaceae) in Sonora, Mexico, and Arizona, U.S.A. *Desert Plants* 10(3):126–43.

Kaufman, Kenn

2000 Hummingbirds. In *A Natural History of the Sonoran Desert,* ed. Steven J. Phillips and Patricia Wentworth Comus, p. 404. Arizona-Sonora Desert Museum Press, Tucson, and University of California Press, Berkeley.

Kelley, J. Charles, and Ellen Abbott

1966 The Cultural Sequence on the North-Central Frontier of Mesoamerica. In *XXXVI Congreso Internacional de Americanistas,* vol. 1, pp. 325–44. Seville, Spain.

Krupp, E. C.

1989 Rayed Disks. *Griffith Observer* 53(12):2–19. [Griffith Observatory, Los Angeles.]

Lamphere, Louise

1983 Southwestern Ceremonialism. In *Handbook of North American Indians,* vol. 10: *Southwest,* ed. Alfonso Ortiz, pp. 743–63. Smithsonian Institution Press, Washington, D.C.

Lee, Georgia

1991 *Rock Art and Cultural Resource Management.* Wormwood Press, Calabasas, Calif.

Lewis-Williams, J. D., and Thomas A. Dowson

1988 The Signs of All Times: Entoptic Phenomena in Upper Palaeolithic Art. *Current Anthropology* 29(2) 201–45.

Lloyd, J. William

1911 *Aw-Aw-Tam Indian Nights: Being the Myths and Legends of the Pimas of Arizona.* The Lloyd Group, Westfield, N.J.

Loendorf, Larry, and Chris Loendorf

1995 *With Zigzag Lines I'm Painted: Hohokam Petroglyphs on Tempe Butte, Arizona.* Loendorf and Associates. Tempe Historic Museum, Tempe.

Lumholtz, Carl

1912 *New Trails in Mexico.* Charles Scribner's Sons, London.

MacMahon, James A.

1985 *Deserts.* Audubon Society Nature Guides. Alfred A. Knopf, New York.

Mallery, Garrick

1893 *Picture Writing of the American Indians.* Annual Report of the Bureau of American Ethnology, Vol. 10. Washington, D.C.

Malmstrom, Vincent H.
1997 *Cycles of the Sun, Mysteries of the Moon: The Calendar in Mesoamerican Civilization.* University of Texas Press, Austin.

Malotki, Ekkehart
2000 The Rake: A Polysemous Motif in the Shamanistic Rock Art Iconography of the Palavayu Anthropomorphic Style. In *American Indian Rock Art,* vol. 24, ed. Frank G. Bock, pp. 13–28. American Rock Art Research Association, Phoenix.
2001 *Kokopelli: The Making of an Icon.* University of Nebraska Press, Norman.

Malville, J. McKim, and Claudia Putnam
1989 *Prehistoric Astronomy in the Southwest.* Johnson Books, Boulder, Colo.

Martineau, LaVan
1973 *The Rocks Begin to Speak.* KC Publications, Las Vegas.

Martynec, Rick, and Sandy Martynec
1995 Did the Tohono O'odham Make Petroglyphs? In *Rock Art Papers,* vol. 12, ed. Ken Hedges, pp. 81–87. San Diego Museum Papers No. 33. San Diego.

McCluskey, Stephen C.
1977 Astronomy of the Hopi Indians. *Journal for the History of Astronomy* 8:175–95.

McCreery, Patricia, and Ekkehart Malotki
1994 *Tampamveni: The Rock Art Galleries of Petrified Forest and Beyond.* Petrified Forest Museum Association.

McGinnis, William G.
1981 *Discovering the Desert: Legacy of the Carnegie Desert Botanical Laboratory.* University of Arizona Press, Tucson.

McKusick, Charmion R.
1976 Avifauna. In *The Hohokam: Desert Farmers and Craftsman,* by Emil W. Haury, pp. 374–77. University of Arizona Press, Tucson.

Michaelis, Hellen
1981 Willow Springs: A Hopi Petroglyph Site. *Journal of New World Archaeology* 4(2):1–23.

Miller, Dorcas S.
1997 *Stars of the First People: Native Americana Star Myths and Constellations.* Pruett, Boulder, Colo.

Miller, Mary, and Karl Taube
1993 *The Gods and Symbols of Ancient Mexico and the Maya: An Illustrated Dictionary of Mesoamerican Religion.* Thames and Hudson, New York.

Mitchell, Douglas R.
1994 Burial Ritual, World View, and Shamanism: Toward an Understanding of the Hohokam World View. In *The Pueblo Grande Project,* vol. 7: *An Analysis of Classic Period Mortuary Patterns,* ed. Douglas R. Mitchell, pp. 181–206. Soil Systems Publications in Archaeology No. 20. Phoenix.

Mitvalsky, Frank
1937 *Arizona Republic.* Newspaper clipping on file, Phoenix Central Library, Arizona Room.

Mixon, Benjamin
1989 Possible Solar Alignments of Room 11 and 10 on the Pueblo Grande Platform Mound. Ms. on file, Pueblo Grande Museum, Phoenix.

Mixon, Benjamin, and Raymond White
1991 Skywatchers of the Salt River Valley Hohokam. *Astronomy Quarterly* 8:245–59.

Molloy, John
1969 The Casa Grande Archaeological Zone: Pre-Columbian Astronomical Observation. Ms. on file, Western Archaeological Center, National Park Service, Tucson.

Monson, Gale, and Allan R. Phillips
1981 *Annotated Checklist of the Birds of Arizona.* University of Arizona Press, Tucson.

Moorehead, Warren King
1906 *A Narrative of Exploration in New Mexico, Arizona, Indiana, etc.* Phillips Academy Department of Archaeology Bulletin 3. Andover, Mass.

Morphy, Howard
1989 Introduction. In *Animals into Art,* ed. Howard Morphy, pp. 1–17. Unwin Hyman, London.

Oster, G.
1970 Phosphenes. *Scientific American* 222(2):83–87.

Patterson, Alex
1994 *Hopi Pottery Symbols.* Johnson Books, Boulder, Colo.

Patterson-Rudolph, Carol
1997 *On the Trail of Spider Woman: Petroglyphs, Pictographs, and Myths of the Southwest.* Ancient City Press, Santa Fe.

Parsons, Elsie Clews
1939 *Pueblo Indian Religion.* University of Chicago Press, Chicago.

Perkins, D. L., and David E. Brown
1981 The Sandhill Crane in Arizona. *Arizona Game and Fish Department Special Publications* 11:1–47.

Peterson, Roger Tory
1961 *A Field Guide to Western Birds.* 2nd ed. Houghton Mifflin, Boston.

Phillips, Allan, Joe Marshall, and Gale Monson
1964 *The Birds of Arizona.* University of Arizona Press, Tucson.

Pilles, Peter J., Jr.
1975 Petroglyphs of the Little Colorado River Valley. In *American Indian Rock Art,* vol. 1, ed. Shari T. Grove, pp. 1–26. San Juan County Museum Association, Farmington, N.Mex.

Preston, Robert A., and Ann L. Preston
1987 Evidence for Calendric Function at Nineteen Prehistoric Petroglyph Sites in Arizona. In *Astronomy and Ceremony in the Prehistoric Southwest,* ed. John B. Carlson and W. James Judge, pp. 191–204. Maxwell Museum of Anthropology Anthropological Papers No. 2. Albuquerque.

Rea, Amadeo M.
1983 *Once a River: Bird Life and Habitat Changes on the Middle Gila.* University of Arizona Press, Tucson.
1997 *At the Desert's Green Edge: An Ethnobotany of the Gila River Pima.* University of Arizona Press, Tucson.
1998 *Folk Mammalogy of the Northern Pimans.* University of Arizona Press, Tucson.

Renaud, E. B.

1938 The Snake among the Petroglyphs from North-Central New Mexico. *Southwestern Lore* 4(3):42–7. [Colorado Archaeological Society, Denver.]

Reynolds, Stephen J.

1985 *Geology of the South Mountains, Central Arizona.* Arizona Bureau of Geology and Mineral Technology Bulletin 195. Tucson.

Richards, E. G.

1998 *Mapping Time: The Calendar and Its History.* Oxford University Press, Oxford, U.K.

Robinson, Andrew

1995 *The Story of Writing: Alphabets, Hieroglyphs, and Pictographs.* Thames and Hudson, London.

Rodgers, James B.

1985 Appendix G: Rock Art Analysis and Regional Comparison of the Terrace Garden Site (AZ T:8:19). In *Hohokam Settlement and Economic Systems in the Central New River Drainage, Arizona,* ed. David E. Doyel and Mark D. Elson, pp. 823–45. Soil Systems Publications in Archaeology No. 4. Phoenix.

Russell, Frank

1975 *The Pima Indians.* University of Arizona Press, Tucson. Originally published as *Twenty-Sixth Annual Report of the Bureau of American Ethnology,* 1904–1905, pp. 3–389, Washington, D.C.

Saxton, Dean, and Lucille Saxton

1973 *O'odham ho'ok a' agitha: Legends and Lore of the Papago and Pima Indians.* University of Arizona Press, Tucson.

Schaafsma, Polly

1980 *Indian Rock Art of the Southwest.* School of American Research, Santa Fe, and University of New Mexico Press, Albuquerque.

1989 Supper or Symbol: Roadrunner Tracks in Southwest Art and Ritual. In *Animals into Art,* ed. Howard Morphy, pp. 253–69. One World Archaeology, vol. 7. Unwin Hyman, London.

1992 *Rock Art in New Mexico.* New Mexico Museum, Santa Fe.

1994 The Prehistoric Kachina Cult and Its Origins as Suggested by Southwestern Rock Art. In *Kachinas in the Pueblo World,* ed. Polly Schaafsma, pp. 63–80. University of New Mexico Press, Albuquerque.

1998 The Paquime Rock Art Style, Chihuahua, Mexico. In *Rock Art of the Chihuahua Desert Borderlands,* ed. Sheron Smith-Savage and Robert J. Mallouf, pp. 33–44. Center for Big Bend Studies, Alpine, Tex.

1999 Tlalocs, Kachinas, Sacred Bundles, and Related Symbolism in the Southwest and Mesoamerica. In *The Casas Grandes World,* ed. Curtis F. Schaafsma and Carroll L. Riley, pp. 164–92. University of Utah Press, Salt Lake City.

2000 *Warrior, Shield, and Star: Imagery and Ideology of Pueblo Warfare.* Western Edge Press, Santa Fe.

Schroeder, K. J., ed.

1999 *McDowell Mountains Archaeological Symposium.* Roadrunner Publications in Anthropology No. 10. Scottsdale, Ariz.

Schultes, Richard E.

1972 An Overview of Hallucinogens in the Western Hemisphere. In *Flesh of the Gods,* ed. Peter Furst, pp. 3–54. Praeger, New York.

Shaffer, Brian S., Holly A. Nicholson, and Karen M. Garner

1995 Possible Mimbres Documentation of Pueblo Snake Ceremonies in the Eleventh Century. *North American Archaeologist* 16:17–32.

Shaul, David L., and Jane H. Hill

1998 Tepimans, Yumans, and Other Hohokam. *American Antiquity* 63(3):375–96.

Shaw, Anna Moore

1968 *Pima Indian Legends.* University of Arizona Press, Tucson.

Slifer, Dennis

2000 *The Serpent and the Sacred Fire: Fertility Images in Southwest Rock Art.* Museum of New Mexico Press, Santa Fe.

Snyder, Ernest E.

1966 Petroglyphs of the South Mountains of Arizona. *American Antiquity* 31(5):705–09.

1975 Petroglyphs of the South Mountains of Arizona. In *American Indian Rock Art,* vol. 1, ed. Shari T. Grove, pp. 105–09. San Juan County Museum Association, Farmington, N.Mex.

Sofaer, Anna

1997 The Primary Architecture of the Chacoan Culture: A Cosmological Expression. In *Anasazi Architecture and American Design,* ed. Baker H. Morrow and V. B. Price, pp. 88–123. University of New Mexico Press, Albuquerque.

Spier, Leslie

1933 *Yuman Tribes of the Gila River.* University of California Press, Berkeley.

Stephen, Alexander M.

1936 *Hopi Journal of Alexander M. Stephen,* ed. Elsie Clews Parsons. Columbia University Contributions to Anthropology Vol. 23. Columbia University Press, New York.

Stevenson, Matilda Coxe

1904 The Zuni Indians: Their Mythology, Esoteric Fraternities, and Ceremonies. *Twenty-Third Annual Report of the Bureau of American Ethnology,* pp. 3–634. Washington, D.C.

Steward, Julian H.

1929 *Petroglyphs of California and Adjoining States.* University of California Publications in American Archaeology and Ethnology No. 24. Berkeley.

Stoller, Marianne L.

1991 Birds, Feathers, and Hopi Ceremonialism. *Expedition* 33(2):35–45.

Strand, Jennifer G.

1993 Faunal Analysis for the SCFAP Sites. In *Classic Period Occupation on the Santa Cruz Flats: The Santa Cruz Flats Archaeological Project,* ed. T. Kathleen Henderson and Richard J. Martynec, pp. 471–92. Northland Research, Flagstaff, Ariz.

Sutherland, Kay

1996 Spirits from the South. *The Artifact* 34 (1 and 2). [El Paso Archaeological Society.]

Szuter, Christine

1991 *Hunting by Prehistoric Horticulturalists in the American Southwest.* Garland Publishing, New York.

Teague, Lynn S.

1993 Prehistory and the Traditions of the O'Odham and Hopi. *Kiva* 58(4):435–54.

Terkanian, Barbara

2000 A Vertebrate Looks at Arthropods. In *A Natural History of the Sonoran Desert,* ed. Steven J. Phillips and Patricia Wentworth Comus, pp. 283–88. Arizona-Sonora Desert Museum Press, Tucson, and University of California Press, Berkeley.

Thiel, J. Homer

1995 *Rock Art in Arizona: A Component of the Arizona Historic Preservation Plan.* Center for Desert Archaeology, Tucson.

Turpin, Solveig A.

1994 On a Wing and a Prayer: Flight Metaphors in Pecos River Art. In *Shamanism and Rock Art in North America,* ed. Solveig A. Turpin, pp. 73–102. Rock Art Foundation Special Publication No. 1. San Antonio, Tex.

Tyler, C. W.

1978 Some New Entoptic Phenomena. *Vision Research* 18:1633–39.

Tyler, Hamilton A.

1979 *Pueblo Birds and Myths.* University of Oklahoma Press, Norman.

Underhill, Ruth M.

1938 *Singing for Power: The Song Magic of the Papago Indians of Southern Arizona.* 1993 reprint, University of Arizona Press, Tucson.

1946 *Papago Indian Religion.* Columbia University Press, New York.

Underhill, Ruth M., Donald M. Bahr, Baptisto Lopez, Jose Pancho, and David Lopez

1979 *Rainhouse and Ocean: Speeches for the Papago Year.* University of Arizona Press, Tucson.

Wallace, Henry D.

1983 The Mortars, Petroglyphs, and Trincheras on Rillito Peak. *Kiva* 48(3).

1989 *Archaeological Investigations at Petroglyph Sites in the Painted Rock Reservoir Area, Southwestern Arizona.* Institute for American Research Technical Report No. 89-5. Tucson.

Wallace, Henry D., and James Holmlund

1986 *Petroglyphs of the Picacho Mountains, Southcentral Arizona.* Institute for American Research Anthropological Papers No. 6. Tucson.

Wallace, Henry D., James M. Heidke, and William H. Doelle

1995 Hohokam Origins. *Kiva* 60:575–618.

Waller, Steven J., David Lubman, and Brenda Kiser

1999 Digital Recording Techniques Applied to Rock Art Sites. In *American Indian Rock Art,* vol. 25, ed. Steven M. Freers, pp. 179–90. American Rock Art Research Association, Phoenix.

Waters, Frank

1963 *Book of the Hopi.* Penguin Press, New York.

Weaver, Donald, Jr.

1985 *Hieroglyphic Canyon: A Petroglyph Record of a Changing Subsistence Pattern.* American Rock Art Research Association Monograph No. 1. San Miguel, Calif.

Weaver, Donald, Jr., and Bettina H. Rosenberg

1978 Petroglyphs of the Southern Sierra Estrella: A Locational Interpretation. *American Indian Rock Art,* vol. 4, ed. Ernest Snyder, A. J. Bock, and Frank Bock, pp. 108–23. American Rock Art Research Association, Tempe.

Wellmann, Klaus F.
1974 Some Observations on Human Sexuality in North American Indian Rock Art. *Southwestern Lore* 40(1):1–12. [Colorado Archaeological Society, Denver.]
1976 Some Observations on the Bird Motif in North American Indian Rock Art. *American Indian Rock Art,* vol. 2, ed. Kay Sutherland, pp. 97–107. El Paso Archaeological Society, El Paso.

Werner, Floyd, and Carl Olson
1994 *Learning about and Living with Insects of the Southwest.* Fisher Books, Tucson.

Whiting, Alfred F.
1939 *Ethnobotany of the Hopi.* Museum of Northern Arizona Bulletin 15. Flagstaff.

Whitley, David S.
1994 Shamanism, Natural Modeling, and the Rock Art of Far Western North American Hunter-Gatherers. In *Shamanism and Rock Art in North America,* ed. Solveig A. Turpin, pp. 1–44. Rock Art Foundation Special Publication No. 1. San Antonio, Tex.

Wilcox, David R.
1980 The Current Status of the Hohokam Concept. In *Current Issues in Hohokam Prehistory: Proceedings of a Symposium,* ed. David E. Doyel and Fred T. Plog, pp. 236–42. Arizona State University Anthropological Research Papers No. 23. Tempe.
1991a The Mesoamerican Ballgame in the American Southwest. In *The Mesoamerican Ballgame,* ed. Vernon L. Scarborough and David R. Wilcox, pp. 101–28. University of Arizona Press, Tucson.
1991b Hohokam Religion: An Archaeologist's Perspective. In *The Hohokam: Ancient People of the Desert,* ed. David Grant Noble, pp. 47–61. School of American Research Press, Santa Fe.

Williamson, Ray A.
1984 *Living the Sky: The Cosmos of the American Indian.* University of Oklahoma Press, Norman.

Woody, Alanah, and Alvin R. McLune
2000 The Distribution of Vulviforms on White Tuff in Nevada. In *American Indian Rock Art,* vol. 24, ed. Frank G. Bock, pp. 29–48. American Rock Art Research Association, Phoenix.

Yarnell, Richard A.
1959 Prehistoric Pueblo Use of Datura. *El Palacio* 66(5):176–78.

Young, M. Jane
1986 The Interrelationship of Rock Art and Astronomical Practice in the American Southwest. *Archaeoastronomy* 10:S43–S57.
1988 *Signs from the Ancestors: Zuni Cultural Symbolism and Perceptions of Rock Art.* University of New Mexico Press, Albuquerque.

Zeilik, Michael
1987 Anticipation in Ceremony: The Readiness Is All. In *Astronomy and Ceremony in the Prehistoric Southwest,* ed. J. B. Carlson and W. James Judge, pp. 25–41. Papers of the Maxwell Museum of Anthropology, University of New Mexico. Albuquerque.
1989 Keeping the Sacred and Planting Calendar: Archaeo-astronomy in the Pueblo Southwest. In *World Archaeoastronomy,* ed. Anthony F. Aveni, pp. 143–66. Cambridge University Press, Cambridge, U.K.

INDEX

C

D

N

O

P

Q

R

S

ABOUT THE AUTHOR

TODD BOSTWICK has conducted research into the ancient Hohokam culture since 1979. He has an M.A. in anthropology and a Ph.D. in history from Arizona State University. Todd has been the Phoenix city archaeologist since 1990, with his office at Pueblo Grande Museum, the site of a prehistoric Hohokam village. Todd is responsible for the management of archaeological sites located within the boundaries of Phoenix, including hundreds of rock art sites scattered throughout the mountain preserves. He has written articles on Hohokam rock art in the *American Indian Rock Art* series published by the American Rock Art Research Association, and in the San Diego Museum of Man's *Rock Art Papers.* He also is a contributing author in the *Handbook of Rock Art Research.*

ABOUT THE PHOTOGRAPHER

PETER KROCEK has found himself exploring remote mountain canyons in the desert Southwest after a life journey that began in Austria, continued in the American Midwest, and eventually led him to teaching high school in Arizona. Although Peter holds degrees in political science and education, he prefers to describe himself as an urban explorer and professional photographer, having worked in both fields in Arizona for the last twenty years. Specializing in large-format photography, Peter has had his work published in *Arizona Highways Magazine* and has made many contributions to various museum exhibits such as at the Pueblo Grande Museum and the South Mountain Environmental Educational Center. He also conducts photographic workshops into the South Mountains for Friends of Arizona Highways.